IRELAND

Gustave de Beaumont at age thirty-five
(Courtesy Beinecke Rare Book and Manuscript Library, Yale University)

IRELAND
Social, Political, and Religious

With an Introduction by Tom Garvin and Andreas Hess

GUSTAVE DE BEAUMONT
Edited and translated by W. C. Taylor

THE BELKNAP PRESS OF HARVARD UNIVERSITY PRESS
Cambridge, Massachusetts
London, England
2006

Originally published as *L'Irlande: sociale, politique et religieuse*
(Paris: Michel Lévy Frère, 1839)

Book design by Dean Bornstein

Library of Congress Cataloging-in-Publication Data
Beaumont, Gustave de, 1802–1866.
[Irlande sociale, politique, et religieuse. English]
Ireland social, political, and religious / Gustave de Beaumont ;
edited and translated by W. C. Taylor ;
with a new introduction by Tom Garvin and Andreas Hess.
p. cm.
Includes bibliographical references and index.
ISBN 0-674-02165-7
1. Ireland—Description and travel.
2. Ireland—Politics and government—1837–1901.
3. Ireland—Economic conditions.
I. Taylor, W. C. (William Cooke), 1800–1849.   II. Title.
DA975.B374 2006
941.5—dc22   2005057032

Introduction: Tyranny in Ireland?

Tom Garvin and Andreas Hess

Ireland in the 1830s was an agrarian country controlled by an aristocracy alien in nationality, language, religion, and culture from the vast majority of the population. The landlords despised the lower orders, who returned the compliment with a ferocious blend of covert contempt and hatred masked by a genial subservience. Arrogant aristocrats used the law and the army to enforce their exploitation of the poor tenants, who defended themselves the only way they could: by collective solidarity, threats, assassination, and mass agitation. These unequal conditions, coupled with the incompetence and greed of the landowners, could only lead to catastrophe. Such is the subject of Gustave de Beaumont's bestselling study of 1839, *Ireland: Social, Political, and Religious.*

Gustave de Beaumont (1802–1866) was, with his friend and lifelong coworker Alexis de Tocqueville, one of the best-known social and political commentators of the mid-1800s. Both men were members of the French gentry and can be described as liberals in the French Catholic tradition. Tocqueville is best known for *Democracy in America,* his monumental two-volume treatise on the United States, published in French as *De la démocratie en Amérique,* and almost simultaneously in English translation, between 1835 and 1840. The book, an instant classic, has never been out of print and has become a key work for the analysis of American society, political culture, and the historical significance of the United States as a new, non-European world power. Beaumont has always been less well known, despite the immediate success of *Ireland,* published in 1839 to great acclaim and reprinted many times. Even today Tocqueville is still celebrated as the political prophet, the time traveler, the man who predicted an inevitable long-term tendency toward democratization; the emergence of the United States and Russia as superpowers in the twentieth century; and the dangers of racism in a future united Germany. Beaumont, by contrast, is usually sidelined as the shadowy travel companion of modern democracy's intellectual seer.[1]

Historical documentation shows that the two men were actually almost inseparable throughout most of their adult lives. They shared their observations and research and rehashed every intellectual conversation either of them might have had with a third party; in effect, they constituted a two-man Department of Political Sociology. They discussed every scholarly line they wrote, whether together or separately. The history of ideas knows very few examples of such intimate intellectual companionship. Benjamin Constant and Madame de Stael, Karl Marx and Friedrich Engels, and Theodor W. Adorno and Max Horkheimer come to mind, but even these examples do not parallel the intimate intellectual friendship between Tocqueville and Beaumont.

Although the Ireland study was one of the first sociological bestsellers in France and has become an important source for historians of nineteenth-century Ireland, it remains an almost forgotten classic in the wider academic world, deserving rediscovery and appreciation. Even less well known is Beaumont's preface to the seventh edition of *Ireland* in 1863. In that piece the author gives a brilliant description of the great Irish Famine, its catastrophic progress, the frantic efforts of the often reviled London government to assuage its impact, its monstrous aftermath in the form of starvation, disease, death on a huge scale, emigration to the United States and the British colonies, and its devastating long-term effects on Irish society and politics. It is here translated into English for the first time.[2]

Parallel Lives: Beaumont and Tocqueville

Gustave de Beaumont de Bonnière was born on February 6, 1802, at Beaumont-la-Chartre in the Sarthe. Beaumont's parents were aristocrats linked to the enlightened circles of the French upper class. Indeed Lafayette, the famous aristocratic soldier who had fought alongside Washington against the British during the American War of Independence, was Beaumont's grandfather. Not much is known of how Beaumont spent his childhood. His first appearance on the historical record as an adult is as a *juge auditeur* and then as a deputy public prosecutor at the court of Versailles.

It was at Versailles that Beaumont first met Alexis de Tocqueville (1805–1859), a fellow student who was also pursuing a legal career. The two young men clicked personally, intellectually, and politically; soon they developed their fabled habit of reading and studying together. Both were passionate admirers of Anglo-American representative institutions and constitutional traditions. They believed that the Americans, in particular, had developed a system involving semi-democratic participation and the exercise of human rights to an extent unparalleled in the early nineteenth century. They admired this liberal democratic

system despite such scandalous features as race-based slavery and the expropriation of native populations. They saw Anglo-Saxon democratic liberalism as a
harbinger of the political future of Europe, which was still ruled mainly by aristocracies and absolute monarchs. As we will see, the two men had an informal
division of labor: whereas Beaumont would do his most important work on the
truly disadvantaged, slaves and Indians in America and the impoverished inhabitants of Ireland, Tocqueville's most powerful work would address the larger
questions of the societal and political institutions of America and France.

The July Revolution (1830) brought an end to the reign of Charles X, and
both young men were faced with difficult decisions. Deeply worried about the
intentions of Louis-Phillipe's new regime, they decided to get away from France
for a while. Beaumont had already written a short study of the French prison
system, in which he had adumbrated a further, comparative study of prisons. To
the friends' surprise, they received funding for a trip to America to investigate
how the French authorities might profit from the new prison systems of the
United States. In April 1831 they left for America, where they were to stay until
February 1832.[3]

The trip was a success in more than one respect. The two men managed to
gather plenty of information about prisons and the American penitentiary systems. Even more important, however, was their discovery that the comparison
of prison systems also provided the key to a new, democratic "philosophy." They
argued that the way a penitentiary system treats its prisoners reveals how a regime treats its individual citizens or subjects in general. American prisons at
that time apparently sought to turn criminals into good citizens rather than
simply mete out retribution or vengeance. This enlightened attitude was the
true revelation of the New World in the eyes of the two Frenchmen: American
institutions, American mores and attitudes, and the new democratic and egali-
tarian approach to social relations that had evolved in the young United States
showed France (and Europe) its possible future.

On their return to France in the spring of 1832 Beaumont immediately
started writing their joint report. In the meantime the news had spread to their
boss, the French state, that the pair were suffering from an apparently incurable
new spiritual disease: love of democracy. Both found themselves peremptorily
dismissed from their duties as public prosecutors, though their careers were not
harmed as a result.

Early in 1833 their report was finally published. *The Penitentiary System of
the United States and Its Application to France* was an immediate success.[4]
The study was widely discussed and was awarded the prestigious Montyon
prize. Second and third editions followed in 1836 and 1844. The book soon
appeared in translation; it was particularly popular in America and Germany.

The Penitentiary System prompted the two friends to carry their studies further. While Beaumont embarked on a new project, a novel about the tragic aspects of their American experiences, Tocqueville turned to his monumental book on American democracy.

Tocqueville and Beaumont continued their travels as far as Ireland, where they toured for six weeks.⁵ During the trip they talked about their publication plans for the future. They agreed on two things. First, they promised to respect each other's writing plans and individual research interests. Beaumont would write on the unfulfilled promises of American democracy, the plight of African Americans and American Indians, and the colonial relationship between England and Ireland, while Tocqueville would focus mainly on America's political system and the prospects for both American and European democracy. Second, to prevent possible misunderstandings, overlapping research efforts, or any intellectual turf war, they decided to show each other their work before publication.⁶

The year 1835 saw the publication not only of the first volume of Tocqueville's *Democracy in America,* but also of Beaumont's novel *Marie, or Slavery in the United States.*⁷ While *Democracy* looked mainly at America's political system, *Marie* was an attempt to take a closer look at the seamier side of American society. The two books have to be read as companion volumes in order to make complete sense of how the two men understood America. *Marie,* like *Democracy in America,* was a huge success and was reprinted numerous times in French. By contrast, the novel remained almost unknown in America for more than a century; American slavery was apparently a more popular topic in Europe than in the United States, and, to put it gently, the book did not harmonize well with American tendencies toward self-congratulation. In fact, the American edition of *Marie* appeared only in 1958, coinciding, probably not by accident, with the emerging civil rights movement.⁸ The two books paid off in career terms; Tocqueville's volume got him elected to the French Academy of Moral and Political Sciences, thus emulating Beaumont's Montyon prize. The friends also made a promising start to their political careers by being elected to the French Parliament.

In the summer of 1837 Beaumont traveled once again to England and Ireland, this time on his own, to gather material for his Ireland project. Two years later *L'Irlande* finally appeared as a two-volume study.⁹ The English edition, translated and edited by William Taylor, was published later that year.¹⁰ The book was an intellectual *tour de force* and even more of a hit than his first two studies.¹¹ It was also a popular sensation; during the author's own lifetime the French edition was reprinted seven times and earned him another Montyon prize.¹²

Quite apart from their publishing record and their political and academic achievements, Tocqueville and Beaumont remained true liberals dedicated to social reform. Unlike many other liberals, however, they also remained internationalist; their opinions were not confined to internal French issues and they argued publicly, for example, against the excesses and abuses of an emergent French colonialism. By now the two friends had perfected their team approach, complementing and supporting each other's efforts. Thus, for example, Tocqueville presented a report on the abolition of slavery to Parliament while Beaumont simultaneously presented a petition to the Chamber on behalf of the French Abolitionist Society.

The Revolution of 1848 ushered in the Second Republic. Beaumont and Tocqueville both became members of the new National Assembly and were selected to join the Constitutional Commission. In the following year Beaumont was appointed Special Ambassador to the United Kingdom and was based in London, while Tocqueville became France's Minister for Foreign Affairs. However, this improvement in political status and achievement did not last for very long. In 1851 they were arrested and imprisoned for opposing Louis Napoleon's *coup d'etat* against the Second Republic. Their arrests, and their almost comically prompt releases, marked their withdrawal from public affairs and the end of two remarkable political careers.

Tocqueville retreated to his home in the countryside and continued his intellectual reflections. Beaumont was less fortunate and could not devote all his time to writing. He had to attend to financial matters out of economic necessity connected with a legally encumbered inheritance from his father-in-law, Georges de Lafayette; this unpleasant experience seems to have informed his strong grasp of Irish land law, the plight of Irish encumbered estates, and the malign social consequences of the interaction of land law and indebtedness, as is illustrated rather vividly in his 1863 Preface to the seventh edition of *Ireland*.

After Tocqueville's death in January 1859, Gustave began editing his friend's published and unpublished writings. Six volumes appeared between 1861 and 1866.[13] Preoccupied as he was with these editorial efforts, Beaumont seems to have found less time to voice his concern for the oppressed and the excluded. Only once more would he succeed in making this concern public. Shocked and disappointed about British attitudes to the Irish tragedy after the Famine, he presented the Irish case (*Notice sur l'état présent de L'Irlande*) to the Academy of Moral and Political Science in 1863; a longer version of this presentation was to become the 1863 Preface.[14] The *Notice* is an old man's impassioned protest at the plight of Ireland combined with an optimism derived from, as ever, his somewhat uncritical admiration for the English constitution. As far as we know this was Beaumont's last major public utterance before his death in Paris on February 22, 1866.

Different Intellectual Passions

Despite their intense intellectual bond, Tocqueville and Beaumont focused on different topics. Gustave's concern with the victims of democratic or semi-democratic societies is perhaps what most clearly distinguishes him intellectually and emotionally from Alexis. A similar sensitivity toward the weak occasionally shows through in Tocqueville's *Democracy* but is never the main thrust of his discourse. In *Marie* Beaumont persistently emphasized the political equality either presupposed or promised in American founding documents. He was shocked by the contrast between their high aspirations and the rather grubby realities of American politics; he noted bluntly that the documents remained mere rhetoric when it came to the systematic dispossession of the Indians and the equally systematic mass enslavement of black people.

The American critics and reviewers who belatedly welcomed Beaumont's sociological novel noted that *Marie* had to be interpreted as the much needed corrective to Tocqueville's omissions in *Democracy*; however, such late and posthumous success came with a price. While American critics praised Beaumont's book as a classic and as a forerunner to the emerging civil rights movement, they seemed quite unaware of the success his work on Ireland had enjoyed in Europe during his lifetime. *Marie* had been celebrated in France when it first appeared there. Viewed retrospectively, however, it was no match for the book on Ireland. *L'Irlande* not only won awards and was reprinted many times up to 1914; it also brought membership in the French Academy for Moral and Political Sciences.

The reason for this success is easily explained: while *Marie* had shed light on the problematic aspects of American democracy, *L'Irlande* had an obvious European context. The book made it clear that even the "oldest democracy in the world," the United Kingdom, had, to put it mildly, a negative side. Of course it could be argued that Beaumont's study and its reception were mainly an expression of French national pride. It could even be argued that, by their enthusiasm for his study of the plight of the Irish, his French readers were showing an ancient antipathy toward *l'Albion perfide*; after all, it wasn't all that long since Waterloo. However, nothing could be further from the author's intentions. As we have seen, like Alexis and like their common intellectual predecessor Montesquieu, Beaumont showed a deep but perhaps somewhat uncritical admiration for the political system of the United Kingdom. Indeed, it is exactly this admiration that helps to explain the immediate success of his book on Ireland. In *L'Irlande*, Beaumont hits all the emotional registers, he weighs all the pros and cons, he appears to be England's advocate and uses all available arguments for the defence of the British government's policies in Ireland, but finally he gives up and concludes reluctantly that Ireland was to the United Kingdom what slavery was to the United States; Ireland was that ironic and tragic entity, a persecuted martyr nation in a free polity.

Beaumont's instinct for the underdog drove his impassioned preface of 1863. In fact, he has been accused of exaggerating the pre-Famine poverty of the Irish; while the potato was free of blight, the Irish were actually unusually well fed, it has been argued, and the Famine came like a bolt from the blue.[15] But Ireland had seen famine before, and 1847 did follow two years of partial crop failure; the British Government had been warned by Mother Nature, *pace* Joel Mokyr. Before the Great Hunger, famine had been endemic on the island for over a century; back in 1740 one-quarter of the population had perished in a huge famine, and smaller starvations had occurred every few years over the next century. Since 1900, paradoxically, perhaps, the Irish have been among the best-fed people on the planet.

Beaumont pursues two lines of argument in *L'Irlande*. In the first half he outlines how in nearly three centuries of rule the English conquerors and the Anglo-Irish aristocracy ("the Ascendancy") never quite legitimated themselves. Naturally, this tiny and fantastically privileged minority would be resented by the mainly folk-Catholic aboriginals and even by people of lower status who happened to be Protestant by religion. However, this minority attempted to constitute itself as the Irish nation *toute courte* in the eighteenth century. In doing so it ignored the millions of men and women of no property below it, poor tenants with their covertly expressed collective ideology of dispossession and sullen dreams of *revanchisme*, commonly expressed in Gaelic prose, poetry, and verse.[16] The Ascendancy essentially drifted between two extreme poles: social, political, and religious indifference to the dispossessed native Irish on the one hand and a passionate wish to exterminate Irish popery by a policy of proselytism on the other.[17] Thus, the English Ascendancy in the conquered island was never able to conceive of a majoritarian project that might have assimilated the Catholic majority to its colonial polity. Edmund Burke's famous pleas for religious tolerance fell on deaf ears, as did the more pragmatic private warnings of the Duke of Wellington. Two generations later, William Butler Yeats was to mourn the passing of a great opportunity: a nationalist Catholic Ireland led by a mainly Protestant Anglo-Irish nobility. Furthermore, while the aristocracy in England was much more open to the industrialization of Britain, in Ireland the landed Anglo-Irish aristocracy was reluctant to get involved in such an enterprise.

In the second half of his Irish study Beaumont describes the political and social consequences of this seemingly irresolvable dilemma. He stresses that through English colonization Ireland had been given all the constitutional tools necessary to free itself from colonial oppression. Daniel O'Connell had grasped that fact as a young man and had, for thirty years between 1815 and 1845, wrested concessions from an unwilling Protestant ascendancy by means of a lethal, very Irish and brilliant blend of mass popular agitation, liberal political principles, and constitutional argument; like the Irish poor, Beaumont admired the beloved Dan, King of the Beggars, and the charismatic leader of the emergent Irish democracy.[18] In the end, however, Beaumont remained skeptical about the prospect of any real sea change in the powerful landed aristocracy of Ireland. It was too out of touch, too arrogant, and too unwilling to learn from past mistakes; like the Bourbons, it learned nothing and forgot nothing. Repeatedly, he referred to the Irish aristocracy as being essentially a collective tyranny. Despite his admiration for Anglo-Saxon constitutionalism, his book could possibly have been legitimately called, following Tocqueville's famous title *Democracy in America*, *On Tyranny in Ireland*.

Ireland, of course, is very much a work of its time, and Irish historians have continually revised Beaumont's diagnosis over the past century and a half. The book's basic argument, however, has not been shaken decisively by later works. In fact, even alleged revisionists such as Roy Foster, Dermot Keogh, and Tom Garvin have built on Beaumont's basic insights, perhaps unconsciously. *Ireland* cannot fairly be compared to *Democracy*, because the two writers set themselves very different tasks. It could be argued that Tocqueville was time-travelling forward whereas Beaumont was looking to the future when Ireland made him look into the deep Irish past; Beaumont had a tougher row to hoe.

Like the majority of Tocqueville's prophecies concerning American democracy, most, but not all, of Beaumont's prophecies concerning Ireland came to pass. The Irish Famine of the 1840s further radicalized the Catholic majority. It also caused the British government finally to write off the Irish Ascendancy. After 1850 Westminster tried to change horses in Ireland and side with the vast peasant-cum-farmer majority against the landlords. Following O'Connell's precedent, a series of mass movements, agitating for land reform and a native government ("Home Rule"), appeared. Beaumont foresaw the land reform and prophesied the emergence of an Ireland of small owner-occupier farmers, as duly happened in the period 1880–1903. But he also expected the Irish to settle down after land reform as part of a British-Irish constitutional democracy. Strangely enough, he did not foresee the rise of a large, successful, and vengeful Irish-American community in the United States that willingly encouraged and financed Irish militant insurgents from 1865. Just after Beaumont's death Irish veterans of the Union Army led the Fenian rising of 1867, which attempted to transform Ireland into an independent republic; these ex-soldiers were referred to respectfully in Ireland as "the men in the square-toed [G.I.] boots." A covert, and later overt, hatred of the British government continued to flourish in Ireland as well as in Irish-America; the Famine had partially delegitimated the British state in Ireland. Beaumont never fully appreciated this fact, but of course he could not have foreseen the calamity of 1914.

With the First World War, Ireland descended, with much of the rest of the continent, into revolution, civil war, and sectarian pogrom after 1918. Eventually an Irish independent democratic state emerged in 1922, shorn of the northeastern counties, with their very different culture and social structure. This new country rapidly evolved into a republican democracy of Catholic yeoman farmers with democratic institutions heavily influenced by both British and American prototypes. The landed ascendancy died out, leaving behind a formidable cultural heritage; the great houses of the aristocracy were burned down, turned into convents, used as schools, or, eventually, converted into hotels, spas, and golf clubs. Despite many backslidings, most of twentieth-century Ireland had achieved an ambivalent freedom, or, as Michael Collins, the Irish revolutionary leader, famously put it in a presumably unconscious echoing of Beaumont, the freedom to achieve freedom. Nonetheless, the sectarian curse of old Ireland lived on in Northern Ireland and has yet to be clearly lifted from Ulster society. Still, in both parts of Ireland equal rights and liberty for all citizens were no longer revolutionary demands but had gradually become practical achievements, in the south in the 1920s and in the north fifty years later. Versions of the English constitution worked in different ways in both parts of Ireland to enable a gradual liberalization and equalization of society to be engineered over the generations.

On reflection, the case of Beaumont and Ireland is more complicated than that of Tocqueville and America. What took the form of an early constitutional promise in America, to be realized only after civil war and a century of discrimination and political struggle, was fought for even more bitterly in Europe, which had to build democracy in the face of entrenched agrarian aristocracies with great social, cultural, and intellectual power. Nonetheless, the messenger should not be blamed for the bad news; Gustave de Beaumont, Ireland's Tocqueville, has given us a classic account of the painful birth pangs of Irish democracy, Ireland providing in miniature a model of the struggle for democracy against feudalism in Europe.[19] For this contribution, Beaumont deserves to be rediscovered and given intellectual recognition by the English-speaking world.

Notes

* The authors would like to thank the Vice Presidency for Research, University College Dublin, the French Embassy in Dublin, and the EU-financed FP6 project ANOVASOFIE for their support.

1. Up to the present day not one study, Ph.D. dissertation, or biography analyzes Beaumont's work comprehensively. Thus far the best studies containing material on Beaumont are:

S. Drescher, *Tocqueville and England* (Cambridge, Mass.: Harvard University Press, 1964); S. Drescher, "Tocqueville and Beaumont: A Rationale for Collective Study," in S. Drescher, ed., *Tocqueville and Beaumont on Social Reform* (New York: Harper and Row, 1968), pp. 201–217; and G. W. Pierson, *Tocqueville in America* (Baltimore: Johns Hopkins University Press, 1938, 1996). Pierson has also published an essay titled "Gustave de Beaumont: Liberal," in *Franco-American Review* I (1936–1937), pp. 307–316. Further helpful information is contained in A. Jardin, *Tocqueville—A Biography* (Baltimore: Johns Hopkins University Press, 1988). Jardin also edited the three-volume set of *Correspondance d'Alexis de Tocqueville et de Gustave de Beaumont* (Paris: Gallimard, 1967). A more thorough study, particularly using the Tocqueville and Beaumont material available in the Yale Beinecke Library, is called for.

2. The 1863 Preface has been translated for this edition by Tom Garvin. It can be found at the end of the text.

3. See Pierson's almost day-by-day reconstruction of the trip in *Tocqueville in America*. Particularly interesting in Pierson's book is the list of acquaintances and contacts, among them John Quincy Adams and Daniel Webster. Beaumont and Tocqueville also had one meeting with then president Andrew Jackson.

4. G. Beaumont and A. Tocqueville, *On the Penitentiary System of the United States and Its Application to France* (Carbondale: Southern Illinois University Press, reprint 1964). Francis Lieber, whom Tocqueville and Beaumont had met on their American trip, translated the American edition.

5. A detailed reconstruction of this trip can be found in E. Larkin, *Alexis de Tocqueville's Journey to Ireland* (Dublin: Wolfhound Press, 1990), and in Drescher, *Tocqueville and England*.

6. Although it cannot be confirmed by any records available to the writers, Beaumont probably met his future translator William Taylor at a meeting of the British Association for the Advancement of Science, at Trinity College Dublin. William Cooke Taylor (1800–1849) was a writer and economist. Taylor had been educated at Trinity College Dublin but later moved to London, where he became a contributor to the whig-liberal, reform-oriented weekly *Athenaeum*. Throughout his life he remained supportive of the Irish cause, following a liberal and reformist agenda and striving to further Irish higher education. He is also known as the founder of the Dublin Society for Statistical and Social Inquiry, which still exists. Two of his books dealt particularly with Ireland: *History of the Civil Wars in Ireland* (1831) and *Reminiscences of Daniel O'Connell by a Munster Farmer* (1847). His magnum opus was *The Natural History of Civilisation* (1840), in which he argued that mankind was created by God to be civilized; savagery, he claimed, is not a natural condition but rather the product of ignorance.

7. There are now a few modern translations available. Particularly good ones are Alexis de Tocqueville, trans. George Lawrence, ed. J. P. Mayer, *Democracy in America* (London: Fontana Press, 1994); and Alexis de Tocqueville, trans. Gerald E. Bevan, ed. and with an Introduction by Isaac Kramnick, *Democracy in America* (London: Penguin, 2003). Gustave de Beaumont's slavery book has been reissued recently in English: Gustave de Beaumont, *Marie, or Slavery in the United States* (Baltimore: Johns Hopkins University Press, 1999).

8. On American self-criticism and intermittent angry awareness of the lack of congruence between American political ideals and the sometimes squalid and brutal realities of American life, see in particular Samuel P. Huntington, *American Politics: The Promise of Disharmony* (Cambridge, Mass.: The Belknap Press of Harvard University Press, 1981).

9. G. de Beaumont, *L'Irlande—social, politique et religieuse* (Paris: Michel Levy Frère, 1839).

10. G. de Beaumont, ed. W. C. Taylor, *Ireland—Social, Political and Religious* (London: Richard Bentley, 1839).

11. Beaumont's modern way of presenting his material and findings resembled what in contemporary social science would be called "thick description," after Clifford Geertz. Beaumont's thick description consisted of a wide range of readings and possible interpretations, usually derived from a broad variety of sources. Detailed note-taking, interviews with experts and other knowledgeable sources, direct observation, the collection and careful study of secondary sources such as journals, government reports, books, and studies, as well as detailed

notes from travel books and diaries, all contributed to the final draft. Beaumont often sent tentative arguments and intellectual trial-balloons to Tocqueville in the form of letters or reports, then awaited his friend's response. On occasion Tocqueville and Beaumont would also discuss and elaborate on a third party's opinion, as was the case with the Comte de Montalambert's study *Lettre sur le catholicisme en Irlande* (Lyon, 1831).

In addition to the modern form of "thick description," the success of *L'Irlande* could also lie in the structure of the book—the political constellation and history were described first, followed by a description of present societal conditions; this scheme very much resembles the structure of Tocqueville's *Democracy in America*.

12. In his correspondence with Tocqueville, Beaumont sometimes mentions reviews of his book. On one occasion (letter to Tocqueville, October 26, 1839) Beaumont refers to a review of the journalist Samuel-Ustazade Silvestre de Sacy, who, in an issue of *Journal des Débats*, had celebrated *L'Irlande* as meriting a place beside Tocqueville's *Democracy*—a remark that the modest Beaumont dismissed as going too far. In the same letter, Beaumont also refers to another favorable review by Jean-Baptiste Biot, a professor at the Collège de France and a member of the Academy of Sciences, who had written a piece for the *Journal des Savants* in which he celebrated *L'Irlande* as a successful follow-up study to *Marie*. The letter is reproduced in full in Jardin, *Correspondance*, vol. 3, pp. 390–395.

13. Alexis de Tocqueville, ed. Gustave de Beaumont, *Oeuvres complètes D'Alexis de Tocqueville* (Paris: Michel Lévy Frères, 1860–1866).

14. G. de Beaumont, *L'Irlande—sociale, politique et religieuse*, 7th ed. (Paris: Michel Lévy Frères, 1863), pp. i–lxxxiv.

15. Joel Mokyr, *Why Ireland Starved* (London: Allen and Unwin, 1985), pp. 6–29. The literature on the Irish Famine is vast; see in particular R. Dudley Edwards and T. Desmond Williams, eds., *The Great Famine* (New York: New York University Press, 1957); Cecil Woodham-Smith, *The Great Hunger: Ireland, 1845–1849* (London: Hamilton, 1962); Cormac O Gráda, *The Black '47 and Beyond: The Great Irish Famine in History, Economy, and Memory* (Princeton, N.J.: Princeton University Press, 1998).

16. See Breandan O Buachalla, *Aisling Ghéar: na Stiobhartaigh agus an tAois Léinn, 1603–1788* (Baile Atha Cliath: Clochomhar, 1996) [Sharp Vision: The Stuarts and the Intellectuals, 1603–1788] on both old Catholic aristocratic and popular Irish-speaking attitudes toward the English Hanoverian and Protestant regime. Essentially these attitudes were rather dreamy, but clearly Jacobite or separatist, and eventually there was a drift toward separatism and republicanism in the late eighteenth century, once the bankruptcy of the Catholic Stuart tradition was understood. The "King across the Water" became the descendant, mythically speaking, not of James II, but of an aristocrat who cared nothing for his people.

17. For a vivid illustration of English proselytism and hatred of Catholicism in Ireland in the early nineteenth century, see Charlotte Elizabeth Tonna, *Irish Recollections* (Dublin: University College Dublin Press, 2004; first published as *Personal Recollections*, 1841).

18. On this extraordinary Irish liberal democratic leader, see Charles Chenevix Trench, *The Great Dan* (London: Triad Grafton, 1986). See also Maurice R. O'Connell, ed., *Daniel O'Connell: Political Pioneer* (Dublin: Institute of Public Administration, 1991); Fergus O'Ferrall, *Catholic Emancipation: Daniel O'Connell and the Birth of Irish Democracy* (Dublin: Gill and Macmillan, 1985). The classic rehabilitation of O'Connell in the face of his hypernationalist republican detractors is Seán O Faoláin, *King of the Beggars: A Life of Daniel O'Connell, the Irish Liberator, in a Study of the Rise of Irish Democracy (1775–1847)* (London: Nelson, 1938, since reissued many times).

19. For a comparative discussion of the much taken-for-granted but actually somewhat problematic birth of Irish democracy, see Tom Garvin, *1922: The Birth of Irish Democracy* (Dublin: Gill and Macmillan, 1996).

Note on the Text

The main text presented here is the 1839 English-language edition of *L'Irlande: sociale, politique et religieuse,* translated and edited by W. C. Taylor (London: Richard Bentley, 1839). The text has been rendered without change, except that the two-volume original edition has been combined into a single volume. The footnotes have been retained and numbered consecutively within chapters wherever their proper placement could be ascertained. In the original English edition, Taylor omitted portions of Part II, which now begins in the middle of Chapter 6.

This edition contains Beaumont's 1863 preface on the Great Famine, newly translated and edited by Tom Garvin, followed by a timeline of important events in Irish history.

Contents

PART I

PART II (ANNEXED TO PART I IN THE TRANSLATION)

IRELAND

Ireland in the nineteenth century

· HISTORICAL INTRODUCTION ·

Translator's Preface

The opinions of an enlightened foreigner, unconnected with the political parties that divide the nation, are always replete with valuable instruction to a people. "To see ourselves as others see us," is as difficult, and at the same time as useful, for societies as for individuals; but to no country is such an aspect of its condition so likely to be of service as Ireland, for in no other part of the world have all circumstances, small and great, connected with the moral, social, and political condition of the country, been so studiously and so grossly misrepresented. The Translator need only mention M. de Beaumont's works on the United States to prove his competency as a political observer; and the extraordinary success which the present work has already had on the Continent, is evidence that his testimony respecting Ireland will guide the opinions of a great part of Europe.

There are some who affect to disregard the opinions which foreigners form of the domestic economy of our empire; "the snail," says the Gentoo proverb, "sees nothing beyond its shell, and believes it the finest palace in the universe;" but though such recklessness may be felt or affected by ardent partisans in Ireland, it is not likely that a similar course will be pursued in England. The political supremacy of the British Empire rests so much on public opinion for its support, that nothing by which that opinion may be changed or modified can be neglected with impunity.

M. de Beaumont designed his work exclusively for continental readers, and therefore, on many points, entered into long and minute explanations respecting the details of British law and administration, which are unnecessary for English readers, and have therefore been omitted. This is the only liberty which the translator has taken with the text, unless the consequent modifications of the division of the matter be deemed changes that ought to be acknowledged.

It was originally designed to add notes and illustrations to the body of the work on the same scale as those appended to the Introduction, but this design has been relinquished to prevent the work from being identified with any of the parties to which the discussions have given rise, and to keep intact its most characteristic and important feature,—its being the record of opinions formed by an enlightened statesman, whose views are obviously beyond all suspicion of being warped by prejudice or passion.

Historical Introduction

The dominion of the English in Ireland, from their invasion of the country in 1169, to the close of the last century, has been nothing but a tyranny.

During the three first centuries they covered Ireland with deeds of violence, the object of which was the completion of the conquest.

The wars of conquest had not ended when those of religion began. England having, in the sixteenth century, renounced the Catholic for the Protestant faith, wished to convert Ireland to the new creed she had adopted, and finding the Irish rebels to her wishes undertook to constrain them; hence the obstinate struggles, the sanguinary collisions, and the terrible catastrophes which lasted more than a century.

When the wars which the Irish maintained for the defence of their religion and country terminated, English oppression did not cease. Seeing that the Irish preserved their religious faith in spite of the violence employed to make them abandon it, England attempted to attain the same end by other means. She had discovered the inutility of force, and she tried corruption. Hence a persecution less barbarous, but not less cruel, more immoral, perhaps, because it assumed the semblance and supported itself by law, which continued nearly a hundred years.

This persecution ceased, not because England brought it to a close, but because Ireland would endure it no longer. One day Ireland undertook to shake off the English yoke, and commenced a struggle for independence, sometimes fatal, more frequently prosperous, which has lasted to our days.

The history of the English dominion in Ireland may be regarded under four principal points of view.

The first embraces the long convulsions of the conquest, from the reign of Henry II. to that of Henry VIII.

The second comprehends the religious drama of the sixteenth and seventeenth centuries; it begins with the Reformation, or Henry VIII., and ends with the Revolution, or William III.

The third comprises the period of legal persecution, extending from the battle of the Boyne, in 1690, to the early part of the reign of George III.

The fourth, which may be considered as the new era of Ireland, because it is that from which the awakening of the country to liberty dates, has for its starting point the independence of the American colonies, and for its most remarkable feature in cotemporary history, Catholic Emancipation, in 1829.

The author is about to cast a rapid glance over those four epochs. These pictures of the past are absolutely necessary for the right understanding of the present.

First Epoch: From 1169 to 1535

CHAPTER I

In 1156, a bull of Pope Adrian IV. bestowed the kingdom of Ireland on Henry II., King of England.[1]

This bull proves, that even at this epoch Henry II. had extended his views to Ireland, whose sovereignty he obtained from the power which then disposed of empires. Adrian IV. was an Englishman by birth, and, doubtless, he felt sympathies for his native land, of which Henry knew how to take advantage.

We read in Hanmer's Chronicle, "Anno 1160, the king (Henry II.) cast in his minde to conquer Ireland; he sawe that it was commodious for him, considered that they were but a rude and savage people."[2]

It was not until twelve years after that the Anglo-Normans invaded Ireland, and the Chronicles give us the following account of the occasion.

"Dermot, king of Leinster, having carried off the wife of O'Rourke, king of Meath, the latter complained to O'Connor, titular monarch of all Ireland, who instantly embraced the cause of the outraged monarch, and expelled the author of the wrong from his kingdom. Dermot, in his despair, went to seek aid from the English king. Henry II., gladly embracing the opportunity of accomplishing a design which he had long projected, promised to do Dermot justice.

"In a short time, Fitz-Stephen, and afterwards Strongbow Earl of Pembroke, landed in Ireland with a numerous suite of Norman knights.

"Nevertheless, scarcely had Dermot introduced the strangers into his country, when, perceiving that he would not be restored to the possession of his states, he endeavoured to persuade Fitz-Stephen to return. But Fitz-Stephen replied, 'What is it you ask? We have abandoned our dear friends and our beloved country; we have burned our ships, we have no notion of flight; we have

---

1. Mac Geoghegan, vol. i. p. 460; Sir R. Musgrave's Irish Rebellion, p. 3; Thierry's Norman Conquest, vol. iii. p. 12.

2. Hanmer's Chronicle, p. 215; Ancient Irish Histories, vol. ii.

already periled our lives in fight, and, come what may, we are destined to live or die with you.'"[3]

Dermot did not recover his crown, and the English remained in Ireland.

They remained there, but not without encountering endless opposition; for if their invasion was singularly easy, the completion of the conquest was a work of extraordinary difficulty.

The first invasion took place in 1169, and, according to the most authentic accounts, we must go down to the reign of James I., in 1603, to find the completion of the conquest. Thus, during more than four centuries, the English only exercised disputed dominion over Ireland.

The spectacle afforded by the native Irish and the Anglo-Normans, struggling to preserve their country, the others to subdue it, must be interesting to all, but especially to Frenchmen.

These native Irish assailed, in their savage but haughty independence, all belonging to the same Celtic race, from which the Gauls, our ancestors, are descended.

And those Normans who invaded them left France in the preceding century. Their names are sufficient to reveal their origin—Raymond le Gros, Walter de Lacy, John de Courcy, Richard de Netterville, and a thousand others of the same sound.[4]

But the history of such distant times would exceed the limits of this introduction.

The author's design, in the sketch he offers of this first epoch (from 1169 to 1535), is merely to give the reader some notions of the people invaded by the Normans; he is also anxious to point out the causes which rendered the invasion easy, and the conquest difficult.

It is not rare to find it alleged by English writers, that at the epoch of the conquest, Ireland contained a wretched, vile, and degraded population; an allegation probably inspired by the desire of imputing the misfortunes and corruption of this people to causes anterior to the English conquest. It is, however, certain that nothing in the contemporary records justifies such an assertion.

"Such," says Campion, "is the character of the Irish; they are religious, sincere, violent in love and anger, compassionate and full of energy in misfortune, vain and superstitious to excess; good horsemen, passionately fond of war, charitable and hospitable beyond expression . . . They have acute minds, are desirous of instruction, and learn easily what they wish to study; they are persevering in labour,"[5] &c.

---

3. Hanmer's Chron., vol. ii. p. 230.
4. Mac Geoghegan, vol. ii. pp. 3–6; Hardiman's Galway, pp. 9–11.
5. Campion, p. 20.

"When Robert Fitz-Stephen and the brave knights of Britain invaded Ireland," says Hanmer, "they did not find cowards, but valiant men, brave both as horse and foot."[6]

"The bodies and minds of the people," says Sir John Davis, at a late period, "are endowed with extraordinary abilities of nature."[7]

Now, how has it happened that this noble population has been surprised by a handful of adventurers? And how, thus invaded, has it for centuries resisted conquest,—too feeble to repulse its enemy, sufficiently strong in its reverses never to submit—equally incapable of enduring or shaking off the yoke—enduring the stranger in its territory without ever losing the hope of his expulsion? How did it happen that these two populations, the one conquering and the other conquered,—the latter sometimes subdued, sometimes in rebellion,—the former always superior without being master—have lived together in a state of warfare for centuries,—either in a state of fierce warfare without one annihilating the other, or in a state of peace without mutual union.

Three principal causes facilitated the Anglo-Norman invasion of Ireland; first, the social and political condition of Ireland in the twelfth century; second, the still recent fact of the Danish invasion; and third, the influence of the court of Rome.

Section I. Political Condition of Ireland in the Twelfth Century

In the twelfth century the political organisation of Ireland was such that its social forces, infinitely divided, could be held together by no common bond. The four provinces, Leinster, Ulster, Munster, and Connaught, had each a separate king.[8] In truth, these four kings recognised one of their number as monarch of all Ireland, but his supremacy was more nominal than real; besides, none of the four provinces having the privilege of conferring on its monarch the power of ruling over the rest, violent quarrels arose at the death of every sovereign, each of the four equal kings claiming the vacant monarchy.[9] The same elements of discord and anarchy which incessantly divided the four provinces externally, were also to be found in their internal condition.

For, as beneath the same monarch were placed kings who were his equals, though subordinate to him, so beneath the king of each province was an infinity of secondary kings and princes, who were also as equal, as independent, and as

---

6. Hanmer's Chron., vol. ii. p. 228.
7. Sir John Davis's Discovery of Causes, &c., p. 2.
8. There was a fifth king in Meath.—*Tr.*
9. Leland, vol. i. The two great families which disputed the supremacy, at the time of the contest, were the O'Connors and Hy Nials, or O'Neills. Dermot was a partisan of the latter, and hence Roderic O'Connor eagerly seized the first pretext for his expulsion.—*Tr.*

divided as their immediate superiors.[10] This fractional division of the social forces did not stop there. After the petty principalities came a multitude of clans, tribes, and families, all separated from each other, not only independent among themselves, but held by the feeblest ties to the sovereignty within whose sphere they were comprised.[11] Besides the inherent weakness arising from this indefinite subdivision of public powers, there was in such a political state another source of exhaustion and ruin; to wit, the perpetual struggles which arose from this great number of equivocal sovereignties, of rights destitute of sanction, of authorities, rivals in fact, though nominally subordinate one to the other, and which incessantly produced opposing pretensions which could only be decided by war.[12] The chiefs of clans presented, within the narrow limits of their authority, the same spectacle of discord and anarchy as the petty princes above them, in less restricted bounds, and as the kings of the provinces in the wider circle of their power.

It may be easily conceived, that a country where the social forces were thus mutilated, and had no point of contact, save for mutual destruction, was of all countries the most favourable for the invasion of a conqueror. However powerful those forces might have been, collected in a mass, each of them was annihilated in isolation. Such was the state of Ireland at the epoch of the Anglo-Norman conquest.

Section II. The Still Recent Invasion of the Danes

Ireland, which has suffered so cruelly from conquest, was the last of the European countries conquered. At the time when the savage nations of the north sought countries to invade, Ireland, separated from them by two seas and one large island, long escaped their notice; the Romans disdained it, the barbarians knew it not. Gaul and England had been each stained by three invasions, while the soil of Ireland remained intact. Still, about the middle of the ninth century, the Danes, a people issuing from the forests of Scandinavia, landed in Ireland; they occupied a part of it without much difficulty; but the opposition to them became vigorous and obstinate. After a series of sanguinary combats, and alternations of victory and defeat, these stern conquerors abandoned the hope of founding an empire in the heart of the country, and limited themselves to the occupation of some points on the south and east coast of Ireland.[13] Dublin, for-

---

10. Leland, vol. i. p. 11.

11. Gordon's History of Ireland, vol. i. p. 31.

12. In the list of one hundred and seventy-eight monarchs of the Milesian line, enumerated by Irish historians, only forty-seven died natural deaths;—seventy-one were slain in battle, and sixty murdered.—*Tr.*

13. Under Zurgesius, the Danes for a brief space established their authority over the whole of Ireland.—*Tr.*

merly Dyvelin, Wexford, and Waterford, are Danish cities.[14] Thus, the Irish, who had been sufficiently strong to check the Danes in their invasion, were too feeble to expel them completely; and at the moment when the Anglo-Normans came into Ireland, the Danes remained masters of all the east coast of Ireland, lived in a sort of tacit peace with the Irish, who were contented to see their conquerors confined to a narrow space, with the understood condition that they would not pass its limits.

However this may be, these struggles, maintained for three centuries, had exhausted the country, and increased the weakness of the body politic, already so great.[15]

The presence of the Danes on the Irish soil at this epoch diminished, for another reason, the strength of Ireland. The Anglo-Normans landed precisely in that portion of the country which was occupied by the Danes; consequently the Danes had to sustain the first shock of the Norman invasion. Now, it is impossible to imagine a more unfortunate circumstance for a country menaced by invaders. On one side the Danes, defending against the Normans a precarious and contested possession, could not display the zeal and devotion of a people summoned to the defence of their country.[16] On the other side, the Irish, seeing the Anglo-Normans engaged with the Danes, their first assailants, fluctuated between the terror which the new conquerors inspired, and the satisfaction with which they beheld the destruction of an enemy established in their territory.

All these circumstances united, sufficiently show how Ireland, both social and political, must have been weak in resisting the Anglo-Norman invasion.

Section III. Influence of the Court of Rome

The third cause favourable to the invasion was, the influence, then all-powerful, of the court of Rome, which gave Ireland to the conquerors.

It was the time of the temporal and spiritual supremacy of the popes, the rivals of kings, the tribunes of the people in the middle ages; it was the time in which, when the most powerful prince resisted the court of Rome, the successor of St. Peter deposed him from his throne, and found the people submit to his decrees. At this time Ireland was eminent for its piety and sanctity amongst the most Christian nations. Its priests were at the head of political as well as religious society.[17] In this country, where the social powers were feeble, uncertain,

---

14. A little before the Anglo-Norman invasion, the Danes in these cities declined the jurisdiction of the Irish prelates, and placed themselves under the see of Canterbury.

15. So weak were the Irish, that the king of the Isle of Man attempted the conquest of their country.—Tr.

16. The Danes were at first disposed to receive the Normans as fellow-countrymen, but the conduct of Fitz-Stephen in Wexford drove them to resistance.—Tr.

17. Mac Geoghegan, vol. i. p. 464.

and ill defined, there was no fixed and invariable rule but that of religion,—no undisputed authority common to all but that of the priest.[18] I find, in 1160, ten years before the Conquest, the Archbishop of Armagh regulating, as supreme arbiter, the quarrels of several Irish kings, between whom he alone could restore harmony.[19] Now, this clergy, supreme in Ireland, had for a quarter of a century been subject to the church of Rome.[20]

It was under such circumstances that Henry II. came to Ireland. He offered himself as a prince, the friend of peace and justice, who came not to strip the Irish of their rights, but to ensure their tranquil enjoyment of them; when he departs, he will leave their political power to the great, their domains to the proprietors, their spiritual authority to the priests, their country, their laws, and their institutions, to all. He only wants one thing, the title of Lord of Ireland, and he will only avail himself of it to promote religion and morality;[21] and he claims not this great mission as his own; he has received it from Pope Adrian IV. and Pope Alexander III.; he seizes Ireland, not to satisfy ambition, but to obey the papal bulls. Religious Ireland, which at this period recognised the authority of the Romish church, could not receive harshly a monarch who presented himself to her with so solemn a mandate as that of the sovereign pontiff. Thus, all the great dignitaries of the Catholic church in Ireland were seen to proclaim the rights of the king of England.[22] It may well be conceived how this moral assistance of the clergy, the most powerful that could be directed against Ireland, must have protected an invasion already favoured by so many other causes.

Thus the social and political condition of the Irish,—the presence of the Danes in the midst of them,—their very religion,—all these causes combine to explain the facility with which the Anglo-Normans gained a footing in Ireland.

CHAPTER II

We are now to inquire how, when the invasion was made without difficulty, the conquest could not be completed without perils continually renewed for centuries.

This fact is also explained by three principal reasons; the first equally derived from the political condition of the Irish; the second, from the relations between

---

18. Gordon, vol. i. p. 105.

19. Mac Geoghegan, vol. i. p. 462.

20. The papal authority was for the first time formally recognised at the synod of Kells, A.D. 1152.—*Tr.*

21. Lingard, vol. ii. p. 205.

22. The sovereignty of Ireland was solemnly granted Henry II. at the council of Cashel, over which the papal legate, Christian bishop of Lismore, presided. The only Irish prelate absent was Gelasius, Archbishop of Armagh, but he subsequently came to Dublin, and publicly gave his full assent to the proceedings of his brethren.—*Tr.*

the Anglo-Normans and England; the third, from the condition to which the natives were reduced by the conquerors.

Section I. Political Condition of the Irish an Obstacle to the Conquest

I have just said that the indefinite division of the social forces in a country singularly facilitate an invasion; I shall add, that nothing is more adverse than this fractional partition to the permanent establishment of the victor in the conquered country. That which is, in the first instance, a source of weakness for the invaded country, becomes, in the second, the principal cause of its strength. In the same proportion as it is difficult for the people resisting the invasion to unite suddenly all its divided elements of action; in the same proportion it is difficult for the conqueror to subdue, after invasion, this multitude of partial forces, spread here and there over a wide extent of territory, all of which bring to the struggle the same tribute of resistance, from the very fact of their being independent of each other.

It may be reasonably said, that a country in which the central power is strong, is at once the most difficult to invade, and that which after invasion presents the fewest difficulties to the conqueror. All the forces of the nation being assembled on a single point, offer a powerful condition of success, which once having failed, leaves the country without defence. It is just the contrary in a country where the national force is not concentrated; it is easy to invade, and difficult to conquer. This is distinctly seen in the first ages of our (French) history. The conquests of the men of the north, which so terribly succeeded each other, were only terminated when a power, feeble in its centre, but strong in its parts, was constituted in the land. Since the establishment of feudality in Europe, there have been several invasions, but there have been no conquests.

The Irish possessed very imperfect notions of the feudal system; but the division and dispersion of the public power over the country, which is one of the characters of that system, belonged equally to their social state. This is the reason why the Danes so easily landed in Ireland, and yet could never establish themselves in the heart of the country. On the arrival of the Anglo-Normans, the same cause produced the same effects.

I believe that this social condition of the Irish injured the Anglo-Normans in the conquest of the country more than it served them in the invasion. For reasons already explained, they easily conquered a part of Ireland, but for several centuries they made vain efforts to complete their conquest. Down to Elizabeth's reign, the conquered part never exceeded a third of all Ireland, and was often less. It was called the *Pale,* on account of the palisades or fortifications with which its borders were sometimes surrounded. The *Pale* was composed of part of Leinster and the south of Munster: sometimes a victory gained over the Irish tribes, sometimes a clever treaty concluded with one of their princes, extended the bounds of the Pale, which, on the other hand, were narrowed after every reverse of the Anglo-Normans. The conquerors often endeavoured to aggrandize the Pale by invasions in Ulster and Connaught, but they were regularly repulsed during four centuries. Even in that part of the island which we call the Pale, their power did not cease to be contested during these four centuries, and history displays to us an uninterrupted series of Irish rebellions, bursting out sometimes at one point and sometimes at another, leaving to the conquerors not a single moment of repose or security.[23]

The Anglo-Normans were thus stopped short in their progress; the great interest of the Irish was to expel them from the space they occupied. But we shall soon see that the same cause which, after having aided the invasion of the Normans checked their conquests, must have assisted them to preserve what they had acquired.

In fact, scarcely had they reached Ireland, when the Anglo-Normans established themselves as feudal lords in all the places of which they were masters.[24] The native Irish and the Anglo-Norman colony were then nearly balanced both in strength and weakness. When the Anglo-Normans wished to extend their conquests, they found scattered here and there among the native Irish an infinity of obstacles arising from their political condition; when, after having repulsed and discouraged their enemies, the Irish undertook to expel them from the countries forming the Pale, the weakness attached to the fractional character of their forces re-appeared; and having become in their turn invaders of their conquerors, they failed before the Anglo-Normans, who, besides the advantage of resisting aggression, feeble, because they were divided, opposed to the Irish the same dispersion of social strength which is so powerful to resist an invasion. Each of the parties was strong when it defended its own territories, and weak when it attacked those of its adversary.

Section II. Second Obstacle to the Completion of the Conquest: The Relation of the Anglo-Norman Conquerors to England, and of England to Them

The conquering population contained two very distinct elements; one party was composed of Norman lords, occupying a secondary situation in England, and who, arms in hand, came to seek in Ireland estates and higher rank; this was the feudal portion of the conquerors; it occupied the rural districts. In the train of the army came a crowd of adventurers of the lowest class, belonging to the British, Saxon, and Danish races, of which the latter had conquered the former, but all had been subdued by the Normans. These came to trade in Ireland, and settled in the cities. The first seized the ground, to live by the toils of the natives

---

23. Geoghegan, vol. ii. p. 74–232.
24. Ibid., vol. ii. p. 26.

reduced to vassalage; the second hoped to enrich themselves in the cities by industrial pursuits. Now, there was one fact which, though favourable to the country of the colonists, was eternally adverse to their establishment in Ireland—I mean the vicinity of England.

For colonists, whether they possess land or ships, it is a great element of success that they should be sufficiently distant from their native soil as to adopt the conquered land for their new country; that they should not have the wish nor the means of leaving it to return to their birthplace; that it should be as difficult to leave it as to reach it; and that, on setting their foot on the invaded soil, they should feel it necessary to become its masters for the future, or to lose their lives in the struggle. Unluckily, such was not the situation of the Anglo-Normans who came from England to Ireland. These emigrants never quitted home without a design of returning. Ireland was never their adopted country: they have always taken it in some sort on trial, and on the condition of separating from it if they were dissatisfied; to them the experiment, if unlucky, was not fatal; they escaped to return to England, where they always had their main interest. Nearly all the Norman lords who obtained land in Ireland did not cease to be proprietors in England,[25] and with most of the merchants in the cities their Irish trade was only a branch of their commercial establishment in some English city. To the Norman lord, Ireland was a farm; to the British merchant merely an office; if both failed, they returned home without much loss. From this state of things it resulted, that a great number of the new inhabitants of Ireland had, at their arrival, an interest more or less great to quit it; and even when they remained, it was always with a resolution not to stay permanently; it was not an honest, definitive residence; when they gave themselves to Ireland, they did not cease to belong to England; hence the perpetual arrivals and departures from one country to another, which gave Ireland, not the appearance of an English colony, but of a place of pilgrimage; hence the absence of the proprietors of Irish lands, so often lamented, and against which the interests of the country and the English government struggled in vain;[26] hence came the passing population of colonists, succeeding each other with frightful rapidity, all bearing in their breasts the same dislike for the new country, the same sympathies for the country they abandoned.

It is a portentous starting point for a new colony, when those who take possession of the land are not bound to it by strong ties, and, as I may say, rooted to the soil. The absolute necessity of living on the conquered land gives the con-

---

25. Mac Geoghegan, vol. ii. p. 70.
26. Absenteeism was made the subject of complaint in the reign of Edward I., was taxed by Richard II., and threatened to be punished with forfeiture by Henry VIII.—*Tr.*

queror greater energy to subdue it, and gives birth to more prudence, more justice, and more humanity, in his relations to the vanquished.

If the Anglo-Normans never completely subdued the Irish, if they were unjust and cruel in their government, is it not especially because they did not look upon themselves as linked, without hope of return, to the destiny of the conquered country, and that, seeing England always near as a friendly land, a refuge in case of shipwreck, they were never excited nor restrained in their actions by feeling that success was necessary, and failure without remedy?

The starting point of the Anglo-Norman population established in Ireland has had a marked influence on the destiny of the country.

When the Normans had conquered England, all the great vassals, having to struggle against the authority of the crown, adopted two principal means of increasing their strength; they formed a strict union amongst themselves, and they mingled with the vanquished populations, in whom they found external support.

The Norman conquerors of Ireland had not a like interest to adopt the same course, because their king resided in England. Scarcely were they masters of a part of Ireland, when they divided amongst themselves, and commenced those deplorable struggles in which the interests of the country were absolutely sacrificed, and into which each of them merely carried views of personal aggrandisement. The strong castles which they constructed, both as residences and fortresses, became the theatre of private quarrels, in which the Normans exhausted against each other the forces which they should have reserved for the common enemy. Some possessed immense domains and great power; they lived almost like kings in the midst of their vassals; their fiefs were erected into palatinates; they created knights at their pleasure; and no authority had access to their domains, not even the officers of the king.[27] These great barons subdivided each of their possessions into an infinite number of sub-tenancies, making grants of land on the condition of military service, just as the king had done to them.[28] Placed at a distance from the only supreme power which could control them, the great vassals, jealous of each other, because they were nearly equal, aspired mutually to destroy each other, and during three centuries Ireland was covered with blood, shed in support of these sad rivalries. The history of the conquest is entirely filled with the quarrels of the Butlers and the Fitzgeralds, who during

27. The Geraldines, in the reign of Henry III., seized and imprisoned a lord deputy for opposing their exactions; and it was not without difficulty that they were persuaded to set him at liberty.—*Tr.*

28. Hence the criminal calendars in the disturbed Irish county exhibit the names which in England would be deemed most aristocratic—Fitzgerald, Burke, Lacy, Grace, Butler, &c.—*Tr.*

four hundred years divided the colony.[29] Thus Ireland had scarcely escaped the first violence of the conquest when she fell into all the evils of feudal anarchy;[30] and feudal anarchy was more disastrous in Ireland than anywhere else, because the Norman vassals, far from their sovereign lord, gave themselves up without restraint or reserve to all sorts of disorders and excesses.[31] It was a feudality without a king. Thus abandoned to the counsels of their own selfishness, the conquerors lost sight of the common interest; each consoled himself for seeing the power of all weakened, provided his own was augmented; and he who had extended his own domain cared little if the circle of English possession in Ireland was restricted. There was not a cause of increase for individuals which was not a cause of ruin for the mass. Strange situation! the vassals of the king of England were too distant to be restrained by his authority, and yet they were sufficiently near to demand assistance when it was required. Hence a sad consequence resulted; their tyranny, unrestricted by superior power, could be exercised with impunity over all the inhabitants of Ireland. They had a very feeble interest in rendering the population happy, whose aid against the king they did not absolutely require; and they could oppress that population without reserve, sure of royal aid to suppress any insurrection.

It may be easily seen how many obstacles to the subjugation of Ireland arose from the situation of the conquerors relative to the native Irish. Other difficulties not less grave arose from their relation to England.

From the very first day of the invasion a violent collision was manifested between two interests widely distinct—the interest of the conquering Norman lords, and that of the king of England.

In order to attain their object, the complete subjugation of the invaded country, the Normans ought to occupy the land, reduce the natives to vassalage, and when once masters of the population, govern it with equity, mingle with it by slow degrees, and, in one word, preserve by peace and justice what had been obtained by all the violence and iniquity of war. It is only at this price that con-

---

29. The Butlers supported the house of Lancaster, the Fitzgeralds that of York; but they cared more about their own rivalry than the disputed succession. In one of their contests, the old Earl of Desmond, desperately wounded, was made prisoner, and borne on a litter from the field. When tauntingly asked by the conquerors, "Where now is the great Earl of Desmond?" he spiritedly replied, "Where he ought to be,—on the necks of the Butlers."—*Tr.*

30. The exaction of "coyne and livery," or food and pay for their retainers, was one of the most ruinous oppressions to which the cultivators of the soil were subject. Baron Finglas, chief justice of Ireland under Henry VIII., declared, "it would destroy hell, if used in the same."—*Tr.*

31. In a curious remonstrance of Fedhlim O'Connor to King Henry III., we find, among other claims for the cruelties and robberies of De Burgho, a charge of three thousand marks for the burning of churches and the massacre of the clergy.—*Tr.*

quest, always founded on usurpation, can render itself legitimate in the course of time.

On the other hand, the English monarchs feared that if their Norman vassals formed too close a union with the Irish population, and were fused with them, a new people might arise from the mixture, sufficiently strong to assert its independence, and too close not to be formidable; they thought, on the contrary, that if the conquerors never ceased to be English, if they never united with the natives, but remained as intermediates between them and England,—if, in a word, they remained simple colonists under the protection of the mother-country, then conquered Ireland would cause no alarm to England, but would become a valuable possession.

The entire evil has originally risen from this opposition of interests; the result was, that Ireland had a mixed government, half feudal and half colonial; the king was too distant to have the feudality well regulated,—the vassals were too powerful to have the royal colony obedient. This conflict between the English kings and their vassals continued during four centuries with various fortunes: in consequence of these vicissitudes, Ireland was sometimes led by the Anglo-Norman feudality, which, in the midst of all its evil passions, often yielded to the interest of all conquerors—that is, to mingle with the conquerors,—sometimes by the royal power, which feared that its supremacy could not be retained, except by preventing the union of the victorious and the vanquished.

Scarcely did Henry II. learn the prosperous issue of the invasion of Fitz-Stephen, and subsequently of Strongbow, than in his quality of king he claimed the advantages; and wishing to ensure his rights, he recalled his victorious vassals to England, forbade them to pursue the conquest, and, in order to complete it himself, went in person to Ireland.

We may well be surprised that Henry II., so jealous of maintaining his royal superiority over his conquering subjects in Ireland, should first have founded for their profit that feudal power which at a later period became the rival of his own. All the power of the barons, in fact, arose from the large grants of land which he made, or permitted them to make; but Henry acted thus because he could not act otherwise.[32]

A conquest was not effected in the middle ages as in the present. In our days, the prince who subdues a country garrisons it with a paid and permanent army; and whether he aids his subjects to become colonists, or leaves the possession of

---

32. Henry II. had formed wise plans for extending and securing his conquests, when he was recalled to England by the alarming intelligence of the rebellion of his ungrateful sons, and the arrival of two papal legates to inquire into the circumstances of Becket's murder. He never afterwards had leisure to return to Ireland.—*Tr.*

the soil to the natives, he remains, by means of his soldiers, master of the conquered country.

Nothing like this could occur at a time when a king possessed neither a permanent army nor soldiers properly so called. His military forces did not belong to him personally, but were furnished by his vassals, who, in return for grants of land, paid a military service restricted within narrow limits. The feudal army could not be required by the king, save in determined cases. Compelled to support a defensive, it was not bound to an offensive, war. When a conquest was undertaken, all who accompanied the king submitted without doubt to feudal rule, but no one was bound to follow him; and when his vassals, in such a case, joined him, it was under the condition, expressed or understood, that the conquered country should be divided between all, according to the rank of each. Henry II. could not have conquered Ireland without his vassals; without them he could not preserve his conquests, and he could not pay their past services, nor ensure their future devotion, without bestowing lands; he granted them in all Ireland, with the exception of some royal reserves,[33] and on this condition he had an army.[34]

The difficulty was, to give them a power which he could not refuse, and at the same time preserve his own. Here we must repeat a fact which constantly presents itself in the history of Ireland, and which, however viewed, is always a misfortune or an embarrassment,—I mean the geographical position of Ireland with respect to England. When we examined the condition of the Anglo-Normans in Ireland, whether as land-owners or merchants, we found nothing more adverse to them than the extreme vicinity of England. If we now consider it in another point, that of the royal interest, we shall find that Ireland, instead of being too near, was too distant. In truth, from the mere absence of the king, the vassals found themselves independent, and beyond the reach of royal authority; and it was commonly said that the king's subjects in Ireland were more Irish than the Irish themselves. *(Ipsis Hybernis Hyberniores.)*[35] We have seen above what a sad use they made of this independence, and how they pursued their selfish designs in despite of the royal power. They had only one common interest in which they could agree with the king; that was, when the existence of the English colony was so menaced, that the vassals ran the risk of losing their estates, and the king his lordship. But when the Anglo-Norman possession was

---

33. Mac Geoghegan, vol. ii. p. 139, gives an interesting account of the levying a feudal army by Edward III.

34. Plowden, vol. i. p. 36.

35. Some of the Norman barons actually abandoned English law, manners, and name, to assume the character of Irish petty princes. Thus two of the De Burghos, having usurped the lands of their nephew, took the titles of Mac William Oughter and Mac William Eighter (the farther and nether Mac William.)—*Tr.*

secured, the quarrel was renewed between the Normans, who, no longer having need of the king, evaded his power, and the king, who, seeing the conquest secure, did not fear to weaken the conquerors.

Doubtless the king would have triumphed in the struggle, if he had been able, if not to reside permanently in Ireland, at least often visit it, to show his power. But we must remark, that from the time of the conquest to Elizabeth, that is to say, during the whole period embraced by our first epoch, the kings of England had not a single moment of political leisure, domestic or foreign. The domestic feuds of the Plantagenets, the wars with Scotland, France, and the barons, and, finally, the murderous contests of the houses of York and Lancaster, spent the blood and wasted the strength of England. None of the monarchs who succeeded each other during this terrible drama could, for the sake of his power in Ireland, leave England, where his life was not less menaced than his crown.[36]

Placed in the absolute impossibility of governing the Anglo-Irish colony themselves, the kings of England were forced to delegate their power to a deputy; but it was a further misfortune that they could never procure good delegates. Their representative, called sometimes viceroy, sometimes lord deputy, lord justice, or lord lieutenant, was, in general, either too weak or too strong. If they selected one of the great vassals in Ireland, they did not find in him a willing instrument for the repression of the Norman lords. A great feudatory himself, he made common cause with his fellows, and turned against the king the arms with which he had been supplied to combat feudality.[37] If, to escape such a peril, the king chose a less considerable personage for his lieutenant, such as a simple knight, whose worth was merely personal, then this deputy, possessing only the royal confidence and his own merit, had no influence over the great vassals with whose government he was charged.[38]

Henry II., John, (when a prince,) and Richard II., are the only kings of England, who, during the four centuries succeeding the invasion, showed themselves in Ireland; and they only appeared there, being always called home by some interest superior to the peace of Ireland. "In 1395," says an Irish historian, with great candour, "Ireland would have been assuredly conquered by Richard II., had he not been called home to resist the Duke of Lancaster."[39]

It is now evident that numberless obstacles, arising both from the relations of

---

36. Richard's absence in Ireland afforded Henry IV. an opportunity of usurping the crown. — *Tr.*

37. This was particularly the case with the Geraldines, whose family connexions were very extensive.

38. To this cause must be ascribed the failure of Sir Thomas Rokeby to tranquillise Ireland. (A.D. 1053.) He was one of the most enlightened governors Ireland ever possessed, but he wanted power to accomplish his designs. — *Tr.*

39. Mac Geoghegan, vol. ii. p. 161.

the Anglo-Normans to England, and from those of the English kings to the feudality established in Ireland, impeded the conquest of that country.

Section III. Third Obstacle to the Conquest: The Condition Imposed on the Natives by the Conquerors

The great interest of the Anglo-Normans was, as I have already said, to unite as rapidly as possible with the natives, and to form with them a single community, completed by sentiments, ideas, and interests. Victory physically unites the conquerors and the conquered, but a moral alliance between them can alone give permanence to the conquest.

Now the first means that presents itself to conquerors for sowing among the vanquished the seeds of union and mutual sympathy, is to give the latter a share in the social and political advantages of the established government, and at once place them under the rule of a common equity. But, whether through pride, selfishness, or weakness, the Anglo-Normans, during four centuries, adopted a contrary course of proceeding towards the native Irish.

No sooner were the Anglo-Normans established in Ireland, than they at once came into possession of the privileges and liberties peculiar to feudal society, which the kings of England had probably no inclination to dispute, even if they possessed the power. They had recognised rights, guarantees formally stipulated, and institutions as free in principles as those of England. Trial by jury was established in Ireland; laws were made in Irish parliaments, composed of Lords and Commons; and shortly after Magna Charta was proclaimed in England, its empire was recognised in Ireland. But when the Anglo-Normans received such liberties, they kept them to themselves, and did not extend their benefits to the Irish population subject to their sway.

The vanquished population, amongst whom the national spirit was deeply rooted, naturally felt no disposition to take the new law of the conqueror; it clung to its ancient traditions and old customs, and perhaps it would have taxed the utmost efforts of the conquerors to obtain the adoption of their laws. But instead of labouring to give such laws, the Anglo-Normans, or rather the kings of England, whom they were forced to obey, were absolutely opposed to the introduction of English law.[40]

We have seen already the interest which the English king had in preventing

---

40. Mr. Beaumont is not quite justified in ascribing the opposition to the introduction of English law either to the Irish people or the English monarchs; both frequently evinced much anxiety for such a consummation, but they were baffled by the local ascendency. In the reign of Edward I., the Irish princes contiguous to the English settlements offered to the king, through his deputy, a subsidy of eight thousand marks, on condition of being admitted to the rights of British subjects. Edward earnestly recommended their petition to the Anglo-Norman parliament, but it was rejected by that body with every mark of indignation.—*Tr.*

the union of the Anglo-Normans with the native Irish, which he feared to see become too strong, and the division of whom was weakness.

The Norman barons, on their side, who committed the greatest disorders, and severely oppressed the native population, were interested in preventing the sufferers from appealing to English law for protection against their outrages.[41]

Thus, after the first chaos of invasion, the Anglo-Norman population and the native Irish, instead of displaying a tendency to unite, ceased not to form two separate communities, having each its distinct government and its own laws.[42]

This separation established by law in political society was introduced into the cities by municipal regulations.

Immediately after the conquest, Anglo-Norman populations were established in the Irish towns: these settlers came for the purposes of commerce and industry, and they failed not to procure for themselves the monopoly of both. These towns successively obtained charters which granted them certain privileges, and constituted them municipal corporations.

As the exclusive interest of a town composed of merchants is a commercial interest, it may be easily understood that the municipal corporations of Ireland were commercial corporations. Now, these corporations followed the inclination natural to all privileged bodies, which is an exclusive tendency.

The Anglo-Norman towns had doubtless an interest in trading with the natives, but they had from the beginning a double interest to exclude the Irish from their walls; first, because this exclusion was ordained by statute, and they could not with impunity break the law; secondly, because to admit a new citizen within their precincts was generally to admit a new commercial rival. So that

---

41. Five Irish septs or families, called the five bloods, were admitted to the benefit of British law by Henry II. In the roll of pleas, 28 Edward III., is the following curious proof that the exclusion of the rest of the natives amounted to a total denial of justice.

"Simon Neal complains of William Newlogh, that he, with force and arms, &c., broke the said Simon's close, &c., whence he says that he is damaged to the amount of twenty shillings, and thereof, &c.

"And the aforesaid William comes now and says that the aforesaid Simon is *an Irishman, and not of the five bloods,* and asks judgment if he be held to answer him."

Fortunately Simon was able to prove himself one of the five bloods, viz. the O'Neills of Ulster, and he therefore obtained compensation.—*Tr.*

42. Hardiman says, "No fact is better authenticated than that, for many centuries, the native Irish continued to enact laws in their own districts to prevent any intercourse whatever with the English settlers, whose rapacity and want of principle, say the native historians, were so notorious, that they became proverbial.

> With one of English race no friendship make;
> Shouldst thou, destruction thee will overtake;
> He'll lie in wait to ruin thee when he can;
> Such is the friendship of an English man."
>
> *History of Galway,* p. 68.

though they were compelled to form commercial relations with the natives, they took care that they should not share in their commercial privileges.

Still such is the irresistible sympathy which leads the best separated populations to unite, that in spite of all these obstacles, the Irish and the conquerors made several efforts to approximate; and as the English law did not permit the Irishman to become an Anglo-Norman, the Anglo-Norman became an Irishman: the vanquished being unable to receive the laws of the victor, the conqueror took those of the conquered.

[43]It was attempted to check this tendency by the STATUTE OF KILKENNY, (A.D. 1366, Edward III.,) an act memorable in the dark annals of Irish legislation. This law provided that marriage, fosterage,[44] or gossipred[45] with the Irish, or submission to the Irish law, should be considered and punished as high treason. It declared that if any man of English descent should use an Irish name, speak the Irish language, or observe Irish customs, he should forfeit his estate, until security was given for his conformity to English manners! It was also declared penal to present a mere Irishman (that is, one not of the five bloods,[46] or who had not purchased a charter of denization) to any benefice, or receive him into any monastery. And finally, it was strictly forbidden to entertain any native bard, minstrel, or story-teller; or to admit an Irish horse to graze on the pasture of a liege subject.

These proscriptions were not idle menaces; in the reign of Edward IV., Fitzgerald Earl of Desmond, one of the greatest of the Anglo-Norman barons, was condemned to death, and executed, for having married a wife of Irish blood.[47]

Thus the link destined to unite the conquerors and the vanquished was broken so soon as it was formed.

---

43. In the translation of this passage, a slight liberty is taken with the text; Mr. de Beaumont took his account of the Statute of Kilkenny from Sir J. Davis, who only quotes the parts which bear on a particular point; it has been deemed better to turn to the act itself.—*Tr.*

44. The custom of placing the children of the chief to be nursed by the wife of a favourite tenant is not yet banished from remote districts in Ireland. The fraternal link was not more binding than that between the foster-children, and the nurse was scarcely less respected than the mother. In spite of the law, the custom was adopted by the English and their descendants to a very late period: the Irish customs and excise are full of records connected with provision made for persons connected by fosterage.—*Tr.*

45. In the Irish church, before its union with Rome, the relation of sponsor to god-child was deemed more sacred than it ever has been in the Latin or English church, and traces of the feeling are still discernible.—*Tr.*

46. See note, page 36.

47. Desmond was put to death, without the formality of a trial, by the Lord Deputy, Tiptoft, Earl of Worcester, who procured an act of attainder against both him and Kildare, for "alliance fostering and alterage with the king's enemies." His real crime was ridiculing the king's marriage with Lady Elizabeth Grey. He had been previously a royal favourite on account of his services against the Butlers, who were partisans of the house of Lancaster.—*Tr.*

The policy of England opposed equally to the Irish becoming English, and to the English mingling with the Irish, compelled the vanquished to become enemies. They remained such, and after a thousand submissions, simulated or sincere, they incessantly renewed their struggles, which, though inadequate to establishing their freedom, rendered the triumph of the conquerors singularly precarious and insecure.

Two facts prove, better than the most laboured reasoning, the sad effects of the plan adopted by the English for the government of Ireland.

In 1406, three hundred years after the invasion, the Irish made war at the gates of Dublin, and ravaged with impunity the suburbs of that city: in the middle of the reign of Henry VIII., when that prince was at the height of his power, the extend of the Pale was limited to a radius of about twenty miles.[48]

Second Epoch: From 1535 to 1690

CHAPTER 1: RELIGIOUS WARS

What four hundred years could not effect, we shall see accomplished in a century—the complete conquest of Ireland. Henry VIII. commenced the work, Elizabeth and Cromwell finished it. Three despots of such a stamp were not likely to wish the same thing without effecting it, and each of them desired ardently, though for different reasons, the conquest of Ireland. It is not the achievement itself that deserves our attention, so much as the causes which produced it, and the consequences which followed. Until then, Ireland had only been to England an object of secondary consideration; how did it suddenly become the principal object of English policy? Elizabeth expended on its conquest all the treasures of England: Cromwell displayed in its reduction all the resources of his valour and intense will; and when the great religious and political drama, which, during the seventeenth century, so fearfully agitated England and the entire world, came to a close, Ireland was the theatre of the combat; the problem of English liberty or servitude was solved on the banks of the Boyne.

Ireland was conquered—all the Irish insurrections stifled; henceforth there is but a single law in Ireland, that of England; there is no more a Pale, no more Irish provinces distinct from the colony; all becomes English Ireland, and every inhabitant is equally subject to the English sovereign. How does it happen that this contest, instead of preparing a union between the conquerors and conquered, establishes between them a new and larger separation, renders hereafter a compact union impossible, and plants in the breasts of both parties germs of mutual hatred, which have only been further developed by the course of years and ages!

---

48. Mac Geoghegan, vol. ii. pp. 167 and 300.

The solution of these questions is found in a single fact, which is, as it were, the soul of this entire period, and the key of all Irish miseries; I mean the opposition which was then established between the religious creed of the conquerors and the vanquished.

Section I. How, When England Became Protestant, It Must Have Desired That Ireland Should Become So Likewise

The philosophic and religious movement which, in the sixteenth century, terminated in the Reformation, and produced such an immense effect in England and Scotland, did not reach Ireland: whilst England and Scotland became protestant, Ireland remained catholic.

From the first moment of its appearance on the stage of the world, the doctrine of Luther had divided nations, and this separation was not accidental.

Although the theory of the innovators was very far from freedom, it had been forced, if not to give it birth, at least to invoke its name, and that was sufficient to ensure the Reformation a natural sympathy among populations in possession of free institutions, whilst the countries subject to despotism naturally rejected a worship sprung from free examination, and attached themselves more closely than ever to the ancient faith, which was based on authority.

This, united with several other causes not connected with my subject, explains why France and Spain continued linked to the court of Rome, whilst England and Scotland separated from it. The religious dispute of the sixteenth century was not merely a dispute of ideas and creeds, struggling with each other in the arena of intelligence and faith; it was a political war of nations; it was a solemn contest between the principle of authority represented by the immovable power of the court of Rome, and the liberty of which the Reformation was the symbol.

I have already said that England took the side of the Reformation; hence the chief cause of the misfortunes of Ireland during the period which occupies our attention. England having become protestant, must have wished that Ireland should become so likewise, and this was to wish an impossibility.

England must have wished it; and, in fact, the spirit of proselytism which then animated the christian world, was not less ardent with her than the other countries of Europe. Her reformers were as enthusiastic and intolerant as the Catholics whom they had conquered; and religious fanaticism by itself would have impelled the English to attempt the conversion of Ireland; but they had, in addition, an imperious political reason: if they did not impose the reformed faith on Ireland, they had reason to fear that Ireland would reestablish the Catholic church. Whilst they stigmatised the Romish creed with the names superstition and idolatry, the Catholics repulsed the reformed doctrine as heretical and impious. In this season of ardent faith, one church could only be preserved by the destruction of the other. In truth, Ireland in the sixteenth century was not formidable to England except on account of foreigners. Scarcely had the great quarrel between Protestantism and Catholicism burst forth in Europe, when Ireland became the aim of all the Catholic countries, eager to overthrow Protestantism in England. It was the hope of the court of Rome, and the centre to which the intrigues of the Papacy, Spain, and France, tended. From the very beginning of the Reformation, the sovereign pontiff indicated his reliance on Ireland, by circulating an old prophecy, intimating that the throne of St. Peter would not be shaken so long as Ireland remained Catholic.[49]

Thus, though England had been led, by intolerant passions, to combat the Catholic religion in Ireland, it would have been compelled to the effort by care for its own defence, and interest in its own liberties.

But I have said, that in wishing to render Ireland Protestant, England desired an impossibility, and this is easily demonstrated.[50]

Section II. Of the Causes That Prevented Ireland from Becoming Protestant

After the long night of the middle ages, light had suddenly sprung up amongst all the nations of Europe, and society had made rapid progress everywhere, except in Ireland, where the civil strife of the conquest having been perpetuated, everything remained stationary.

In the midst of a political chaos and a moral anarchy, faith in the Catholic and Romish church had alone remained in the creed of the Irish people. This faith reigned in absolute sovereignty over their minds, without any other idea to divide its empire.[51] Whilst the successive efforts of a philosophical spirit prepared Europe for religious reform, Ireland, in a remote corner of the world, distant from every intellectual movement, was still safe from doubt; she had learned nothing of Wycliffe or Huss; she had not heard the mutterings that preceded the eruption of the volcano; she had seen none of the brilliant flashes which heralded the great conflagration of the sixteenth century.

Of all European countries, Ireland was consequently the most attached to its

---

49. Plowden, vol. i.

50. The claim of England to supremacy over Ireland for four centuries rested on a papal grant, and that grant was conditional. This fact had been so repeatedly recognised by parliaments, ecclesiastical synods, and all other public authorities, that it was universally regarded as a first principle. By adopting the Reformed religion, England clearly voided the grant; and if Ireland remained Catholic, every Irishman acknowledged the pope's right of resumption. England had, therefore, no alternative but to abandon the country, or to change the conditions of allegiance; which could not be done to all appearance at the time without subverting the ancient faith.—*Tr.*

51. It must also be added, that the native Irish clergy won the affections of their flocks by frequently interfering to check the oppressions of the oligarchy; the Irish, therefore, valued their religious system as the only institution which afforded them any protection from the tyranny of the aristocracy.—*Tr.*

ancient creed, and the least capable of comprehending the new religion which the English wished to establish.

It must be added, that had these dispositions been different, the Reformation presented itself under such circumstances that it could not be accepted.

Who, in fact, brought to Ireland a creed which the country neither desired nor comprehended? It was brought by a people with whom the country had been at war for four hundred years, by a people whom it hated as a mortal foe, and from whose yoke it still hoped to escape. It might be said with confidence, that if the Irish were inclined to reform their faith, this attempt of England would have prevented them; under existing circumstances, it would only be an additional motive to combat an adversary, who not only wished to conquer the country, but to impose upon it a religion.

Besides, when the monarchs of England invited the Irish to shake off the yoke of Rome, they found themselves in a dilemma, which must have invited the Irish to resistance, if they had not been impelled by more serious motives. It was from the pope that the English monarch had originally received his rights; how then could he contest the power from which he held his sovereignty? how throw doubt on the spiritual authority of the pope, whose temporal power had not been contested when it was exerted to bestow a kingdom?

The enterprise of England was clearly impossible. Thus the despotism of the Tudors, which established the Anglican church in England, only revolted Ireland. Henry VIII. and Elizabeth seized all the monasteries, greedily confiscated all ecclesiastical wealth, commanded the use of the Anglican ritual in all the Catholic churches,[52] subjected to severe penalties those who absented themselves from church, and made the oath of supremacy necessary for sharing in all

---

52. It was a ridiculous but a very mischievous blunder of the English rulers, that they did not cause the Prayer-book to be translated into Irish; for to the mass of the people English was as much an unknown tongue as Latin. This violation of the very first principle of the Reformation, which required that prayers should be offered in a language understood by the people, excited hostility and ridicule. It was, of course, fair game for a satirist like Ward, and his attack on it is far the most pungent part of his Hudibrastic History of the Reformation.

> They cried the mass down, 'cause (they said)
> The priest in unknown language pray'd,
> And yet themselves their prayer-book sent
> To such as knew not what it meant.
> And it was read, and psalms were sung,
> And sermons preach'd in English tongue,
> Among wild Irish; where not one
> Knew what they said; but cried O Hone!
> O Hone! they cried, and shook their heads,
> With grief to change their mass and beads,
> For what they knew to be a pray'r,
> No more, poor souls, than Banks his mare.

acts of social and political life. They had acted the same way in England, but the two countries were in a different position. After the sanguinary wars of the Roses, the English wished, at all hazards, to give their monarchs power, which indeed they were capable of taking by force. Religious supremacy could not be refused to Henry VIII. without diminishing his royal authority, of which it formed a part, and to this the English people had no inclination. It was quite the contrary with the Irish, who, far from seeking to strengthen the power of the English monarch, were eager to escape from it, and eagerly seized an additional reason for detesting it. Thus, while Henry VIII. and Elizabeth established the reformed faith in England, according to their will and pleasure, all their efforts to fix it in Ireland terminated in three or four insurrections against England, to which, without doubt, the national sentiment was no stranger, but which, nev-

---

The best passage in the book is a whimsical description of an English clergyman reading prayers to an Irish congregation; the people make responses in the wrong places, and occasionally raise an Irish howl which frightened the poor stranger.

> He came at last out of his fits,
> And gather'd up his scatter'd wits;
> Assum'd new courage, and grew brisk,
> And took his journey to his desk:
> Where, being seated in his chair,
> Gives laud and praise, and falls to pray'r;
> When, lo! another hill-lil-lil-im,
> Which he mistook for kill, kill, kill him,
> So stunn'd him that he could not pray
> One word, but strove to get away;
> Then in a cold sweat down he fell,
> Alive or dead he could not tell.

The congregation believing the parson dead, raise a lament over him in a truly Irish style.

> Oh! hub-bub-boo! (for all did weep
> To see the parson dead asleep);
> What made thee die? Oh, dear Aroon,
> What made thee go away so soon,
> And leave thy tythes behind? Hubboo,
> Hadst thou not tythe of calf and cow,
> Of lambs and ewes, and new-shorn fleece,
> Of honey, wax, and bees, and geese?
> O Hone! tythe-duck, and sow, and pigs,
> Tythe-chickens, hens, and Easter-eggs.

He is finally brought home by the sexton and his wife.

> Being thus in safety home convey'd,
> He gets his supper, and to bed:
> For always, whether well or ill,
> His stomach was infallible;
> Their church itself was never so
> Infallible as parson's maw.—*Tr.*

ertheless, were principally derived from the new source of hatred springing from religion.[53]

Ireland was, in truth, subdued by Elizabeth.[54] This princess, in less than ten years, spent three millions and a half of money, an immense sum for the sixteenth century; and lost an incalculable number of her bravest soldiers in effecting this conquest. But the result of the submission of Ireland was the cessation of the war, not the adoption of the Anglican worship. Perhaps it might have been foreseen that the Irish, whilst submitting to civil and political laws, would retain their religious creed and worship; for it is the natural disposition of man, when he undergoes physical violence, to take refuge in his soul, and proclaim himself free there, while his body is loaded with chains.

The first efforts of despotism had been vain; the Irish retained only the recollection of the tyranny; they remembered that, to conquer them and change their worship, Elizabeth had waged a cruel war, followed by frightful famine and destructive plague.[55]

The Stuarts ascended the throne of England; the English became more protestant, because they suspected that their rulers were not so. The Irish, on the contrary, believing the Stuarts Catholics, were encouraged to remain such. This is the reason why, after Charles I., the Irish, who hated the English, generally loved the king of England. The fear of fines, the dread of confiscation, the terror of imprisonment, often produced external conformity to the English worship in the towns; all those who executed any public, even a municipal office, were obliged under heavy penalties to comply with the English ritual;[56] finally, there was always a current of new comers from England, who were Protestants when they arrived, and remained what they were. Nevertheless, in consequence of political events, the English government which imposed this worship lost its power in Ireland; the English settlers, as well as the Irish natives, abandoned the

---

53. The Irish Juvenal, written in the beginning of the last century, but for some unknown reason never published, says,

> "You'll scarce believe it, 'tis so wondrous odd,
> They hate each other for the love of God."—*Tr.*

54. The semi-official history of the conquest was called Hibernia Pacata.—*Tr.*

55. More than one half of the population perished by the sword, famine, or pestilence. "The country," says Hollinshed, a contemporary writer, "which was before rich, fertile, populous, abounding in pasturages, harvest-lands, and cattle, is now deserted and barren; no fruit or corn grows in its fields, no cattle is found in its pasturages; there are no birds in the air, no fish in the streams; in a word, the vengeance of Heaven is so heavy on the land, that it may be traversed from one end to the other almost without meeting man, woman, or child."—Hol. 460. It was on this occasion that the principal woods of Ireland were destroyed, and several bogs formed by the decay of the falling timber and the stoppage of the mountain streams.—*Tr.*

56. The Elizabethan Act of Uniformity (2 Eliz.) obliged all public functionaries, from the highest to the lowest, to take the oath of supremacy.

Anglican church, and spontaneously returned to the Catholic religion. This happened after the death of Elizabeth, to whom James I. succeeded, a monarch believed in Ireland favourable to catholicism.[57] It was the same under Charles I. in 1642, when the population believed it possible to take up arms against the English parliament, and at the same time remain faithful to the king. Even during the periods of tranquillity and submission, observance of the Anglican worship was with difficulty obtained from the English inhabitants of the towns themselves. During Elizabeth's reign, the greatest persecution of the Catholics was the prohibition of their own ritual; no serious efforts were made to enforce the adoption of that of England. James I. was more enterprising without being more fortunate. During his reign it once happened that the town of Galway could not find a mayor willing to take the oath of supremacy;[58] and Chichester, viceroy of Ireland,[59] giving an account of the vain efforts he had made to bring over some leading personages to the Anglican church, whose conversion was eagerly desired, depicted very accurately the state of the country when he declared that the atmosphere and even "the soil of Ireland were tainted with popery."

Such was the state of affairs in Ireland, that the reformed religion could not be supported by a regular and durable persecution. Circumstances necessarily and suddenly led to a general war. In England it was a struggle of parties so nearly balanced, that one was ultimately the master of the other; in Ireland it was an entire Catholic population driven to revolt when its religion was assailed.

Section III. How England Rendered Ireland Protestant—Protestant Colonisation—Elizabeth and James I

It was impossible to convert Ireland to Protestantism, and yet it was necessary that Ireland should become Protestant.

This necessity was every day more imperious for England; for, besides its hatred against a religious and political principle hostile to its own, it feared Catholic Ireland, and the more, as its own liberties were disputed, and as the absolute governments of the continent formed many intrigues in Ireland to strike with the same blow the Protestant religion and the liberties of England.

The first means derived from persecution and war having failed, another was tried: wholesale confiscation; the expulsion of the Catholics from the Irish soil,

---

57. James I. was obliged to issue a proclamation to disabuse his Irish subjects of the notion that he was disposed to grant liberty of conscience. The proclamation is too long for insertion, but is in its way a perfect curiosity.—*Tr.*

58. Hardiman's Galway, pp. 212, 213.

59. See his letters in the collection of State-papers. Chichester's honesty may be doubted; he was anxious to make a fortune by trafficking in Irish confiscations, and the reconciliation of the Irish owners to the English church would have impeded his designs. He finally acquired immense estates in Ulster, and bequeathed to his posterity a princely fortune and a detested name.—*Tr.*

and their immediate replacement by Protestant colonists. This violent and odious means had nothing repugnant to the manners of the times; for confiscation
and death had been at the bottom of all the political and religious quarrels from
the time of Henry VIII.; it could only be said, that when tried on so vast a scale
it was of difficult execution; for how could an entire population be driven from
its natal soil? What was to be done with the people torn from their dwellings?
How could all be massacred? If not massacred, how were they to live when
plundered? And further, how could an entire people be found ready to take their
place? It is not so easy as people think to practise injustice. Still the obstacles did
not daunt the projectors.

The first attempt of this kind was made in the reign of Elizabeth. The genius of this queen discovered the object to be attained, and her tyranny easily
adopted the means. Desmond's revolt was the opportunity.[60] Near six thousand
acres in the province of Munster having been confiscated, proclamation was
made in England, offering these lands to all who would take them on certain
conditions, of which the first was, that not a single farmer or labourer of Irish
birth should be employed on these lands.[61] About two hundred thousand acres
were thus distributed to the new settlers of English descent. The old inhabitants
of the soil, dispossessed of their domains, only found shelter in the depths of the
forests, or on the uncultivated sides of the mountains.

The work begun by Elizabeth was continued by her successors.

In the reign of James I., the real or imaginary plot of the Earls of Tyrone and
Tyrconnell, and Sir Cahir O'Dogherty, having been detected, the six northern
counties which belonged to them, (as suzerains,[62]) Donegal, Tyrone, Derry,
Fermanagh, Cavan, and Armagh, were confiscated to the crown; rather more
than half a million of acres were thus placed at James's disposal. As, after Elizabeth's first confiscation, several of the English on whom lands had been be-

---

60. Desmond was driven into rebellion by the subtle malignity of the Earl of Osmond and
others, envious of his power and estates. He offered to surrender to Admiral Winter, on condition of being conveyed to England to plead his cause before the queen, but this was sternly
refused. To take his trial in Ireland, was voluntarily to submit to ruin, for the political trials of
that day, at least in Ireland, are edifying comments on the maxim, "It is quarrel and cause
enough to bring a sheep that is fat to the shambles."—Tr.

61. Leland, vol. ii. p. 301.

62. The Irish chiefs possessed the *suzerainité* but not the property of the soil: consequently
the guilt of O'Donnell, though even so clearly proved, could not affect the right of their feu-
datories, who were not even accused of treason. The English law of forfeiture, in itself sufficiently unjust, never declared that the interests of innocent tenants should be sacrificed for
the rebellion of the landlords; it only placed the king in the place of the person whose property
had been forfeited, and left all the relations of the tenantry unaltered. Yet were all the actual
holders of lands in these devoted districts dispossessed without even the shadow of a pretence;
and this abominable wickedness is even at the present day eulogised by many as the consummation of political wisdom.—Tr.

stowed had not entered on the possession, James permitted the Scots on this occasion to share with the English in the division of the confiscated estates, under the pretence that they were nearer Ireland, but in reality through partiality for his countrymen.

The regulation of this new colony was not precisely similar to that which had served as a base for the first.

In Elizabeth's colony, the occupant of the soil should be an Englishman—in that of James I., it was necessary he should be a Protestant of the Anglican church.[63]

Experience had consequently shown a defect in the first colony, which an effort was made to avoid in the second.

"The original English adventurers," says Leland, "on their first settlement in Ireland, were captivated by the fair appearance of the plain and open districts. Here they erected their castles and habitations, and forced the old natives into the woods and mountains, their natural fortresses: thither they drove their preys —there they kept themselves unknown, living by the milk of their kine, without husbandry or tillage—there they increased to infinite numbers by promiscuous generation, and there they held their assemblies, and formed their conspiracies without discovery." (Lel. vol. ii. p. 431.)

To escape this peril, quite a different plan was adopted for the second plantation; the confiscated lands were given to the new settlers, on condition of their residing in the woody and mountainous part of the country, whilst the dispossessed natives were left free in the plains, where they would be more easily watched. A still more important innovation was made—the Irish whose lands were confiscated, and the new English settlers who had been intermingled in Elizabeth's plan, were settled in distinct and separate districts.[64] It is from this colonisation that the city of Londonderry, founded by the corporation of London, arose; from it also dates the Scotch and Presbyterian settlement in Ireland; and this starting point of puritanism in Ireland is too important not to be demonstrated.[65]

James I. had made great advances in his iniquitous work, and he was so proud of his success that he had nothing more at heart than its continuance. The dif-

---

63. This rule was not enforced against the Scottish Presbyterians, who were just as unwilling to take the oath of supremacy as the Irish Catholics.—*Tr.*

64. Leland, vol. ii. p. 431.

65. Most of the Elizabethan settlers were attached to puritanism, as were also the Protestant clergymen sent over during her reign: hence the Irish church has been always more deeply tinged with Calvinistic principles than the church of England. The Elizabethan adventurers, particularly those who accompanied Sir Walter Raleigh and Richard Boyle, (afterwards Earl of Cork,) were chiefly the younger branches of noble and respectable families in Devonshire and the western counties of England; they were long remarkable for their steady adherence to Whig principles, and many of them so continue to the present day.—*Tr.*

ficulty in his view was not to dislodge the natives and replace them by new settlers, for his wisdom had solved all the difficulties of execution; the obstacle was,
that there were no more lands to confiscate; and though nothing was easier than
to expel the Irish from their houses and estates, it was necessary to assign a motive for such conduct. The subtle spirit of James was not long at fault. This
monarch, who, according to Sully, was "the wisest fool in Europe," this pedantic
spirit waged war against Ireland like a pettifogging attorney.

After ages of civil war and anarchy, there necessarily existed great uncertainty
and confusion in the titles to estates in Ireland; no doubt many usurpations had
been committed, but the chief defect in the titles was irregularity. Taking advantage of this irregularity, a trick well worthy of his limited understanding, James
resolved to deprive of their lands all whose titles were not strictly regular, and
seize them for the crown. In consequence, a crowd of lawyers, interested in the
plunder by the hope of sharing the booty,[66] pounced upon Ireland like a flock of
harpies, shook the dust from old parchments; and by their chicanery, their ingenuity in discovering flaws and errors of form, and their diligence in hunting out
defects, real or imaginary, succeeded so well, that there was not a proprietor who
enjoyed the shadow of security; the king obtained a vast number of estates, and
was able to stock them with Protestant colonists in place of the Catholic proprietors so cleverly ruined.

Section IV. Protestant Colonisation—Charles I

James had discovered a tyrannical expedient, of which his successor, Charles I.,
did not fail to take advantage.

There was in Ireland one province which had hitherto escaped every attempt
at colonisation, that of Connaught. The viceroy, Wentworth, afterwards Earl of
Strafford, resolved to dispossess all the inhabitants of this vast country, and confiscate it to the king, who might afterwards dispose of it at his pleasure. To accomplish this enterprise, he took with him judges and soldiers, the first to falsify
the law,[67] the second to violate it.[68] Both agents admirably answered his expectations. The lawyers suddenly discovered that all the grants made by preceding

---

66. At the head of "The commission for the discovery of defective titles" was placed Sir
William Parsons, an unprincipled adventurer, on whom craft and crime have conferred an un-
enviable notoriety. Through his exertions and those of his brother "discoverers," half a million
of acres was forfeited to the crown.—*Tr.*

67. Strafford's own letters contain the most minute accounts of this mystery of iniquity.—
He tells his correspondent that "he obtained a grant of four shillings in the pound, out of the
first year's rent of every estate vested in the crown by these inquisitions, to the judges who presided at the trial."—*Tr.*

68. Strafford says, "He took with him to each town where an inquisition was held five hundred horsemen as *good lookers on.*"—*Tr.*

kings to the actual proprietors or their ancestors were null and void, and that Connaught had no lawful proprietors but the king. It was not sufficient to discover the defect of titles, it was further necessary that the proprietors should recognise it, and withdraw; if they did not go of their own accord, they should be constrained to abandon their estates by force, and this was the business of the soldiers. Preceded by an imposing army, Strafford traversed the country, spreading terror everywhere, and receiving everywhere the most servile submission. Still, when he reached the county of Galway, Strafford was stopped in his progress by the resistance of the inhabitants: in this county, though bent under severe despotism, there were still certain legal forms inherent in the government and the manners of the conquerors. A jury was empannelled in Galway to decide between the crown and the occupants of the land. Strafford spared no pains to obtain a verdict for the king.[69] Still the jurors found for the defendants.[70] This fact alone would be sufficient to prove that there are guarantees and protection in a jury, which will triumph over the chicanery of fraud and the menaces of force. When Strafford heard the verdict he flew into a passion—on his own authority he fined Darcy the sheriff 1,000*l*. for empannelling an improper jury—he arrested the jurors themselves, and brought them before the Court of Starchamber in Dublin, where each of them was sentenced to pay a fine of 4,000*l*., and to acknowledge himself guilty of perjury on his knees. All had the courage to refuse this humiliating proposition. Some time after, Strafford wrote to Wandesford, another servant of Charles, and Strafford's successor in the government of Ireland—

"I hope that I shall not be refused the life of Sheriff Darcy; my arrows are cruel that wound so mortally, but it is necessary that the king should keep his rights."

Darcy was not executed, but he died of severe treatment in prison. A new jury was summoned, which, under the salutary influence of terror, found that in all time the county of Galway, like the rest of Connaught, belonged to the king; and this sentence placed all the proprietors at the mercy of the king.[71] Trial by jury, though one of the most vital institutions, does not save a country from the insolence of despotism, when despotism is established; still a jury defends the citizens better than any other tribunal. If it yields to corruption, it

---

69. Strafford himself says, that "he inquired out *fit* men to serve on juries."—*Tr.*

70. They took courage, because they hoped that they would be supported by the influence of the Earl of Clanricarde.—*Tr.*

71. The narrative would not be complete unless it was added, that the Irish proprietors had actually paid one hundred thousand pounds to the king for the concession of certain graces, of which the security of property was one. Charles took the money, but, by Strafford's advice, refused to perform the conditions.

surprises the people, who believed it independent; if it resists, and fails in its resistance, it does not save those whom it wished to protect; but, associated with their misfortunes, it renders their cause more popular, and the oppression which weighs upon them more striking. In either case it sets tyranny in bolder relief.

If we consult the sentence pronounced against Strafford by the parliament of England, we are led to believe that the violence offered to the Galway jury was not the only nor the worst outrage of the kind committed by Strafford in Ireland. One of the reasons assigned for his condemnation was, "Considering that juries who had given their verdict according to their consciences have been censured in the court of Star-chamber, severely fined, sometimes exposed in the pillory, have had their ears cut off, their tongues pierced, their foreheads branded," &c.[72]

Too happy to be able to please his English parliament by exercising his royal prerogative, Charles I. would have gladly plundered all the Catholics of Ireland, and bestowed their estates upon English Protestants, but even his tyranny in Ireland could not procure him pardon for his arbitrary government of England. To such a degree was popular indignation excited, that the tyranny towards Ireland was actually made a ground of complaint against Strafford. The royal authority was already greatly shaken (A.D. 1640); the king then suddenly ceased from oppressing the Irish, whose support he was anxious to secure in case of a reverse. The entire project of colonisation was abandoned; the Irish were assured that there never was a thought of plundering them. When you see a Stuart just towards Ireland, be well assured that his authority is tottering in England.

Section V. Civil War—The Republic—Cromwell

It may be said that from the moment when Charles I. no longer persecuted Ireland, and abandoned the great project of the time, to make it protestant at all hazards, he was no longer king of England.

Thenceforward the true sovereign was the parliament; it was no longer an English king nor his delegate that was at war with Ireland,—it was England herself, puritan and protestant England, no longer restrained in its hatred by a prince less the enemy of the Catholics than of the Puritans. England henceforth enters into close contact with Ireland, which had become more free in its hostility to England, since the king, who favoured the Catholics in combating the Puritans, lost his power.

Two terrible cries of destruction were raised; one in England, "War against the Catholics of Ireland!" The other in Ireland, "War against the Protestants of England!" It is difficult to say which of these clamours was first raised, just as

---

72. See Parliamentary History, and Hardiman's Galway, 105.—*Tr.*

when two armies meet eager to engage, it is often impossible to decide which has begun the battle.

The day in which Scotch puritanism became master of the king and of England, Catholic Ireland was at once menaced with extermination. It did not wait for aggression to commence its defence, and in the month of October 1641 a terrible insurrection burst forth. All the Irish of Ulster whom James had so ingeniously expelled from their habitations and lands, to put English and Scotch in their places, rose in masses and fell on the Protestant settlers. In a few days, O'Neill, the Irish leader, was at the head of thirty thousand soldiers.

In this awful moment, when all the passions of the Irish were at work, we may judge which passion was predominant in their souls; and it is remarkable that in the first moment not a single Scotchman was killed; their vengeance in the beginning was directed against the English. Was not this because the national sentiment was still superior to religious passions? The Scotch, from their puritanism, were the most terrible enemies of Catholic Ireland; but they were new enemies, whilst their inveterate enemies, the enemies of five centuries, were the English, the English of Henry II., the first invader, the English of Henry VIII. and Elizabeth, the last conquerors, the English of James I., protestant and plundering settlers.

In the execution of this terrible vengeance, in which so many ancient resentments were united, cruelties were committed which will scarcely bear recital.

The insurrection was at first regular; the insurgents limited themselves to resuming the property of which they had been deprived, without committing any useless violence. Their rapid success, at first undisputed, gave them the generosity of strength, and their first triumphs having been followed by some reverses, their violence knew no bounds; they became sanguinary and murderous; they vowed not to leave an Englishman alive.

It was then that a civil and religious war displayed itself in all its horrors.

Leland, speaking of the treatment which the prisoners received, says, "Their miserable prisoners, confined in different quarters, were brought out, under pretence of being conducted to the English settlements. Their guards goaded them forward like beasts, exulting in their sufferings, and determined on the destruction of those who had not already sunk under their tortures. Sometimes they enclosed them in some house or castle, which they set on fire, with a brutal indifference to their cries, and a hellish triumph over their agonies. Sometimes the captive English were plunged into the first river to which they had been driven by their tormentors. One hundred and ninety were at once precipitated from the bridge of Portadown. Irish ecclesiastics were seen encouraging the carnage. The women forgot the tenderness of their sex; pursued the English with execrations, and embrued their hands in blood; even children in their feeble malice lifted the dagger against the helpless prisoners." (Leland, vol. iii. p. 127).

In a short time more than twelve thousand Protestants, Anglicans or Presbyterians, were massacred.[73] Those not deprived of life were driven from their lands and houses, which were resumed by the old possessors.

The impulsive and determining cause of this sanguinary insurrection has long been disputed by historians. Inveterate hatred of England,—the desire of recovering the property of which they had been plundered—religious animosity —emulation of the Scots, who had forced a presbyterian covenant from the king, leading the Irish to hope for success in extorting a catholic covenant—fear of being exterminated by the Protestants—the intrigues of the Catholic powers on the continent, have been all assigned as motives by different writers. Is it necessary to choose amongst these causes, and declare any single one the real cause! I think not: it seems to me more just and true to say, that all these motives, and all these passions, have more or less concurred in a single result, which doubtless would have been produced without their union.

Whether the Irish were the aggressors or the attacked in this bloody tragedy remains undecided; still it is very certain that the English Protestants and Scotch Presbyterians accepted with a sort of joy the struggle of extermination which was offered.

It is a generally accredited opinion, that the lords justices of Ireland could have destroyed the insurrection in its bud, and that, instead of doing so, they endeavoured to render it more terrible and extensive.[74] One of these lords justices, Sir Wm. Parsons, whose name deserves to be recorded that it may be branded with infamy, fomented the revolt, hoping to enrich himself by the confiscations of the insurgents; and the plan of this ruler and his colleagues was to engage as many as possible in the outbreak, in order that, by augmenting the number of the culpable, the harvest of confiscations, after the conclusion of the war, should be increased.[75]

I have no doubt that sordid passions played their part at the epoch of which I write; for never are sordid passions more abundant than when they are shaded by great passions; but what I more firmly believe is, that it was not in the power of any of the governors of Ireland to prevent a sanguinary conflict between implacable enemies, when an opportunity of battle was offered.

---

73. It cannot be necessary to enter here into any examination of the very different statements given of the numbers slain at the first outbreak of the insurrection; they vary from five thousand to one hundred thousand; still less need we balance the account with the massacres perpetrated by the officers of government at Bantry and the Island Magee. Beaumont adopts Warner's calculation, which, however, is higher than that of Cromwell's commissioners, who estimated the number of Protestants not slain in fair fight throughout Ireland during the whole war at nine thousand.—*Tr.*

74. Warner, 103—Leland, iii. 140—Hallam, v. 279. (See also the autobiography of Borlase, who was one of the lords justices.)

75. Leland, vol. iii. pp. 160, 161.

Remark—that the combatants were Protestant England and Catholic Ireland.

The English nation then declared by its parliament that it would no longer tolerate popery in Ireland, (Dec. 8th, 1641;) all England then cried out with one voice, Catholic Ireland must be destroyed; Protestantism must be established in Ireland; the last Irishman must be exterminated, rather than allow Catholicism in the country.[76]

To sustain the expense of this merciless war, parliament borrowed an immense sum of money, for the payment of which it mortgaged beforehand the properties of the Catholics of Ireland. Two million five hundred thousand acres were thus pledged to the fanatic lenders. This war of destruction was to be waged against the Irish wherever they were found; an ordinance of parliament prescribed "that no quarter should be given to any Irishman, or Papist born in Ireland, that should be taken in hostility against the parliament, either upon the sea or in England." A captain of a parliamentary frigate, named Swanly, having seized a ship with seventy Irishmen on board, tied them back to back, and threw them into the sea. After the battles of Philiphaugh and Corbie's Dale, the Scotch shot all their Irish prisoners without mercy. It is wondrous to see how faithfully laws are observed when they are executed by the passions.[77]

It seemed, at this moment, as if the whole life and power of England were directed against Ireland: all the puritan passions which had been so impetuous in England, rushed with far different force on catholic Ireland. These passions were assuaged in England by the sympathy they met, but in Ireland they found a barrier which irritated them and rendered them violent. It was no longer the fanatic puritanism which made an irruption from Scotland into England in the midst of an army of saints; the puritanism that invaded Ireland rushed like a bird of prey to its quarry, bringing in its train some generous emotions, but many ignoble calculations and mercenary desires.

England sent to Ireland an army of fifty thousand English and Scotch Presbyterians and Independents, more desirous of vengeance than justice, more greedy of blood than truth, more desirous of adventures and riches than of religious success.[78]

---

76. Hallam, vol. v. p. 276.

77. Dr. Borlase, who wrote a history of what he is pleased to call the rebellion of 1641, professedly to vindicate the character of his near relative, the lord justice, *boasts* that Sir W. Cole's regiment killed two thousand five hundred rebels in several engagements, and adds, with horrid complacency, "there were starved and famished of the vulgar sort, whose goods were seized by this regiment, seven thousand."—*Tr.*

78. The army which Cromwell led to Ireland was composed chiefly of the Levellers, fanatics so called from their opposition to every rational form of government, and who were intent on establishing a species of theocracy, which they denominated "the dominion of the Lord and his saints." The future Protector feared these wild visionaries, and resolved to avert their

Scarcely had the insurrection commenced, even before orders could be received from the English government, when the English army in Ireland gave a specimen of its zeal and sanguinary passions by the cruel manner in which it treated the revolted country. Among other deeds of extraordinary barbarity, it is recorded that, five or six days after the outbreak, Colonel Matthew massacred a hundred and fifty peasants, "starting them like hares out of the bushes." The lords justices, the deputies of the English parliament, at the same time gave the most sanguinary instructions to the Earl of Ormond, the commander of the Anglo-Irish army.

He was directed not only to kill and destroy "rebels, and their adherents and relievers," but also "to burn, waste, consume, and demolish all the places, towns, and houses, where they had been relieved and harboured, with all the corn and hay there, and also to kill and destroy all the male inhabitants capable of bearing arms.'"

One example will suffice to show how these instructions were fulfilled.

The Scottish soldiers who had reinforced the garrison of Carricfergus were possessed with an habitual hatred of popery, and inflamed to an implacable detestation of the Irish by multiplied accounts of their cruelties, horrible in themselves, and exaggerated, not only by the sufferers, but by those who boasted and magnified their barbarities. In one fatal night they issued from Carricfergus into an adjacent district called Island Magee, where a number of the poorer Irish resided, unoffending and untainted by the rebellion. If we may believe one of the leaders of this party, thirty families were assailed by them in their beds, and massacred with calm and deliberate cruelty.

But it was especially when the English republic was established, and when the head of Charles I. fell on the scaffold, that the irruption of the English into Ireland became more fierce and irresistible; then the predominant sentiment of England was no longer concealed, the desire for the destruction of Ireland was openly avowed; the English generals landing in Ireland brought with them carnage, pillage, conflagration. Treaties made with the insurgents were openly violated.[79] Ireland must perish, and, to attain this object, what matters it that moral law should be outraged? It is no longer a question about reducing the people to

---

opposition to his meditated scheme of invasion, by sending them to Ireland. When the army assembled at Bristol, the object of the selection could not be concealed; the soldiers mutinied and refused to embark. But Cromwell's personal influence produced obedience; at the same time their preachers worked upon the spiritual pride of these stern enthusiasts. They compared them to the Israelites proceeding to exterminate the idolatrous inhabitants of Canaan, and declared that they were a people chosen to inherit a land of promise, and purge it of idolatry and superstition. The baser motives described by M. de Beaumont arose from the belief that they were about to conquer a land which "the Lord had granted as an inheritance to his saints."—*Tr.*

79. For instance, the capitulation of Galway.—See Hardiman, p. 133.

subjection; their extermination is required; it is even advantageous that they should resist—let them fight that they may be annihilated. Everything is consequently done to exasperate Ireland; the sacred places are profaned; tombs are robbed; Catholic churches are changed into barracks: the very graves are searched for plunder, and insulted by impious fanaticism.

"Ireland must be destroyed" is the cry of England, and extermination has selected its most formidable instrument. Cromwell is named general of the English army. This occurred in 1649. Nearly two centuries afterwards, I passed through the country traversed by Cromwell, and found it still full of the terror of his name.[80] The bloody traces of his passage are effaced from the soil, but they remain fixed in the minds of men. Cromwell met but two instances of firm resistance in Ireland, and let us see how he overcame them. The town of Drogheda refused to open its gates; he employed two weapons of a very different nature for its reduction. At the moment of assault, he offered life to those who capitulated. The town surrendered at discretion. Cromwell then, with great coolness, ordered that the garrison should be put to the sword.

"His soldiers, many of them with reluctance, butchered their prisoners. The governor and all the gallant officers, betrayed to slaughter by the cowardice of some of their troops, were massacred without mercy. For five days this hideous execution was continued with every circumstance of horror. A number of ecclesiastics was found within the walls, and Cromwell, as if commissioned to execute divine vengeance on these ministers of idolatry, ordered his soldiers to plunge their weapons into the helpless wretches. Some few of the garrison contrived to escape in disguise. Thirty persons only remained unslaughtered by an enemy glutted and oppressed by carnage, and these were immediately transported as slaves to Barbadoes."

Wexford likewise closed its gates against Cromwell, and his soldiers proceeded to put all to the sword, who were found in arms, with an execution as horribly deliberate as that of Drogheda.

The memory of Cromwell continued sullied with these horrors; but all the infamy must not be attributed to him. He had only his share; even the initiative does not belong to him. Two years before, one of these indiscriminate massacres had been perpetrated by the parliamentary army in Ireland, under the command of Colonel Jones, when three or four thousand Irish prisoners were mercilessly put to the sword, after the victory at Danganhill.

It must be frankly confessed that these crimes belong less to the men than the time and the frightful passions of the epoch. They have been charged on a single man, because this man, more extraordinary than the rest, drew all atten-

---

80. One of the most bitter execrations in the mouth of an Irish peasant is, "The curse of Cromwell be on you."—*Tr.*

tion to himself. Cromwell in Ireland was an agent rather than a mover; he made the most energetic use of the English hatred against Ireland, but he did not create it. If his army had not conquered Ireland, one of double or triple the force would have been sent. Constant mistakes are made respecting the power of a man; it is always set down too low or too high.

I could refute several other prejudices existing against Cromwell; and if this were the proper place, I could show that his was the first English army in Ireland that ever observed strict discipline, respected the inoffensive inhabitants, scrupulously paid for every article supplied on its march, and showed itself an instrument of order as well as of terror. The very same man who had so coolly commanded the massacres of Wexford and Drogheda, hanged two of his own soldiers for having stolen a couple of chickens from an Irish cabin. I might say, if I had leisure, that Cromwell was the first man before our time who had appreciated the future destiny of Ireland—its union with England; he realised not only the political but the parliamentary union, for in his time Ireland sent thirty members to the English parliament. Finally, I might add that his son, Henry Cromwell, was the most honest governor that Ireland had hitherto possessed: so disinterested was his administration, that at its close he had not money to defray the expenses of his passage to England.

Besides, Cromwell had not the omnipotence, even in Ireland, usually attributed to great actors on the stage of life. The conqueror of Marston Moor and Naseby was stopped in his march before the little town of Clonmel, in the attack of which he began by losing two thousand soldiers, and which he did not take until after a siege of two months. The destructive fanaticism of which Cromwell was the instrument and the guide, had encountered in Ireland a more pure and noble fanaticism,—that of a country defending its religious worship, and of religion defending a country. During the siege of Clonmel, the (Catholic) bishop of Ross, who had displayed great zeal in raising an army to relieve the besieged place, was made prisoner by Lord Broghill, who had become an auxiliary of Cromwell. He had been too distinguished in the war against the parliament to hope for mercy. Still Broghill promised the prelate his life, on condition that he would use his spiritual authority with the garrison of a fort near the field of battle, and persuade it to capitulate. The bishop of Ross allowed himself to be led to the front of the fort, so that the garrison could hear his words. The holy man then raising his voice, without losing for a moment his calmness and serenity, strenuously exhorted the soldiers to hold out against the enemies of their religion and their country. He then came back, and resigned himself to his fate.[81]

---

81. "His enemies," says Leland, "could discover nothing in this conduct but insolence and obstinacy, for he was a papist and prelate."

Individual and indiscriminate executions greatly advanced the work of destruction; but three circumstances impeded it; first, the recall of Cromwell to England; secondly, the disgust for blood which indulgence produces in the most sanguinary; and finally, the terror caused by these murders, which, leading the insurgents to submission, gave some respite to the wearied cruelty of the conquerors. After the exterminations of war came those of peace—that is to say, judicial executions. These were few, if we consider the time. There were not more than two hundred, on the severest inquisition, condemned to death. The tribunal by which the sentences of death were pronounced, has kept the name of Cromwell's slaughter-house. We must add to this number several priests who were subsequently hanged for the mere fact of remaining in the country. Means were adopted to drive the Catholic proprietors and soldiers of Ireland into exile, but, after all, the Catholics remained in the proportion of eight to one of the Protestants.[82] It must be confessed that persecution is an ungrateful task, and that the extirpation of an entire people is very difficult, in spite of the assistance derived from massacres and proscriptions—in spite of the most murderous scourges.

Death and exile not having accomplished all that was expected of them, recourse was had to a last expedient, less violent, but not less iniquitous. It was resolved at all hazards to separate the English Protestants from the Irish Catholics; for the fate of the settlers sent by James I. was remembered, massacred by those whom they had plundered, and in the midst of whom they had the imprudence to live. The following expedient was adopted when it was found impossible to expel all Irishmen from Ireland. It was resolved to people three out of the four provinces, of which Ireland is composed, exclusively with Protestants, and to admit Catholics only into the fourth; not that even this was to be without Protestants, but that it was the only one in which Irish Catholics should be permitted to reside. This province, the last refuge of the Irish Catholics, was the province of Connaught, to which was added the county of Clare. All that war had ruined, all that poverty had protected from hatred or persecution—in a word, all the misery of Ireland, fled or was driven, into Connaught. But this wretched population was still the most noble in Ireland; it bore with it the faith of its ancestors and the love of its country. The whole future of Ireland was there. Having once entered Connaught, the Catholics were penned there like sheep; they were forbidden under pain of death to pass the borders. Their southern boundary was the right bank of the Shannon, and every Irishman found on the left bank could be slain with impunity. This right bank, where Ire-

---

82. Sir William Petty calculates that more than half a million of Irish perished by the sword, pestilence, famine, or exile, between 1641 and 1652.

land was sentenced to perpetual imprisonment, was the famous county of Clare, which ten years ago sent the first Catholic member to parliament. Singular expiations often arise from great iniquities.

Thus, when the poor Irish, in the excess of their distress, dying with hunger, themselves, their wives, and their children, lifted their hands to heaven and implored mercy from their persecutors, Cromwell and his saints replied, *"Go to hell or Connaught!"*

I have said that Connaught was the only province in which Catholics were received, though it ceased not to be occupied by Protestants. It may easily be imagined how dangerous to their neighbours such an agglomeration of enemies, exasperated by their misery, must have proved, if they had not been restrained by some power in the midst of them. This power was that of the cities, which it was resolved to make Protestant, leaving only the rural districts to the Catholics. This was a more delicate task than the other, because the cities were almost exclusively inhabited by Catholics of English origin, who seemed to excite more interest than the native Irish. This, however, proved no obstacle. The English Catholics were expelled from their houses in the town, as the Irish had been from their cabins in the country. English or Scotch Protestants were immediately put in their place; the municipal offices were supplied from the army; captains became mayors, and sergeants aldermen. Sir Charles Coote, the republican general and president of Connaught, charged with the expulsion of Catholics from the town of Galway, called it "clearing the town." In his report of his mission to the government, he says, that he had only left in Galway some persons of such advanced age and delicate health, that he could not drive them out on account of the severity of the season. The council of state approved the exception, but only on condition of his "taking care that the few so dispensed with should be removed as soon as the season would permit."

We have already seen that the English, on their first landing, expelled all of Irish descent from the towns. We now see the English Protestants similarly banish all Catholics from these same towns; these Catholics were the descendants who, some centuries before, under the pretext of right of conquest, exercised towards the Irish the same violence which now in the name of religion was practised on themselves.

All these means having been employed, death, transportation, voluntary exile, and finally the removal from one part of Ireland to another, three fourths of the country were nearly vacant, and nothing remained but to take possession. This was the hideous moment of the civil war, when the division of the confiscated lands was made; it was the moment when cupidity showed itself more odious than even the sanguinary excesses of fanaticism; it was the moment when virtues, hitherto unassailable, were corrupted by the chance of wealth. Two classes of people especially profited by the rich spoils; Cromwell's soldiers, that is, those who had served in the army since his landing in 1649; and the speculators or adventurers who had advanced money to the English government on the security of the soil of this unhappy country devoted to destruction.

Thus the sentence of extermination pronounced by England was executed. The Irish Catholics were driven from the soil; they were expelled from the cities; property and commerce had passed into the hands of Protestants; the Irish were struck with death or isolation.

Section VI. The Restoration of Charles II

The restoration of Charles II. proved how inevitable was the destruction of the Irish Catholics by English Protestantism.

Never was so favourable an opportunity offered to the Catholics of Ireland as on the day when the English nation, weary of revolutions, reverted to the fundamental principles of the constitution, and restored the Stuarts to the throne of England.

There was not assuredly a Catholic in Ireland who, seeing Charles II. restored to the throne of his ancestors, did not believe that he was about to recover the plenitude of his political and religious rights. On the other hand, the actual possessors, most of them soldiers of Cromwell, and rigid republicans, or adventurous speculators, who had lent their money to wage war on "popish Ireland," trembled at a restoration, whose first result would be, as they believed, the restitution of their estates to the ancient proprietors. All were deceived; the first in their hopes, the second in their fears.

Charles II. proscribed the Catholic worship in Ireland, as his predecessors had done; he ordered that the penal laws should be executed against Catholics in Ireland; he suspended individual liberty; for fear that the Irish should come to demand justice in England, he forbade them to leave Ireland; he imprisoned as factious those who came to London to make complaint; and as a great number of the Irish had not waited for his permission to resume the possession of their properties, the king proclaimed them *rebels,* ordered them to be apprehended and brought to trial, and decreed, on his own royal authority, that all the actual possessors of land in Ireland, English and Scotch adventurers, Cromwellian soldiers, or others, should not be troubled in the possession of their lands, with the exception of those who occupied church property, or who had taken a personal share in the trial and execution of Charles I. Still it was said that the king did not refuse justice to his Irish subjects; he recognised that many of them had been unjustly dispossessed. Means were appointed for their redress; it was to establish their *innocence* before the court of claims. Those whose innocence should be recognised were to resume their lands and houses, but with the following restriction: the lands of these Catholics were occupied by Protestants, to whom, above all things, it was resolved that no injury should be done; it was, therefore, well understood that in all cases even *acquitted* Catholics should not enter on their estates until the Protestant possessors had been reprised with equivalent properties.

In the eyes of every Irishman there was gross injustice in this royal proclamation. All those whose properties had been confiscated in England at once entered again on their ancient rights when the king resumed his crown, though the properties thus recovered had been sold after their confiscation, and fairly purchased by those who were now dispossessed. But in Ireland the spoliators were assured possession of property for which none, except the London speculators, had paid a farthing. Thus the Scotch Puritan, or English Independent, on whom the republic had bestowed the lands of the Irish royalists, found favour with the king, whilst the Irish Catholic, crushed by the republic for his devotion to the royal cause, was declared a rebel! It was indeed said that he might obtain justice; but what form of justice was offered? He was proclaimed culpable, and required to prove his innocence.

Still there was a great number of Irishmen whom such justice and such a mode of administration did not discourage, and they presented themselves, at all hazards, before the court of claims. This tribunal was composed of judges hostile to the Catholics; still it so happened that a great number of claimants obtained decrees of innocence. This spread alarm among the Protestant proprietors, some of whom were forced to quit, and establish themselves elsewhere. It was calculated, from the number already pronounced innocent, that if the tribunal continued thus to act, lands would be wanting to indemnify the Protestants whose places would be taken by the acquitted Catholics, and the spirit of justice assuredly could not resist such a consequence. The cry of popery was raised; it was thought that if any one should be sacrificed in such a conjuncture, it should be a Catholic rather than a Protestant. Consequently the court of claims was suddenly ordered to suspend its labours; and in one day three thousand Irishmen, who aspired to no other favour than being permitted to establish their innocence, were told that their case would not even be taken into consideration.

The king of England believed it necessary that all these measures should be sanctioned by an Irish parliament, which was convoked for the purpose. This parliament was full of Protestants, which may easily be conceived, as the Protestants provisionally held the confiscated estates. Still, for fear that any dissident should step into the House of Commons, the assembly itself decreed that no member should be permitted to take his seat who had not first taken the oath of supremacy; and the House of Lords, on its side, ordained that each of its members should be obliged to receive the Sacrament of the Lord's Supper from the Archbishop of Armagh.

I have said that these acts were the consecration of gross iniquity; but the Irish must not attribute the blame entirely to Charles II.

It is certain that this prince, on ascending the throne of England, was resolved, if not to establish Catholicism as a legal, obligatory worship, at least to render its exercise as free as that of the Anglican and Presbyterian forms. One of his first acts was to promise this toleration; but he promised what he could not perform. He owed his crown to a political re-action; the two parties whose coalition had placed him on the throne, were royalists and Presbyterians, leagued against the independents and anarchists. Now the royalists, who for the most part belonged to the Church of England, were not less enemies of the Catholics than the Presbyterians. The prince whom they had raised to the throne could not, at a time when religion and politics were intimately connected, preserve his royal power, save on the condition of not opposing the religious passions of his subjects, and he would have offended them violently by the toleration of Catholicism. At the restoration, Anglican episcopacy was re-established, almost of itself, as a fundamental law of the kingdom existing before the revolution. Hatred against the Catholic religion was thus completely renewed; popery was still the common enemy, the bugbear for frightening women and children, whose very name was sufficient to rouse all the passions. The toleration of Catholicism was the most dangerous act of hostility which could be committed against the public spirit of the times. It was, moreover, a violation of the laws of the kingdom; for these laws prescribed uniformity of religious worship according to the rites of the Anglican church, and inflicted penalties on those who worshipped God with any other forms.

Charles II. was thus condemned by the laws and passions of the country to act contrary to his inclinations. It is but just to say that he did everything in his power to pass the limits of his royal authority. When blamed for continuing papists in public employments, he justified himself by whimsical excuses. "One," he said, "was an amateur of cock-fighting, another skilled in hunting, a third kept good fox-hounds," &c. He made use of other tortuous expedients: not being able openly to tolerate Catholicism, he wished at least to exempt the Catholics from the penalties of non-conformity; but a dispensation with these laws was manifestly a violation of them. This was clearly demonstrated by the ministers of the Anglican church, who hitherto, it is true, had professed the doctrine of passive obedience, but who, when the king wished to employ his power in favour of the Catholics, suddenly discovered that obedience was only due to the sovereign within the limits of the law and constitution. He was therefore obliged to renounce his bias in favour of the Catholics; he made, however, some other efforts which had no better success; and in order to reign, he was compelled to become the persecutor of those whom he had undertaken to defend.

When Plunket, Catholic Archbishop of Armagh, one of the victims of the pretended popish plot, was condemned to death, Essex, who had been viceroy of Ireland, solicited his pardon from Charles II., avowing that the charges were, to his knowledge, utterly false and unfounded. "Well, my lord," said the king, "his blood be upon your conscience; you could have saved him if you pleased; I cannot pardon him, because I dare not."[83]

I well believe that the persecution of the Irish cost Charles less pain than that of the English Catholics, because at all times the destiny of Ireland and its people was little regarded by the English sovereigns, except when they had need of them; and Charles, being forced to persecute Catholics, hoped, by severity to the Catholics of Ireland, to obtain milder treatment for the Catholics of England.[84] Thus Ireland was always a resource for the Stuarts; in their days of distress, they employed the money of Ireland against England, and promised eternal friendship for a little money and soldiers; when their fortune changed—when they again ascended the throne, they endeavoured to obtain pardon for their despotism in England by crushing Ireland with more grievous tyranny.

Charles might be pardoned for the wrongs which he committed from mere weakness of position; it is easy to see that he could do nothing for the Irish Catholics, since, in doing them justice, he must have acted harshly to the English Protestants; but what cannot be pardoned is, that he himself took a share in the confiscations. Ormond, his favourite, obtained land to the amount of 70,000*l.* annually; the Duke of York also obtained a large donation; and there was scarcely a person about the court, down to the wife of the king's scullion, who did not get some share of the booty.[85]

Charles, while he persecuted the Irish, need not have stained himself with the spoils of the unhappy people. But I have already said that it was not in his power to avoid persecution. If he had wished to grant the Catholics toleration of their worship, that is, according to the presbyterian phrase, "to legalise blasphemy and idolatry,"—if he had attempted to release them from the penalties of nonconformity, and restore them to the privileges of civil and political life, he would have done exactly what James II. attempted, and for attempting which he was deprived of his throne.

---

83. Royalist historians have frequently brought forward this anecdote to extenuate the iniquity of Charles in consenting to the execution of an innocent man. But assuredly the same excuse is equally valid for the Earl of Essex; in the moral madness which had then seized the people of England, the character of "a stifler of the plot" was scarcely less dangerous than that of an actual participation. Plunket's execution, moreover, was not merely a violation of substantial justice, but of legal forms; and it had at least this good effect, that it was one of the first circumstances which led the English people to suspect the monstrous artifices of which they had been the dupes, and to doubt the "thousand and one tales" of Oates and his associates.—*Tr.*

84. Down to the very close of the reign of Charles II., the penal laws against Catholics were executed far more rigorously in Ireland than in England.—*Tr.*

85. The profitable lands forfeited in Ireland amounted to 7,708,236 statute acres, leaving undisturbed 8,500,000 acres belonging to the Protestants, the constant-good-affection men of

It must be fully recognised, that in the seventeenth century every king of England was obliged to be unjust and inhuman to one portion of his subjects, to obtain the power of governing the rest.

Thus everything conspired to the destruction of the Catholics of Ireland, and to the violent plantation of Protestantism in the country—everything. Tudors, Stuarts, republic, monarchy, friends and enemies, because the dominant power in England for more than a century was but the instrument of a general movement, which might be moderated or accelerated by accidents and human passions, but which no person or thing could repress.

We have now reached the close of the second epoch, that included between the commencement of the Reformation in England, and the definitive establishment of the Reformation in Ireland. Having pointed out the great movement of the sixteenth century, I have endeavoured to show why England, a nation of free

---

the Irish, the church, and the crown, besides some lands never seized or surveyed. The forfeited estates were thus distributed:—

GRANTED TO THE ENGLISH.

	Acres.
Adventurers	787,326
Soldiers	2,385,915
Forty-nine officers	450,380
Royal Highness Duke of York	169,431
Provisors	477,873
Duke of Ormond and Col. Butler	257,716
Bishops' Augmentations	31,596
Total	4,560,037

GRANTED TO THE IRISH.

	Acres.
Decrees of innocence	1,176,520
Provisors	491,001
King's letters of restitution	46,398
Nominees in possession	68,360
Transplantation	541,530
Total	2,323,809

The forty-nine officers are those who claimed arrears for service under the king before 1649, (when Cromwell landed in Ireland;) the Duke of York received a grant of all the lands held by regicides who had been attainted; provisors were persons in whose favour provisoes had been made in the Acts of Settlement and Explanation; nominees were the Catholics named by the king to be restored to their mansion-houses, and two thousand acres contiguous; transplantation refers to the Catholics whom Cromwell forced from their own lands, and settled in Connaught.

There remained 824,391 acres which were still unappropriated; these were parts of towns, or possessed by English or Irish without title, or, on account of some doubts, had never been set out.—*Tr.*

institutions, having adopted the reformed creed, must necessarily have wished that Ireland should do the same. I have related how she tried to convert the Irish to the new faith, who still remained, and must necessarily have remained, faithful to Catholicism. I have also shown that when England failed to convert the Irish, she must of necessity have employed terror and violence to render Ireland protestant. I have added that all that happened was inevitable. Am I then about to support the new school of philosophy, which bows before every popular movement, when these movements bear the impress of a certain fatality, which doubts not the sanctity of a cause when it is stamped with the seal of irresistible necessity? It would be a strange mistake to suppose that such was my belief.

When I see a man the prey of ardent or criminal passion,—when I see him, either from obliquity of intellect or hardness of heart, animated by an imperious thirst for vengeance, or an ardent sentiment of cupidity,—I can, estimating the consequence of such a depraved passion, declare that it will hurry the person on whom it has seized to crime; I may, seeing to what an extent it has subjugated his soul, foresee that it will necessarily hurry him to spoliation, or even murder. I do and can judge thus; but I do not proclaim the perpetrator of the crime innocent; I do not declare this necessity for crime just, which I deem inevitable. I say that when error or passion exists in a certain degree, crime must follow; the effect is predestined, but the cause is not so. It was in the power of him who has gone astray to avoid error; it was in the power of him who is enslaved by passion to refuse that passion access to his heart. I say that the robber, who through cupidity seizes another's property, the murderer, who through vengeance slays his fellow, might both have resisted inclinations which, when once masters of their soul, became sovereign and irresistible.

The passions of a nation are like those of an individual. The passions which impelled England to destroy Ireland present the same character of fatality; these passions once admitted, Ireland must have perished, as fatally as the victim marked by the vengeance of an assassin—as necessarily as the weaker party in a mortal struggle. But what we want to appreciate is not the consequences of these passions, but the passions themselves,—not the fated effect, be it as necessary and inevitable as you please,—it is on the cause that we must pronounce sentence—the cause which was free, voluntary, and independent. Now, what was the cause? It was the spirit of religious intolerance; the false belief that truth must be imposed by force; the hatred of one creed towards another. Now these errors and these passions were inherently bad; they ought never to have existed; they do not, at least to such an extent, in our days. But if it be true that Ireland, delivered up to these errors and omnipotent passions, must have perished, was not such a destruction supremely unjust, and an imputation on the moral government of the universe? It might be replied that the murder of an innocent man attaches itself only to the assassin, and does not ascend to Providence; but here another consideration presents itself to our notice.

Assuredly the spite of England against Ireland in the seventeenth century had produced the most terrible and iniquitous acts of violence ever perpetrated by one people on another. But if we trace back the principle of the evil, has Ireland such a right to complain? Ireland itself was the first depository of that intolerant spirit of which it became the victim. Does any one believe that if the fortune of the two countries had been reversed, Ireland would not have massacred the English Protestants, just as England immolated the Irish Catholics? Let us not forget the dominant passion and fatal error of this unhappy period. Ireland was the persecuted instead of the persecutor—the victim instead of the assassin; and, in my opinion, hers was not the worse part. But these considerations, which should silence Ireland, do not acquit England; they merely show that Ireland, like England, misunderstood the essential principle of society, which is, that man is as free in his external worship of God as in his internal conscience. Both countries were guilty of this violation; the one in design, the other in deed. The stronger and the more fortunate in the struggle was the more criminal; but the victim herself was culpable. For my part, I find no reason to accuse the justice of God in these cruel wars and sanguinary controversies; I only see that forgetfulness of a single principle costs mankind much blood and much iniquity; and instead of lamenting it, I perceive in these frightful calamities the sanction of the great truths which are important to the happiness of nations; all that is most revolting in the violence of this dreadful epoch only serves to prove that there are certain principles which cannot be mistaken with impunity, and the violation of which entails the most fatal consequences. This is my interpretation of fatality.

Third Epoch: From 1688 to 1755

CHAPTER I: LEGAL PERSECUTION

On the 1st of July, 1690, William of Orange, a Protestant prince, and under this title chosen as king by the English aristocracy, gained in person the famous battle of the Boyne over James II., a Catholic prince, the champion of absolute power, and under both titles expelled from the throne of England. Thus Catholic Ireland fell in its last struggle with Protestant England; henceforth resistance was impossible; Ireland made a final effort—it failed—the war was ended.

Catholicism, conquered once again, must pay for its audacity in daring to raise its head.

After the Restoration of 1660, some Catholics, whose loyalty was recognised by the king himself, or who were declared innocent by the court of claims, resumed possession of their estates. Amongst these restored Catholics, a great number joined James II,, when that prince, expelled from England, appealed to the fidelity of his Irish subjects. Four thousand of them were declared rebels and traitors, and their property, amounting to sixty thousand acres, was confiscated. Although this act of public robbery[86] was perpetrated under the reign and with the consent of William III., it would be unjust to charge it on his memory, for he tried to prevent it. The treaty of Limerick obliged him to use his utmost efforts to obtain from parliament the security of Irish Catholics in their religion and property; but though a Protestant king, and the chosen head of a new dynasty, he had not sufficient credit with his parliament to obtain this justice: the passions of England against popish Ireland were too strong to lose an opportunity of confiscation; and though the king had signed the treaty of Limerick with his own hand, the parliament ordained that the adherents of the dethroned prince should be prosecuted and dispossessed of their lands.

By the Act of Settlement only two millions out of the eleven millions of acres which Ireland contains were left to Catholic proprietors.[87] Out of these two millions one was now taken; so that, by successive confiscations, the Irish Catholics retained only one million of acres, or one eleventh of the (arable) soil; and even this small portion was not divided among a great number; it was concentrated in the hands of five or six Catholic families, English by descent, who, from private considerations, found favour when justice was refused. Thus the Protestant population, which was to the Catholic in the proportion of one to four, possessed ten-elevenths of the soil,—a feeble minority in presence of a plundered majority.

It is true that an attempt had been made to separate the two populations by enclosing the Catholics in one particular district, with fixed limits. But this plan could only be imperfectly accomplished. The only proscription completely executed was that which deprived one party of its property for the benefit of the other; no Catholic proprietor retained his forfeited estate; but many poor and ruined persons, who were ordered into Connaught, remained in some one of the other three provinces: they remained concealed during the first burst of extermination, and when the storm had passed by, they appeared again.

Ludlow, a general of Cromwell's army during the Irish war, depicts in his memoirs, with remarkable energy, the terror of the Irish papists at the approach

---

86. So little regard was paid to ordinary decency by the Irish parliament, that many of the Catholics were attainted for acts performed on the day when the Prince of Orange landed in Torbay.—*Tr.*

87. Ireland contains more than twenty millions; but it appears that the old writers only took into account the land which in their days was deemed capable of cultivation. M. de Beaumont deems it unnecessary to correct the estimate, especially as it is the basis of the calculations used by most historians.—*Tr.*

of his army; they disappeared, as if by enchantment at the mere sound of its name; they were vainly sought in their houses, in the woods, in the plains; not a trace of them could be discovered. His conduct to a band of these unhappy wretches, which he once surprised, is thus related by himself:—

"I went to visit the garrison of Dundalk, and being upon my return, I found a party of the enemy retired within a hollow rock, which was discovered by one of ours, who saw five or six of them standing before a narrow passage at the mouth of the cave. The rock was so thick that we thought it impossible to dig it down upon them, and therefore resolved to reduce them by smoke. After some of our men had spent most part of the day in endeavouring to smother those within by fire placed at the mouth of the cave, they withdrew the fire; and the next morning, supposing the Irish to be made incapable of resistance by the smoke, some of them, with a candle before them, crawled into the rock. One of the enemy, who lay at the entrance, fired his pistol, and shot the first of our men into the head, by whose loss we found that the smoke had not taken the designed effect. But seeing no other way to reduce them, I caused the trial to be repeated; and upon examination found that a great smoke went into the cavity of the rock, yet it came out again at other crevices; upon which I ordered those places to be closely stopped, and another smother to be made. About an hour and a half after this, one of them was heard to groan very strongly, and afterwards more weakly; so, therefore, we presumed that the work was done; yet the fire was continued till about midnight, and then taken away, that the place might be cool enough for ours to enter the next morning, at which time some went in armed with back, breast, and head piece, to prevent such another accident as fell out of their first attempt; but they had not gone above six yards before they found the man that had been heard to groan, who was the same that had killed one of our men with a pistol, and who, resolving not to quit his post, had been, upon stopping the holes of the rock, choked by the smoke. Our soldiers put a rope about his neck, and drew him out. The passage being cleared, they entered, and having put about fifteen to the sword, brought four or five out alive, with the priest's robes, a crucifix, chalice, and other furniture of that kind. Those within preserved themselves by putting their heads close to a water that ran through the rock. We found two rooms in the place, one of which was large enough to turn a pike; and having filled the mouth of it with large stones, we quitted it."

This recital contains the history of all the violent expedients employed to kill or banish the Catholics of Ireland. The unfortunate man, menaced by a fatal decree, hides himself whilst the peril is imminent: for a moment he is deemed dead or exiled—but when the passions of the persecutor abate, the proscribed reappears, and it is surprising to see the victim resume his place by the side of the assassin.

The Irish Catholics were exposed to two sets of tyrants; the English Protestants established in their land, and England itself, by which they were supported. The two oppressors were closely united by one common interest, keeping down the Catholics. But they had also distinct and sometimes opposite interests.

To understand their mutual situation and their respective position to the nation that groaned beneath their yoke, it is necessary to distinguish the new state of things from preceding circumstances. Before the disputes of religion, England had many interests and embarrassments in Ireland, but she had no great passions engaged in the country. The struggles of the conquest interested the sovereign more than the nation. The English settlers were the means by which the king remained master of Ireland, and the Irish tribes enabled him to check those settlers whose efforts for independence he always dreaded. England, which detested one party as enemies, had little sympathy for the other. In this state of things, its policy to Ireland was marked out; England supported the settlers against the natives, but did not hesitate to support its own interests at the expense of the settlers.[88]

When the Reformation came, and Ireland preserved its ancient faith, the mutual relations of the countries were simplified. All the inhabitants of Ireland, natives or settlers, being Catholics, England regarded both without distinction as enemies, enveloped them in the same proscription, blindly struck all Ireland, exterminating natives and settlers as odious papists.[89]

But when, at the end of the civil wars, a Protestant population was established in Ireland, the condition of England in relation to Ireland was very different from what it had been after the conquest, and after the earlier periods of the Reformation.

Doubtless, England was then more animated than ever by implacable hatred towards the Catholics of Ireland; but as the detested Catholics were intermingled with Protestant friends, the indulgence of hate was not easy—it was difficult to strike the one without injuring the other by the same blow. The embarrassment of England was extreme; she felt a warm sympathy for the young Protestant nation she had just founded in Ireland, composed of men who had fought with her under the same banner for the same liberties and the same religion, and which not only had the merit of braving the terrible hydra of popery in Ireland, but was moreover destined to rear the young plant of the Protestant faith in that accursed land. The passion of England was then as friendly to the Protestant settlers as it was hostile to the Irish Catholics.

---

88. By an act of Henry VIII. (1542) the importation of Irish wool into England was prohibited. The only custom-houses in Ireland were at Cork and Drogheda, and vessels from every other port of Ireland were obliged to go to one or other of these ports for a clearance.

89. Immediately after the Restoration, the English parliament prohibited the importation of Irish cattle.

There were doubtless many cases in which it was easy for England to oppress the one without ceasing to protect the other; but there were some occasions in which it was impossible to make a distinction. Thus, in commercial affairs, the restrictions on the Catholics necessarily touched the Protestants; but at this epoch such restrictions appeared to England a fundamental condition of her industrial prosperity. The English nation which, at the close of the seventeenth century, was profoundly religious, was also at the same period essentially commercial. Thus she was at once under the yoke of two passions very different in their nature, whence resulted opposite sentiments towards the Protestants of Ireland,—an ardent sympathy for them as brothers in the faith, an anxious jealousy of them as commercial rivals.

Divided on one point, the England and the Irish Protestants were closely united on another. The annihilation of Irish Catholicism had been their common work, and England was as interested as they were in maintaining their social and political ascendency over the Catholics of Ireland.

In this state of things England deemed, that by lending the strength of her army to enable the Protestants of Ireland to maintain their ground, she might claim in turn an equivalent concession. A sort of tacit compact was then formed between England and the Irish Protestants, which might be expressed in the following terms:—

"England will aid the Protestants of Ireland, with all her might, to oppress the Catholics of that country, and keep them in servitude and misery; for which purpose she will place at their disposal her treasures, her army, her parliament: in return for which, the Protestants agree to impoverish Ireland, and sacrifice her industry and commerce to England." In other words, England said to the Protestant faction, "Resign to me the general interests of the country, and I will ensure you dominion over the nation in which you live." The Irish Protestant answered, "I am willing to be your slave, provided you will aid me to tyrannise over others."[90]

Thus the Irish Protestants were secured in the conquered country, and England was gratified in her two most ardent passions, religion and love of money.

Doubtless the treaty was never reduced to writing, but what I have stated, if not its exact words, were its genuine spirit.

The mutual situation of England and the Protestants of Ireland must be taken into account, to comprehend the two kinds of oppression which weighed down the Catholics of Ireland; one which we may call *general,* and which the Protestants had to endure likewise; the other *special,* which fell exclusively on

---

90. It was, in fact, the argument of the fond father to the naughty child: "Take your physic, Master Tommy, and you shall have the dog to kick." The Irish Protestants took the physic, and kicked the popish dogs with a vengeance.

the Catholics; the first striking at the interests of the entire nation for the profit of England—the second falling only on the Catholic population of Ireland.

Let us now see how the Protestants of Ireland kept their engagement to England.

The first sacrifice required was the recognition of the supremacy of the English parliament over the Irish parliament. In former times, England had attempted to establish this legislative supremacy. Poyning's law was nothing else than an organisation of this dependence of Ireland on the English government; but, before as well as after Poyning's law, the Irish parliament, though yielding to superior force, had always protested against it, and claimed its national independence. Now the Irish parliament abandoned all its prerogatives; England declared it in a state of absolute subjection, and it kept silence.

The Irish parliament was then as much at the service of England as the English parliament itself. What the latter decreed was directly binding on Ireland; if England willed the acts of its parliament to be ratified by the Irish parliament, the latter granted the approbation requested, and if any act originating in this parliament displeased England, it was rendered null and void. Thus, the English parliament could impose any laws (save those for taxation) on Ireland without the approbation of the Irish legislature, and the latter could make no law for Ireland without the express or tacit sanction of the English parliament. Reduced to this passive condition,[91] the Irish parliament perfectly accomplished its object; it

---

91. Swift lost no opportunity of expressing his contempt for the degraded parliament of Ireland. In his Legion Club he thus describes their houses, which stood near Trinity College, and are now a bank:—

> As I stroll the city, oft I
> See a building large and lofty,
> Not a bow-shot from the college;
> Half the globe from sense and knowledge,
> By the prudent architect,
> Plac'd against the church direct,
> Making good my grandam's jest,
> Near the church—you know the rest.

The following less known fragment of rhyming vengeance was written when the Irish parliament sought to punish the author of Drapier's Letters.

> Ye paltry underlings of state:
> Ye senators who love to prate;
> Ye rascals of inferior note,
> Who for a dinner sell a vote;
> Ye pack of pensionary peers,
> Whose fingers itch for poets' ears;
> Ye bishops far remov'd from saints,
> Why all this rage? Why these complaints?
> Why against printers all this noise?
> This summoning of blackguard boys?

was an excellent agent to consent to all the acts of oppression which should be asked of it in execution of the treaty. When a question was debated between Irish Catholics and Protestants, it was allowed full scope within this narrow sphere, and might persecute, ruin, and crush its enemies without English interference. But when a question arose between Ireland and England, the Irish parliament bowed to that of England.

I shall only cite one example of this legislative despotism imposed by the parliament of England, and accepted by that of Ireland.

One branch of industry had attained a high degree of perfection in Ireland at the close of the seventeenth century, and was especially a source of wealth to the southern provinces; this was the woollen manufacture. It had a double influence on the prosperity of the country. Numerous flocks were required to produce the wool, which engaged vast pasturages for their support—this was the advantage of the landed proprietor; manual labour was required for the manufacture—this was the poor man's profit. Still, as the superiority of the Irish stuffs injured English fabrics, the parliament of England resolved that they should be annihilated. This resolution, which included the ruin of Ireland, was transmitted to the Irish parliament, and accepted.[92]

Such a decree, which suddenly destroyed industrial establishments, founded under the protection of the laws, was difficult of execution; and as there was reason to fear that the magistrates of Ireland would not be quite so servile as its

---

Why so sagacious in your guesses,
Your *effs* and *tees* and *airs* and *esses;*
Take my advice; to make you safe,
I know a shorter way by half;
The point is plain—remove the cause—
Defend your liberties and laws,
Be sometimes to your country true,
Have once the public good in view—
Bravely despise champagne at court,
And choose to dine at home with port.
Let prelates, by their good behaviour,
Convince us they believe a Saviour—
Nor sell what they so dearly bought,
This country now their own for nought:
Ne'er did a true satiric muse,
Virtue or innocence abuse,
And 'tis against poetic rules
To rail at men by nature fools;
But · · · · · · · ·
· · · · · · · ·

92. In June 1698, the English parliament addressed William III. to discourage the woollen manufactures of Ireland, and the king promised compliance; in the following year the Irish parliament levied a duty on the export of their own woollens, which amounted to a total prohibition. The manufacture was of course ruined.

parliament, England decided that every violator should be liable to trial before both English and Irish tribunals, and that though acquitted in Ireland, he should be liable to a new prosecution in England: that is to say, to sustain iniquity, the forms and first principles of justice were violated. The Irish parliament made no objection to this injustice, and thus showed that it comprehended its mission of dependence.

Such was the oppression which weighed down all Ireland, and was equally supported by Catholics and Protestants.

Let us now see how the Protestants of Ireland were indemnified for the oppression which they endured from England, by being enabled to tyrannise over the Catholics in their turn. The means employed by the Irish Protestants, assisted by England, to crush the Irish Catholics during the sixteenth and seventeenth centuries, were the persecuting statutes called "the Penal Laws," enacted by the parliament of Ireland, and enforced by the army of England.

Violent persecution ceased—pacific persecution came in its stead, adopting all the forms of justice, and covering its most oppressive acts with the semblance of regularity; believing itself just because it was legal, and humane because it shed little blood; but which, nevertheless, was the more iniquitous of the two, because it was more designed—the more odious, because it killed in cold blood, and would not excuse itself by heat of combat or violence of passion.

CHAPTER II: THE PENAL LAWS

To comprehend the tyranny of the penal laws, we must not lose sight of the starting-point. There is no power that oppresses for the mere sake of oppression, or at least which does not cloak its oppression under some cause or pretext. Hence so much iniquity is committed in the name of justice—so much tyranny in the name of the law—so much impiety in the name of God. The primary cause of English oppression in Ireland during the eighteenth century—a real cause with some, a mere pretence with others—was religious proselytism. It was deemed necessary to destroy Catholicism in Ireland, and make the country Protestant. The sanguinary violence employed to attain this end had failed; men got tired of Irish rebellions and their suppression—another influence was tried, that of the penal laws. Let us see how the English governors advanced in this way, and follow them through their whole course of experiments.

The national religion of Ireland must be destroyed! Observe, that to tear from a people its religion and its creed, is a fearful enterprise. In truth, it was designed to accomplish this without driving the Irish people to revolt; but what is the difference between persecution by the sword and persecution by the law? The tyranny is still the same, and it is the most depraving of all persecutions, for it strikes the most deeply into the soul.

It is designed to persecute without driving to revolt—to practise oppression without provoking resistance; but this is a difficult problem. How can it be solved? In truth, a law existed from the very commencement of the Reformation, which absolutely interdicted the exercise of the Catholic worship;[93] this law had not been abolished, but its application was suspended.

Another law of the same epoch ordered all Catholics, under certain penalties, to attend Protestant places of worship;[94] this law was allowed to stand, but it had long ceased to be enforced.

Thus the Irish Catholic, who had proved that no violence, however cruel, could lead him to forsake his religious faith, was nominally allowed his church and priest, and might be led to suppose that he would not be deprived of either.

But at the same time that the practice of the Catholic worship, and the presence of the Catholic priest, were, at least, tacitly tolerated in Ireland, a law was passed commanding "all popish regular clergy, jesuits, friars, and bishops, or others, exercising ecclesiastical jurisdiction, to depart the kingdom before May 1st, 1698, or be committed to gaol until transported."[95] This was to declare, in other words, that the Catholic religion should cease with the generation of priests actually existing.

Return from exile was declared high treason.[96] Irishmen who harboured them, or concealed them, were liable to a penalty of twenty pounds for the first offence, forty pounds for the second, forfeiture of lands and goods during life, for the third.[97] At the same time the law provided rewards for the discovery of popish prelates, priests, and teachers, according to the following scale.

For discovering an archbishop, bishop, vicar-general, or other person exercising any foreign ecclesiastical jurisdiction	£50 0 0
For discovering each regular clergyman, and each secular clergyman not registered	20 0 0
For discovering each popish schoolmaster or usher	10 0 0

The twenty-first clause of the same act, (that of 1709,) empowers any two justices to summon before them any papist over eighteen years of age, and interrogate him when and where he last heard mass said, and the names of the persons present, and likewise touching the residence of any popish priest or school-

---

93. 6 Edward VI., six months' imprisonment for the first offence, a year for the second, imprisonment for life the third.

94. 1558. Eliz. ch. ii. sect. 14., a penalty of twenty pounds per month for non-attendance at church; banishment from the kingdom in case of refusal.

95. Will. III. ch. i. (See collection of Irish Statutes for this and the other laws subsequently quoted.)

96. 2 Anne, ch. iii.

97. The act of 1709 prohibits a papist from teaching even as an assistant to a Protestant master.—*Tr.*

master; and if he refuses to give testimony, subjects him to a fine of twenty pounds, or imprisonment for twelve months. At the same time, the entrance of foreign ecclesiastics into the kingdom was strictly prohibited.

The Catholic clergy was thus reduced to the proportions strictly necessary for the exercise of a temporary worship, and was destined to be gradually extinguished in the midst of a population whose religious belief, it was supposed, would vanish at the same time.

But was even this limited practice of the Catholic worship free? No: the exercise of their religion was provisionally allowed the Catholics only to avert insurrection, but it was subjected to every possible restraint, short of actual prohibition.

Priests were only permitted to remain in Ireland on three conditions; first, that they should take the oath of abjuration;[98] secondly, to register their names at the court of quarter sessions, and give two sureties in fifty pounds each, that they would not go out of the county; and thirdly, that they would officiate only in the parish for which they were registered. Thus the religious ministers of the Catholic population were treated as malefactors, obliged to find security for their good behaviour, and to remain in a fixed residence, where they would always be within the reach of the public authorities.

The law then explains how the right granted to each priest of officiating in his parish must be understood. No external sign was allowed to indicate the spot where the Catholic rites were celebrated. No steeple should catch the eye of the believer, no bell should sound his summons to prayer. The priest might remain in his parish, but he was refused his ecclesiastical title, and his professional dress. He could not celebrate the rites for the burial of the dead at the grave of any of his flock. Every infraction of these prohibitions incurred the penalty of transportation.[99] Such was the mysterious and clandestine form under which the law endured rather than permitted the practice of the Catholic faith.

---

98. This was purely a political oath, directed against the claims of the House of Stuart; it is still administered in Trinity College, Dublin, to every candidate for a degree. The other conditions form part of the statute of 1709.—*Tr.*

99. These exceptions occur in an act of toleration, (21 and 22 George III. ch. 24,) one section of which is headed, "No benefit hereby to extend to any ecclesiastic officiating in church or chapel with steeple or bell; or at funeral in church or churchyard, or exercising the rites, or wearing the habit, save in usual places of worship, or in private houses, or using marks of ecclesiastical dignity or authority, or taking ecclesiastical rank or title." The modern custom at Roman Catholic funerals in Ireland is merely to recite the psalm *"De profundis"* and nothing more, though, in the recent controversies about allowing Roman Catholic priests to perform the rites of burial in churchyards, it was said that these places would be polluted "by superstitious and idolatrous practices." A penitential psalm is clearly neither the one nor the other. The dread of popery injuring the dead reminds one of the old jest, "They have buried a child who died of small-pox next to mine, who never was vaccinated, and never had the disease."—*Tr.*

Doubtless, the legislators supposed that the Irish priest, thus placed in a state of legal suspicion, subjected to rules whose violation entailed terrible penalties, would often bewail his lot, and fail in courage to support it; they counted on the weakness of the priest, and opened a way of escape. If he only would turn Protestant, the law ceased to be severe, and even became generous. The state offered an annuity of twenty pounds for apostasy,[100] and when this prize appeared inefficient, it was raised to thirty pounds,[101] and even to forty-eight pounds at a later period.[102]

At the same time that the law deprived the Catholic ritual of all its external pomps, it prohibited everything which in the religious customs of Ireland addressed itself to the heart or the imagination. It was an old custom in Ireland to undertake a pilgrimage at certain seasons to some holy isle, some sacred well, blessed by St. Patrick, some particular crucifix, or image of the Virgin. The images were destroyed, the crosses thrown down, the pilgrimages forbidden under pain of whipping.[103]

Ireland possessed the liberty strictly necessary for remaining Catholic, and yet suffered incessantly for its attachment to that faith; its religion was not taken away, but the profession of it entailed a thousand grievances, and this was what the law desired. The law willed that the Irish should suffer incessantly for keeping their ancient religion, and not adopting the new creed; and this suffering was felt not only in religious, but still more severely in civil and political life. In fact, the penal laws struck the citizen more heavily than the Catholic, because the blows directed against the former, though they affected his dearest interests, irritated the passions, whose effervescence was dreaded, much less than an attack on the second. Here was demonstrated in its true aspect the legal system of corruption substituted in the government of Ireland, for the brutal violence which had been hitherto predominant. Here was the system described with equal force and truth by Edmund Burke: "It was a system of wise and elaborate contrivance, as well fitted for the oppression, impoverishment, and degradation of a people, and the debasement in them of human nature itself, as ever proceeded from the perverted ingenuity of man."[104]

This system attacked the infant in its cradle. Conversion being the great ob-

---

100. 2 Anne, ch. vii. sect. 2.

101. 8 Anne, ch. iii. sect. 18.

102. 11 and 12 Geo. III. ch. 27.

103. "Pilgrimages and meetings at wells deemed riots: magistrates to destroy all crosses, pictures, &c., publicly set up, and occasioning such superstitions." (2 Anne, ch. vi. sect. 26 and 37.) The hostility of the Irish Protestants to the emblem of the cross is utterly incomprehensible to Englishmen; it is not allowed as an ornament inside or outside their churches, and few of them, without ocular demonstration, would believe that the symbol they so detest is erected on almost every church in England.—*Tr.*

104. Burke's Letter to Sir H. Langrishe, p. 87.

ject, every Catholic school was prohibited. It is true that Protestant instruction was not imposed on the Catholics; but no other was permitted in the country, and the father of a family had to choose between the apostasy or the ignorance of his children. If he became a renegade, a convert was gained to the reformed worship; if he remained faithful to his creed, the child of a Papist was placed in a state of intellectual inferiority to Protestants. But how could such a law be enforced? All Catholic schoolmasters were banished from Ireland, under penalty of death in case of return.[105] The law pushed its foresight and care still further, making a provision of five pounds sterling for the transportation of every Catholic schoolmaster, teacher, or usher, to the West Indies.[106]

Under the influence of such prudential measures, it is easy to see that the immense bulk of the people must have been consigned to profound darkness. It was foreseen that the richer Catholics might send their children to be educated on the continent; provision was made for this difficulty, and sending children beyond sea, without special license, was prohibited under the gravest penalties:[107] and as this prohibition might be secretly infringed, power was given to the magistrates to demand the production of the child on mere suspicion, and if not produced, its parents or guardians were liable to the penalties for removing it beyond sea.[108]

Assuredly it would be difficult to find a more minute law of persecution; the child of every faithful Catholic was doomed to grow up in ignorance.

Let us follow the Catholic in every phase of civil life. All roads of honourable ambition were shut against him. He was ineligible to parliament;[109] he was deprived of the elective franchise;[110] he could hold no commission in the army or navy, and no office under the crown.[111] He was excluded from every liberal profession save that of medicine: nothing was left him but the indus-

---

105. "Schoolmasters and other Papists liable to transportation shall in three months, by order at assizes, be transmitted to the next seaport town, and remain in gaol till transported." 8 Anne, ch. iii. sect. 41.

106. "Collector to pay five pounds for each Popish schoolmaster, teacher, or usher, transported to the West Indies. The money to be received by master or freighter of ships. If schoolmaster, teacher, &c., found out of such master's or merchant's custody, to suffer as regular returning." 8 Anne, ch. iii. sect. 32 and 33.

107. "Sending, or suffering to be sent, children beyond sea without special license, liable to penalties of præmunire." 2 Anne, ch. vi.

108. "Judges, or two justices, may on reasonable suspicion convene the parent, guardian, &c., and require production of the child in two months; if not produced, nor cause assigned for further time, to be deemed educated abroad." 2 Anne, ch. vi. sect. 2.

109. "No person to be a member of the House of Lords or Commons without first taking oaths of allegiance and supremacy." 3 Will. and Mary.

110. 2 Anne, ch. vi. sect. 24.

111. See the celebrated Test Act, 2 Anne, ch. vi. sect. 16.

trial professions, and here new obstacles were placed in his path.[112] The sixth clause of the act of 1703 (2 Anne, chap. vi.) renders Papists incapable of purchasing any manors, tenements, hereditaments, or any rents or profits arising out of the same, or holding any lease for lives, or other lease whatever for any term exceeding thirty-one years. And with respect even to such limited leases, which must have been considered short when the greater part of the land in Ireland was absolutely waste, it is further enacted, that if a Papist should hold a farm producing a profit greater than one third of the amount of the rent, his right to such should immediately cease and pass over entirely to the first Protestant who should discover the rate of profit. Restricted within such limits, the agricultural industry of the Catholics presented nothing formidable to the Protestant party; but it is clear that it could have little interest for the Catholic.

Let us now examine the condition of the Irish Catholic in relation to trade and commerce. Without doubt, he might (with a few trifling exceptions[113]) adopt any industrial or commercial pursuit he pleased; but, in order to exercise it, he must be dependent on a corporation naturally hostile to him as a privileged body, and his religious enemy as a Protestant body.[114] Though the corporation did not actually prohibit his enterprise, it placed him in the most disadvantageous position possible. Catholics were excluded from corporations, and subject to the tolls from which Protestant freemen were exempt. One employment only was open freely to the Irish Catholic—that of a labourer or journeyman; but even here the poor Irish Catholic was subject to a tyranny. The law compelled him to labour, and subjected him to an arbitrary fine if he refused to work on any holiday not recognised in the Protestant ritual.[115] Thus a double violence was done—first, to the man, who has always a right to give or refuse his labour; secondly, to the Catholic, whose conscience forbade him to work. The legislator still feared that commercial and manufacturing industry might afford the Catholic too speedy means of elevation, and in order to limit further the in-

---

112. "Every barrister, attorney, or solicitor, before application to be admitted, must take the oaths, 2 Anne, ch. vi., and subscribe the declaration against Popery." 1 George II. ch. xx.

113. The exceptions refer merely to the possession of arms or ammunition. "No Papist to be employed as fowler, or keep fire-arms for Protestants." 10 William III. ch. viii. sect. 4. "No Papist shall keep for sale or otherwise, warlike stores, blades, gun-barrels, &c., under penalty of twenty pounds fine, or a year's imprisonment." 13 George II. ch. vi. sect. 13.

114. In some corporations, freemen alone were permitted to carry on any business; in all, the goods of the non-freemen were subject to heavy tolls. Almost every corporation in Ireland became a rotten borough, and excluded from its privileges Catholics and Protestants alike.—*Tr.*

115. "Holidays in the year, limited to thirty-three, (besides Sunday,) enumerated, and refusing to work on other days punished." 7 William III. ch. 14.

dustry already so trammelled, a law was passed that no Catholic should take more than two apprentices.[116]

Even if a Catholic was enriched by his industry, he could not make that use of his gains which reason, necessity, or inclination suggested; he could not purchase an estate, or hold a mortgage. He was even prevented from displaying luxuries offensive to the Protestants above whom he was raised by fortune. To prevent this peril, Catholics were prohibited from possessing horses of higher value than five pounds sterling, and the law authorised any Protestant to seize even the best horse from a Catholic, on the payment of that sum; furthermore, penalties were inflicted on the Catholic who concealed his horse.[117] One exception was made, which reason showed to be necessary. Protestants would not allow Catholics to possess showy horses, whose possession implied a superior condition; but in order to keep up a good breed of horses, they were permitted to retain even the best horses under the age of five years.[118] The Catholic was permitted to rear horses in which he could not have final property, just as he was allowed to farm the lands he was forbidden to acquire.

But the Catholic was not even certain of retaining the wealth acquired by his industry. There is no security for property but in law, and in Ireland the Catholic was placed beyond the protection of law.[119] The legislators and electors being Protestants, it is not surprising that laws were frequently passed which placed the property of Catholics in peril. Was the country agitated, and was it necessary to embody the militia?—the law pointed out a simple expedient; it declares that all the horses of Catholics might be seized without any reference to their value,[120] and the militia thus drawn out must be paid by contributions levied on Catholics.[121] And finally, the law declared that all public robberies should be indemnified by taxes levied on Catholics, as also the losses which Protestant merchants suffered from privateers when the country was at war with a Catholic potentate.[122] Thus Catholic property was incessantly charged with the most iniquitous and arbitrary taxes. It was taxed for the necessities of the state by a Protestant parliament; for the necessities of the county by a Protestant grand

---

116. "Papists not to keep above two apprentices, nor under seven years." 7 Will. III. ch. 14.

117. "Authorising Protestants to seize the horses of Papists above the value of five pounds sterling. Penalties on Papists for concealing horses." 7 Will. III. ch. v. sect. 10 and 11.

118. "Papists may, notwithstanding, 7 Will. III. ch. v., keep stud mares and stallions, or their breed, under five years of age." 8 Anne, ch. iii. sect. 34, 35, and 36.

119. It was solemnly declared by the Irish judges, that the law did not recognise the existence of a Papist in Ireland.—*Tr.*

120. "Horses of Papists seizable for militia." 2 Geo. I. ch. ix. sect. 4–18.

121. "Twenty shillings per day for refreshment of each troop of militia while drawn out, leviable by presentment on Papists of the county." 6 Geo. I. ch. iii. sect. 4.

122. "Presentment on Popish inhabitants of the county to reimburse robberies, losses by privateers," &c. 9 Geo. II. ch. vi.

jury, for the necessities of the parish by a Protestant vestry, and for the necessities of the town by a Protestant Corporation. What security could Catholic property have, when thus exposed and thus menaced?

Even those few Catholics whose estates had been spared, were denied the protection of the rules of inheritance which preserved properties in Catholic families. By the tenth clause of the Act of 1703, the estate of a Papist not having a Protestant heir is ordered to be gavelled, or divided in equal shares amongst his children.[123] Thus there was, on the one hand, an obstacle to the acquisition of wealth by a Catholic family; and, on the other hand, the certainty that it would be lost in a given time.

The interests of riches, property, and industry, having been swept away along with political interests, nothing remained but private life and the domestic circle. Even this simple life, exempt from ambition and accidents, was rendered bitter to the Irish Catholic. When he went to select a partner for life, he was not always free to choose according to the dictates of his heart. Such a power seemed to the Irish legislator open to great inconvenience. A Catholic was not allowed to take a Protestant wife.[124] This law, which contradicts the first law of nature, was enforced by the most terrible sanctions. The penalty of death was denounced against any priest who married a Protestant and a Catholic; and, to remove all hope of escape, his knowledge of the religion of the parties was presumed unless he could prove his ignorance:[125] a strange law, which released the prosecutor from the care of proving the crime, and threw upon the accused the charge of proving his innocence.

Let us suppose the Catholic to have chosen a wife of his own persuasion; his children grow; he is poor, but he has rich friends; but if they be Protestants, they cannot give him, during life, or bequeath to him after death, any portion of their properties.[126] Even in the hour of death, the unhappy Irish Catholic was assailed with fresh peril and terrible disgrace. He could not entrust his wife or his friend with the guardianship of his children;[127] his choice would be null, and the wardship would lapse to the chancellor of Ireland, who had the privilege of naming Protestant guardians to Catholic minors.[128] This last stroke of penal law was directed against a principle rendered sacred by every consideration, human

---

123. 2 Anne, ch. vi. sect. 10.

124. "Penalties to prevent Protestants marrying with Papists." 9 Will. III. ch. iii.

125. "Priest marrying Protestants, presumed knowingly, unless minister's certificate that they were not." 8 Anne, ch. iii. sect. 26.

126. "Papist to take no benefit by descent, devise, gift, remainder, or trust of lands, whereof any Protestant, seised in fee or tail." 2 Anne, ch. vi. sect. 7.

127. "No Papist to be guardian. Penalty on any Papist taking guardianship, £500." 2 Anne, ch. vi. sect. 4.

128. "Chancery may dispose custody of Popish minors to near Protestant relations, and if not fit, to other Protestants." 2 Anne, ch. vi. sect. 4.

and divine. As a temptation to apostasy, a child that turned Protestant became at once independent of his Catholic parents; a suitable maintenance was assigned him out of his father's property by the chancellor of Ireland,[129] and if he were an eldest son, the father became a mere tenant for life, and was not only deprived of the power of disinheriting his son, but of encumbering that property with portions for younger children.[130] This was a fearful law, incessantly suspended like a sword over the head of the father of a family, who every day trembled lest he should hear some fatal seduction, and who, while bestowing his last blessing on his children, had reason to dread the face of an apostate.

A persecuting code had been instituted, which held the people of Ireland in debasement and misery, without driving them to revolt. Still there was reason to dread a Catholic attempt at insurrection, and, to prevent the danger, all the Catholics were deprived of their arms.[131]

Such were the legal rigours to which the Catholics of Ireland were subject for more than a century.

Special Character of the Penal Laws

The more this collection of laws is studied, the more clearly we see that the constant design of the legislator was to attack the Catholics by a double interest; one interest acting to withdraw them from Catholicism, the other to lead them to Protestantism. Persecution is always double-edged—it employs fear and hope, menaces and promises. If terror fails, bribes may succeed.

The peculiarity of these persecuting laws was, that, though political in their consequences, they always contained a principle exclusively religious. Thus it was only because the Irish were Catholics that they were excluded from parliament, the corporations, the elective franchise, and public employments. If they ceased to be Catholics, and abjured their religion, the exclusion ceased. The law did not directly say, "Irish Catholics shall be excluded from parliament;" it expressed itself thus—

"And be it further enacted, that no person shall vote or sit in the House of Lords or House of Commons of Ireland, who shall not first have taken the oaths of allegiance and supremacy, and subscribed a declaration against transub-

---

129. "On bill in Chancery by Protestant child against Popish parent, suitable maintenance ordered." 2 Anne, ch. vi. sect. 3.

130. "From enrolment in Chancery of bishop's certificate of eldest son's conformity, Popish parent made tenant for life-reversion in fee to the son, maintenance and portions of children, (Protestant or Papist,) not exceeding one-third." 2 Anne, ch. vi. sect. 3.

131. "Papists, notwithstanding any license heretofore, shall deliver up arms to magistrates." 7 Will. III. ch. v.

"Refusing to deliver on demand or search, and also to declare what arms, &c., they or any with their privity have, &c., fine and imprisonment, or pillory, or whipping, at court's discretion." 15 and 16 Geo. III. ch. xxi. sect. 17.

stantiation, the sacrifice of the mass, the idolatry of the church of Rome, the invocation of the Virgin Mary and the saints," &c.

The greater part of the political laws are conceived in the same terms; the same spirit predominates in the civil laws; the Catholic excluded from property, incapable of purchasing lands, or inheriting by succession, gift, or devise, became on his conversion immediately capable of acquiring property and estate.

We see that these laws were constructed so as to strike obliquely; their blows were indirect, and therefore the more dangerous and treacherous; they did not say, we forbid the Catholics to practise their worship; but they banished the priest, without whom the worship could not be performed. They did not say, no Catholic shall enjoy the benefits of instruction and education, but they inflicted a severe punishment on every Catholic who exercised the profession of a teacher.

Furthermore, if we only look at the surface, we find them apparently full of solicitude for the education of the Catholics. Schools were founded for the education of poor Catholics;[132] but these schools were Protestant, and Catholics did not want a Protestant education for their children.

It follows that the Catholics were deprived of religious worship and moral instruction, though no law forbade them to worship God according to their conscience, and schools were provided for their education.

There is no real difference between direct and indirect persecution; but the first, more open and frank, has fewer chances of being endured, because it is comprehended by all; the second, not being avowed, escapes the numerous multitudes in every country, who only see what is pointed out to them, and comprehend what is told.

Another Special Character of the Penal Laws

We have seen how all these laws were linked together, and formed a complete whole: still it would be a mistake to regard them as a rational system, all at the same time conceived, deliberated, and decreed. No; these laws came piece by piece, one after the other, without order, method, or visible connexion. Some openly sin against logic, such as that of 1692, which excluded Catholics from parliament, and left them the elective franchise; that is to say, disputed the ends, and left the means. This anomaly lasted until 1727, when the Catholics were deprived of their right of voting at elections.

Moreover, the law which established uniformity on one point, presented in itself a remarkable dissimilarity to all the rest. Thus, preceding laws excluded

---

132. The charter-schools, founded in 1747. These schools were infamously managed, and became perfect nuisances. After many and repeated complaints, their state was investigated by a royal commission, and the parliamentary grants, by which they were chiefly supported, were withdrawn.—*Tr.*

Catholics from parliament and public employments; they even recognised all sorts of rights, provided they gave any sign of conformity to Protestantism: in this last law, on the contrary, the exclusion is direct and straightforward; the last law declares in express terms, "No Papist shall be permitted to exercise the elective franchise." In the first case, the exercise of civil rights was subjected to a condition morally impossible; in the second, a direct and absolute prohibition was enacted against the Catholics.

Were I asked the cause of these different forms in laws which so constantly and uniformly tended to a common end, I should say that this irrational form belongs to the English character, which always proceeds by precedents instead of principles, by facts instead of theories; and that the logic at bottom belongs to the passions by which the legislators were then animated. I do not know if in the annals of English legislation there could be found a series of acts presenting so much harmony of spirit, and at the same time united together by no apparent chain. The English or the Anglo-Irish legislator, whilst persecuting the Catholics, did not proclaim the principle of persecution, because he never recognised it in any way; he did not organise the general system on rules solemnly established, because this is not his mode of action. But he was animated by an ardent hate of the Catholics, the more solid as it was supported by his interests; indefatigable in advising, because it was always heard with favour; unequal in its movements, but always operating; and this hatred, which reigned despotically over the legislator's soul, did not cease during sixty years to inspire all his actions.

In the operations of a long passion, there is always an instructive logic, which can with difficulty be traced in the more regular combinations of reason and genius.

Legal Persecution Was Not Restrained by the Limits of Law

It would be a great error to believe that the persecutions of which the Catholics were the objects, were limited to those prescribed or authorised by the law.

It might be supposed that the Catholic, in virtue of these laws, banished from political society, driven from the civil professions, deprived even of family rights, would have suffered enough from legal exclusion, without any idea being formed of searching beyond the law for means to aggravate his lot. It might naturally be supposed that, subject to so many interdictions, he should have full and free enjoyment of the small number of rights of which he was not deprived. These rights were to enjoy with security the little which belonged to him, to be protected in person and property, to have free access to courts of justice, whether as plaintiff or defendant, to find an equitable tribunal, an independent judge, and an impartial jury.

Still, a little reflection will show that the Irish Catholic was too severely crushed by persecuting laws, to breathe freely the small portion of air allowed him by law. Where tyrannical laws failed, public opinion carried on the oppression.

In 1771, the Lord Lieutenant of Ireland was on the point of pardoning a Catholic unjustly condemned; but seeing to what unpopularity this act of mercy, or rather justice, would lead, "I see," said he, "that his death is resolved; let him die;" and the warrant for his execution was issued.[133]

How could the Protestants, daily executing iniquitous laws against Catholics, adhere strictly to legal injustice, and not pass the bounds against those whom they persecuted for conscience sake, and who were too enfeebled and troubled by legalised oppression to resist usurped tyranny?

It may be stated with certainty, that every political constitution which bestows extraordinary power on the governing body, does not give analogous means of resistance to the governed; it organises a tyranny which exceeds its legal bounds in a proportion that it is impossible to estimate.

The following example of the tyranny practised on the Irish peasantry by their superiors, is given by the author of "An Inquiry into the Causes of Popular Discontents in Ireland." (London, 1804.)

"It has not been unusual in Ireland," he says, "for great landed proprietors to have regular prisons in their houses for the summary punishment of the lower orders. Indictments preferred against gentlemen for similar exercise of power beyond law are always thrown out by the grand juries. To horsewhip or beat a servant or labourer is a frequent mode of correction."

In 1718, a comedy, called the Non-juror, was represented at the Theatre Royal, Dublin, and the prologue contains the four following lines:—

> To-night ye Whigs and Tories both be safe,
> Nor hope at one another's cost to laugh;
> We mean to souse old Satan and the Pope,
> They've no relations here, nor friends, we hope.[134]

No law forbade the pleasures of the theatre to an Irishman, but it was a right of which he could not take advantage, without seeing himself and his country held up to ridicule.

To leave some rights to those deprived of their essential rights is a worthless semblance of indulgence; the defect of the one renders the other void: power is

---

133. Plowden, vol. i. page 414.

134. Miscellaneous Tracts, Irish Office, vol. xxix. This is by no means a solitary instance; even in plays which had no conceivable relation to politics or popery, songs were frequently introduced, ridiculing the religion of the Irish people.—*Tr.*

too strong by what it has already taken, not to render illusory what it has left when it pleases.

All the relations of men with each other are not written in the law; those of sympathy are not susceptible of rule. Can we be surprised if the Protestant proprietor was a severe and merciless master to his Catholic tenants? When he maltreated them, who was to check his excesses? When he demanded more than was due, who was to restrain his exactions?

In order to form a correct estimate of the condition of the Irish Catholics, we must take into account not only the penalties inflicted by the judge, but all the injuries to which the feeble are subject, when brought into contact with the arbitrary power of the strong. Let those who doubt that such has been the state of affairs in Ireland, read what Arthur Young has said; he travelled through Ireland in 1778, and, though an Englishman and a Protestant, he judged the country with an impartiality far from common among his compatriots.

"The landlord of an Irish estate," says he, "inhabited by Roman Catholics, is a sort of despot who yields obedience, in whatever concerns the poor, to no law but that of his will. . . . .

"A landlord in Ireland can scarcely invent an order which a servant, labourer, or cottar, dares to refuse to execute. Nothing satisfies him but unlimited submission. Disrespect, or anything tending towards sauciness, he may punish with his cane or his horsewhip with the most perfect security. A poor man would have his bones broken, if he offered to lift his hand in his own defence. Knocking down is spoken of in the country in a manner that makes an Englishman stare. Landlords of consequence have assured me, that many of their cottars would think themselves honoured by having their wives and daughters sent for to the bed of their master—a mark of slavery which proves the oppression under which such people must live. Nay, I have heard of anecdotes of the lives of people being made free with, without any apprehension of the justice of a jury. But let it not be imagined that this is common; formerly it happened every day, but law gains ground. It must strike the most careless traveller to see whole strings of cars whipt into a ditch by a gentleman's footman, to make way for his carriage; if they are overturned or broken in pieces, no matter—it is taken in patience; were they to complain, they would perhaps be horsewhipped. The execution of the laws lies very much in the hands of the justices of the peace, many of whom are drawn from the most illiberal class in the kingdom. If a poor man lodges his complaint against a gentleman, or any animal that chooses to call itself a gentleman, and the justice issues out a summons for his appearance, it is a fixed affront, and he will infallibly be *called out*. Where *manners* are in conspiracy against *law*, to whom are the oppressed people to have recourse? It is a fact, that a poor man, having a contest with a gentleman, must—but I am talking nonsense—they know their situation too well to think of it; they can have no defence but by means of protection from one gentleman against another, who probably protects his vassal as he would the sheep he intends to eat."[135]

In all the actions of oppression recorded by Young, there was not one legal, and yet not one which was not a direct consequence of the laws.

Why Persecutions Continued When Religious Passion Ceased

We have seen that the persecutions in Ireland were derived from two principal causes—religious passion and self-interest.

For a long time these influences were so intermingled and confounded, that it is impossible to distinguish the special action of each. When any violence was exercised against the Catholics, it cannot be determined whether it was prescribed by some general interest, or commanded by the secret voice of some private interest. When a Catholic priest appeared in Ireland with the ensigns of his order, the cry of *No Popery* was raised.

Was an independent voice raised to claim for Catholics the right of acquiring property in land?—the cry of *No Popery* was raised again. The two cries are the same, but do they proceed from the same cause?

From the middle of the eighteenth century, England could no longer fear Ireland as an ally of the Stuarts. In 1746, the young Pretender was overthrown at Culloden; and this circumstance might have proved that the Jacobite party was extinct in Ireland, where previously the Scotch insurrection of 1715 had not produced the slightest movement.

On the other side, Catholicism, by the aid of time, had reformed those principles which were most frequently and most justly the text of the attacks of which it was the object. The Catholic church no longer insisted on obedience to the Pope in the sense formerly attached to the phrase; the most fervent Irish Papist did not look upon the Pope as his temporal sovereign, nor recognise his right to depose princes, or absolve subjects from their allegiance.

These new circumstances were sufficient to moderate Protestant passions; but they were further weakened by the utter barrenness of persecution. Many vain efforts were made before its impotence was discovered; but when, after sixty years of useless exertions, the persecutors had not advanced a step, the sad truth could not fail to be recognised. It might then be said, that the fire of religious passion, which had hitherto nourished persecution, was extinct; the passions disappeared from the scene, self-interest alone remained; it was a sad spectacle.

When the Irish Catholics, seeing that their creed was no longer assailed, at-

---

135. A. Young's Tour in Ireland, vol. ii. page 29.

tempted to claim civil liberty or political rights, passion, it is true, was silent, but mercenary interest raised the old cry of *No Popery*, and there were many in the multitude who were duped into believing the clamour conscientious.

In 1761, the poor peasants of the south, reduced to the lowest degree of misery by the insatiable cupidity of the landlords, revolted, and the House of Commons voted that it was "a popish insurrection."[136]

From this time, Ireland was subject to a new tyranny, that of selfish interest, reigning apart from the passions which had hitherto shaded its naked deformity.

Which of the Penal Laws Were Executed, and Which Not

There are people who deny the Protestant persecutions against Catholic Ireland, because their rigour was occasionally relaxed. It is certain that penal laws, as we have described them in their completeness, were never uniformly executed. There were some which never ceased to be enforced; such, for instance, as those which prohibited public functions and civil professions to the Catholics, and did not allow them the rights of property or trade, save on certain conditions: but the laws relating to religion were modified by circumstances; the Catholic worship was often tolerated without being prohibited; Protestants shut their eyes on religious ceremonies, feigned not to see priests, whose presence the law punished, nor chapels nor convents, which were presumed not to exist.

Sometimes the laws against the Catholic worship slumbered so long, that the Irish might have imagined that they had fallen into desuetude. Still the mistake could not be durable. Some political event, imprudence of the Jacobite party in England, a Scotch insurrection in favour of the pretender, intelligence of a French or Spanish invasion, sufficed to revive persecution; the Catholic worship was prohibited with greater severity, chapels were closed, priests banished, monasteries proscribed, and convents demolished.

Still it is a very remarkable fact, that in a country where persecutions had a religious principle and aim, the only persecution that abated was that against worship; the religious object of the persecutions was dropped out of sight, but the physical advantages which the Protestants derived from them did not cease to be present and vividly felt.

In general, the persecution against worship, the war upon Catholicism itself, was made at the suggestion of England; that which attached to the persons and properties of the Catholics, was the spontaneous work of the Protestants settled in Ireland. The former resulted from passion, the latter from interest.

The instinct of the Irish Protestant was only to take from the penal laws the enactments which assured him the monopoly of social and political advantages;

---

136. Plowden, vol. i. p. 355, 416. In a very admirable treatise on Irish disturbances, by G. C. Lewis, Esq., the glaring falsehood of this assertion is decisively exposed. See pages 6–12.—*Tr.*

but from time to time the English government commanded the literal execution of all the laws against all Papists; such was the injunction sent from England after the Scotch rebellion of 1715; and again in 1731, Ireland saw the zeal for persecuting the Catholic faith revived, when, after a solemn discussion in the English House of Lords, it was resolved—"That the insolence of the Papists in the kingdom was great."[137]

From this time England left the Protestants of Ireland to themselves, and then the Catholics were more attacked in their social life than in their religion.

Arthur Young justly says, "These laws seem directed against the property rather than the religion of the Catholics. According to law, a priest should be hanged or transported for saying mass, but he is allowed to do so with perfect impunity; but if the same priest made a fortune by his masses, he would at once become an object of persecution."

There are some who look with great indulgence on the persecutions exercised against the Irish Catholic, on account of their frequent relaxations. I have never been influenced by such a consideration. Though persecution was suspended, it could always be renewed. Now the legal power of inflicting a penalty is in fact a penalty to the person menaced. I pity the man who believes himself free because he is not imprisoned, when a law exists which permits his imprisonment. In such a case, there is not a slave who has not his hours of liberty; nevertheless, when his hands and feet are loosed to allow him repose, he does not cease to be in a state of bondage.

Far from admitting that the suspension of bad laws allows some happiness to the people, I say, on the contrary, that bad laws are never so pernicious as when they are dormant. There is no tyranny worse than that which moderates itself to become supportable. A government erected for oppression, and which does not oppress, is a deceiver and a liar; and it is to be reproached with the additional vice of hypocrisy. If the penal laws against the Catholic worship had been so faithfully executed as those of which spoliation was the object, they would have driven the Irish to revolt, who, in vindicating their religion, would have reconquered their other rights. But it is one of the most dangerous acts of tyranny, to choose among its instruments those which plunder without wounding.

It must never be forgotten, that a fact, however grave, is far less important than a right, for a fact has no to-morrow. He who is indifferent to the right, because he is in possession of the fact, resembles some domestic animal which believes itself free when set loose, and exhibits stupid astonishment when the owner comes to replace the chain.

---

137. See Parliamentary History. From an abstract of a Report of a Committee of the Irish House of Commons, (A.D. 1731,) it appears that in the entire kingdom of Ireland there were, besides huts, sheds, and movable altars, eight hundred and ninety-two mass-houses, fifty-four private chapels, nine nunneries, and five hundred and forty-nine popish schools.—*Tr.*

When, under the empire of just laws, I find myself loaded with chains, I feel my liberty protected by the very act which deprives me of it; for the law which casts me into prison, fixes the day when I shall come out, and punishes any who would illegally detain my person. But what is a liberty which I enjoy, only because it does not please a tyrant to take it away? The man who goes to sleep, trusting his freedom to the faith of another man, deserves to awake a slave.

The Whiteboys

Religious persecution was so tempered as to render it endurable; in this respect the authors of the penal laws attained their objects; but social oppression, of which these laws contained the source, became too heavy to be endured in silence; and one day the Irish population, weary of the burthen, made an effort to throw it off.

The revolt was not general—it was not founded on a plan common to all the sufferers; it consisted of partial, successive movements, without relation or connexion—it was absolutely devoid of intelligence, such as might be expected from a population kept in profound ignorance.

The revolt displayed itself in acts of the most atrocious and revolting barbarity—it was such as should be expected from a people systematically demoralised by misery, and degraded by slavery.

The first insurrection of the Whiteboys, or Levellers, began in 1760; they received their first name from wearing their shirts over their dress as a kind of uniform, and their second from levelling the hedges erected round new enclosures.[138] The Whiteboys were driven to revolt by an infinity of causes, of which the most prominent were, the exorbitant rents demanded by the landlords, and the exactions of the agents (tithe proctors) employed by the Protestant clergy to raise tithes from the Catholics.[139]

Arthur Young gives the following description of the outrages usually committed by the Whiteboys:—

---

138. Many of these enclosures were illegal; commons were seized without the consent of the commoners, and wastes seized by neighbouring proprietors without a shadow of right. Such things were occasionally done in the early part of the present century.—Tr.

139. I am far from being convinced by Mr. Lewis's arguments, that whiteboyism was wholly unconnected with the cause of the pretender; it was, perhaps, not so in its origin, but assuredly efforts were made to render the popular discontent subservient to the restoration of the Stuarts. I find in my collection of popular Irish ballads, several mystical songs written about 1770, in praise of the young pretender. One of these, "The Royal Blackbird," is still a great favourite with the peasantry of Munster, though it is rare to find any who sing it aware of its signification. The French also had agents to enlist soldiers for the Irish brigade, and many of these alimented the disturbances in order to obtain recruits. The simple truth appears to be, that the revolt was caused by the rapacity of landlords and tithe-proctors, but that the enemies of England naturally took advantage of it to forward their own purposes.—Tr.

"It was a common practice with them to go in parties about the country, swearing many to be true to them, and forcing them to join by menaces, which they very often carried into execution. At last they set up to be general redressers of grievances, punished all obnoxious persons, and having taken the administration of justice into their own hands, were not very exact in the distribution of it; forced masters to release their apprentices, carried off the daughters of rich farmers, ravished them into marriages, of which four instances happened in a fortnight. They levied sums of money on the middling and lower farmers, in order to support their cause, by paying attornies, &c., in defending prosecutions against them; and many of them subsisted for some years without work, supported by these contributions. Sometimes they committed several considerable robberies, breaking into houses, and taking the money under pretence of redressing grievances. In the course of these outrages, they burnt several houses, and destroyed the whole substance of men obnoxious to them. The barbarities they committed were shocking. One of their usual punishments (and by no means the most severe) was taking people out of their beds, carrying them naked in winter on horseback for some distance, and burying them up to their chin in a hole filled with briers, not forgetting to cut off one of their ears."[140]

Certainly no complete association could exist among rude and uncultivated men, for nothing separates men more than ignorance; nevertheless the Whiteboys attempted to establish a permanent association throughout Ireland, founded on a certain number of common sentiments and necessities.

This confederation, which has served as a model for all the associations of the same kind subsequently formed under other names,[141] was marked from the beginning by two essential characteristics.

First, all the members were compelled to keep the secrets of the association, under pain of death.

Secondly, (and this is the principal trait,) every member of the society engaged to do all that the society should command;[142] a formidable engagement,

---

140. Young's Travels, vol. i. p. 82. In the debate on the Whiteboy Act in 1786, Lord Luttrell related the following anecdote, which there is reason to believe was but too true:—

"A friend of mine, a few days since, after riding through Urlingford early in the morning, overtook, beyond that town, a person, who proved to be a clergyman, riding seemingly in pain, with his head muffled to a monstrous size, and bound over with a napkin. My friend addressed him, being a very compassionate man, and inquired what was the matter. 'Ah! Sir,' said he, 'did you see, as you rode through that town, two ears and a cheek nailed to a post?' I did, said my friend. 'They were mine,' the clergyman replied."—*Tr.*

141. The Rightboys in 1785; Peep-of-day Boys in 1772; Steelboys and Oakboys in 1764; Thrashers in 1806; Carders, Caravats, Shanavests, Rockites, &c., down to the present day.

142. In the county of Leitrim, in 1806, the Thrasher's oath is stated to have been,—"To keep secret; to attend when called upon; to observe the Thrasher's laws; not to pay tithes but to the rector, and to pay only certain fees to their own clergy." For the county of Longford it is given in similar terms, viz.—"To be true to Captain Thrasher's laws; to attend when called

placing him who contracts it at the mercy of another's caprice, deprives him of his free will, subjects him to laws of which he is ignorant, and whose execution he has blindly sworn to accomplish at all hazards, even at the expense of crime.

When the Whiteboys were excited by the secret bonds of a fearful oath and of mutual obedience, they proceeded to act by terror.

They proclaim their code, and announce its sanctions. Woe to him who is guilty of any forbidden act! Woe to him who resists their pleasure! The command is usually given in a printed or written notice, which is either sent to the individual, or posted on his door, or some conspicuous place in the neighbourhood.[143]

If a proprietor demands an extravagant rent from his tenants, he finds some morning a notice to the following effect, posted on his door:—

County of Kildare, to wit.
Take notice, That we will no longer bear the oppression of paying *double rent* to farmers for land, and the gentlemen so favourable to the poor. Therefore all farmers will be obliged to return their under-tenants to the head landlord, at the same rates an acre for which they hold the land themselves. And we trust the gentlemen will not allow them any longer to tyrannise over the poor of this impoverished nation. Any farmer demanding rent from his under-tenants, or any under-tenants paying rent to the farmer, either party so *violating this notice* shall be used with the utmost severity imaginable, and *We* their cause forsake in every measure.

So I remain your most humble servant,
A son to that poor old woman called

Terry's Mother.[144]

If his labourers are employed at too low a rate of wages, the Whiteboy society issues a decree establishing a minimum.

Take Notice,
From this day forward, that no man will be allowed to work in any boat without having regular wages, 10s. per week. Any person or persons daring to violate this notice, will be visited by night by those people under

---

upon; not to prosecute Captain Thrasher or any of his men, and to meet them the following night."—*Trials of the Thrashers*, pp. 257 and 303.—*Tr.*

143. When a boy, I unwittingly tore down a Rockite notice posted on a gate; several peasants seized me, but finding that I had no design in taking the placard beyond the gratification of curiosity, they let me go, warning me not to commit so perilous an act for the future.—*Tr.*

144. H. C., 1832, Appendix, p. 9. This notice was in print, and was posted in different parts of the county Kildare.

the denomination of Whitefeet, or Terry Alts. Any man putting us to the necessity of paying him a visit will be sorry: therefore any man who has not the above wages, let him not attempt to leave Athy.

I remain your humble servant,

Terry Alt.[145]

It is worthy of note, that here the menace is addressed to the labourer who works for low wages, and not to the master who employs him.

In the same way, when they wish to prevent the payment of Tithes, notices of the following description are posted.

Remarke the concequence Thomas Wardren dant pay the tithe far if you do you may prepare your coffin you may be assured that you will loose your life either at hame or abraad.

Captain Rock.

No Tithes

No Tithes   Coffin.

No Tithes.

If a landlord threatens to eject his tenant for non-payment of rent; if he announces an intention of raising his rents; if he invites strange labourers into the country;[146] in all these cases he encounters the penalties of the Whiteboy code, and receives notice of the menaced chastisement.

The intimidation produced by such proceedings is extreme; and when men-

---

145. This and the following notices are taken from various reports of Committees of the House of Commons. I have seen some in very tolerable rhyme. They were generally written by the hedge schoolmaster, who was usually Rockite secretary to a district. The establishment of national schools has been of great service to Ireland, by removing this very dangerous class of men.—*Tr.*

146. The following threatening letter, addressed to a person in the barony of Gallen, county of Mayo, (which contains a different expression of the same feeling,) is cited from a Mayo newspaper in the *Times* of 11th December, 1835:—

NOTICE.

Take notice Mr. John Waters of Stripe that unless you give up your transgressing and violating and attempting persecuting poor objects or poor miserable tenants remark that the country is not destitute of friends or otherwise if you do not give over your foolishness or ignorance *you will be made an example in the country that never was beheld*

Here is to our foe of Stripe

Mr. John Waters of Stripe Esq & I would be sorry to be in your clothes.

CAPTAIN ROCK ESQ

Tr.

aces fail, vengeance follows close behind. The following are the punishments usually inflicted by the Whiteboys for the violation of their ordinances.

First, death. Second, corporeal inflictions, such as severe beating, mutilation, tearing the body with briers, thorny bushes, or wool-cards; abduction of young girls with small fortunes,[147] who are forced to marry their ravishers. Destruction of property.

The usual modes of destroying property are, the burning of houses and haggards, the houghing of cattle. In some cases, the ears and tails of horses, and the teats of cows, are cut off; sheep are likewise shorn and mangled in a barbarous manner, not for the sake of the wool, but in order to spoil the sheep. Windows are likewise often broken, and other property in and about houses damaged or burnt. A short and easy mode of arriving at a desired end is the *turning up of grass land,* sometimes practised by the Whiteboys. By these means, the farmers are compelled to let their ground for setting potatoes, without the long and troublesome process of notices, burnings, beatings, and murders. This method was practised to a great extent by the Terry Alts in the last disturbances in Limerick and Clare; bodies of several hundred or even several thousand men with spades used to assemble, sometimes in the daytime, and turn up a meadow in a few hours.

Barbarous as is this penal code, its execution is conducted with considerable regularity. The Whiteboy association points out the members who are to inflict the required punishment, and the members obey. The Whiteboy is often ordered to go forty or fifty miles to kill an obnoxious individual, and he yields implicit obedience to his instructions. Men who would shudder at the idea of being assassins, do not hesitate to become executioners.[148]

---

147. This is not a common Whiteboy outrage; it was more frequently perpetrated by the underlings of the aristocracy, called in Ireland *Squireens* or *Buckeens—Tr.*

148. The utter disregard for human life shown on these occasions is most fearfully illustrated at Irish assizes. At the trial of Lacy for the murder of the Maras, who were sacrificed to Whiteboy vengeance, because their brother had given evidence against a Whiteboy on a former occasion, the principal witnesses for the prosecution were two approvers, Fitzgerald and Ryan. It appeared that the assassins had watched the Maras for ten days before a convenient opportunity for the murder was found. I took down at the time the following portion of Ryan's cross-examination respecting his employment on one of those days.

"Well, Ned Ryan, where were you on the Wednesday?"—"I went to Ballingany, sir."

"And what did you want at Ballingany, Ned?"—"Och, then, nothing that has anything to say to this business, at all at all."

"But I must know what it was, Ned?"—"Well, then, I wanted to rob arms and shoot a man."

"To shoot a man! Gracious Heaven! Who was he?"—"Faix, I don't know."

"What was his name?"—"Why, then, I heard tell his name, but I forget it."

"And what had the man done to you?"—"He never done nothing to me, only Paddy Lacy axed me for to go and help him."

"Did you shoot the man?"—"No; he wasn't at home."

The vengeance of the Whiteboys being accomplished, universal terror prevails, which generally prevents what they wish to hinder, and obtains what they desire.

Still this is the time when regular society, whose institutions they openly attack, appears armed against them with all its powers and attempts to enforce obedience of the laws.

But here the Whiteboys find in their association singular resources to combat justice and society; nowhere does their power appear more formidable than in resistance to the magistrates; for if they have a severe penal code to enforce their own laws, they have one still more severe to combat the laws by which they are menaced themselves.

The first article of this second code may be stated in these words: "Whoever will give evidence against a Whiteboy will be punished with death."[149]

Scarcely has a judicial pursuit commenced against a Whiteboy, when the whole association is set in motion to prevent the due course of law. The most dreadful menaces against witnesses are posted up; the victims of Whiteboy violence are forbidden to complain, under pain of new tortures; and nothing is so difficult as to collect the elements of conviction for a Whiteboy crime.

It often happens that a witness who has had the impudence to give information to a magistrate, is murdered before he can be produced to give his evidence in court.

"So great indeed," says Mr. Lewis, "is the danger to which witnesses for the crown are exposed in Ireland, and so great the probability of their being murdered, if not put in a place of safety, that it has been found necessary to provide, by a special enactment, that the depositions of murdered persons may be read in evidence."[150]

"Would you have shot him if he was at home?"—"To be sure we would, after all the trouble he giv'd us."

"He was a lucky fellow to escape you?"—"Faix, then, you may say that."

While listening to this display of unmitigated ferocity, I could scarcely believe the testimony of my own ears.—*Tr.*

149. The menace is extended to all the relatives and friends of the informer. It appeared on the trial of the murderers of the Maras, that vengeance was extended not only to the brother of a witness, but even to that brother's apprentice.—*Tr.*

150. The 50 George III. ch. cii. sect. 55, having recited that "whereas it has happened that persons who have given information against persons accused of crimes in Ireland have been murdered before the trial of persons accused, in order to prevent their giving evidence, and to effect the acquittal of the accused," proceeds to enact, that "if any person who shall give information on oath against any person for any offence against the laws shall, before the trial of such person, be murdered, or violently put to death, or so maimed or forcibly carried away and secreted, as not to be able to give evidence on the trial of such person, the information so taken on oath shall be admitted in all courts of justice in Ireland as evidence on the trial of such person." This provision was extended to grand juries by 56 George III. ch. lxxxvii. sect. 3. The former act likewise contains a clause enabling grand juries in Ireland to present such a sum as

In such a state of things, the magistrates have recourse to extraordinary means to procure the elements of conviction against the guilty. Payment is offered for information;[151] after the deposition of a witness is taken, he is lodged in a place of security, generally the gaol, where he remains until the day of trial. When the trial is concluded, the witness is protected by a guard of police until he can be removed from the county. Every individual who has figured as a witness in such a case has no choice between death and exile.[152]

Some writers have attributed Whiteboy insurrections and associations to political causes; they were first excited, according to these authorities, by the intrigues of France and the pretender. It is now generally recognised that the cause of these insurrections was social, not political; the insurrection was directed against the landlord and the rich, not against the Protestant: it was misery, not the spirit of party, that armed the Whiteboy.

Ireland had no share in the rebellion of 1745; the first Whiteboy movements began in 1761. It would be strange if the Irish, who made no effort when the pretender had some chance of success, should have risen in his favour twenty years afterwards, when his cause was utterly hopeless and forgotten. This error has been propagated by those best acquainted with the truth: the men who had produced and profited by the misery of Ireland, seeing the outrages which their oppression had generated, endeavoured to assign another source to those crimes, and, by ascribing them to the spirit of party, to enlist on their side all the opposite political prejudices. They attained their end without much trouble, as most of the insurgents were Catholics, and those against whom they revolted Protestants; they said, and it was believed, that the insurrection was excited by religious fanaticism; people would not see that in a country where all the rich were

---

they shall think just and reasonable to be paid to the personal representative of any witness who shall be murdered before trial, or to himself if maimed. Sect. 6. Lewis's Irish Disturbances, p. 269.—*Tr.*

151. It could not be obtained otherwise, but the hope of blood-money has sometimes led to the accusation of innocent persons.—*Tr.*

152. Exile is not always sufficient protection. An attempt to kill an informer among the Irish at Wigan, although his offence had no Whiteboy complexion, is mentioned by Mr. Lord, a magistrate of the borough, in his evidence taken for the Irish Poor Commission.

"A young Irishman, about October last, gave information to the magistrates that two Irishmen who had recently come here, and followed the trade of selling oysters, had committed a rape and robbery in Ireland, and had fled from justice. They were apprehended and detained more than a week; but, in consequence of a delay in receiving an answer from Ireland, they were liberated; the day they were liberated, the warrant came from Ireland for their apprehension. Several attempts were made by the Irish to murder the young man who gave this information, and his brother; the attempts were made openly by several persons, and he was once struck on the head so severely that he was nearly killed. I believe they have both since left the town." Lewis's Irish Disturbances, p. 267. I have heard of similar hatred shown to informers who had emigrated to America.—*Tr.*

of the reformed religion, and all the poor Catholics, that a revolt of the poor against the rich must necessarily have been an insurrection of Catholics against Protestants.

Doubtless, political passions hostile to the government might be found amongst the Whiteboys, as well as enmity against the rich; but the former were not predominant; they were mingled with the sentiments of hate which drove the peasants to revolt; but they were not the moving power of their conspiracies. There are, moreover, two undeniable facts which show very clearly how far political passions were strangers to these agrarian insurrections.

The first is, that when the Catholic clergy levied severe dues on the peasants, the Whiteboys resisted them, and adopted measures against their own priests— measures of repression not less severe than those directed against the ministers of the Anglican church;[153] and on their side, the priests excommunicated those who joined Whiteboy associations. The second is, that the outrages were directed against landlords and persons who took land without distinction, and that the greater part of the latter were Catholics.[154] Finally, there is a third fact not less grave than the preceding; the same insurrections raised by the Catholic peasants of the south appeared soon after, from similar causes, among the Protestant peasants of the north, who, in 1764, under the name of Oakboys, took up arms against the Pressure of rent and tithes; and others, in 1772, rose as Steelboys, because the Marquis of Donegal, a large proprietor, had ejected numbers of his tenants. Assuredly the northern Presbyterians would not take arms in favour of the pretender. They were still far from the time when they would make common cause with the Papists.

"All the insurgents of the south," says Lord Charlemont, "were Catholics; it was generally believed by Protestants that the gold and intrigues of France were at the bottom of all these rebellions; but they were not the real causes, which are very easy of detection. The causes manifest to all eyes, were misery, oppression, famine!"[155]

The Whiteboy insurrections are not directed against the government, but against the landlords. "They are," says Mr. Justice Jebb, "a war of the peasantry against the proprietors and occupiers of land." If any further proof were wanting to show that such has ever been their character, it would be sufficient to consider their character at the present day. They have been constantly reproduced, under

---

153. Captain Rock's tariff always contained a clause regulating "the priest's dues," that is, the fees to be paid for christening, marriage, &c.—*Tr.*

154. The truth is, that in all these agrarian insurrections, more Catholics were murdered than Protestants. Religious rancour, no doubt, mingles with these disturbances; but I doubt on which side the greater share of it would be found.—*Tr.*

155. Hardy's Life of Lord Charlemont, vol. i. p. 173.

various denominations, from 1716 to the present day, and have always originated in the excessive misery of the people, and the starting point of this misery is the persecution which arose from the penal laws.[156]

Fourth Epoch: From 1776 to 1829

REVIVAL AND ENFRANCHISEMENT OF IRELAND

For nearly a hundred years Catholic Ireland was as if it had not existed. The Protestants established in Ireland, a feeble and almost imperceptible minority, presented themselves to England as the Irish nation, and under this title regulated everything foreign and domestic. They said that they were Ireland, and ended by believing it. They proclaimed their tyrannical power legitimate, and probably thought it was so. Sufficiently strong to divide amongst themselves in the presence of a humbled enemy, they ended by forgetting this enemy was in possession of a terrible power, that of numbers; when they saw their foe asleep, they forgot that he might wake again; full of confidence in themselves, they lost sight of their enemy, and acted as if he had not been amongst them; they thought no more about him; but constituting their own society independent of his wants, habits, and all his interests, they regarded this as the only existing, the only real, and the only possible society; all that did not belong to this society was

---

156. It is of importance to show that M. de Beaumont's views of the causes of Whiteboy insurrection are the same as those of the most enlightened partisans of Protestant ascendency in Ireland.

"In the particular regions of disturbance," says Mr. Baron Foster, "I consider that religious animosities are and always have been less frequent than in other parts of Ireland. The great theatres of those differences are the northern counties of Ireland, in which the Insurrection Act has never been applied. Those religious animosities, however much to be regretted, have never led to insurrectionary movements; they have led to quarrels and personal outrages, but never to an attempt against the government." H. L., 1825, p. 72.

Similar testimony was given by Mr. Justice Day.

"Have the actual disturbances in Ireland originated in religious differences, or in what other causes?"—"The recent disturbances in Ireland have not had anything to do with religion."

"In what causes did they originate, in your opinion?"—"The poverty of the people, which exposes them to the seduction of every felonious or turbulent leader; the want of employment; the absence and non-residence of landlords, who might superintend, control, and advise; the want of education, which leaves them in a semi-barbarous state, and incapable of judging for themselves. These are some of the various and combining causes which may be enumerated. The severe and unconscionable rents, too often exacted from the peasantry, ought not to be forgotten."—H. L., p. 552.

The same account is given by the Rev. Mortimer O'Sullivan:—

"Were there no instances of the hostility of the people creating those disturbances being directed against Catholics as well as Protestants?"—"Yes, numerous instances; I believe I stated, that I conceived the disturbances to have commenced in the struggles of poverty; of course it was a war against property principally, and the religious spirit was a thing that mingled in it, but was not the mainspring."—H. C., 1825, p. 464.—Tr.

nothing in their eyes—all outside its circle seemed contemptible and unworthy of attention.

There is a capital fault, and there is serious danger, in such a position; for whilst this minority, in its selfish confidence, shuts its eyes to everything around, and turns entirely to itself, storms which it does not perceive are forming in the distance; the oppressed majority devises plans of freedom, has its dreams of freedom, raises itself slowly from its degradation; it labours, it grows rich, it acquires strength, resumes its courage, takes up the abandoned arms, and prepares for the combat. The dominant faction perceives none of the preparations made by a people it is accustomed to despise. Its form of Protestant administration is complete; it has docile agents and a devoted legislature; not a hostile voice is raised against it; it has all the illusions of a good government, and thus, by a mild and easy navigation, it arrives in the midst of a sea full of quicksands, and rife with shipwreck.

When a subjugated people secretly nourishes projects of independence, and contains the germs of regeneration, it may long remain inert and mute; but often, also, nothing is wanting to rouse it from silence and slumber but an extraordinary event, a fortuitous accident. This favourable event—this lucky accident, was not wanting to Ireland.

CHAPTER I: 1776—EFFECTS OF AMERICAN INDEPENDENCE ON IRELAND

I do not know whether there is any single political event in the history of the world, which has produced so great an influence on the history of all nations as the struggle sustained by the United States of America at the close of the eighteenth century.

The American revolution was the first great revolution effected in the light of the press, and reflected in the discussions of a free representative government. Observe what an impulse this revolution gave to the debates of the English parliament! It appeared that until then parliamentary liberty of speech was mute, or at least that liberty spoke without being heard at a distance; the press alone has given it loudness of voice. Without it the thirteen colonies of England might have separated from the mother country, but without it the world would have known nothing further of the matter than that they were rebels chastised by their master.

The minor events mingled with the war of independence have a trifling appearance. "It was," said Lafayette, "a war of patrols," in which the destinies of the world were decided. If you inquire why small events are really so great,—why this war of skirmishes should decide the fate of nations, you can find no other reason than the principle on which the war was grounded. That principle was just and legal resistance against tyranny and oppression. It was the idea, not the fact, that troubled the world. Attila passed over nations like a hurricane over the ocean. The tempest passed by—it was cursed and forgotten. But a petty people revolted; scarcely had blood flowed, though at the distance of two thousand leagues from us, when, though we had nothing to fear from the agitation, we were profoundly affected by it; the fact was the smallest possible, but the principle was immense.

The great impression of the American crisis on nations arose from the circumstance of a just cause having never before been so clearly stated; it is not that the cause should be just, it is further requisite that its equity should be apparent. The Americans did not revolt against England, simply because it is better that a nation should be free than dependent; their cause thus presented would have been open to dispute, for there was a contract existing between the parent state and the colonies. But according to the very contract which linked them to England, the colonies could only be taxed through their representatives. Still England wished to tax and constrain them by violence; resistance was their right; they fought, triumphed, shook off the yoke; and the whole world applauded the triumph of right over might. A movement of independence was made amongst all nations. As tyranny was everywhere, efforts for freedom were made everywhere. These great epochs of simultaneous effervescence, and a common struggle for rights, are rare; nations should employ them to conquer security; for when once they are passed, general apathy succeeds to universal agitation.

Nowhere was the effect of the American revolution more potent than in Ireland. There was an analogy in the situation of the two countries. The colonies of North America were indeed far more prosperous than Ireland; though they were merely colonies, and treated as such, they had the good fortune to be distant from England. Ireland, which was not a colony, for it had never been occupied under that title,—nor a part of England, for it had never been governed by English laws,—nor a free people, for England made laws to govern it,—Ireland, I say, had one point in common with the United States, that it contended against England for its rights: it demanded liberty to escape from poverty and wretchedness, whilst the American colonies, rich and prosperous, wished only that their dependence should not be increased.

These analogies seized on all minds in England and Ireland. In the English parliament, there was not a discussion on America which did not direct attention towards Ireland. See, said the Whig orators in the English parliament, see the effects of the unjust pretensions of governments towards their subjects; fear to engage in an iniquitous contest with Ireland when the state of your colonies forewarns you of the result. "England," cried an enemy[157] of Irish liberty, in 1774, "has as good a right to tax Ireland as the colonies." "Yes," replied an opposition

---

157. Rigby, Master of the Rolls, whom the pen of Junius has consigned to immortal shame.

member, "and the colonies are in revolt precisely because you have taxed them." It may well be conceived what an effect was produced in Ireland by those great parliamentary discussions, where in marvellous encounter met the greatest and most extraordinary oratorical powers that England has ever produced—Burke, Pitt, Fox, Sheridan,—splendid talents, noble souls, bright geniuses, in whom the love of glory was intimately blended with the love of country!

Ireland was inflamed by these discussions; in 1776 America was free; Ireland resolved to be so likewise. The declaration of American independence was likewise the great instrument of Irish independence.[158] America taught Ireland that a dependent people might become free, and taught England that it is perilous to refuse liberty to those who can take it.

The impulse given to England and Ireland by American emancipation had consequences which it is necessary to demonstrate. The first and most important, without doubt, was the abolition of some of the penal laws enacted against the Catholics of Ireland; the first stone taken from the edifice of persecution, and the first step of reform. Let us see in what it consisted.

Section I. First Reform of the Penal Laws, 1778

1. Catholics were granted the right of holding land on leases of a hundred and ninety-nine years. They thus obtained the right of unlimited possession without the right of property. One reason for this limitation was, that conceding this limitation might give the Catholics too much influence at elections.

2. The son of a Catholic turning Protestant had no longer a right to seize on his father's property, or make him only tenant for life in his estate.

3. The law requiring Catholic property to be gavelled was repealed, and the rules for Catholic and Protestant inheritance became the same.[159]

Such a reform was doubtless incomplete, and persecution remained armed with sufficient rigours to strike severely those whom it attacked. But the first wound was given to the tyrannical code, and we shall soon see it fall asunder piece by piece. An impulse was given to reform; henceforth no great event could be without its fruit. As the events arise, we shall point out their consequences, and immediately connect the effects with the causes. Just as there was no rationality in the establishment of the penal code, we shall find a want of order and logic in the acts by which it was repealed. The reform seemed to be made by chance or accident, according to the circumstances and necessities of the moment. The legislature abolished as it created the penal code, without plan or method.

---

158. "A voice from America shouted liberty," was Flood's fine description of the time. See Hardy's Life of Charlemont, vol. i. p. 387.

159. 17 and 18 George III., chap. xlix.

Section II. Second Effect of American Independence
on Ireland (1778 to 1779). The Irish Volunteers

The war between England and her colonies not only exercised a moral influence on Ireland, but produced results in that country which may almost be called physical.

On account of America, England was at war with France, Spain, and Holland, as well as the United States; it was necessary to withdraw a part of the English army from Ireland to send it to America.

The Irish coasts were daily menaced with hostile invasion; Ireland demanded aid, but was told to defend herself the best way she could.[160] England at the moment was stunned by the number of embarrassments pressing on her from a distance and close at hand.

These embarrassments of England added to the strength of Ireland, already encouraged by her success in having obtained the first concession. Besides this movement, Ireland was greatly irritated at being refused the commercial and maritime liberties which she claimed. Associations were formed to refuse the use of English manufactures,[161] in order that the English, who resisted the commercial advantages of Ireland, should be deprived of them themselves.

In this state of things, the viceroy declared that in consequence of the failure of the public revenue, the laws for raising a militia could not be executed.[162] Immediately, by a universal and spontaneous movement, Ireland was covered with a volunteer militia, self-armed, self-regimented, self-organised, which elected its own chiefs, and formed its own rules of discipline, without the government taking any share, direct or indirect, either in its formation or superintendence. The commercial association was transformed into a military association.

The government appears to have acted imprudently in allowing the formation and organisation of these "independent companies;" but how could it have opposed them? Doubtless it had the rigorous right, but it had not the inclination; it was, above all things, necessary to avert an invasion, which was imminent, and to conjure away this peril, which was a peril of death.

It is very unfortunate for tyrannical governments to have sometimes imperious need of the people; when once this recourse has taken place, the delusion is

---

160. The people of Belfast, alarmed at their unprotected state, petitioned the government for a garrison, and received as an answer, that half a troop of dismounted cavalry, and half a company of invalids, constituted all the force that could be spared.—*Tr.*

161. One of these associations had the humorous motto, "Burn everything that is imported from England except coals."

162. His Majesty's ministers were obliged not only to pay the Irish troops on service abroad from the British exchequer, but also to remit fifty thousand pounds to Ireland to complete the sum necessary for the payment of the few troops who had been left in that kingdom.

dissipated: the people discovers that it is strong, and the tyrant weak. It cannot defend the government without learning the art of defending itself against the government.

The English government felt the necessity of throwing itself into the arms of Ireland, and entrusting the country with the care of its own preservation. The viceroy distributed sixteen thousand swords and muskets to the volunteers. An imposing force was soon on foot; forty thousand men organised themselves in the twinkling of an eye at their own expense, and without any other impulse than national feeling. Ireland was, without doubt, saved for the moment from hostile invasion, but from that day she also learned the secret of her strength against England.

These armed bodies, having no other discipline than that which they imposed on themselves, and refusing all royal regulations, proclaimed themselves sovereign, in so far as they refused to derive their rights as armed citizens from any power but their own.

They then discussed affairs of state, and regarded themselves as the true representatives of the nation; they formed a kind of military parliament, and Ireland no longer presented a petition to England, save at the point of the bayonet. They asked why the rights of the citizens should be limited to bearing arms, and why they should not have the right of debating on public affairs. They assembled on fixed days; each corps named representatives; assemblies elected by the majority of citizens passed resolutions, approved or blamed the conduct of the government, recommended such and such measures, censured severely the acts of parliament which appeared injurious to the country. In truth, the parliamentary power was in the popular masses, and the masses were armed. A memorable circumstance prevented the disorders with which such a state of things was rife; it was that the rich, the landlords, the chief men of the country in commerce, amongst the citizens and amongst the nobility, were at the head of the volunteer battalions; they at first entered them from the feeling of nationality which pervaded Ireland on the menace of a foreign invasion; and afterwards, when the volunteer companies organised themselves into political deliberative assemblies, these noblemen and gentlemen remained at their posts from prudential motives. They saw the march of events with terror; they comprehended all the peril of a deliberative army, but they knew how much more dangerous it would become if the chiefs withdrew from the direction.

The volunteers taught England that there was such a thing as formidable Ireland, with which she would have to reckon. Composed for the most part of Protestants, they taught England and Ireland itself, that with most of the Protestants the prejudices against the Catholics were weakened; since the delegates from one hundred and forty-three of these companies, who met at Dungannon, on the 15th of February 1782, to demand in the name of their armed constituencies free trade and an independent parliament, adopted also the following resolutions:—

"Resolved, (with two dissenting voices only, to this and the following resolution,) that we hold the right of private judgment in matters of religion to be equally sacred in others as ourselves.

"Resolved, therefore, that as men and as Irishmen, as Christians and as Protestants, we rejoice in the relaxation of the penal law against our Roman Catholic fellow-subjects, and that we conceive the measure to be fraught with the happiest consequences to the union and prosperity of the inhabitants of Ireland."

It is from this day that the origin of the party of liberal Protestants in Ireland must be dated. Until then, Protestants had only been patriots so far as they wished that Ireland should not be subject to England; but these patriots, so impatient of the English yoke, were satisfied that the Catholics should endure theirs. But now they began to invoke liberty, not only for themselves but for their fellow-citizens.

It is true that they only claimed, with a timid voice, the cessation of the persecutions against the Catholics; but they demonstrated their injustice in demanding their cessation; and the population which groaned under the penal laws had henceforth auxiliaries in the ranks of its oppressors.

The volunteers, their acts, the impulse which gave public opinion in Ireland, and their moral effect on England, produced the independence of the Irish parliament.

Section III. Independence of the Irish Parliament

Poyning's Law, so called from the name of the viceroy during whose administration, in the time of Henry VII., it had been enacted, declared that no Irish parliament should be holden until "the causes and considerations" of its convocation, and the projects of laws to be discussed, had first been approved by the English government. This law, which rendered the Irish parliament absolutely dependent upon England, had never ceased to excite the complaints of Ireland. On the 19th of July 1782, the Irish parliament declared itself independent of the English parliament, and adopted the principle publicly deliberated by the volunteers, "That no power on earth, save the King, Lords, and Commons of Ireland, had the right to make laws binding on Ireland."

Amongst the crowd of parliamentary combatants, one great chief deserves to be distinguished—HENRY GRATTAN. It is rarely the privilege of an individual to bear so signal a part in a national movement, and to contribute so much to the success of an enterprise otherwise effected by general causes. It was in his living and powerful words that the Irish parliament sent this energetic address to the King.

"To assure his Majesty, that his subjects of Ireland are a free people. That the crown of Ireland is an imperial crown inseparably annexed to the crown of Great Britain, on which connexion the interests and happiness of both nations essentially depend: but that the kingdom of Ireland is a distinct kingdom, with a parliament of her own—the sole legislature thereof. That there is no body of men competent to make laws to bind this nation, except the King, Lords, and Commons of Ireland; nor any other parliament which hath any authority or power of any sort whatsoever in this country, save only the parliament of Ireland. To assure his Majesty, that we humbly conceive, that in this right the very essence of our liberties exists; a right which we, on the part of all the people of Ireland, do claim as their birthright, and which we cannot yield but with our lives."

This address, supported by an army of nearly a hundred thousand men, had full success with the Irish parliament, which expressly abolished the laws on which England founded its right of predominance and legislative supremacy over Ireland.[163]

---

163. The following statement of the Volunteer force is too important a document to be omitted:—

Abstract of the effective men in the different volunteer corps, whose delegates met at Dungannon, and those who acceded to their resolutions, and to the requisitions of the House of Commons of Ireland, the 16th of April; 1782, (viz. "That there is no body of men competent to make laws to bind this nation, except the King, Lords, and Commons of Ireland, nor any other parliament which hath any authority or power of any sort whatsoever in this country, save only the parliament of Ireland.

"That in this right, the very essence of our liberties exists: a right which we, on the part of the people of Ireland, do claim as their birthright, and which we cannot yield but with our lives.")

COMMANDER-IN-CHIEF.
EARL OF CHARLEMONT.

GENERALS.

DUKE OF LEINSTER,	SIR JAMES TYNTE,
EARL OF TYRONE,	EARL OF CLANRICARDE,
EARL OF ALDBOROUGH,	EARL OF MUSKERRY,
LORD DE VESCI,	SIR WILLIAM PARSONS,
SIR B. DENNY,	HON. J. BUTLER,
RIGHT HON. GEORGE OGLE,	RIGHT HON. HENRY KING.

PROVINCE OF ULSTER.

Dungannon meeting, 153 corps	26,280
Twenty-one corps since acceded	3,938
Infantry since acceded, two battalions	1,250
Six corps of cavalry	200
Eight corps of artillery	420
Total	32,088

Section IV. Legal Consequences of the Declaration of Irish Independence

We may consider the act by which the Irish parliament asserted its independence as an echo of the declaration of independence by the American colonies.

Ulster Corps which have acceded since the 1st of April.		
Thirty-five of infantry and one battalion		1,972
Two of cavalry		92
Total of Ulster		34,152
Artillery.		
Six pounders		16
Three pounders		10
Howitzers		6
Total pieces of artillery	32	

PROVINCE OF CONNAUGHT.

Ballinasloe meeting, fifty-nine corps		6,897
Thirty-nine corps of infantry who since acceded		5,781
Cavalry light corps		421
Artillery		250
	13,349	
Acceded since 1st of April.		
Four corps of infantry and one of cavalry,		987
Total of Connaught	14,336	
Artillery.		
Six pounders		10
Three pounders		10
Total pieces of artillery	20	

PROVINCE OF MUNSTER.

City and county of Cork		5,123
Sixty-eight corps of infantry in the province		7,987
Cavalry of the province, returned fifteen corps		710
Artillery, nine corps		221
Total	14,041	
Acceded since 1st of April.		
Fifteen corps of infantry		3,921
Two corps of cavalry		94
Total of Munster	11,056	
Artillery.		
Six pounders		14
Three pounders		14
Howitzers		4
Total pieces of artillery	34	

PROVINCE OF LEINSTER.

One hundred and thirty-nine delegates met at Dublin, April 17th		11,983
Ten corps of cavalry who before acceded, and no delegates sent		580
Nineteen corps of infantry		4,398
Artillery, nine corps		322
Total of Leinster	22,283	

North America inspired the movement, the association of the Irish Volunteers gave Ireland the strength necessary to execute it. It would, however, be a mistaken view of the relations between England and Ireland to compare it to that of the colonies with the metropolitan state. Nothing is more common than to institute such a comparison. Ireland appears for centuries governed by force alone, and hence some have supposed that force was the only bond which united the country to England. To adopt such a view, is to mistake completely the nature of the contract existing between Ireland and England.

There is no doubt that after the conquest, and for a long period subsequent, Ireland was at the mercy of England, and might, if she had pleased, inflict on that country a government purely despotic, founded simply on the right of force and conquest. But the question is, not to know if such a course was possible, but if it was really adopted. Now it is clear that such was not the line of conduct pursued towards Ireland. Scarcely had England subdued the country, when she bestowed upon it free institutions, especially recognising the right of Ireland to have a parliament of her own, and to pay no taxes but those which should be voted by her parliament. Scarcely was England mistress of Magna Charta, when she extended its principles to Ireland; a conquered country obtained possession of these rights, not because she constituted an independent state, but because the people on which she depended had granted these franchises; she held her liberties from the very power which might have given chains if it had pleased.

Now, if we reflect on the circumstances which accompanied and followed the conquest, we shall see that this generosity of England was feudal. We have already seen under what circumstances and by what title the vassals and subjects of Henry II. established themselves in Ireland. These Anglo-Normans, for the most part noble by birth, preserved in Ireland all the privileges inherent to their rank; and the king no more thought of taking these away than the adventurers did of disputing with the king his quality of liege lord of Ireland.

Artillery.	
Nine pounders	2
Six pounders	16
Three pounders	14
Howitzers	6
Total of artillery	38

Total Number.	
Ulster	34,152
Munster	18,056
Connaught	14,336
Leinster	22,283
Total	88,827
Twenty-two corps also acceded, but made no returns, estimated at	12,000
Making in all, nearly a general grand total of	100,000

Artillery, one hundred and thirty pieces.

After the conquest, therefore, it is important to regard England as not only engaged with the native Irish, and making them bow beneath the yoke of the conqueror; we must especially consider her in her relations with the conquerors that issued from her own bosom, all freemen, Anglo-Normans by race, in whose presence she stood, and whom she was obliged to treat like the inhabitants of every other province belonging to the crown. There were men in Ireland more or less degraded in the feudal scale, at the top of which the king was placed; but they were all, in the style of the period, free men, not conquered subjects.

In truth, for a long time the conquerors of Ireland did not occupy the entire country; for a long time the unsubjugated population of natives which surrounded *the pale* was treated by England as an enemy, and deprived of all the privileges granted by England to her children; and whilst this state of things endured, we may say that there were two Irelands in the country: one English, and conqueror, the other vanquished or rebellious;—the first sharing in the free institutions of England—the second, enduring all the servitude of conquest. But when the potent hand of Henry VIII. weighed upon the country, the two Irelands became one; those of English or Irish birth were equally subjects of the same empire; one and the same law existed for all—so that, from this time, the condition granted to the Anglo-Norman colonists became the common right of all Ireland. Henry VIII. was not very prodigal of rights and privileges; we cannot tell whether, in his plans of tyranny, he intended to raise the Irish to English liberty, or to depress his English subjects to the servitude of barbarous Ireland.

However that may be, the despot established a level in Ireland, and at a later period, the Englishman in this country could not invoke a single political right which did not equally belong to every Irishman. This principle of political liberty, due to the feudal character of the conquest, received a singular development in the religious wars of the sixteenth century.

When Protestant England entered into a contest with Catholic Ireland, the question of race was lost in that of creed; there was no debate about reducing the sons of old Erin to the yoke, the point was to stifle the hydra of superstition and popery which had found refuge in Ireland; and this was the reason why England, fanaticised by Scotland, rushed on Ireland. The English settlers, who at this time invaded the Irish soil, seized it, not only to possess the land, but "to plant and nurture the tree of true religion."[164] Thus acted the Scotch settlers of

---

164. This was the cant of the sixteenth century; its meaning is best developed in the following resolutions adopted by the puritans of Massachusetts, when about to seize on lands belonging to the Indians.

"Resolved, That the earth is the Lord's, and the fulness thereof.

"Resolved, That the Lord hath given the inheritance of the earth unto his saints.

"Resolved, That we are the saints."—*Tr.*

James I., the fanatics of Cromwell, and the partisans of William III. Between 1615 and 1688, that is to say, in less than eighty years, Ireland was three times invaded under the pretext of religion, and the religious occupants remained there.

Thus, in the same way as England, in 1172, found herself in the presence of a feudal society whose rights she would not refuse to recognise; so, during the agitations of the sixteenth century, Protestant England beheld a Protestant society arise in Ireland, whose rights she was neither able nor willing to restrain.

In these times of enthusiasm, with which sometimes a singular spirit of universal levelling was singularly mingled, it was impossible that the notion of placing the Protestants of Ireland in an inferior condition to the Protestants of England could have entered the minds of Englishmen; every privilege granted to Englishmen, exclusive of their Protestant brethren in Ireland, would have been then regarded as an act of impiety and odious injustice

There were then, it is true, terrible conflicts between England and Ireland; there is no doubt that there were then conquerors and conquered, and that England was still victorious. But the vanquished were not Irish, they were Catholics, some of English race, others of Irish descent. A religious party was beaten down, not a nation conquered. During nearly two centuries, the majority of the inhabitants of Ireland enjoyed neither rights nor political privileges, but this majority was not oppressed as a people, but only as a sect.

The moment in which the Papists of Ireland endured the most terrible tyranny, was precisely that in which England showed itself most liberal to the only Irish population which it then recognised, that is to say, the Protestants. Never did such a sympathy exist; as they had the same religious passion, they seemed also to have the same common interest; and Cromwell only gave expression to the existing public feelings when he did that which was not finally completed until after another century and a half, that is to say, *united* Ireland to England.[165]

It must be remarked, that this immense portion of the inhabitants of Ireland, which did not enjoy the privileges of the constitution, was not directly excluded by law; all Irishmen had alike the right of invoking its protection: their incapacity only arose from the repugnance of their consciences to an oath which the law made a condition of exercising nearly all rights, civil and political. Thus, on the day when Catholics and other dissenters obtained a dispensation from the oath, they had entered *ipso facto* on the enjoyment of all their privileges, the right to which they had never lost, though the exercise had been suspended; and thus they at once participated in the advantages of the free society which had not ceased to exist in Ireland.

---

165. In Cromwell's plan of a parliament, (A. D. 1651,) Ireland was to be represented by thirty members.

From the preceding statement, we see how great is the mistake of those persons who believe that they can explain the respective situations of England and Ireland, by the nature of the relations which usually exist between a colony and the metropolitan country. Ireland has never been a colony but in name. The state of a colony implies a political and legislative dependence, a condition of inferiority to the parent state, which would not have been endured by the feudal Ireland of Henry II., nor the Protestant Ireland of Cromwell and William III.

Ireland is, besides, too near England to fulfil the conditions of an ordinary colony, which distance from the mother country protects in some sort, and which finds a certain independence in the very impossibility of the metropolitan country's governing it perpetually. No conquered country close to the conquering can remain in the intermediate position that a colony holds between political independence and entire subjection. Ireland, placed under the English sceptre, must necessarily have been treated as an equal or as an enemy, as free or enslaved; we have seen that it could not be placed in a state of servitude; it consequently received, theoretically at least, the privileges of liberty. There is no doubt that England frequently outraged the liberties she had consecrated; she violated them every time she pleased, for though Ireland had a free government, England did not cease to be the stronger, and her interests frequently hurried her beyond her engagements and even her passions. It was thus that Henry VII., by Poyning's law, subjected Irish acts of parliament to a sort of preliminary censorship: and at a later period, when England wished to annihilate Irish industry and trade by a single blow, she went so far as to assert that the laws of the English parliament were binding on Ireland.

But even whilst submitting, Ireland protested against such an abuse of strength, and England herself formally recognised her excesses when she declared, by her parliament in 1782, "that the English parliament had never the right to make laws for Ireland, nor to interfere with the independence of the Irish parliament." Before England had recognised this principle, Ireland had herself proclaimed it; and it is worthy of remark, that in declaring herself free, Ireland acted not as a colony breaking its chains, but as a people asserting its rights. Far different from the American provinces, whose declaration of independence was a signal for war in England, never was Ireland more closely united to that country than on the day when her parliamentary independence was established, for that independence was the first condition of the social compact; the United States broke that compact by their emancipation, to which Ireland remained faithful by becoming free. Burke well described the event of 1782, when he called it the 1688 of Ireland.[166]

---

166. Plowden, vol. i. p. 521.

Section V. 1782—Abolition of Certain Penal Laws.
Consequences of the Declaration of Parliamentary Independence

The movement of the volunteers, which produced the declaration of independence by the Irish parliament, had two very distinct effects—the one general, which interested all the inhabitants of Ireland, Catholic and Protestant; the other special to the Catholics.

In the first respect, the independence of the Irish parliament, though profitable to all, was especially an advantage to the Protestants, who, being in possession of all social advantages, were the more impatient to acquire a free government. Those who are dying of hunger do not look upon parliamentary independence as a means of getting bread; they are too wretched to envy political rights; their ambition leads them only to the immediate object of their wants, and they do not consider that political liberty is the best instrument for constructing social happiness.

Nevertheless, the Irish parliament, though exclusively Protestant, could not recover its independence without manifesting it by some acts favourable to the Catholics.

Thus, at the same date, (1782, by Act 21 and 22 George III., ch. xxiv.) the laws were abolished which hindered Catholics from acquiring, disposing, selling, purchasing, inheriting, and possessing property like Protestants. This was the completion of the law of 1778; it was the concession of the right of property without restriction; henceforth the Catholic was not a mere tenant on lease, but might be a proprietor like the Protestant.

The law was repealed that prohibited Catholics from possessing a horse of higher value than five pounds, and which permitted the horses of Catholics to be seized in time of war, or in case of invasion. Catholics were, therefore, free to possess any goods or chattels.

The law was repealed that inflicted punishment on a Catholic priest for performing any office according to the ritual of the Catholic church. The only penalty left was for officiating in a chapel with a bell and steeple.

The law was abolished which subjected to imprisonment every Papist who refused to denounce a priest and his assistants for celebrating mass. It was a step to the full toleration of the Catholic worship; the Catholics could not, it is true, perform their worship with pomp and splendour, but still they could pray in silence, according to the forms of their religion. The penalties of imprisonment and transportation denounced against the Catholic priests were repealed.

Finally, the law was revoked which prohibited Catholics from being instructors of youth, and guardians to their own children, or those of others.[167]

167. The sacramental test, which excluded Presbyterians and Protestants from offices of trust under the crown, was also repealed in the session of 1782.—*Tr.*

This was the second act of Catholic emancipation; from this epoch also two changes date, which, though equally advantageous to Protestants and Catholics, ought to be considered especially useful to the latter; to wit, the law which secured their places during good behaviour, (*quamdiu se bene gesserunt,* and not *durante bene placeto,*) and a similar law of *habeas corpus* to that possessed by England. These laws were particularly favourable to the Catholics, for guarantees and tutelary laws are most needed by the poor and oppressed.

Section VI. Continuation of the Volunteer Movement. Convention of 1783

It would not be reasonable to suppose that so powerful a body, representing the nation, having strong feelings of its rights, and a consciousness of its power, after having decreed resolutions, immediately transformed into laws by the parliaments of England and Ireland, should rest satisfied there.

After the independence of the Irish parliament had been proclaimed and recognised, another matter naturally presented itself—reform of the representation. This parliament was a delusive representation even of the Protestant population; under the influence of corruption, it voted anti-national laws, and popular laws when coerced by fear. It was vainly proclaimed free, for it was so only in name. And as its vices were derived from its very source, that is to say, the electoral system, a radical reform was necessary. Consequently, the National Convention of volunteers, assembled in 1783, proclaimed the necessity of parliamentary reform.[168]

The subject was brought before parliament at the very moment it was debated in this great assembly of the armed nation; so that Ireland might be said to have had two representative assemblies at the same moment; one perfectly legal, but unpopular; the other irregular, but possessing the confidence of the people.

Nevertheless, the Irish parliament rejected the proposition of reform by a majority of one hundred and ninety-nine against seventy-seven. More was asked of this parliament than it could effect. In fact, to change the basis of election, would be to ensure that the great majority of its members would not be re-elected; it was asking bad citizens to commit patriotic suicide. The House of Commons also resolved, "that they would support the rights and privileges of parliament against all encroachments."

Perhaps the Irish parliament might have yielded from fear what it would not grant to justice and reason, if there had been any peril in rejecting parliamentary reform; but no such danger existed. The armed volunteers, who had so energetically demanded and obtained parliamentary independence, did not manifest

---

168. Nov. 29th, 1783.

similar zeal for parliamentary reform. Divisions began to creep in amongst them; many believed that when this independence was obtained, everything was accomplished; others, and they were very numerous, began to fear that the prolongation of these discussions, and the consequent reforms, might effect a perilous revolution in the condition of the Catholics. Now, most of the volunteers were Protestants.

Observe that the political emancipation of the Catholics was discussed in parliament; it was debated whether they should be admitted to the elective franchise at the same time that the general questions of parliamentary reform were discussed. The two questions were thus linked, and were debated conjointly by the volunteers. These, disposed to alleviate the sufferings of the Catholics, but not to emancipate them, had resolved "that parliamentary reform was necessary, but that Catholics ought not to be admitted to the elective franchise." Still the two questions were confounded and discussed together in parliament; it may then be easily conceived why the Protestants should fear lest the triumph of the one which they desired might lead to the success of the other: and they had reason to do so, as it was a logical consequence. How could the principles of parliamentary representation, founded on property, be rationally discussed, if the rights of a number of proprietors were resisted on the mere ground of religion, and that too at a moment when the injustice of the penal laws had been fully recognised and proclaimed?

This explains the indifference with which the resolution of the Irish House of Commons rejecting parliamentary reform was received.

Section VII. Corruption of the Irish Parliament

Parliamentary reform was rejected, and yet the corruption of parliament was extreme. The Commons were composed of three hundred members; it would have been a difficult and troublesome task to bribe three hundred independent deputies; but of this number the greater part were mere creatures of the aristocracy; more than two hundred were members for rotten boroughs,[169] belonging either to peers or rich proprietors, who were also members of the House of Commons; so that it was only necessary to purchase a few in order to have nearly the entire; sometimes a single person could dispose of twenty boroughs, or forty votes.

There were two modes of purchasing members of the House of Commons, by places and pensions. The first was the *honourable* mode of sale; government had a multitude of places at its disposal. When there was not a sufficient num-

---

169. Some were members for still more rotten corporations, the leaders of which combined to exclude the inhabitants of the towns, whether Protestant or Catholic, from the franchise, so as to enable themselves to sell the representation to some peer who trafficked in boroughs, receiving in return places in the customs or excise for themselves and their children.—*Tr.*

ber, new places were created; when existing salaries were not sufficient for remuneration, they were augmented.[170] With regard to the petty offices of judicature and administration, unsuited to the dignity of national representatives, they were publicly sold, and the money thus raised was employed to purchase votes. When places were exhausted, pensions were given out of the Irish revenue;[171] the money thus employed was that of poor Ireland, who thus paid those that sold her while they sold themselves. Those pensions, which in 1756 were 44,000*l.*, rose in 1793 to 120,000*l.* Finally, when places and the fund for pensions were exhausted, the government took what it wanted from the treasury. A viceroy rarely quitted Ireland without leaving an arrear of 200,000*l.*, and sometimes 300,000*l.*

This corruption was practised with incredible openness. Grattan[172] challenged its denial in the midst of the corrupt parliament, and no voice dared to contradict it. Sometimes, after a strong opposition had been remarked in parliament, people were surprised to see it suddenly vanish; this happened in 1765, on the bill relating to the exportation of grain. But corruption was actually and openly avowed by the officers of the crown.[173] During the debate on giving the

---

170. M. de Beaumont deems that his account of the venality and profligacy of the Irish parliament will be scarcely credited; but every one acquainted with the history of the country must be aware that the systematic corruption both of the Irish Lords and Commons is understated. Everybody has heard the story of Mr. Hutchinson, founder of the Donoughmore family, whose vote, on a particular occasion, was purchased by giving *his daughter* a cornetcy of dragoons.—*Tr.*

171. "Infamous pensions to infamous men."—*Grattan's Speeches*, vol. i. p. 23.

172. Mr. Grattan, in the name of the little minority that opposed the destructive and disgraceful system pursued by the Irish administration, used the following pointed and powerful words:—"We charge them publicly, in the face of the country, with making corrupt agreements for the sale of peerages; for doing which, we say they are impeachable. We charge them with corrupt agreements for the disposal of the money arising from the sale to purchase for the servants of the Castle seats in the assembly of the people; for doing which we say that they are impeachable. We charge them with committing these offences, not in one, nor in two, but in many instances; for which complication of offences we say that they are impeachable—guilty of a systematic endeavour to undermine the constitution, in violation of the laws of the land. We pledge ourselves to convict them; we dare them to go into an inquiry; we do not affect to treat them as any other than public malefactors; we speak to them in a style of the most mortifying and humiliating defiance. We pronounce them to be public criminals. Will they dare to deny the charge? I call upon and dare the ostensible member to rise in his place, and say, on his honour, that he does not believe such corrupt agreements have taken place. I wait for a specific answer."

Major Hobart, the Irish secretary, refused to give any reply, on the ground that an inquiry of the motives of raising persons to the peerage was trenching on the royal prerogative.

173. "The threat was proceeded on, the peerage was sold, the caitiffs of corruption were everywhere—in the lobby, in the street, on the steps, and at the door of every parliamentary leader, whose thresholds were worn by the members of the then administration, offering titles to some, amnesty to others, and corruption to all."—*Grattan's Letter to Lord Clare. Miscellaneous Works*, p. 107.

regency of Ireland to the Prince of Wales, the Irish attorney-general, Mr. Fitz-gibbon, afterwards Earl of Clare, said to an astonished house and an indignant nation,—"You have set up a little king of your own; half a million, or more, was expended some years ago to break an opposition, the same or a greater sum may be necessary now."

Their original parliaments were annual; by corruption they became rare, and were gradually protracted during the life of the king. Hence it followed, that if government purchased a majority in the first year, it remained its master, and disposed of it at its pleasure until the accession of a new king. To avoid the evil chance of too short a reign, it was once proposed to vote the supplies for twenty-one years; this was proceeding direct to the object, but the motion failed.[174]

In the reign of George III. a different system was established; the parliament became octennial, and was obliged to assemble once every two years at the least. The consequence was, that there was a new parliament to purchase every eight years; the members who sold themselves generally disappeared, and were not re-turned at the new elections; but others, equally venal, came in their stead, and what was regarded as a guarantee of independence, appeared to several a mere increase of expense to the English government, or rather to Ireland, which had to supply the funds for corruption.

The House of Lords was still more easy to gain. The crown exercised over it that ascendency which a superior necessarily possesses over those who derive from him all they have. Besides, they were almost all a new nobility, and conse-quently had no root in the country. Occupied with their pleasures in London, or attending on the King of England, they were more eager to pass for English lords than to be courageous defenders of the interests of their country. The ses-sion of the Irish House of Lords was only marked by some interchanges of courtesy with the viceroy;[175] and every time that these took place, the Irish lords displayed fresh meanness. "Never," says the biographer of Lord Charlemont, "did any nobility equal that of Ireland in varying the forms of obsequiousness and servility."

In truth, the Irish House of Lords neither was nor could be a source of em-barrassment to the English government. It was too feeble, as a national institu-tion, to render its support valuable; but it offered the British government a re-source of another nature which had its value. It sometimes happened that the pension fund was exhausted when money for corruption was wanting; in such a case, peerages were sold to persons who had no claim to nobility, and who were,

---

174. It was lost by a majority of one. The casting vote was given by Col. C. Tottenham, who rode up from the country, and arrived barely in time to turn the contest; hence, "Tottenham in boots" became a popular toast.—*Tr.*

175. For several successive days the journals of the Irish House of Lords present the same record. "Met—heard prayers—ordered the judges to be covered—adjourned."—*Tr.*

therefore, eager to become purchasers, and the sums of money derived from this traffic served to purchase the consciences which still remained free. The great merit of the peerage in the eyes of the government consequently was, that the sale of its honours supplied money for bribing the Commons. "Thus," said Grattan, in the Irish parliament, (Feb. 8th, 1791,) "The ministers have sold the prerogatives of the crown to buy the privileges of the people."

The legal agent between England and the two Irish houses of parliament was the viceroy of Ireland. For a long time, this high functionary attended to no part of his office but the emoluments. The charge of viceroy was regarded as a sine-cure which the English government bestowed to arrange some political exigency. When a great lord or borough proprietor demanded some ministerial employment in spite of his absolute incapacity, he was named Lord Lieutenant of Ireland; it was also occasionally a means for some great person, poor or ruined, to make or repair his fortune. The viceroy possessed two magnificent palaces, one in Dublin, the other in the suburbs, but he did not reside in either. Dublin could not compensate him for London, where he was detained by his habits and his pleasures. There were some viceroys who never appeared in Ireland, such as Lord Weymouth, who was nominated to the office in 1765. They generally went over only for a few months to attend the opening of parliament, after which they returned to England. Although his sojourn in Ireland was so brief, the viceroy derived large profits from his office. Lord Wharton, in two years, is said to have netted 45,000*l.* So unusual in Ireland was a resident viceroy, that when Lord Townshend established himself as such in Dublin (1768) people looked upon the event with amazement, and seemed almost to doubt such a phenomenon.

During the absence of the viceroy, the government was entrusted to three lords justices, selected either from the privy council, the judges of the four courts, or the dignitaries of the Anglican church. These were employed by the English government to negotiate the majority in parliament.

"There were always three or four influential persons in the Irish parliament," says Dr. Campbell, "whose coalition necessarily produced a majority on any question whatever. These were the individuals whom it was important to gain, and with whom the lords justices treated; the most immoral and scandalous transactions followed. The lords justices leased out the Irish administration; they gave up to those influential members of parliament the disposal of all the employments and dignities dependent on the executive power, the revenue of Ireland, and the funds for pensions; bargaining that those persons in their turn should carry through parliament all laws desired by the English government. The vile agents thus employed by the English ministers were usually called "undertakers."

In virtue of the powers thus delegated to them, the undertakers appointed to all offices, selecting governors of counties, sheriffs, justices of peace, crown lawyers, collectors of excise and customs, &c.: they could even bestow peerages, or rather, as they never did anything gratuitously, they sold all that was given them. Parliament—justice—administration—everything was venal in Ireland.

The undertakers had every sort of advantage over the viceroy; as they were always on the spot, they knew better than he did the actual state of affairs, and the course of intrigues. Besides, they lent themselves more pliantly than the viceroy to all the base manœuvres in which they were required to act as instruments. The office of viceroyalty was become so degraded, that no viceroy would execute it. All the power being placed in the hands of the undertakers, the viceroyalty was but a nominal dignity; and if a Lord Lieutenant had employed his right to dispose of places and honours, the undertakers would have complained of a breach of contract. In general, the recommendations of the viceroys were utterly disregarded.

Out of twenty viceroys, who, in the course of a century, succeeded each other in Ireland, Lord Townshend was the first who, in 1767, formed the project of administering the government himself. His intentions were pure and honourable; he wished to remove the dominant cabal, and govern Ireland directly, without the intervention of the undertakers.

But though the corruptors were removed, all those whom corruption had tainted remained, with the wants and habits they had acquired. Henceforth there were several members of the Irish parliament in both houses, accustomed to live on the pension of England, and whose hostility was to be expected if payment was suspended. Lord Townshend who, above all things, wished to be responsible for Ireland to his own country, had recourse to the only means of success then known. He governed alone, but he governed by bribery, like those whom he had supplanted; but with this difference, that, being a novice in corruption, he submitted to exorbitant conditions from the consciences he purchased; though he reserved no personal gains for himself, he spent more than the undertakers, who never made a bargain without reserving something for their own share. On the whole, it cost Ireland more to be governed by a man of honour than by a set of political intriguers.[176] He was honourable, and the system was not. There is not a more ludicrous exhibition in the world than an honest man practising corruption; he understands nothing of the roguery with which he has to deal; vile intrigues should be left to mean minds; in such they are sure to be superior.

---

176. When Lord Townshend left Ireland, the treasury was in an arrear of 265,000*l.*

Section VIII. Is a Servile Parliament of Any Use?

It is impossible to glance at the parliament of Ireland and its venality, without raising a doubt whether it would not have been better for Ireland to be without any parliamentary representation, than to possess one so corrupt. Of what advantage to a country are representatives setting themselves up for sale? Is it not merely an additional load upon the people that has to pay them? Is not the authority of these pretended representatives a mantle with which power may veil itself, and from which it may derive greater strength for evil, than if abandoned to its own forces?

There are, doubtless, immense perils in the corruption of parliament. Still the executive has not always the power of purchasing members, even when it has the will. It sometimes happens, that people are not in a humour to sell themselves; and there are some difficult steps to be taken in the bargain which greatly impede the progress of corruption; finally, so great is the love of liberty, that even apostates to it endeavour to keep something in their own power; they equivocate with the purchasers, and make strange conditions with their own consciences; they endeavour to retain some little honour in the depth of their degradation, and are tempted to display independence at the very moment they accept servitude. Placed between the trust reposed in them by their constituents, and the engagements they have made with the power to which they have yielded, they doubtless belong to those whose money they have received, but not without some tendency towards those whose esteem they wish to preserve. A power hostile to the people, acting independent of any assembly, would simply do as it pleased, without any regard to the interests of the country; the assembly sold to it will not contravene the course of power; but if there exist means of accomplishing what power requires without injuring the people, such means will be adopted even by a venal assembly. In the most venal and corrupt minds there is a kind of tacit compromise between honour and infamy, in consequence of which, the man who, in one way, most treacherously sacrifices the interests of his country, defends it most intrepidly in another.

It often happens, also, that the members of parliament who have sold themselves, compel the government to understand, that in order to be strong, they must not be too unpopular; and when a measure of tyranny is required, though they consent to it, yet, to escape execration, they demand that the oppressive act should be accompanied by some national measure.[177]

---

177. Thus, in 1769, a money bill planned by the British cabinet, certified in England by the Lord Lieutenant and Irish privy council, and returned under the king's great seal, was rejected by the Commons after the first reading, because it had not originated in their house. On this occasion the patriots were aided by some pensioners and placemen, who had reserved to themselves a right of opposing the government in questions of importance. . . . On the motion

We must also remember, that corruption is vainly practised on a large scale: it does not taint everybody. There are always some souls elevated above the reach of corruption. We may instance Grattan, Curran, Ponsonby, Lucas.[178] The minority that remained pure, became powerful by its virtue alone, which brought out in high relief the vices of the majority: and eventually this minority became formidable when supported by the wants and sympathies of the nation.

The practice of corruption is beset by a multitude of obstacles and difficulties. If the man purchased be worth little, his defection makes little noise, but also the purchase is of little value. If he possesses importance, without doubt he is worth the money paid for him; but then the intrigue makes a noise. See what a clamour was excited by the defection of the patriot Flood,[179] when named to an employment revocable at the pleasure of the crown. One matter deserves to be specially remarked. It is not rare in the midst of corruption to find honest men, who resist temptation, treated as dupes or fools, blind to their own interest; and yet where can we find in history an independent character that is not remembered with honour, or a servile creature that is not branded with infamy?

The most venal parliament has sometimes another advantage. It is true that it generally aids power against the country; still, when a liberal administration

---

of the prime-serjeant (Mr. Hussey Burgh) Oct. 12th, 1799, the House of Commons unanimously resolved that, in their address to the king, these words should be inserted: "We beg leave, however humbly, to represent to your Majesty, that it is not by temporary expedients, but by a free trade alone, that this nation is now to be saved from impending ruin."—*Tr.*

178. The name of Hussey Burgh should not be omitted from this list. The following fragment, almost the only specimen of his eloquence that remains, is said to have produced the most electrical effect ever witnessed in a deliberative assembly.

"The usurped authority of a foreign parliament has kept up the most wicked laws that a jealous, monopolising, ungrateful spirit could devise to restrain the bounty of Providence, and enslave a nation, whose inhabitants are recorded to be a brave, loyal, and generous people; by the English code of laws, to answer the most sordid views, they have been treated with a savage cruelty; the words penalty, punishment, and Ireland, are synonymous; they are marked in blood on the margin of heir statutes; and though time may have softened the calamities of the nation, the baneful and destructive influence of those laws has borne her down to a state of Egyptian bondage. The English have sowed their laws like serpents' teeth, and they have sprung up in armed men."

179. The following character of Flood is contained in Grattan's reply to Lord Clare's pamphlet:—

"Mr. Flood, my rival, as the pamphlet calls him, and I should be unworthy the character of his rival, if in the grave I did not do him justice. He had faults, but he had great powers; great public effect; he persuaded the old—he inspired the young; the Castle vanished before him; on a small subject he was miserable; put into his hand a distaff, and, like Hercules, he made sad work of it; but give him the thunderbolt, and he had the arm of a Jupiter; he misjudged when he transferred himself to the English parliament; he forgot that he was a tree of the forest—too old, and too great, to be transplanted at fifty; and his seat in the British parliament is a caution to the friends of union to stay at home, and make the country of their birth the seat of their action."

comes, which may happen, it will be seen voting laws useful to the country with more ardour than it displayed in the support of anti-national measures. A sudden revolution seizes all the members; what they are commanded to do accords with their desires; they have always been the friends of liberty; they display marvellous zeal in defending the principles which they have hitherto combated; they give more than is asked, so happy are they to have the power of being popular without ceasing to receive the wages of servility. Finally, however prevalent corruption may be, a time comes when it is impotent; those who have been regularly paid for a long time, end by believing that what they receive is their due, and some day or other, in spite of their engagement to servitude, they will be found speaking and acting as if they possessed their liberty.

Sometimes, also, public opinion manifests itself so imperiously, that whatever may be the desire which members of parliament feel to resist it, though additions may be made to their pensions, and a barrier raised by money between them and the patriotism outside, it is impossible for them to refuse what the country demands; and then this servile parliament becomes a precious instrument to proclaim the will of the people, which could only be manifested by irregular and violent acts, if it did not possess a constitutional organ for its expression.

When a government beholds the members of parliament it has purchased resume their liberty, it sometimes makes bitter complaints. It is wrong; for the consciences it bought had no right to sell themselves. More frequently it is silent; it fears lest one defection should bring several others: if it withdraws the pensions from those who acted independently, they are indignant at being deprived of a property which they regarded as sacred, and become from that moment adversaries of power, the more dangerous as they know all its secret turpitudes; and they become patriots the more zealous as they have the more need of proving the sincerity of their attachment to the popular cause.

When persons are alarmed at the cost of a venal parliament, they do not take into account all that would be spent and lavished without any limit or public advantage if there were not a parliament.

These considerations, which are in some sort a history of the Irish parliament, perhaps prove that for a nation there is something worse than a corrupt representation, namely, to have none.[180]

---

180. M. de Beaumont's views in this section are so admirably illustrated in the account which Grattan gives of the occasional bursts of patriotism in the Irish parliament, that it is worth while to quote the passage. It is taken from his celebrated reply to Lord Clare's Union Pamphlet:—

"Those servants of the crown proved themselves to be Irishmen, and scorned to barter their honour for their office; that parliament, whose conduct the pamphlet reprobates, had seen the country, by restrictions on commerce, and by an illegal embargo on her provision trade, brought, in 1779, to a state of bankruptcy; that parliament had reposed in the liberality

CHAPTER II: THE FRENCH REVOLUTION—
ITS EFFECTS IN IRELAND

Section I. 1789

The French revolution found an immense echo in the miseries and passions of Ireland; it introduced new elements of reform into that country.

Until then, the chiefs of the popular party, that is to say, the Whigs, having at their head Grattan and Lord Charlemont,[181] pursued liberty, such as it is under-

---

of the British parliament an inexorable confidence—that parliament waited and waited, till she found, after the English session of 1778, nothing could be expected; and then that parliament—(and here behold the imperative principles of our constitution, and contemplate parliament as the true source of legitimate hope, though sometimes the just object of public disapprobation)—that parliament at length preferred a demand—I say a demand—for a free trade, and expressed in a sentence the grievance of a country. They shorten the money bill, assert the spirit of the country, and break, in one hour, that chain which had blocked up your harbours for ages. They follow this by a support of government and of empire as ample as was their support of their country and of her commerce, bold and irresistible, and do more to intimidate and deter the common enemy than all your present loans and all your establishments.

"I come to the second period, and here they fall back; here they act reluctantly; but here you see again the rallying principle of our constitution; that very parliament whom the pamphlet vilifies, whom the minister thought he had at his feet—those very gentlemen whom the pamphlet disparages—whom the then secretary relied on as a rank majority, made a common cause with the people, (made a common cause with liberties,) and, assisted and backed by the voice of that people, preserved, carried, and established the claim, inheritance, and liberties of the realm, and sent the secretary, post, to England—to recant his political errors in his own country, and to register that recantation in the rolls of his own parliament. These achievements we are to estimate, not by the difficulties of the day, but by the difficulties resulting from the depression and degradation of ages. If we consider that the people and parliament, who had thus associated for the defence of the realm, and had added to the objects of their association the cause of trade and liberty, without which that realm did not deserve to be defended, had been in a great measure excluded from all the rest of the world, had been depressed for one hundred years, (by commercial and political oppression, and torn by religious divisions,)—that then ministers had not seldom applied themselves to taint the integrity of the higher order, and very seldom (except as far as they concurred in the bounties of the legislature) applied themselves to relieve the condition of the lower order; that such a people and such a parliament should spontaneously associate, unite, arm, array, defend, illustrate, and free their country; over-awe bigotry, suppress riot, prevent invasion, and produce, as the offspring of their own head, armed cap-à-pee, like the goddess of Wisdom, issuing from the Thunderer, *commerce* and *constitution*. What shall we say of such a people, and such a parliament? Let the author of the pamphlet retire to his closet, and ask pardon of his God for what he has written against his country!

181. The following character of this distinguished nobleman is taken from Grattan's reply to Lord Clare's pamphlet:—

"In the list of injured characters, I beg to say a few words for the good and gracious Earl of Charlemont: an attack, not only on his measures but on his representative, makes his vindication seasonable. Formed to unite aristocracy and the people, with the manners of a court and the principles of a patriot, with the flame of liberty, and the love of order; unassailable to the approaches of power, of profit, or of titles, he annexed to the love of freedom a veneration for order, and cast on the crowd that followed him the gracious light of his own ac-

stood by the English, that is to say, feudal liberty, claimed and obtained as a privilege and under the name of concession.

When the influence of France made itself felt, the liberals of Ireland invoked liberty as a right—a right natural, general, and imprescriptible. The radical who demanded reform in the name of Magna Charta, henceforth claimed it as part of the rights of man.

Irish reform thus assumed a philosophical character, which it had hitherto completely wanted; its circle was enlarged, it had higher aims, and it advanced farther. All those who were embued by this philosophical spirit, could not comprehend the refusal to Catholics of the rights recognised as belonging to Protestants; all men being equal, they ought to share equally in the benefits of the constitution, and hence universal suffrage followed as a necessary consequence.

All minds were then seized with an ardent fever of general innovation. Society was to be made anew; all reforms were to be proposed at once; social reform, political reform, religious reform. Everybody had his system, and everybody had speculated on the plan of a new constitution.[182]

The French revolution agitated all nations; but there was not a country in the world to which the impulse was communicated so quickly and so faithfully as Ireland.

Henceforth Irishmen had their eyes fixed on France, and everything which passed in that country excited their deepest sympathy. The cause of France was, in their eyes, that of all enslaved nations who aspired to freedom. "Right or wrong," said Wolfe Tone, who only gave vent to sentiments generally felt, "right or wrong, success to the French. They are fighting our battles, and if they fail, adieu to liberty in Ireland for another century!"

---

compliments; so that the very rabble grew civilised as it approached his person. For years did he preside over a great army, without pay or reward, and he helped to accomplish a great revolution without a drop of blood.

"Let slaves utter their slander, and bark at glory which is conferred by the people—his name will stand; and when their clay shall be gathered to the dirt to which they belong, his monument, whether in marble or in the hearts of his countrymen, shall be resorted to as a subject of sorrow, and an excitation to virtue.

"Should the author of the pamphlet pray, he could not ask for his son a greater blessing than to resemble the good Earl of Charlemont; nor could that son repay that blessing by any act of gratitude more filial, than by committing to the flames his father's publications."

182. The very able sketch of the state of the public mind in Ireland during the French revolution, given by M. de Beaumont, will be recognised as perfectly accurate by all acquainted with the publications of that period. The principal authorities quoted by M. de Beaumont are Tone's Memoirs, Hardy's Life of Lord Charlemont, and a collection of detached papers called Belfast Politics, published at Belfast, 1794. The mention of these authorities here will supersede the necessity of further reference.—Tr.

Not only did Ireland sympathise with France and assume its passions, but it even adopted its manners, its language, the style of its laws, and all its new revolutionary allurements.

The volunteers of Dublin assumed the name of a national guard, (but a proclamation was issued against their meeting, and they never assembled on parade). The triumph of French liberty was annually celebrated at Dublin and Belfast. The anniversary of the capture of the Bastile became a national festival. In public assemblies the cap of liberty was substituted for the Irish harp. Orators at clubs and meetings styled themselves citizens of the world.

The following toasts were given at civic banquets, (in 1792,) "The sovereignty of the people," "The rights of man," "May philosophy illuminate all nations and people, and make them one great family." At a national festival, a flag, bearing the goddess of liberty, was displayed with the inscription, "To our sister of Gaul. She was born the 14th of July, 1789,—we are yet in embryo."

Ireland rejoiced in all the triumphs of France, and grieved at her reverses. A victory obtained by the French on the Rhine was celebrated by a general illumination in Dublin. The press shared the imitation of French language: patriotic letters bore the signature of "A Liberty Boy;"[183] friends gave each other the title of "Citizen," and United Irishmen raised the cry of "Long live the Nation!"

When a French expedition, sent in 1798 to revolutionise Ireland, landed in Killala bay, on the western coast, the following song was widely circulated through the country.

A Song of the United Irishmen.[184]

I.

Rouse, Hibernians, from your slumbers!
See the moment just arrived,
Imperious tyrants for to humble,
Our French brethren are at hand.
    Vive la united heroes,
    Triumphant always may they be,
    Vive la our gallant brethren,
    That have come to set us free.

---

183. This is a cant phrase in Dublin, and not an imitation of the French; part of Dublin is called "The Liberty."—*Tr.*

184. This song was found on the mother of Dogherty, a United Irishman, who was killed at Delgany, in the county of Wicklow, in the autumn of 1798.—*From Mulgrave's Irish Rebellions, Second Edition, p. 78 of Appendix.*

II.

Erin's sons, be not faint-hearted,
Welcome, sing, then, Ca ira,
From Killala they are marching,
To the tune of Vive la.
    Vive la united heroes, &c.

III.

To arms quickly, and be ready,
Join the ranks, and never flee.
Determined stand by one another,
And from tyrants you'll be free.
    Vive la united heroes, &c.

IV.

Cruel tyrants, who oppress you,
Now with terror see their fall!
Then bless the heroes who caress you,
The orange now goes to the wall.
    Vive la united heroes, &c.

V

Apostate Orange, why so dull now?
Self-will'd slaves, why do you frown?
Sure you might know how Irish freemen
Soon would pull your orange down.
    Vive la united heroes, &c.

Sometimes Irish patriotism blundered in its adoption of French language and symbols; thus, in one song the Fleur-de-lys appears to have been mistaken for a symbol of republican France.

The Fleur-de-lys and harps we will display,
While tyrant heretics shall mould to clay.

But it is to the French revolution that we must especially attribute the immense change which took place in the feelings and principles of the Irish Volunteers. Liberal as the volunteers were, they did not cease to be Protestants, and they sought for themselves only the liberties and privileges of which, either from prejudice or religious passion, they believed the Catholics unworthy. They had, it is true, claimed for them some modifications of the penal laws, but they rather sought an abatement of persecution than a return to justice. Their liberalism was never entirely free from a sectarian spirit. They treated the Catholics as inferiors, even when they lent them aid, and exercised over them a sort of patronage; but in 1792, in order to unite all ranks and parties, they took the name of United Irishmen.[185]

This new union between Protestants and Catholics was not only manifested by political acts, it was manifested in the minor details of social life. A patriotic dinner was given at Belfast, where Protestants and Catholics sat side by side in token of their harmony. The metamorphosis of the volunteers into United Irishmen is one of the most remarkable facts of this epoch, and deserves especially to fix the attention of the reader.

And, in the first place, the principal trait in the character of the United Irishman was, that they derived the greater part of their inspiration from France. We see in Tone's Memoirs, that one of the principal objects of the committee was, to verify and publish everything of importance which occurred in France. This was a new starting-point for Irish freedom. Until then, the Irish revolutionist had been chiefly inspired by American genius; now he invoked at the same time the names of Washington and Lafayette, of Franklin and Mirabeau.

The military organisation of the United Irishmen was entirely modelled on that of the volunteers, but their principles were not the same. The volunteers of Ireland were associated to protect Ireland from an invasion of the enemies of England. The United Irishmen were openly friends to France, and bargained with her for an invasion. But what especially characterises the transformation of the volunteers into United Irishmen was the sudden and fundamental change wrought in their political principles.

They suddenly exhibited a violent hatred of the Whigs, and a thorough contempt for the slow and regular progress of reform. Hitherto they endeavoured to obtain the abolition of oppressive statutes, and the enactment of good laws from the English government and their own parliament; they now required an entire change of system. They wanted either a complete, absolute reform, or to have nothing altered. We find from his Memoirs that Tone was grieved because a partial emancipation (1793) might give the Catholics some satisfaction. "The English yoke must be shaken off!"—"The connexion with England, the source of all Ireland's woes, must be broken!"—"To ameliorate the condition of the people, a vile and odious aristocracy must be humbled."—"In emancipating Ireland, the right arm of England must be cut away." Such were the wishes, the sentiments, and the new principles of the Irish reformers.

In proportion as republican France advanced in revolutionary paths, they followed her. The doctrine that "the end justifies the means" was established in

---

185. This name was first proposed by T. W. Tone.

Ireland, and ardent friends of their country and of freedom were seen using their utmost endeavours to produce a French invasion. Here is the order of their ideas: "Ireland must be delivered from the English yoke; she is too weak to emancipate herself; there is consequently a *necessity* for asking assistance from a stranger." All the ardent patriots eagerly invoked the aid of the French armies. "Ten thousand men would suffice to separate Ireland from England," said Tone, in 1793. And what will be done when the government is overthrown? Terrible dreams of vengeance and extermination presented themselves to the minds of some of the reformers. "The aristocrats," said Tone, "have no mercy, and deserve none."

Still, in the midst of these revolutionary meditations, Wolfe Tone, the head of the United Irishmen, who came to France to negociate for an invasion with the Directory, was brought into connexion with General Hoche, the head of the intended expedition, who, in a private conversation with the Irish patriot, used the following memorable words: "When you guillotine a man, you get rid of an individual, it is true, but then you make all his friends and connexions for ever enemies to the government." Struck by this language, Wolfe Tone adopted the opinion that, in case of a revolution, it would be better to avoid sanguinary retaliation.

Section II. Other Effects of the French Revolution. Abolition of Penal Laws

England, hearing the echoes of the French revolution in Ireland, in order to calm the popular passions, hastened to make some of the concessions loudly demanded by the reformers.[186]

In the first place, the bar was opened to Catholics; the right of taking more apprentices than two was conceded to Catholic merchants and artisans; the law which prohibited marriages between Catholics and Protestants was abolished.[187]

Other concessions were soon added to these. At the beginning of the war with France in 1793, the English government, feeling the necessity of tranquillising Ireland, abolished the most severe laws which still pressed on the Catholics. Thus the law of conformity to the Anglican rites was abolished; the penalties against Catholic instruction were removed; the elective franchise was given to Catholics; but they were not yet made eligible to parliament.[188] Finally, with a

---

186. In 1792, the Catholic petition was rejected with the greatest contumely; in 1793, more favours than that petition sought were granted.

187. 1792, 32 Geo. III. ch. xxi.

188. 1793, 33 Geo. III. ch. xxi. These concessions would have been more full and complete, had not a portion of the Catholic aristocracy declared themselves satisfied with a part when so much was still due. To this dereliction of their own rights and those of their countrymen may be attributed no small amount of the subsequent evils of Ireland.—*Tr.*

few reservations, they were admitted to all civil and military employments in the state and the municipal corporations.[189]

The preceding reforms compose what is sometimes called the third emancipation of Ireland, or the emancipation of 1793. The first was produced by the American war; the second by the independence of the Irish Parliament; and the third emanated directly from the French revolution.

Section III. Other Consequences of the French Revolution.—Reaction

After this exaggerated, and in some cases stupid imitation of French revolutionary movements in Ireland, excesses of infamous memory sullied the cause of liberty in France, and a re-action fatal to reform soon appeared in Ireland. The Protestants, who had reluctantly embraced the Catholic cause, seized this opportunity for abandoning it, and many of the Catholics, disgusted by French infidelity, rejected every reform that came from such a source. The republic, which henceforth appeared a blood-stained phantom, terrified the world, and dissension appeared in the body of United Irishmen.

The Parisian massacres of September (1792) are a remarkable epoch in the history of Ireland. Until that time, republican principles spread rapidly in Ireland; but they then stopped short—re-action commenced. In August, 1792, the Whig leaders were still on terms with the party of the United Irishmen. At the same epoch (August 7th, 1792,) the Catholic clergy made common cause with them; and their union with the Catholic proprietors was still unbroken.

The year 1793 arrived, and the patriot party of Ireland was struck to the heart; the public mind suddenly changed; the dreams of progress were dissipated, and the illusions of liberty vanished. The great Burke, whose talents had been devoted to the Irish cause, withdrew from it. From the month of October, 1792, the Catholic clergy separated in a body from the reformers; and when the question of universal suffrage was proposed in the House of Commons, Grattan, the chief of the Whigs, resisted it with all his might. "Compare," says Tone in his memoirs, "our committee in 1793 with what it was in 1792."

The most ardent Irish democrats, when they heard of the fatal days of September, could not avoid feeling some degree of terror. Tone comforted himself by considering the Irish character. "In France," said he, "the people assassinate, and do not plunder: an Irish mob would do just the contrary; it would rob everybody, and kill nobody."

The English government, long alarmed by the agitations of Ireland, eagerly

---

189. The clauses admitting the Catholics to municipal offices were clogged by subsequent provisos which neutralised their effects. The corporations took advantage of the legislative blunder, and, in spite of the manifest design of the law, Catholics are, in many places, practically excluded to the present hour.—*Tr.*

seized an opportunity of striking a mortal blow at the revolutionary spirit. Without encountering any formidable opposition from the Irish people, it dissolved and suppressed the volunteers, forbade the formation of armed bodies without the authority of the executive power, disarmed the citizens, sent strong garrisons into the towns, prevented public discussions at clubs or meetings, prohibited the sale of munitions of war, and finally passed a law (the Convention Act) which prohibited every assembly of delegates for deliberating on public affairs. These energetic measures were everywhere put into execution; they were resisted nowhere but in Belfast, and there the laws were easily enforced by the strong arm of power.

Ireland, hitherto so agitated, was paralysed. It was almost ready to become a republic; but it now murmured at the very name of liberty. Still, notwithstanding the decay of public spirit, some isolated but ardent patriotic passions survived in Ireland.

Deprived of all public means of action, the reformers sought others. The association of United Irishmen still subsisted; but, as it was menaced by law, it acted in the shade instead of the open day. It attacked the government previously at meetings and through the press, or in national conventions, but now it conspired secretly. Formerly, free to consult the nation, it received its instructions from the people, and was more or less obliged to conform to them; now, forced to act secretly, the leaders of the United Irishmen received no mandate but from themselves, and conducted Ireland according to their personal views and passions. The Irish people could no longer dictate to its agents when and how reform should be effected; the leaders were to determine both the moment and the means. Now the chiefs of the popular party, seeing that the nation had fallen again under the yoke, and was too much humbled to rise, believed that Ireland could not effect a revolution by herself. Consequently they resolved to invite a foreign army into Ireland to deliver the country from its fetters. Hence three attempts to invade Ireland were made by France between 1796 and 1798, in consequence of negociations between the Directory and the head of the United Irishmen. Hence arose the fatal insurrection of 1798, and hence, finally, the parliamentary union between England and Ireland, which was completed in 1800.

Section IV. French Invasion of Ireland. Insurrection of 1798

Tone's Memoirs contain the most interesting account of this insurrection, and of the three French expeditions. The Irish insurrection and the French invasion were to be so combined as to afford each other mutual aid; and Wolfe Tone had been accepted by the Directory as a general of brigade, though he was in reality only the diplomatic agent of the United Irishmen with the French government. Tone, Irish to the heart's core, an enthusiast by nature, an ardent partisan of French and republican ideas, displayed extreme zeal and rare intelligence in engaging the Directory to send an expedition to Ireland. He cleverly dispelled the fixed notion of all the French politicians of the time, which was a descent upon England, and succeeded in persuading the members of the French government that England could be best attacked through Ireland.

We see in his Memoirs, that at the close of the year 1796, an expedition commanded by General Hoche was prepared, and that the fleet separated by a storm from the vessel that carried the general; it was compelled to return to Brest, from whence it had started, without even attempting a debarkation.

If we believe Tone's Memoirs, it depended on a mere trifle, whether Napoleon might not have made an expedition to Ireland instead of a campaign in Egypt. Two reasons prevented him; he was reluctant to execute an enterprise which Hoche had planned; and secondly, he displayed at this time a singular repugnance for the French Jacobins, with whom the United Irishmen had formed very close connexion.

Hoche's expedition failed from a concourse of unfortunate circumstances; a thousand other events retarded the execution of French designs on Ireland. Still the French were expected in that country, and the plan of a vast insurrection was prepared without relaxation. This insurrection was immediately to follow the landing of the French troops; but such was the dominion of events, that the insurrection took the lead. After a thousand successive adjournments, which could not be renewed without the greatest peril to most of the conspirators, the insurrection exploded.

It had been too long uncertain and languishing for the people to have faith in it; badly concerted, badly directed, received with coldness by some, and with terror by others—guided by men divided amongst themselves, some of whom wished for reform, and others for revolution—rejected by the aristocracy in a body,[190] and even by the middle classes themselves—reduced to support itself solely on the lowest of the people—composed of the most heterogeneous elements, of Presbyterians fighting for a republic, and Catholics contending for the freedom of their creed[191]—mutual enemies associated by surprise in a common course, though they aimed at different ends. Guided by such chiefs, sustained by such a base, the insurrection could not succeed. It might be said to have died before it was born: its only effect was to bring from the British government the most atrocious and sanguinary measures of repression.

The recital of the horrors committed during this fatal crisis would of itself be

---

190. With one splendid exception, Lord Edward Fitzgerald. The life of this amiable and unfortunate young nobleman, by Moore, is, perhaps, the most interesting piece of biography in any language. It unites all the charms of romance to the importance of truth.

191. In some cases, no doubt, for its supremacy; they had been taught the lesson of exclusion by the ascendency, and had they succeeded, they would have in all probability proved themselves apt scholars.—*Tr.*

a long and mournful history; luckily for the author, the limits of this summary do not allow him to discuss the details of this terrible epoch.[192]

I do not know if the sanguinary annals of Ireland exhibit war in a more horrible aspect; I speak not here of the acts of barbarity committed in the heat of action, and by which the insurgents and their opponents were equally sullied. What civil and religious war is there that does not bring frightful violence, murder, pillage, devastation, and flame? I mean to speak of the cruelties committed in cold blood by the victorious party.

Perhaps one sentence will suffice to show all the miseries of Ireland at this moment; even after the war, the country was delivered over to the mercy of the soldiery.[193] In the middle of the insurrection, martial law was proclaimed; when the revolt was subdued military justice was not withdrawn; and the English army, after having struck down the enemy on the field of battle, pursued them still with sentences of death pronounced by courts-martial. A few examples will suffice to show the proceedings of this soldier-justice, stimulated by passion and unrestrained by rule.

Lord Charlemont declares in his Memoirs, that suspected and accused persons were, without any form of trial, tortured, flogged, and half hanged, in order to extort confessions.[194] A gentleman of eminent merit, Sir Edward Crosbie, had declared himself favourable to reform in parliament; the military judge concluded that he was a republican, and had him brought to the bar. At the trial, "Protestant loyalists, witnesses in favour of the accused, were forcibly prevented by the bayonets of the military from entering the court."[195] This was not all: "Catholic prisoners had been tortured by repeated floggings, to force them to give evidence against him, and were promised their lives upon no other condition than that of his condemnation." Notwithstanding these and other violent measures, no charge was proved; of which the members of the court-martial who sentenced him to death were so sensible, that, in defiance of an act of parliament, the register of the proceedings was withheld as a secret from his wife and family. The court was irregularly constituted, and illegal, destitute of a judge advocate. The execution of the sentence was precipitate, at an unusual hour, and attended with atrocious circumstances, not warranted even by the sentence. After he was hanged, his body was abused, his head severed from it, and exposed

192. The most impartial history of the Irish insurrection yet published is that by the Rev. Mr. Gordon, a Protestant clergyman.—*Tr.*

193. A soldiery, be it remembered, so totally demoralised, that General Abercromby declared it to be "formidable to everybody but the enemy."—*Tr.*

194. On this repulsive subject it is not necessary to enlarge; but it is sufficient to say, that the torture of the suspected was made the subject of boast in public, and was even vindicated in pamphlets.—*Tr.*

195. See Gordon, vol. ii. p. 393. See also Curran's speech in the case of Heavey *versus* Sirr.

on a spike.[196] The president of the court was an illiterate man, unable to write the most common words of English without mis-spelling.

In the course of this savage administration of justice, every art was employed to accumulate proofs of guilt; even proofs of innocence were used for the purpose. Who would believe it? It was a grave subject of charge before these military tribunals to have rescued Protestants from the fury of the rebels; for this influence over the insurgents was deemed a proof of attachment to their party. "I thank my God that no person can prove me guilty of saving any one's life or property!" was the sudden exclamation of a Catholic gentleman in a company where the notoriety of the practice was the subject of conversation. These, and many similar facts, are recorded by the Rev. Mr. Gordon, a clergyman of the Established Church, all whose sympathies were in favour of the men whom impartiality forced him to condemn.

In a short time two hundred victims fell by the hand of the executioner. The legal punishment of the condemned did not always satisfy the passions by which it had been procured. When the sentences pronounced by the court-martial at Wexford were executed, the bodies of the victims were mutilated, insulted by a thousand indignities, and thrown into the river, after their heads had been severed and spiked on the walls of the court-house. Sometimes, after the victim was turned off, he was lowered on his feet until he recovered; he was then again suspended, and thus the tortures of strangulation were multiplied at pleasure.[197]

The deep wounds which Ireland received from these dreadful measures of repression long remained open and bleeding. The English army destroyed all the harvests on its march, and the consequence to the people of Ireland was a general famine, which lasted two years. The number of individuals slain on both sides during this calamitous period has been estimated at thirty thousand men, and the destruction of property during the continuance of the civil war, at 2,000,000*l.*

The insurrection was suppressed in Ireland when two French divisions arrived. The first, amounting to about one thousand men, sailed from Rochelle, under the command of General Humbert, and, on the 22d of August, 1798, landed in Killala bay, on the coast of Connaught. After gaining a victory at Castlebar, it was met by Lord Cornwallis, the viceroy, who took the command

---

196. The rank of the unfortunate baronet rendered it impossible to conceal the iniquity of his fate; but there were many other victims to brutal ignorance invested with power, whose cases were not less atrocious, but for obvious reasons they may now be permitted to rest in oblivion.—*Tr.*

197. Prisoners were sometimes strangled by being suspended from the shoulders of tall men; an officer in his Majesty's army, for his services in this way, was honoured with the title of "the walking gallows."—*Tr.*

in person, with an army twenty times its strength; it was defeated and made prisoner. The armament, consisting of three thousand men, embarked in a ship of the line and eight frigates, sailed from the bay of Camaret, on the 20th of September, 1798, and on the 10th of the following October reached the entrance of Lough Swilly, in the province of Ulster. Preparations for landing were made, when a superior fleet, under the command of Sir John Borlase Warren, appeared, and, after a terrible engagement, the French squadron was compelled to surrender. Wolfe Tone shared in this expedition; he was taken, recognised,[198] tried, and condemned to death.

Such was the sad and fatal termination of those attempts at invasion from which some ardent spirits expected the regeneration of Ireland, but which were to her only the cause, or the pretext, for new and terrible persecutions.

Consequences of the Insurrection of 1798. The Union

After the insurrection of 1798, England, holding Ireland under her hand as a vanquished rebel, punished her without reserve or pity. Twenty years before, Ireland had entered into possession of her political liberties. England preserved a better recollection of this success of Ireland, and hastened to profit by abasement to place her again under the yoke.

The Irish parliament, after the recovery of its independence, became a subject of annoyance to England; to become its master, required an endless care of corruption, notwithstanding which, opposition was occasionally experienced; the opportunity seemed favourable for its suppression, and England resolved to abolish it altogether.

At this news poor Ireland was agitated, as a body about to be deprived of life still moves under the irons by which it is mutilated and torn. Out of thirty-two counties, twenty-one protested energetically against the destruction of the Irish parliament. This parliament, from which an act of suicide was demanded, indignantly refused, (in 1799,) and voted the maintenance of its constitutional existence.

Indignant at the servility demanded from the body of which he formed a part, Grattan vehemently denounced the ministerial proposition. But all resistance was vain. The only serious obstacle to England was, the reluctance of the Irish parliament to vote its own annihilation. Hitherto its acts were bought, but now its death was to be purchased. Corruption was immediately practised on a large scale; places, pensions, favours of every king, peerages, and sums of money, were lavishly bestowed; and the same men who had rejected the Union in 1789,

---

198. The British naval officers were willing that Tone should escape, and affected to believe that he had fallen in the action, but he was recognised and denounced by Sir George Hill, who had been his fellow-student in the Dublin University.— *Tr.*

adopted it in 1800 by a majority of 118 to 73. It has been calculated, that out of the 118 votes, 76 were pensioners or placemen.[199] One of the greatest difficulties arose from the number of boroughs belonging to rich proprietors, who made a lucrative traffic of seats in parliament. To silence these complaints, every rotten borough was valued at 15,000*l.*, and this sum was proffered as an indemnity to all those who by the Act of Union would lose their political privileges.[200] The engagement was kept, and the total indemnity amounted to 1,260,000*l.*

Thus was completed the self-destruction of the Irish parliament, an act imposed by violence and sustained by corruption; but it was not effected without rousing in Ireland all that remained of national feeling and patriotic sentiment.

When Lord Castlereagh moved "that the bill should be engrossed," Mr. O'Donnell moved as an amendment, "that the bill should be burned:" to which Mr. Tighe also moved as an amendment, "that it should be burned by the hands of the common hangman." (But these were vain exhibitions of the *"iræ leonum vincla recusantium."*)

Constitutional and Political Effect of the Union

Nothing is more common than to mistake the real effect of this measure, and the error arises from taking the word *union* sometimes in a moral sense, and sometimes in too extensive a political sense.

If by *union* we understand the concord and sympathy of two nations formerly divided, we must confess that this term is quite unsuited to the act under consideration; for England and Ireland were, perhaps, never more hostile to each other than after the union of 1800.

It would also be a great error to suppose that the act of 1800 identified England and Ireland, so as to make this latter a province, subject in all points to the same government, the same police, and the same laws.

Before the act of union, Ireland had its own institutions; it preserved them after the union, with the single exception of its parliament.

When England added Ireland to herself, she did not resolve that Ireland should for the future be governed by the laws and principles of the English constitution; she did not and could not do any such thing. The English constitution is not a charter in a hundred articles which may be granted hastily to a nation in urgent want of a government. It is especially composed of usages, traditions,

---

199. Their names are given in Mr. O'Donnell's remarkable amendment, that the Address to the Lord Lieutenant should be presented by the pensioners and placemen. (See Grattan's Speeches, vol. iv. p. 5.)—*Tr.*

200. A most extraordinary claim for compensation was made by the Bishop of Ossory; his petition averred, that his predecessors had got promotion in consequence of their influence in the borough of St. Canice: he therefore claimed to be remunerated for having his chances of promotion diminished by the disfranchisement of the borough.—*Tr.*

habits, and a multitude of statutes, connected with the usages from which they cannot be separated, whether they annul or confirm them. Now, though the observance of a law may be prescribed to a people, a usage or custom cannot be so enjoined: a custom is a complex fact, the result of a thousand preceding facts; it is consecrated, not imposed; were it possible to remove its prescriptions to a people with whom it had not originated, it would be impossible to transfer its spirit. What, then, did England do, when she proclaimed the union with Ireland? She declared that for the future all laws necessary to the two countries should be made in a common parliament, to which each should send representatives; but whilst providing for the future, she left the past untouched; and Ireland, united to England, remained in possession of all her laws and usages, except that which assigned her a separate parliament.[201]

Thus, after the act of union, there was always *an Ireland;* in the terms of this act, the three kingdoms form a single empire, under the title of the United Kingdom of Great Britain and Ireland. After the Union with England, Scotland lost its name, but Ireland kept hers; and she will still longer keep her national habits and passions.

CHAPTER III: CATHOLIC EMANCIPATION IN 1829

The convulsions in 1798, of which the union in 1800 was the last episode, were followed by a long repose, or at least order was re-established in Ireland, such as it had been before the nation made an effort to break its fetters. The Protestants resumed their habits of oppression, the Catholics submitted in silence: this sort of peace reigned twenty years in Ireland.

Nevertheless, at the moment when the act of union was formed between England and Ireland, the latter engaged to the former that all the political incapacities to which the Catholics were subject should be abolished. This abolition was promised as an alleviation of the rigours of the act of union. But when this act was accomplished, the measures of grace and generosity stipulated to accompany it were not realised. Mr. Pitt, then prime minister, evinced, it is true, some anxiety to keep his engagements, but his wishes were powerless before the obstinacy of George III., who believed that he would violate his coronation oath by consenting to Catholic emancipation. The minister behaved nobly: not being able to keep his promise, he resigned his office.[202] Ireland had not less reason to complain of a breach of faith; warned by past misfortunes, she had not recourse to violence and revolt, in order to obtain justice; for the assertion of her rights,

---

201. By the eighth Article of the Union, it is enacted, "That all laws in force at the time of the union, and all the courts of civil and ecclesiastical jurisdiction within the respective kingdoms, shall remain now as by law established."

202. But he resumed it again without making any stipulation in favour of the Catholics.— *Tr.*

she only employed the legal means offered to her by a free constitution. The press and the association were her two most potent instruments. About the year 1810, a Catholic committee was organised, and took in hand the direction of all the national efforts which tended to reform.[203] John Keogh directed this body until O'Connell appeared, and ruled over it as it ruled over Ireland. The Catholic association took for its object and motto the parliamentary emancipation of the Catholics: public opinion excited on this point grew warm by degrees; the press stimulated it incessantly; the people, convened in meetings, grew animated at the voice of the leaders; petitions were sent to parliament; they failed, but their rejection alimented the passions that had dictated them. O'Connell, who soon became powerful with the people, guided them with prudence and skill; thus, reform advanced with equal wisdom and boldness. England refused the emancipation demanded by the Irish Catholics; Ireland sent a Catholic to represent her in the English parliament; the representative was O'Connell, the county that elected him, Clare; and this act was accompanied by demonstrations too imposing to be despised. Ireland, cloven down and mutilated thirty years before, began to rise from her ruins; recourse to violence had destroyed her, adherence to right restored her power.

On the 13th of April, 1829, the English parliament adopted the bill by which every Catholic may, for the future, enter parliament without taking an oath repugnant to his conscience. Thus fell the last link of the chain of the penal laws by which persecution was supported. This is the term of the fourth epoch,—the close of the period which separates the past from the present.

---

203. The very interesting history of the struggles made by this body is now out of print, and a copy can scarcely be obtained. It is to be hoped that its amiable and highly-gifted author, Mr. Wyse, will favour the world with a second edition.—*Tr.*

· PART I ·

I

External Appearance of Ireland. Misery of Its Inhabitants

Ireland, by a fatal destiny, has been thrown into the ocean near England, to which it seems linked by the same bonds that unite the slave to the master.

Its coasts are high; differing from England, the soil of which, elevated in the centre, gradually falls towards the shores; it exhibits in its midland a vast table-country, of which the surrounding peaks seem to form the borders.

This external conformation explains the short and rapid course of its rivers, which, issuing from the mountains, seem only born to perish instantly, and find their tomb in the depth of the seas by the very side of their source.

Nevertheless, there is one great river in Ireland, such as neither England nor Scotland possesses; this is the Shannon, which, by an extraordinary accident in Ireland, rises in the inner table-land of the country; and thus, placed on a level surface surrounded by eminences, it seems, as it were, imprisoned in a great vase, from which it could not escape save by overflowing. But its privileged waters find no obstacle to their passage; a gentle and almost insensible declivity offers to their course no asperities by which it might be precipitated or suspended. Abundant and flowing near its source, where more feeble streams are exhausted, —majestic and tranquil where other rivers are hurried onwards and lost in torrents, the Shannon, in a course of more than two hundred miles, distributes the benefit of its stream to half of Ireland, and gently advances to the ocean, into which it does not throw itself, but imperceptibly mingles with its waters.

Nature seems to have bestowed its most bounteous gifts on Ireland; she has enriched the bowels of its ground with the most precious metals, poured with lavish hand the most fertile soil in the world over the rock that serves as its base; she has bestowed on its maritime commerce the finest harbours, fourteen of which are fit to receive ships of war; and, as if she had destined the country to high fortunes, she has placed it on the west of our continent as an advanced out-post, the depository of the keys of ocean, charged to open to European vessels the highway to America, and to offer the American vessels the first European harbour.

Having made these rich presents, Nature further laboured to embellish the country; she has traced the forms of its mountains with infinite grace, interspersed its valleys with prairies and lakes, and, covering the whole with a brilliant robe of verdure, has desired that it should be called, in the language of the poet, "*Green Erin, the lovely Emerald Isle,*"

First flower of the earth, and first gem of the sea.

Still, in spite of the ornaments it bears, and the treasure that it contains, Ireland is neither a smiling country nor a prosperous land.

The most beautiful natural prospect wants life when it is not animated by the sun. These beautiful mountains, these immense lakes, these endless meadows, these hills as verdant as the vales, doubtless present the most charming landscapes when accidentally seen under a clear sky; but the atmosphere of Ireland is generally dark and clogged with mists and fogs. The west and south-west winds blow on it almost without intermission; they bring to it the storms[1] and tempests of the Atlantic; the ocean masters Ireland, and has sovereign rule over its temperature: it is the tyrant of its climate.[2]

Formerly Ireland was a vast forest; so powerful was the vegetation there, that it was called "the island of wood."[3] It is now almost destitute of trees; and when, on a fine day in spring, it appears, though bare, full of sap and youth, it seems like a young and lovely girl deprived of her hair.

It is not exactly known at what time and by what process this great destruction was effected. We may, however, be assured that it was before the christian era, and probably at a much more distant date. Some attribute it to an extraordinary inundation, which uprooted the trees, levelled the forests, and buried them in the bosom of the earth. Others, whose opinion is better supported by scientific study, believe that the ruin of the forests was the result of violent storms. When the lofty forests that covered the country were compact and entire, they afforded each other mutual support against the violence of the tempests; but, in proportion as man requiring an open space for his house and field, effected clearances here and there, the trees near those that had been cut down were without support against the fury of the hurricane, and fell before blasts that were previously powerless; every ruin occasioned by a tempest produced a thousand others, rendered more easy as they were multiplied: the work of destruction

---

1. Wakefield's Ireland, i. 416.
2. Campion's Irish Histories, 13.
3. Mason's Survey, ii. 501.

went on, and all the fallen trunks, descending by the natural declivities to the lakes and the marshy parts of the soil, were stopped on this liquid base, where, heaped one above the other year after year, they were mingled together, some preserving their natural form, others decomposing into vegetable matter, until they formed that spongy, combustible substance, sometimes red and sometimes black, of which the vast turf-bogs of Ireland are composed.[4]

But the greatest convulsions and most terrible shock to Ireland came not from the ocean, from winds, or from tempests—they were the work of man.

We have seen in the foregoing historical introduction to what cruel sufferings Ireland was subject during the three centuries which followed the landing on her shores of the Anglo-Normans, so prompt to invade, so slow to effect a conquest,—how, whilst Ireland was still palpitating from the struggles of the invasion, she endured the terrible shocks and sanguinary trials of a civil and religious war;—finally, how, after having been mutilated and crushed by the arms of Protestant England, Catholic Ireland endured the tyranny of law. The struggles of the conquest have long ceased; the wars of religion are at an end; persecuting laws have disappeared; and, towards the close of the last century, Ireland commenced a new era of independence. Nevertheless, Ireland is unhappy and poor; all the sources of its misery have not been dried up; and amongst the causes of its misery there are some whose consequences still exist, and are destined to a long duration.

I do not believe that there is any country where a conquest of so distant a date has left impressions at once so old and so vivid. It seems that ages as they roll have not healed one of its scars. The soil is still bleeding with its wounds; everywhere war has left its devastations—everywhere confiscation has struck its blows. It is impossible to travel in Ireland without meeting a ruin which was the witness of some sanguinary struggle; it is scarce possible to stir a step without treading on land which, by the fortune of civil war, has not passed through the hands of three or four sets of possessors, the last of which, remaining master, represents the cause that triumphed. The vanquished may be seen beside the conquerors still full of the recollections of more prosperous times. These fields, they tell you, "belonged to our ancestors; Cromwell gave them to one of his soldiers, who has transmitted them to his children. That castle, now occupied by an English lord, whose nobility is of recent date, was confiscated by William III. from an Irishman of illustrious race and royal blood, whose descendants now till the soil over which their ancestors reigned."

But the wounds made by the wars of religion are those which are still the deepest and most grievous in Ireland.

---

4. Bogs are sometimes confounded with marshes; but the latter are always in low levels, while some of the Irish bogs have an elevation of more than five hundred feet above the sea.

Everything in Ireland is mingled with religion; the recollections of its history from the time when it was called the Island of Saints, down to the last century, when it was persecuted for its faith,—the struggles of the conquest,—the revolutions that followed it,—the governments which succeeded it,—its social condition in our days,—the classes and political parties that divide it, the passions that animate it,—the character, the manners, and the intellectual developement of its inhabitants, even the geographical distribution of its territories,—all bear the stamp and impress of religion.

We cannot hope to learn the misfortunes of Ireland without thoroughly understanding Ireland in its religious aspect.

It is divided into two distinct zones, the northern Protestant, the southern and western Catholics; the former is limited to Ulster, the second extends over the other three provinces, Leinster, Munster, and Connaught.

Connaught is, in our days, the type of ancient Ireland. It would seem as if Nature had been anxious to distinguish it from the other provinces. The ocean bounds it on the west, the river Shannon girds it on the south and east, forming it into a peninsula separated from the rest of Ireland. It was thither, in the time of Cromwell, that the unfortunate persons were driven, who had to choose between death and that place of retreat. "To hell or Connaught," said the tyrant to the proscribed. Those who sought shelter in that wretched land brought with them the ancient faith of their ancestors, their banished religion, their exiled country. Since that time, Connaught has not ceased to be the great focus of Catholic Ireland. Nowhere is the remembrance of the civil wars more vivid— nowhere are the Englishman and the Protestant detested with a hatred more religious and more national.[5]

The characteristic of the north is not merely that it is Protestant, but that it is puritan: Ulster is the Scotland of Ireland. This province has preserved, in all their bitterness, the old antipapal passions which the settlers of James brought with them, and which the soldiers of Cromwell and William III. revived. The inhabitant of Ulster is not merely separated by a river from the native of Connaught, religion has established a still more powerful barrier; and a great length of time must elapse ere the Scotch puritan of the North of Ireland will regard and treat as brethren the Catholics of Connaught. In Connaught, most of the people speak the primitive language of the country; in Ulster, English (or rather Scotch) is the only language. Ulster is the type of Protestant, and Connaught of Catholic Ireland.

In general, the primitive Irish are Catholics, the English Protestants, at-

---

5. The Irish language is also more generally spoken in Connaught than in the other provinces.

tached to the Anglican church, and the Scotch also Protestants, but adopting the Presbyterian ritual.

I have said, that in Ireland everything is mingled with religion, that parties and the state of society bear its imprint. Protestantism, which since the age of Elizabeth has been the creed of the conquerors of Ireland, is the religion of the upper classes. The Protestant is rich, the Catholic poor. In general, the former governs; the latter, consigned to an inferior condition, obeys the Protestant as a political master for whom he labours.

The Protestant religion is a sign both of fortune and of power. Not only is the Catholic poor and the Protestant rich, but each seems to think that such is the natural condition of both; the Catholic accepts his humble destiny, and the Protestant places implicit confidence in his pride of place. The latter, in his relations with the Catholics, displays some of that superiority which Europeans in the colonies exhibit to persons of colour who retain traces of their African descent.

The Protestant is not only a descendant of conquerors, the inheritor of their glory and of their power, established by seven centuries of domination, he believes himself of a race superior to that of the Irish; and as in Ireland religion marks the race, Protestantism is regarded as a species of nobility. This opinion, it is true, grows weaker every day, but sufficient traces of it remain in the mutual relations between Protestants and Catholics to allow of its escaping notice.

The Catholic of Ireland is in that dubious state in which a freedman finds himself when first delivered from servitude, and who makes his first essay of liberty—obliged suddenly to change the manners of a slave, that no longer suit him, for the deportment of a free man, which is as yet unknown. In spite of fact and right, he still regards as his master the person who has been so. Vainly does he protest, by external acts, against this inward sentiment: the cry of conscience, depraved by former servitude, gives him the lie within his own bosom; and sometimes the grossness and insolence which he displays in asserting his equality with the Protestant, serve in reality only to place him below the latter.

Nothing is more rare than to find, with the Irish Catholic, a just appreciation of his actual condition; in his intercourse with Protestants, you will always find him take his ground too high or too low; either, forgetting his emancipation, he offers himself in an humble and obsequious attitude to his former master, or, intoxicated by the victory over his oppressors, he is not contented to be their equal, but wishes to prove himself free by oppressing them in his turn.

There is another circumstance in the social condition of Ireland not less remarkable than this aristocracy of race and creed; that is, the feudal aspect which the country offers in the middle of the nineteenth century.

The government of the English in Ireland has been for the last hundred and fifty years a Protestant aristocracy, grafted on a feudal aristocracy. Great reforms have been made in the laws which established the Protestant ascendency, but the feudal base of the edifice has for the most part remained unshaken.

The country, after the religious confiscations, was divided amongst large proprietors, and has still remained in the possession of their descendants, who have received the large estates of their ancestors entire, under the protection of the laws of primogeniture and entail. These lands are cultivated by the Catholic population, theoretically free to detach itself from the soil, but bound to it as the only means of existence, and in reality in a condition worse than that of the serfs during the middle ages.

This state of things presents only a deceptive analogy with England. In the latter country, as in Ireland, the feudal law, doubtless, keeps the property of the soil in a small number of families, who receive and transmit it without the power of dividing estates; but, by the side of these fortunes derived from land, there have risen fortunes made by industry and commerce; whilst the feudal principle operates to maintain the rich in his wealth and the poor in his misery, the industrial and commercial principle is incessantly at work to displace fortune, to diminish the number of the poor, and to raise new men to wealth. These two rival powers are in a state of incessant war, which leaves no repose to the combatants. The industry which creates is superior to the feudal principle which preserves; the rich, armed with his fruitful land, is vanquished by the activity of an industrial producer; between the lord of the soil and the *prolétaire,* an infinity of new existence is constantly rising, which collectively forms the middle class. This class is almost unknown in Ireland.

Ireland presents an eternal contrast of riches and poverty, of which it is singularly difficult to form a correct idea.

When the traveller, approaching the Lakes of Killarney, halts near Muckross Abbey, a double spectacle is offered to his view; on one side, uncultivated plains, barren marshes, monotonous flats on which meagre rushes and rickety firs miserably vegetate; extensive heaths, through which appear here and there some rocks of moderate elevation, whose uniform aspect, destitute even of savage beauty, attests only the poverty of nature; it is impossible to imagine a land more indigent or more desolate.

But on the opposite side a far different scene bursts upon the view; at the foot of a chain of mountains, gracefully divided and separated from each other by a series of lovely lakes, are extended rich and fertile plains, verdant and smiling meadows, forests full of sap and vegetation; here there are cool shades, secret grottos, mysterious shelter; there are open spaces, bold peaks, an horizon without bounds; by the side of silver streams are fields covered with yellow ears of corn; abundance, riches, and beauty everywhere;—everywhere the extraordinary of nature as graceful as she is fruitful. Thus, from the same point may be seen two landscapes absolutely opposite; on one side extreme wealth, on the other extreme wretchedness; it is the image of Ireland.

The traveller in Ireland meets only magnificent castles or miserable hovels; but no edifice holding a middle rank between the palace of the great and the cabins of the lowly; there are only the rich and the poor.

The Catholic of Ireland, or the man of the lower class, finds only one profession within his reach, the culture of the soil; and when he has not the capital necessary to become a farmer, he digs the ground as a day labourer.[6] Two-thirds of the English population are industrial or commercial, only about a fourth part is agricultural. In Ireland, less than a fourth part is manufacturing or commercial, more than two-thirds are exclusively devoted to agriculture. He who has not a spot of ground to cultivate, dies of famine.

From what has been stated, it may be seen that the incredible variety of classes, ranks, and degrees, which infinitely divide the social scale in England, cannot be found in Ireland, where the limit which separates the aristocrat from the *prolétaire* is marked by a narrow line, on which no intermediate existence can be placed.

The Protestant in Ireland, who has the privilege of rank, of political power, and of wealth, has likewise the monopoly of education. Until very recent times there existed no primary schools, save for the Protestants; even at the present day, Catholics have not the same advantage as Protestants in the establishments consecrated to the higher branches of education. Thus, whilst everything is calculated to develope the intellectual faculties of the rich, the poor man is abandoned to himself, and left in his ignorance.

It may easily be conceived how these two opposite classes, each constituted on an immutable base, must have developed and extended themselves, the one in the sphere of its power, the other in the circle of its misery and servitude.

It is necessary to reflect long on what has passed during several centuries; it is necessary to represent the rich and poor following invariably for ages two opposite roads, the one leading to extreme wealth, the other to extreme misery; it is necessary to estimate the logical and necessary results of these two principles, the first of perpetual increase, the second of progressive ruin, fortifying each other, and finding a new power of action in each of their consequences; it is necessary, I say, to meditate long on these causes, to comprehend the excess of luxury to which the Irish aristocracy has reached, and the inveterate leprosy of misery that covers poor Ireland.

The revenues of the rich in Ireland sometimes amount to sums that appear chimerical. In this country of misery, the rich man has made for himself a mag-

---

6. Surlly's Penal Laws, 143.

nificent destiny: he possesses splendid castles, boundless domains, mountains, parks, forests, lakes, and he sometimes possesses them two or three times over.

Whilst millions of unhappy beings ask every day by what means they shall provide for their most imperious necessities, the rich man inquires by what art he can stimulate a passion in his cloyed soul, or awake the half-extinguished appetite of his pampered body. Does he wish to remove his person, wearied of itself, from one place to another? The finest roads, well able to rival those of England, are at his service. Luxury and riches travel, with all their comforts and all their ostentation, across the suffering and the misery of the country.

Such is Ireland, which was created rich! To see Ireland happy, you must carefully select your point of view, look for some narrow isolated spot, and shut your eyes to all the objects that surround it; but wretched Ireland, on the contrary, bursts upon your view everywhere.

Misery, naked and famishing, that misery which is vagrant, idle, and mendicant, covers the entire country; it shows itself everywhere, and at every hour of the day; it is the first thing you see when you land on the Irish coast, and from that moment it ceases not to be present to your view; sometimes under the aspect of the diseased displaying his sores, sometimes under the form of the pauper scarcely covered by his rags; it follows you everywhere, and besieges you incessantly; you hear its groans and cries in the distance; and if the voice does not excite profound pity, it importunes and terrifies you. This misery seems inherent to the soil, and one of its natural products; like some of those endemic scourges that pollute the atmosphere, it blights everything which approaches it, smites the rich man himself, who cannot, in the midst of his joys, separate himself from the miseries of the poor, and makes vain efforts to rid himself of the vermin which he has produced, and which cling to him.

The physical aspect of the country produces impressions not less saddening. Whilst the feudal castle, after seven centuries, shows itself more rich and brilliant than at its birth, you see here and there wretched habitations mouldering into ruin, destined never to rise again. The number of ruins encountered in travelling through Ireland is perfectly astounding. I speak not of the picturesque ruins produced by the lapse of ages, whose hoary antiquity adorns a country—such ruins still belong to rich Ireland, and are preserved with care as memorials of pride and monuments of antiquity—but I mean the premature ruins produced by misfortune, the wretched cabins abandoned by the miserable tenants, witnessing only to obscure misery, and generally exciting little interest or attention.

But I do not know which is the more sad to see—the abandoned dwelling, or that actually inhabited by the poor Irishman. Imagine four walls of dried mud, which the rain, as it falls, easily restores to its primitive condition; having for its

roof a little straw or some sods, for its chimney a hole cut in the roof, or very frequently the door, through which alone the smoke finds an issue. One single
apartment contains the father, mother, children, and sometimes a grandfather or
grandmother; there is no furniture in this wretched hovel; a single bed of hay or
straw serves for the entire family. Five or six half-naked children may be seen
crouched near a miserable fire, the ashes of which cover a few potatoes, the sole
nourishment of the family. In the midst of all lies a dirty pig, the only thriving
inhabitant of the place, for he lives in filth. The presence of the pig in an Irish
hovel may at first seem an indication of misery; on the contrary, it is a sign of
comparative comfort. Indigence is still more extreme in the hovel where no pig
is to be found.

Not far from the cottage extends a little field of an acre or half an acre; it
is planted with potatoes; stones heaped on each other, with rushes growing
through the interstices, serve it for a fence.

This dwelling is very miserable, still it is not that of the pauper, properly so
called; I have just described the dwelling of the Irish farmer and agricultural labourer.

I have already said that there are no small proprietors under the great, and
that below the opulent there are none but the poor: but these are wretched in
various degrees, and with shades of difference, which I shall endeavour to indicate.

All being poor, the only food they use is the cheapest in the country—potatoes;[7] but all do not consume the same quantity: some, and they are the privileged class, eat potatoes three times a day; others, less fortunate, twice; those in a
state of indigence only once; there are some still more destitute, who remain one
or even two days without receiving the slightest nourishment.[8]

This life of fasting is cruel, but nevertheless it must be endured under the
penalty of still greater evils. He who eats a meal too much, or fasts once too little, is sure to have no clothes; and moreover, this prudence and resignation to
suffering are often unavailing.[9]

Whatever may be the courage of the poor peasant to endure hunger in order
to meet other demands, he is in general naked or covered with rags handed
down in the family from generation to generation.[10]

In many poor hovels there is often only one complete suit between two indi-

---

7. Third Report of the Irish Poor Inquiry, 1836. The disadvantages of the potato as a staple
food are, difficulty of transport, difficulty of preservation, and the small proportion of nutritive
matter.

8. Selections from the evidence received by the Irish Poor Inquiry Commissioners, 220.

9. Ibid. 296.

10. Ibid. *passim.*

viduals; and hence the priest of the parish is almost always compelled to say several masses on the Sunday. When one of the family has heard an early mass, he returns home, strips off his clothes, and gives them to the other, who goes then to hear the second mass.

I have seen the Indian in his forests, and the negro in his chains, and thought, as I contemplated their pitiable condition, that I saw the very extreme of human wretchedness; but I did not then know the condition of unfortunate Ireland. Like the Indian, the Irishman is poor and naked; but he lives in the midst of a society where luxury is eagerly sought, and where wealth is honoured. Like the Indian, he is destitute of the physical comforts which human industry and the commerce of nations procure; but he sees a part of his fellows enjoying the comforts to which he cannot aspire. In the midst of his greatest distress, the Indian preserves a certain independence, which has its dignity and its charms. Though indigent and famished, he is still free in his deserts, and the sense of this liberty alleviates many of his sufferings: the Irishman undergoes the same destitution without possessing the same liberty; he is subject to rules and restrictions of every sort: he is dying of hunger, and restrained by law; a sad condition, which unites all the vices of civilisation to all those of savage life. Without doubt, the Irishman who is about to break his chains, and has faith in futurity, is not quite so much to be bewailed as the Indian or the slave. Still, at the present day, he has neither the liberty of the savage nor the bread of servitude.

I will not undertake to describe all the circumstances and all the phases of Irish misery; from the condition of the poor farmer, who starves himself that his children may have something to eat, down to the labourer, who, less miserable but more degraded, has recourse to mendicancy—from resigned indigence, which is silent in the midst of its sufferings, and sacrifices to that which revolts, and in its violence proceeds to crime.

Irish poverty has a special and exceptional character, which renders its definition difficult, because it can be compared with no other indigence. Irish misery forms a type by itself, of which neither the model nor the imitation can be found anywhere else.

In all countries, more or less, paupers may be discovered; but an entire nation of paupers is what never was seen until it was shown in Ireland. To explain the social condition of such a country, it would be only necessary to recount its miseries and its sufferings; the history of the poor is the history of Ireland.

It is necessary to renounce all the notions which in other countries serve to distinguish comfort from poverty, in order to comprehend Irish misery. We are accustomed to call those paupers, who are out of work and driven to beggary. There is not an Irish peasant that abstains from beggary, who is not in want of such a resource. It is impossible to compare the Irish pauper with the pauper of any other country. The independent labourer cannot even be compared with the pauper of England. There is no doubt that the most miserable of English paupers is better fed and clothed than the most prosperous of Irish labourers.

There are sad theories, according to which there is a pretty nearly equal sum of happiness and misery, of comfort and of suffering, in every country; whence it has been inferred, that it is idle to take any thought about evils which man can neither alleviate nor remove. Those who hold such discouraging language, have doubtless never seen the United States nor Ireland; they neither know the country where misery is the common rule, nor the land in which destitution is the exception.

The misery of Ireland descends to degrees unknown elsewhere. The condition which in that country is deemed superior to poverty, would in any other be regarded as a state of frightful distress; the miserable classes in France, whose lot we justly deplore, would in Ireland form a privileged class. And these miseries of the Irish population are not rare accidents; nearly all are permanent, and those which are not permanent are periodic.

Every year, nearly at the same season, the commencement of a famine is announced in Ireland, its progress, its ravages, its decline.

In the month of February, 1838, the French press registered this annual cry of Irish misery, and told the number of persons who, in a single month, had perished by famine. Whether through selfishness or humanity, many persons flattered themselves that the accounts of Irish indigence were exaggerated; and the word *famine*, employed to describe the misery of Ireland, appeared to them a metaphorical expression for great distress, and not the exact term to express the state of human beings *really* famishing and perishing from sheer want of food.

It was in England, especially, that persons were pleased to keep themselves in this state of doubt, from which, however, they could be relieved without much difficulty.

In 1727, that is, rather more than a hundred years ago, Primate Boulter, who was the principal agent of the English government, thus wrote from Ireland (to the Duke of Newcastle.)

"Since my arrival in this country (in 1725) famine has not ceased among the poor. There was such a dearth of grain last year, that thousands of families were obliged to quit their dwellings to look for support elsewhere; *many hundreds perished.*"[11]

When Bishop Doyle was asked, in 1832, what was the state of the population in the west, he replied, "The people are perishing as usual."[12]

---

11. Baulter's Letters, i. 181.
12. Tithes Inquiry, House of Lords, second report, 95.

In 1817, fevers produced by indigence and famine attacked one million five hundred thousand individuals, of whom sixty-five thousand perished;[13] and it was calculated in 1826, that twenty thousand persons were attacked by disease arising from the use of bad food.[14]

During the important inquiry into the social condition of Ireland, made by the British government in 1835, the following question was addressed by the commissioners to their correspondents in every parish.

"Have you known of any deaths in your parish, during the last three years, arising from urgent want?"

This inquiry established a multitude of deaths, occasioned solely by sheer destitution. Here were wretches manifestly killed by famine, there miserable beings whose end was hastened by misfortune. The former sank from long exhaustion, the latter were victims to famine and disease together.[15]

It would be a painful task to go through this immense report, which extends to ten folio volumes, some of which contain nine hundred pages, every page, line, and word of which establish Irish misery, but where, nevertheless, all the miseries of Ireland are not reported.

The commissioners entrusted with this inquiry calculate that there are in Ireland nearly three millions of individuals who are subject every year to the chances of absolute destitution. These three millions are not only poor, they are indigent.[16] Besides the three millions of paupers, there are millions of unhappy beings, who, as they do not die of famine, are not counted.

The author of this book, to whom such evidence ought to have sufficed, still was anxious to see with his own eyes what his reason hesitated to believe. Twice, in 1835 and 1837, whilst travelling through Ireland, he visited the counties where famine is accustomed to rage with most violence, and he verified the facts. Shall he relate what he saw?—No. There are misfortunes so far beyond the pale of humanity, that human language has no words to represent them. Besides, were he to recal the scenes of sadness and desolation he has witnessed;—to repeat the howlings and yells of despair he has heard;—were he required to relate the anguishing tone of a mother's voice refusing a portion of food to her famishing children;—and if, in the midst of such extreme misery, he were required to portray the insulting opulence which the rich ostentatiously displayed to all eyes;—the immensity of those demesnes where the hand of man has created artificial waters, vales, and hills;—the magnificence of the lordly palace sustained

---

13. Irish Poor Inquiry, 1836, p. 4.
14. Ibid.
15. Wakefield, i. 224.
16. Beaumont adopts the calculations of the first Commission for Inquiry into the State of the Irish Poor. He rejects the calculations of Mr. Nicholls, because he believes that gentleman to have been influenced by English prejudices.

by columns of the finest marble from Greece or Italy, and which the gold of America, the silks of France, and the tissues of India, vie to decorate;—the splendid residence designed for servants, the still more superb building destined for horses;—all the wonders of art, all the inventions of industry, and all the caprices of vanity, accumulated on a spot where the owner does not even deign to reside, but makes his visits "few and far between;"—the sumptuous and indolent life of the wealthy landlord, who knows nothing of the misery of which he is the author;—never has glanced at it;—does not believe its existence;—draws from the sweat of the industrious poor his 20,000*l.* a year;—every one of whose senseless and superfluous luxuries represents the ruin or destitution of some unfortunate being;—who every day gives his dogs the food of a hundred families, and leaves those to perish by hunger who support him in this life of luxury and pride;—if the author of this book were required to recal the sinister impressions produced by such contrasts, and the terrible question which such appositions raised in his soul, he feels that the pen would fall from his hands, and that he would not have courage to complete the task which he has undertaken to accomplish.

II

A Bad Aristocracy Is the Primary Cause of All the Evils of Ireland. The Faults of This Aristocracy Are, That It Is English and Protestant

We have just seen how wretched is the condition of Ireland. The first anxiety felt at the aspect of such misery is to discover its cause; and this anxiety is the greater, because, in order to remedy an evil, it is necessary to know its origin and nature.

Let us begin, then, by declaring the cause of the ill; we shall afterwards seek the remedy.

It is impossible to observe Ireland attentively, to study its history and its revolutions, to consider its habits, and analyse its laws, without recognising that its misfortunes, to which so many sad accidents and fatal circumstances have contributed, had, and still have, one principal cause,—a cause primary, permanent, radical, which predominates over all others,—and this cause is *a bad aristocracy*.

All aristocracies founded on conquest and on inequality, doubtless contain many inherent vices, but all do not possess the same, nor in equal number.

Suppose conquerors, who, after the first convulsions of the conquest, were fast endeavouring to efface the memory of it, by mingling with the conquered people, assuming their language, adopting a portion of their habits, appropriating to themselves most of their laws, and practising the same forms of religious worship; suppose that these conquerors, formed into a feudal society, having to struggle against powerful and tyrannical kings, sought an auxiliary in the conquered population; and that afterwards, united by the bonds of mutual interest, the conquerors and conquered blended their cause in struggling against the common enemy; suppose that these struggles lasted during several centuries, and that the lords in their quarrels with the kings never failed to make stipulations in favour of the rights of the people whenever they conquered privileges for themselves; finally, suppose that these conquerors, after having thrown the violence of the conquest into oblivion by a rapid fusion with the vanquished, continually laboured to redeem the injustice of their privileges by the benefits of patronage; that, superior in rank, wealth, and political power, they incessantly showed themselves equally superior in talents and virtue; that taking in hand the affairs of the people, they mingled in all their assemblies, discussed all their interests, directed all their enterprises, sacrificed half their revenues to banish poverty from their domains, gave instruction to one, capital to another, enlightened, charitable, and benevolent support to all;—that, placed at the head of a commercial society, they admirably comprehended genius and its requirements, gave it, with the freedom of industry, all the civil and political liberties which are the soul of that freedom; and in order to procure for that society a magnificent destiny, they opened for it the markets of the entire world, established for it flourishing colonies, founded for it colossal empires in India, rendered its vessels sovereign on every sea, and made the nations of the earth its tributaries; and that, finally, after having opened all the paths of fortune to commercial industry, these same men, throwing down the barrier which separated them from the *prolétaire*, should say to the latter, "Get rich, and you may become a lord:" without doubt, such an aristocracy may conceal within itself many germs of oppression, and more than one principle of ruin; still it is easy to comprehend how such an aristocracy may for a long time maintain itself in strength and prosperity, and that even succeeding to a conquest, and charged with all the injustice of feudal privilege, it may give to the country it holds under its sway the illusion, if not the absolute reality, of a just and national government. It is easy to conceive the long and brilliant rule of the English aristocracy.

Suppose, on the contrary, conquerors who, instead of arresting the violent outrages of conquest, should lend all their efforts to the perpetuation of them—should open a hundred times the wounds of the conquered country—instead of uniting with the vanquished, should force them to keep separate—refuse to adopt their laws or impart their own—suppose this conquering race to preserve its language, its habits, and to erect an insurmountable barrier between itself and its subjects, by declaring it a kind of high treason to celebrate a marriage between the descendants of the victors and the offspring of the vanquished; suppose that having been thus constituted in the face of the conquered people, as a faction distinct by race and power, the conquerors are still further separated by a deeper cause, difference of religion; that not content with having deprived a people of national existence, they should endeavour to wrest from it its creed; —that having spent centuries in despoiling it of its political independence, they should pass a second series of centuries in disputing its religious faith; suppose that these conquerors, political tyrants, despising the conquered nation because of its race, hating it because of its creed, should be placed in such an extraordinary position that it has no interest in the protection of the people, and no peril in their oppression;—it may well be conceived, that an aristocracy composed of such elements could only produce selfishness, violence, and injustice on one side —hatred, resistance, degradation, and misery on the other. Such is the picture of the aristocracy of Ireland.

The English aristocracy, clever and national as it is, would not perhaps have been able to maintain itself, if, while it concealed its defects by splendid virtues, it had not been protected by fortunate accidents.

Subject like all aristocracies, whose principle is privilege to employ its strength for the promotion of selfish interests, it has carried to excess the resources by which it is supported, and disproportionately concentrated in its hands the property of the soil, which has become the monopoly of a very small number; the landed proprietors of England form so small a minority compared to the non-proprietors, that landed property might be placed in peril, if it were a desirable object in the eyes of the people.

But, by a fortunate event rather than any result of wise policy, the soil of England has not hitherto excited the envy of the lower classes; the English people leaves its aristocracy the monopoly of the land, so long as it resigns to them the monopoly of industry. The immense estates of a peer excite no unpleasant feeling in the mind of a merchant to whom the commerce of the whole world presents an unlimited arena, and who thinks that if he makes a great fortune, he may perhaps some day obtain the estates of a lord with the title and honours.

The English agriculturist cares little about a political system whose effect is to drive the peasantry from the country into the towns, when this labourer, removed from the soil, finds in the factory equally regular work, and much better pay. This, we must confess, is the great guarantee of the English aristocracy, a frail and feeble guarantee, which will only last so long as English industry will supply the world with its products.

The Irish aristocracy, full of defects from which that of England is free, far from being aided like it by favourable circumstances, has to struggle against pernicious accidents.

It is a fatal chance for the Irish aristocracy that has placed Ireland in such close proximity to England; for this aristocracy has never ceased to be English in heart and almost in interest. Here is the cause why the aristocracy has always resided, and at the present day resides, more in England than in Ireland; and this material fact, which most frequently divides it from the people subjected to its sway, is in its case the source of the evil most fatal to every aristocracy, which really exists only on the condition of governing. It is common to hear all the evils of Ireland attributed to absenteeism, but this is to mistake a consequence of the evil for the evil itself. The aristocracy of Ireland is not bad because it is absentee; it is absentee because it is bad, because nothing attaches it to the country, because it is retained there by no sympathy. Why should it, loving neither the country nor the people, remain in Ireland, when it has England near, inviting it by the charms of more elegant and refined society, which attract it back to its original country?

In general, every aristocracy contains within itself the corrective which tempers, if it does not arrest, its aberrations and its selfishness. It usually happens, that the very class which does not love the people fears them, or at least has need of them; it then performs from calculation what it would not do from sympathy. It does not oppress too far, through fear of revolt; it spares the national strength from which it derives profit; it may even happen that it appears generous when it is only clear-sighted and interested.

The Irish aristocracy has always had the misfortune of fearing nothing, and hoping nothing, from the people subject to its yoke; supported by England, whose soldiers have always been placed at its disposal, it has been enabled to give itself up to tyranny without reserve: the groans, the complaints, the menaces of the people have never tempered its oppressions, because popular clamour had for it no terrors. Did insurrections break forth in Ireland? The aristocracy of the country never stirred; it was English artillery that subdued the insurgents; and when everything was restored to order, the aristocracy continued to receive the revenue of its lands as before.

The Irish aristocracy has exercised an empire of which no other country furnishes an example; during six centuries it has reigned in Ireland, under the authority of England, which abandoned to that body half the advantages of its dominion, and spared it all the expense. Furnished with rights, privileges, and constitutional guarantees, it has employed all these instruments of freedom to practise oppression; Ireland has thus been constantly the prey of two tyrannies, the more dangerous as they mutually protected each other. The Irish aristocracy, regarding itself as the agent of England, for that reason granted itself absolution for all its excesses and all its personal injustice; and England, whose rights this aristocracy exercised, was contented to throw upon that body the blame of any abuse of its power.

There are few countries in which the governors have not an interest, greater or less, in inducing the people subject to their laws to cultivate the arts of industry and commerce. Of what use, in fact, would large revenues be to the rich man, unless they served to obtain the objects fit to render his life pleasant and comfortable? And how could he procure them if the people did not work? But it is an additional fatality of the Irish aristocracy that it is abundantly supplied with all the most precious productions of art and commerce, though no industrial employment exists in Ireland; it has ready to its hand the products of English industry to satisfy its wants and caprices, as well as armed regiments to ensure the payment of its rents. In order to possess comfort and elegance, it has no need of exciting the people to industrial labour. Commerce and industry are, nevertheless, the means by which the lower classes may escape from their misery. Thus, the people of Ireland, to whom the land is inaccessible, see in the hands of the aristocracy an immense privilege for which they possess no equivalent. Thus the aristocracy of Ireland, deficient in all the primary bases on which that of England rests, is also deprived of that condition of existence without which probably the English aristocracy could not sustain itself. It is immovable and closed. As a principle, its ranks are open to all, but, in fact, access to them is nearly impossible; to enter them, it is necessary to become rich; but what means are there of becoming rich in a country where commerce and industry are dead? So that this aristocracy, motionless in its wealth, living on the life of others, has for its support a population also motionless in its misery: in Ireland, poverty is a caste. Finally, this aristocracy, attached by no natural sentiment to the people, has the misfortune to be further removed from it by difference of creed.

Religious sympathy is, beyond contradiction, the most powerful tie that unites men together; it has not only the power of bringing nations together, but, what is still more difficult, of mingling classes and ranks, raising the most humble to the level of the most proud, mingling the rich and the poor; it is religion that invests alms with the dignity of christian charity, and which, stripping the benefit of its pride, renders the bestower and the recipient both equal. But, in the absence of religious sympathy, what is there to unite the rich and the poor, the Englishman and the Irishman, the race of the conquerors and that of the vanquished? What power shall bring them together when religion herself separates them? And in a country where all the laws are made against the poor for the profit of the rich, what will be the result if religion, instead of checking the powerful, actually fortifies it, and, instead of supporting the feeble, crushes him to the earth?

The Irish aristocracy has two inherent vices, which include all others; it is *English* by origin, and has never ceased to be thus alien: it became *Protestant*, and has had to govern a people that remained Catholic.

These two vices contain the principle of all the evils of Ireland; in them are the key to all its miseries, and all its embarrassments: if this starting point be attentively considered, all the extraordinary circumstances, whose causes will be vainly sought elsewhere, will be found to flow from it as natural consequences. These consequences are of three sorts; the first, which we may call civil, because they relate to habits and manners; the second political, because they concern institutions; the third religious, because they arise from difference of creeds. The first more especially affect the relations between rich and poor, between landlord and tenant; the second, the reciprocal relations between the governors and the governed; and the third, the mutual position of Catholics and Protestants.

Section I: Civil Consequences

SUBSECTION I

Extreme Misery of the Farmers—Accumulation of the Population on the Soil—Absenteeism—Middlemen—Rack-Rents—Want of Sympathy between Landlord and Tenant

In England and Ireland the lower classes cultivate the soil under the same title—they either take a farm from the rich man, or hire out to him their daily labour.[1] Theoretically, their condition is the same in both countries. Whence does it arise that in reality their lot is so dissimilar? Why is the one as happy as the other is miserable? How does it happen that the first is well lodged, well clothed, well fed, surrounded by a family prosperous like himself, living in comfort and contentment, scarcely imagining a lot more fortunate than his own; whilst the other, covered with rags, lives on potatoes when he is not forced to fast, has no other shelter than the filthy hovel which he shares with his pig, and sees during the winter his poor children perishing from cold, without being able to clothe them, and hears during the whole year their cries of hunger which he cannot appease?

It is because that in England the large proprietor is the patron of the soil and its inhabitants; he does not limit himself to receiving his rents and claiming his rights; he also fulfils his duties, and believes that he is bound to return a portion of what he receives. And in the first place, engaging, in some sort, his fortune in the land that he possesses, he invests in it considerable capital. See what a residence he prepares for his tenant. It is composed of several buildings; nothing is wanting to render the life of the resident pleasant and comfortable: it is the centre of an extensive culture; round it extend vast domains that depend on it; the best agricultural implements are there waiting for the hand that is to employ them. After he has formed this great farm, he keeps an eye on its fortune. Watching the efforts of his tenants, he rejoices in his success, and compassionates his reverses; and by a sympathy as enlightened as it is generous, he soothes the misfortunes which, if they remained unredressed, would prove injurious to himself. He is not always liberal, but he is rarely destitute of intelligence. Thus the relations between landlord and tenant have for their primary base the wis-

---

1. The class of farmers called yeomen in England, is almost unknown in Ireland.

dom or the benevolence of the one, whence naturally arise the deference and re-spect of the other.

Matters are not managed in this way in Ireland. The proprietor, as we have said, is often an absentee; it often happens that he is unacquainted with his own estates; he knows vaguely that he possesses some hundred, or hundred and fifty thousand acres in the county of Cork or Donegal; that it is bounded on one side by the sea, and on the other by the loftiest mountain perceptible in the horizon. Desirous of deriving from these possessions the greatest profit possible, he is also resolved not to spend a single farthing in improving their value. He or his ancestors obtained this vast tract by confiscation; who knows but some new rev-olution may take away what the preceding revolution has thrown into his fam-ily? This reasoning of the absent proprietor is very nearly repeated by the resi-dent landlord; for though he touches the soil, he rarely takes root in it, and Ireland is not the country to which he believes that his cares and sacrifices are due.—Thus a large proprietor in Ireland generally aims at managing his estate without any expenditure of capital; that is to say, he expects to reap without hav-ing sowed. But how is he to obtain the smallest profit without some preliminary expense?—Here is the way in which he solves the problem. He gives up the rental of his domain to an agent, either for a round sum at once, or an annual payment, of which the amount is secured by penalty of forfeiture. This under-taker, a rich capitalist, residing either in London or Dublin, does not take Irish land to turn farmer, but he takes it on lease as a matter of speculation; and when the bargain is concluded, he aspires only to transmitting the culture of the land to another, on condition of his being insured a beneficial interest. It is then usual to divide the estate into a certain number of lots of a hundred, five hundred, or a thousand acres, which he farms out to secondary agents, called *Middlemen*. Sometimes the resident proprietor makes this division of his estate himself, which he lets out to the secondary agents.

But how will these agents of the first or second degree derive profit from the land they take on lease? Will each establish a large farm?—If he did so, he would have to risk a large capital. Now, how could an agent have more confidence in the land than the lord of the soil himself?—What then does he do?—He estab-lishes no farms on the land he has taken, small or great; he in general limits himself to manuring the surface. When this work is done, he subdivides his lot, (on what is called in Ireland the *cornacre system*,) and lets it out at the highest rent he can get, in parcels of five, ten, and twenty, acres to the poor peasants of the country, the only persons who take ground with the intention of cultivating it;[2] that is to say, on the most moderate advance of capital he expects to realise the highest profit.

---

2. Larger farms are sometimes held in joint-tenancy.

But how will all these petty agriculturists cultivate the land they have taken? Where will they establish themselves? Will the proprietor or agent take care to erect a dwelling on each of the small allotments?—Assuredly not: this building would require capital, which no one is inclined to advance. The land is then given to them entirely naked;—but where are they to lodge? They build for themselves a shapeless mass of mud, wood, and straw, which they call their cabin! At least, do they find any agricultural implements at their disposal? Not one; they are left to procure them the best way they can.

Thus, in England, the landed proprietor furnishes his tenant with a house and agricultural implements. In Ireland, the poor man who takes a "bit of ground," must build his own dwelling, and find all his own farming implements.

It may be asked, when the rich do not supply capital, how is the poor peasant to procure it? It must be answered, that for the most part he does not obtain it, and that he only applies brute force to an enterprise for the success of which capital would be necessary. He cultivates badly, because the means of cultivation are wanting. Now, how can he, cultivating badly, pay the exorbitant rents demanded by the proprietor, the middleman, and the subordinate tenants? For it is the poor tiller of the ground who must bear the weight of all the successive engagements of which the land has been the object. The chief proprietor, who leases his land to an undertaker, receives from him a sum of money, which he gets back again with profit from the inferior middlemen; and these again, subletting to small farmers, not only receive what they have paid the undertaker, but realise a profit-rent; so that the actual tillers of the soil have to pay a rent in the first place, equivalent to the sum which the undertaker pays the proprietor, and to which must be added the profits of the undertaker, and the beneficial interest of all the intermediate rates. It is in vain that the poor agriculturists of Ireland labour to satisfy all these interests, and at the same time to derive from the land a sufficiency for the sustenance of themselves and families. However fruitful the land of Ireland may be, it cannot give all that is required of it; incessantly, in spite of all his efforts and his labours, the poor Irish peasant finds it impossible to pay his rents. What then happens? The middleman or the proprietor ejects him from his land, seizes his few moveables, and sells them by auction. And what becomes of the peasant, whose entire crime is having attempted an impossibility? As no other branch of industry is open to him but the land, he goes to seek a small farm elsewhere, and until he finds it, he, his wife, and children, beg or starve.

Here is doubtless a great misery, which appears particularly enormous when viewed in contrast with the comfort and prosperity of English farmers. But it would be a great mistake to attribute the entire to undertakers, agents, and middlemen. These middlemen are an effect, and not a cause. Assuredly they are an evil,[3] and nothing can be imagined more disastrous than these successive trans-actions, of which the first effect is to give up the soil to speculators who feel no interest in the property, and take the culture of a farm as a temporary employ-ment; and of which the no less immediate consequence is, to place between the proprietors and tillers of the soil three or four traffickers, who only come upon the land for hire. But who is the real author of this evil? Is it not he who, in his indifference for the country and those who cover it, has delivered the soil and its inhabitants into alien and avaricious hands?

Whether the Irish agriculturists have to deal with the owner of the soil, or his agent, there is no difference in their condition. They find no sympathy in one or the other; the same spirit of cupidity animates both, the same selfishness hardens and blinds them; both have only one object—to get the highest rent out of the land they can. The moral and physical condition of the tenant is equally indifferent to both. They feel and display the same insensibility in presence of his prosperous efforts or barren toils, his successes or his reverses; the man occu-pies their ground, but still is to them as a stranger. Provided he pays, it is all they require. Thus, when they see him weak and broken down, they leave him in his distress, and turn away their eyes; they only come to ask him for the rent that has fallen due; or if, by any accident, relations are established between the land-lord and the tenant—if, by any chance, the latter works for the former, or sells him any article, it is certain that the landlord will take a gross and unfair advan-tage of the poor agriculturist's simplicity, and that the latter will always be the dupe in the bargain.[4]

And of what importance are these miseries of the wretched peasant to the middleman, who only sees them in his hasty transit, and who will fly the coun-try of the miserable beings he has tortured so soon as he has made his fortune. "What do you want with me?" the proprietor exclaims at the sight of these frightful evils; "I have ceded my rights to my agents, who must exercise them as they please." But most frequently the proprietor does not pronounce these words of regret, for he does not see the misery of which he is the author. Se-cluded in his mansion in London, he does not hear the cries of despair which is-sue from the Irish cabin; under the pure and serene sky of Italy, he knows not that a storm in Ireland has destroyed the poor man's harvest; he knows not at Naples that, for want of a genial sun, the fruits of the earth have failed in cold Hibernia: if, by any unexpected event, the poor peasants that cover his estate have fallen into distress, he is ignorant whether any unexpected blow of fortune

---

3. There are sometimes six or seven removes between the landlord and the occupying tenant.

4. Wakefield's Ireland, i. 287. A decided change for the better is in progress during the last three years.

has struck down the wretches, such as a long sickness of the head of the family, or the loss of agricultural cattle; he knows none of these things, and it would be inconvenient for him to know them. What he knows well is, that £20,000 are annually due to him from his Irish estates; that his mode of life is regulated by the amount; that this sum must be paid at every term; and that if the payment were delayed for a single day, it would trouble the order of his habits and the arrangement of his pleasures.

Besides, whether he manages his affairs personally or by agents, whether he is absentee or resident, you may be well assured that the proprietor who has no "bowels of compassion" for the country, and for whom his country has no voice; who does not regard as fellow-citizens the peasants by whom his land is cultivated, will never be beneficent to the soil or its inhabitants. This is a starting-point of which sight is constantly lost, but which must be kept steadily in view, unless we wish to go astray.

Nothing is more common than to attribute the misery of the Irish peasant to defects in the agricultural systems practised in Ireland. If we believe some, the leases are too long, which destroys the proprietor's interest and care of his property; according to another, leases are too short; their brief duration renders the farmer's condition precarious; the evil, says a third, arises from there being no leases, which places the tenant completely at the mercy of his landlord.

There is no disputing the pernicious or beneficent effect that different systems of agriculture may exercise on the fortune of the proprietor and the condition of the tenant; but what is not less certain is, that, under the best agricultural management, the farmer's lot may be miserable, whilst, in spite of the most defective method, his condition may be enviable and prosperous. I have seen counties in England and Scotland where leases are long, and others where they are short; I have even seen some where the land is held by tenants at will; but I have not remarked that these diversities in the form of engagement, which doubtless have some influence on agricultural produce, modify to any extent the condition of the farmer, which I have found everywhere uniformly prosperous.

Whatever may be the terms of the law between landlord and tenant,—whatever the text of the contract by which they are united,—whatever attention may be bestowed in assuring to the poor agriculturist rights, sureties, and guarantees, —the *letter* of the engagement will always be barren, unless the *spirit* give it life. Now the spirit, the soul of the obligations by which a landlord is bound to his tenants, is *good-will*—the only shield of the feeble against the strong, of the poor against the rich. The abstract right will be more cruel than the sympathy. No law, however liberal, can supply the place of absent charity; and there is no law so cruel as not to be alleviated by charity; this is the reason why the poor Irish peasant, who finds in his landlord neither kindness nor pity, is so miserable.

SUBSECTION II

Competition for Land—Whiteboyism—Social Evils—Inutility of Coercive Measures—Terror in the Country—Disappearance of Landlords and Capital

We have just seen how, by the effect of the selfishness or carelessness of the rich, the land in Ireland is covered with a number of petty cultivators, between whom it is divided into portions of five, ten, or twenty acres. If it be asked, how it was possible to find such a number of agriculturists, I would reply, that it is easy to lead all the inhabitants of a country to tillage where there absolutely exists no other form of industry. It was doubtless at first a great advantage to the proprietor to find such a multitude of petty farmers at his disposal; for without them he could not obtain any profit from his estates, unless he made an outlay of capital which he was unwilling to risk.

However, a time came when all these lands were occupied; and this was not long in coming, for all the Catholic population, excluded from public employments, liberal professions,[5] prohibited from becoming proprietors, incapable through poverty of engaging in commerce or manufacture, even if it had not been prevented by the political condition of the country, having absolutely no career open but that of farming,—this population, I say, precipitated itself on the offered land, and overwhelmed it as the overflow of a torrent soon covers a vast plain with its waters.

But in a country where the land is the sole means of existence, what is the fate of those to whom land is wanting? What becomes of an ejected tenant, if he can find a farm nowhere else? What is to become of his children? Here is a little plot on which a poor peasant procured a moderate subsistence; he has five children, (an inconsiderable number in an Irish family;) his only thought and his only ambition is to find a farm for each; but he cannot succeed, because all the farms are occupied. What then is to become of his children? Observe that the question is rigorously put, for tillage, as I said before, is the only resource, the only available employment, to an Irishman; and yet the land fails him; nevertheless, employment is most wanting to the poor in a country where the rich possess no charity. The peasant must possess a plot of ground, or starve.

This is the secret of that extraordinary rivalry of which land is the object in Ireland. The land in the country resembles a fortress eternally besieged and defended with indefatigable ardour; there is no safety unless within its precincts; he who makes good his entrance, leads a life of labour, privation, and peril, but still he lives; he holds fast to the rampart—he clings to it; and in order to remove him, it is necessary to tear him limb from limb. The condition of the unfortu-

---

5. Except medicine.

nate being who has failed in attaining this object is lamentable; for, unless he yields himself to starvation, he must either beg or rob.

What is the consequence? The farmer who is anxious to ensure the existence of his family, has no resource but to subdivide his little farm into as many parts as he has children; each of them, then, possesses four or five acres, instead of the twenty which the father held, and several mud cabins are built on the farm instead of one. The son has children himself; he must do for them just what his father did; and thus, from generation to generation, this fractional division at length reaches a half or even a quarter of an acre for each family, and the occupant of the soil finds it physically impossible to live on so restricted a portion. This is the reason why, at the present day, three or four hundred cottiers are found crowded and living miserably on some domain which formerly contained a very small number.[6] In spite of this accumulation, it often happens that a time comes when space is physically wanting, and a certain quantity of those born on the ground must quit it.

They remove from the land, and nevertheless the land alone can support them. What follows? That the number of farmers being greater than the number of farms, the competition immeasurably raises the rents. The Irish peasant must have an acre or half an acre of ground, or die; he must have it at any price, or on any conditions, however severe they may be. The reasonable rent of this acre would be four pounds; I offer the landlord double; another offers ten pounds; I raise my bidding to twenty; the land is adjudged to me; at the rent-day I will not be able to pay;—what matter?—I shall have lived, or tried to live, for a whole year.

Thus he who already pays an exorbitant rent, is obliged by competition, in order to keep his farm, to pay a still higher sum.[7] To be sure, he is free to refuse any increase of rent; but a two-edged sword is suspended above his head; if he resists the demand of the landlord, he is ejected from his farm; if he submits to the severe conditions, it is nearly certain that he will be unable to fulfil his rash engagements, and that he will soon be dismissed by the landlord, perhaps at the instigation of some other competitor. After all, the worse condition is to quit the ground in a country where ground is the only means of livelihood; he remains then on his farm—consents to everything; he knows that scarcely one in a thousand succeeds in such an enterprise, and he resigns himself to the chances of this cruel lottery.

The competition of the farmers perhaps raises rents higher than the avidity of the landlord or the middleman. A worse condition cannot be imagined than

---

6. Lewis's Irish Disturbances, 79 and 320.

7. Farms are too often let to the highest bidder, without any previous investigation of his character or solvency.

that of all these poor labourers vegetating on the ground, clinging to it like vermin, and adding to their misery by their supernatural efforts to overcome it.
This misery is augmented in the exact proportion of the increase of population,[8]
until there are, in our day, two million six hundred thousand paupers; that is to
say, two million six hundred thousand persons destitute of land, or having too
small a portion of land for their support.[9]

This lamentable condition of the farmer is not profitable to the landlord; he
or his agent, deceived at first by the promises of the competitors, soon discovers
the falsehood; he receives but little from the land thus highly rented, and he is
disgusted by rigorous proceedings, in which his profits are swallowed by the legal expenses; he discovers that by ruining his tenants he has not enriched himself. Sometimes he says, "All the mischief has risen from this accumulation of
cottiers, who devour the soil instead of fertilising it. The evil would cease if a
few large farms were substituted for this multitude of small holdings; this is the
agricultural system in England and Scotland; the time is favourable for imitat-
ing it in Ireland; the age of revolutions is gone, their remembrance is effaced; the
soil, once so precarious, is now secure; capital may with safety be invested in
land."[10]

His plan is then fixed; he is about to substitute some large farms for a multitude of small holdings; but how is this end to be attained? By ejecting the cottiers that cover his land, and proceeding to a new distribution of property; that is
to say, after having made use of the cottier tenants during the period when from
want of capital he had need of them, he casts them off at the moment when the
return of capital affords him the means of establishing a more lucrative means of
cultivation. But what is to become of the two or three hundred peasants who in
one day receive an order to quit their cabins? The blow is fatal. For here it is
necessary to observe, that this is no common removal; usually the outgoing tenant succeeds some one else—here hundreds of peasants depart, two or three only
remain, no one comes in; so that three hundred desperate wretches are created
by a single blow, whose removal does not open any opportunity for the relief of
other unfortunates.[11]

We can now see what contrary interests and what different passions control
the possession of land in Ireland. The order to quit being given to the poor tenant, he resists it; this order is to him a sentence of death; he sees rising before
him the hideous spectre of hunger, which is ready to seize upon him, his wife,

---

8. The supply of labour in Ireland is so limited, that the peasants are for the most part
without employment during six months of the year.

9. Third Report of Irish Poor Commission, *passim.*

10. This evil is fearfully on the increase: Lord Courtown has just commenced a clearance
which will consign hundreds to starvation.

11. Inquiry of 1832 into the State of Ireland, 471.

and his children; he then contemplates the entire extent of his misfortunes, passes from grief to despondency, and from despondency to utter despair. Still one ray of hope comes to illumine his forehead: "If I went *to the master,*" says he, "and showed him the misery which overwhelms us—if he saw my wife pining with hunger, my children pale and famishing, surely he would feel for us, and would leave us our little cabin at least for a few days longer!" The wretch is mistaken—he throws himself at the feet of his master, he supplicates, he implores in vain; the rich in Ireland have no compassion for the poor. In that country, the poor man may preserve his pride, for he humbles himself unprofitably before the rich, who rejoice in his abasement without alleviating his misery. The poor peasant, harshly repulsed, regains his cabin in silence, brings back there an additional sorrow, and, struck with a misfortune too great to be combated and too great to be endured, crosses his arms and remains immovable. The proprietor then claims the assistance of the law, which at great cost pronounces sentence, by which the poor agriculturist is condemned to quit his land; the judgment triples the sum which the wretch before had to pay. He had been ejected for not being able to pay his rent; how is he now to raise three times that sum? He soon sees two constables appear, bearing a sentence in proper form, according to the tenor of which he must immediately leave the place; and at once these agents of public power begin by seizing every article which they can find in the cabin. It is very necessary that the lawyers, without whose aid justice cannot be had, should be paid for their trouble. All this is done amidst the most heart-rending cries, which burst forth from the cabin; imprecations are heard, which if they reached the ear of the rich man would mingle remorse with his pleasures: but, finally, justice takes its course—everything is seized and sealed in the farmer's dwelling; the bailiffs are its masters, the poor family is gone.[12] The constables disappear with their plunder. The next morning the farmer and his family are again in possession of the poor cabin; force alone removed them, they reappear when that force is withdrawn. They have been driven from their land, but since this land is their only means of subsistence, they must of sheer necessity return. The proprietor then takes the only means that can rid him of these obstinate wretches—he pulls down the cabin, and thus gets rid of its inhabitants.

These rigours accumulate, these cruelties are multiplied; the poor occupants of the soil are pursued from cottage to cottage, thrown with their families out on the public road, everywhere exposed to the same legal violence, to the same extremity of misfortune.[13]

Some day or other a voice is raised amongst these poor farmers, which exclaims—

---

12. Lewis's Irish Disturbances, 225.
13. Ibid. 164

"The earth alone supplies us with food, let us cling to it closely, and not quit it. The landlord or agent bids us depart—let us stay. The courts of justice order it —still let us stay; an armed force is sent to compel us—let us resist it; let us oppose all our forces to an unjust force, and in order that the injustice should not reach us, let us enact the most terrible penalties against those by whom it is committed.

"Be it enacted,—

"That whoever shall attempt, directly or indirectly, to deprive us of our farms, shall be punished with death.

"That the landlord, middleman, or agent, who shall eject a tenant from his estate, shall be punished with death.

"That the landlord who demands a higher rent than that which we have fixed, shall be punished with death.

"That he who bids a higher rent for a farm, takes the place of an ejected tenant, purchases by auction or otherwise goods that have been distrained, shall be punished with death.

"Let us strike the culpable, not only in their persons, but in their dearest interests and affections; let not only their cattle be houghed, their houses burned, their land turned up, their harvests destroyed, but let their friends and relations be devoted to death, their wives and daughters to dishonour.[14]

"And as, in order to be strong, it is necessary that we should have arms, let us haste to seize the arms of which we have been deprived. Hitherto isolation has been our weakness; let us associate—let us solemnly engage to enforce our laws, and, in order that the engagement should be sacred and inviolable, let us give it the sanction of an oath—let us cover it with the veil of inviolable secrecy[15]—let us extend our confederation over the entire country—let whoever refuses to join us be regarded as an enemy, and treated as such; and, in order that our laws should not be idle commands, let us solemnly promise, that whichever of us shall be appointed to execute the punishment for a breach of our code, shall instantly obey and execute in all its rigour the prescribed sentence."

These are, doubtless, dreadful laws,—they are those of the Whiteboys,[16] an atrocious savage code, worthy of a semi-barbarous population, which, abandoned to itself, has no light to guide its efforts, finds no sympathy to assuage its passions, and is reduced to look to its rude instincts for the means of safety and protection.

Terror then spreads through the country; dangerous plots are formed in

---

14. Ibid. 58.
15. Ibid. 232.
16. Ibid. 23.

darkness; strange figures appear here and there; houses are attacked during the night; every one is obliged to fortify his dwelling;[17] but all resistance is vain—sometimes it is necessary to give up arms, sometimes to take oaths. These are banditti of a singular kind; to obtain arms or vengeance, they commit all sorts of outrages, while they abstain from the gold and silver under their hands. A murder is committed; it is soon discovered that the victim is a proprietor whose tenant has been ejected the evening before.[18] The perpetrators have been seen, but no one in the country knows them, and everything proves that they have been brought from a distance to execute vengeance for another. A second similar crime is committed; it is the murder of a middleman who has seized his tenant's goods. The whole proprietary class is alarmed, an appeal is made to the laws, it issues its mandates, but no one points out the traces of the guilty; justice discovers them after an active search; they resist, she seizes them, but an insurrection rescues them from her hands; at length she seizes them again; the guilty are under lock and key. It is then necessary to search for witnesses; all who are summoned declare that they have seen nothing: one presents himself and tells the truth. Two days afterwards it is discovered that this witness has been assassinated. What is to be done? It is very necessary that justice should have its course. The witnesses do not appear. Well, they must be arrested and brought before justice by force; but there, they refuse to give evidence. It is necessary to purchase their evidence. Their existence is menaced; it is necessary to protect them. How is this to be done? No one will give them an asylum. Well, they must be committed to gaol. But what reward will be sufficient to induce a witness to make a declaration which endangers his life, and the first effect of which is to deprive him of liberty? However high his price, he must be paid in full. But who will admit the sincerity of a witness under the double influence of the money which he receives, and the death which he dreads? Necessity, however, decides that he must be believed. But will not this witness, dismissed after the trial, be assassinated? No, he will leave the prison and leave Ireland at the same time. Thus, the condition of every witness for the prosecution in criminal affairs must be, to remain in prison until the trial, and afterwards go into exile. But what honest man will be a witness? Honest witnesses will be dispensed with—stern necessity demands it. But what honest man will act as judge? . . . . . Thus have we gone from consequence to consequence, until we have reached the sad alternative, that justice must either be powerless or immoral—must either acquit the accused for want of witnesses, or condemn by the aid of purchased witnesses. Finally, the verdict is given, the guilty man is sentenced and

---

17. Ibid. 119.
18. Ibid.

put to death. The informer and the witness go into exile. Next day it is found that the brother of the informer, the mother or sister of the witness, have been assassinated.[19]

When you have reached this point, you may be well assured that all rigorous means to restore peace and order will be useless. In vain will you employ a Draconian code to repress atrocious outrages; in vain will you enact cruel laws to arrest the course of revolting excesses; in vain will you affix the penalty of death to minor crimes;[20] in vain, actuated by the terrors of weakness, will you suspend the ordinary course of law, and proclaim entire counties under the Insurrection Act;[21] in vain will you violate the principle of individual liberty,[22] create martial law and special commissions,[23] and, to produce a salutary impression of terror, multiply to excess capital executions.

All these rigours will be vain; instead of healing the wound, they will irritate it, and render it more painful and dangerous. The peasants who, in 1760, revolted against a bad social system, under the name of Whiteboys, renewed the insurrection some years after under the name of Oakboys; in 1772, under that of Steelboys;[24] in 1788 they were called Rightboys; at a later period they took the name of Rockites or Clarites, subjects of Captain Rock and Lady Clare;[25] in 1806 they called themselves the Thrashers; in 1811, 1815, 1820, 1821, 1823, and 1829, they resumed the name of Whiteboys; in 1831 they were Terry-Alts; in 1832, 1833, and 1837, Whitefeet and Blackfeet;[26] and under these various denominations you may see them actuated by the sense of the same miseries, committing the same acts of violence, followed by the same cruel means of repression, which have been always powerless.

All your vigorous measures to restore peace and order will be abortive, because the order you design to make supreme is actual discord; because the peace you wish to establish is violence and oppression. This violence, this oppression, this disorder, have produced a state of war; and this social war is not between the honest man and the malefactor, between the labourer and the idler, between the industrious man and the robber,—it is a war between the rich and the poor, between the master and the slave, between the proprietor and the cultivator; and

---

19. See Historical Introduction for an account of the Whiteboys.

20. See Whiteboy Act of 1775.

21. Lewis's Irish Disturbances, 43.

22. By the Insurrection Act, persons found out of their houses between sunset and sunrise are liable to be arrested.

23. See Coercion Bill of 1833.

24. Those were chiefly in Ulster.

25. An imaginary queen.

26. There are many other names, such as Carders, Shanavests, Caravats, Blackhens, Magpies, &c.

this war has arisen because the selfishness of the rich has been carried to an excess which necessarily drove the poor to revolt.[27]

Now say what are the means to escape from this vicious circle? Here is an aristocracy that, either by its faults or its vices, has allowed such a mass of evil to accumulate in the country entrusted to its care, that the wretches on whom the burden presses, shake it off from sheer inability to sustain it longer. There is no longer a social state: it is war—it is anarchy.

What is the consequence? Half of the resident gentry depart; many, not driven away by terror, remove from the aspect of such great evils, which it is not in their power to alleviate; the attempt at a remedy is no longer a feasible enterprise, and the sight of so much misery is especially dreadful to the compassionate: hence it follows, that those whose presence would be a blessing to the country, have not the courage to remain there.

Still there are some whom social war and its horrors do not drive from the land; but whilst they remain, they feel their hatred for a population already detested continually increase; and their severity continually adds to the distress of the people, and its thirst for vengeance.

Capital is wanting; the terror which reigns in the country, drives it farther away. Industry alone could raise from indigence the multitude of cottiers that contend for the land; and capital, without which no industry is possible, has fled from poor Ireland for ever.

Thus, the sources of Irish misery mutually increase, and reciprocally produce each other; all proceed from one common cause, and ascend in uninterrupted chains to the first link—a bad aristocracy.

Section II: Political Consequences

But it is especially in the political institutions of Ireland that we incessantly discover traces of the fatal principle which has vitiated the aristocracy of that country.

Those who imagine that they can explain all the evils of Ireland by the despotism of England, fall into a great error, for this absolute despotism has never existed.

We have seen, in the Historical Introduction, how the conquerors of Ireland, having established a feudal society in the country, the only one of which men had any notion in those times, this society, by the mere fact of its institution, found itself in possession of rights, privileges, and franchises which England could not dispute.

We have seen how, after the conquest of Ireland, the English, wishing to in-

---

27. Religion is but slightly mingled with agrarian revolts.

troduce the reformed religion into the country, founded there a Protestant society, to which England could still less refuse the civil and political liberties already enjoyed by the feudal society.

Finally, we have seen how the native Irish, at first as a vanquished people, and afterwards as Catholics, were excluded from the benefit of these institutions; in what manner this exclusion ceased, and how at present the laws of the country recognise no inequality founded on race or creed.

Dependent, then, as Ireland is upon England, she has always possessed her own free institutions.

It would be a great error to look upon Ireland as making with England one and the same people, subject to the same government and the same laws. We have seen, in the same Introduction, that Ireland has always had her own government and peculiar laws. Thus, Ireland not only possesses free institutions, but, though united to England, she has still her own peculiar institutions. These free and distinct institutions which Ireland preserves, seem exactly modelled from those of England.

Like England, Ireland is in possession of all the essential rights on which the civil and political liberties of nations rest, such as trial by jury, independence of the judges, responsibility of public functionaries, the right of petition, the right of union and association, individual liberty, freedom of the press, and such like.[28]

In both countries the organisation of the different political powers presents, at least externally, a perfectly similar though distinct aspect.

The supreme authority, which in England is vested in the sovereign, is in Ireland entrusted to the viceroy.

The government of which the viceroy is chief, employs in its executive similar instruments to those used by the English government.[29] With both nations there are connected with the central power four supreme courts of justice, which are, as it were, the soul and source of public power in countries where justice and administration are perpetually confounded; these are the courts of Chancery, Queen's Bench, Exchequer, and Common Pleas.

Both countries are equally divided into counties, over which the state preserves rather than exercises its sovereignty: and in both, the agents by which the central power displays its authority are the same. The principal representatives of the state in an Irish county are the lord lieutenant, the sheriff, and the justice of the peace.

In Ireland, as in England, there are within the state, but independent of the counties, a certain number of incorporated cities or boroughs which do not de-

---

28. The exercise of these rights is, however, more jealously watched in Ireland than in England.

29. There are some differences which are noted in a subsequent page.

pend on the central government for their administration, because they have received the privilege of self-government: these are called municipal corporations.

Finally, in both countries, we find at the base of the powers already mentioned, that of the parish; a power sovereign in its sphere, independent of all the rest, and which, in both nations, presents the same external structure.[30]

Not only is the political edifice, which appears to view, the same in England as in Ireland, but furthermore, the authorities are instituted on the same basis; they bear the same names; all are theoretically created for the same object; they exercise their power according to the same laws; they are nominally subject to the same rules, and restricted by the same limits. And in both countries, the aristocracy is the fundamental principle of all public power.

Whence, then, does it arise, that, with similar institutions, the two nations have had such different fortunes, and that one has fallen into a state of abasement and misery, with a form of government which has placed and kept the other at the summit of greatness and prosperity?

It is because that, though the form is important in political institutions, the spirit is still more important. Now the institutions of Ireland present to the eye the same body as those of England; what is wanting is the soul. The Protestant aristocracy, which in England is the very heart of all political powers, seems in Ireland to be their cancer.

Let any person examine the government of Ireland in all its parts successively, in the state, the county, the municipal corporation, and the parish, and he will find that the same original and permanent vice which corrupts civil society, carries the same corruption into political society; he will find that the same causes which poison the relations between rich and poor, landlord and tenant, do not less materially affect the mutual relations of the governors and the governed.

SUBSECTION I: THE STATE

Influence of the English and Protestant Aristocratic Principle on the Powers of the State—Hatred of the People to the Laws—A Public Accuser in Ireland—The Unanimity of the Jury in Ireland—Why Ireland Has Several Official Institutions Not Found in England

The Irish viceroy endeavours to reproduce the image of royalty; he holds a brilliant court in Dublin, the etiquette of which is regulated by that of London; he has two palaces, a splendid staff, and his salary, with the allowances, is about 30,000*l.* annually.[31]

---

30. The Irish parish is now of little importance.
31. This sum is, however, barely adequate to the necessary expenses of his station.

The viceroy of Ireland, like the sovereign of England, has a privy council; he nominates to all the public offices, which in England are in the gift of the sovereign; he has the same right of pardoning or commuting punishment; and he is equally invested with the singular power of suspending the law, under certain grave circumstances, at his discretion, for which he is responsible only to parliament.[32] The Irish viceroy possesses also some extraordinary powers which the sovereign has not in England, but which the peculiar circumstances of Ireland have rendered necessary to its first magistrate.[33]

Until 1800, Ireland had its own parliament, consisting of hereditary lords and elected commons; for it never enters into any Englishman's head that any human law could be framed unless by two houses, of which one should be called Commons, and the other Lords.

The legislative power of Ireland was, therefore, composed of three powers designed to balance each other, as in the English constitution. But is not the fundamental error of such an organisation, applied to Ireland, at once apparent? Is it not manifest, that these powers, instead of controlling, would mutually support each other, and that their harmony would not be a union of rival powers, but that of accomplices banded together for a single and common object, the enslavement of the people? In the days of the Tudors, the parliament did what the viceroy pleased; after William III., the viceroy did what the parliament pleased. England had full confidence in the aristocracy of Ireland, and entrusted to it the entire government of the country. It might then be said, that the laws were made in full freedom by the two parliamentary bodies that represented Ireland, but who does not immediately see that such a system of representation was a falsehood?

Who does not at once comprehend the spirit in which laws were made by those lords who, English and Protestant by birth, were the natural enemies of Catholic Ireland; and by this house of commons, which, not less English and Protestant at heart, was in reality a mere creature of the lords, though it was presumed to be elected by the people?

No one could sit in either house, unless he gave proof of his "having taken the Lord's supper," according to the Anglican ritual. Could such a parliament, framing laws for a Catholic country, be anything else but the representative of a

---

32. The exercise of the prerogative of mercy by an Irish lord-lieutenant was never questioned until the present year. It might be asked, of the expiring Orange faction as it was of Edward I.,

> And must their word at dying day
> Be nought but quarter, hang, and slay?

33. He can proclaim counties or baronies, and thus put them under the restrictions of the Coercion Bill.

faction; a mere instrument to maintain the power of a narrow oligarchy, and furnish it with constitutional means of practising oppression?

Having once established this starting point, need we be surprised that the Irish legislature, during the entire course of its long existence, cruelly tyrannised over the country, formed a selfish compact with England, of which poor Ireland paid all the costs; abandoned to England the political and commercial liberties of Ireland, on condition of being maintained in its own domination over the Catholics; subjected the people that it governed to an anti-social code, the cruel and ingenious system of which has been exposed in the Introduction; and finally, by a course of falsehood and blunders, went so far as to proclaim that there were legally "no Papists in Ireland;" in other words, that a nation was blotted from existence! The Irish aristocracy terminated its parliamentary career by an act which pictures its entire life.

One day,[34] England came to the resolution that it was bad for Ireland to have its own parliament, deeming it better that the country should be ruled by laws emanating directly from herself; she therefore resolved to abolish the Irish parliament; but how was this to be accomplished? Ireland possessed the right of making laws, and who could take this right away? At the instant of the proposal, all Ireland was in movement; the parliament of Ireland was anti-national, but the right to have a parliament was a national right.[35] The aristocracy itself, usually so obedient to the English government turned restive; for it was about to be deprived of its power of giving law to Ireland.

The difficulty was great, and yet it was easily overcome. The self-same aristocracy, which at the outset disputed with England the right of taking away its privileges, suddenly abandoned them; and, in a short time after it protested against the attempt upon its life, the Irish parliament put an end to its own existence. Why did it commit this suicide? The explanation is simple; the principle parliamentary undertakers, the chiefs of parties, sold their privileges to England for the sum of 1,260,000l. paid down in hard cash, and renounced their parliamentary prerogatives. After all, what cared they for the legislative independence of Ireland, which was never their real country? Besides, the existence of an Irish parliament was not exempt from annoyance. Did it not oblige them every year to spend at least a few months in Ireland? After the union, they would no longer be burdened by this charge; some became peers of England, others members of the British house of commons; all could pass their lives in London, all be delivered from Ireland. They then renounced their rights for the stipulated price; an infamous bargain, in which the corruption of those who bought was surpassed by the baseness of those who sold themselves; a worthy end of a parliament

---

34. In 1800.
35. The Union was a most unpopular measure.

which, during the course of its existence, was rarely independent, almost always servile, never national; and which, when condemned to perish, disposed of its carcass like a criminal selling his body for dissection.[36] It was this bargain which brought about the legislative union between England and Ireland, in the opening of the present century.

Since that time, Ireland has had no parliament, but we must not conclude that she has no parliamentary representation. By the articles of union, a part of her lords sit in the English house of peers;[37] and the counties, cities, and boroughs of Ireland elect members to the British house of commons;[38] these members are elected by the people, according to a system nearly the same as that of England;[39] and under which the Irish aristocracy formerly exercised considerable influence over the elections; but this influence, though it has not quite ceased, has been greatly weakened.

Thus, for the last forty years, the Irish aristocracy has ceased to give laws to Ireland, and this is one evil the less, no doubt; but nearly all the laws which were the work of that aristocracy still exist; and if it no longer makes the laws, it still retains their administration.

We have seen, in the Historical Introduction, that the act of union had no other effect than to abolish the Irish parliament, and confer its legislative privileges on the British parliament, which has not only continued the ancient peculiar institutions of Ireland, but has continued to give the country special laws, adapted to these institutions, though analogous to the laws of England. Thus the legislative power of Ireland has been displaced, but no change has been made in the mode of administering the laws.

Of all the general interests with which the state is charged, there is doubtless none more important than the judicial administration; let us take this as an example of the influence produced on government in Ireland by the radical defects of the aristocracy.

The judicial organisation of Ireland is precisely the same as that of England.

The four supreme courts are quite independent of those of England; they are the sovereign guardians of individual liberty, which is placed in their hands by the *habeas corpus* act; their jurisdiction has the same extent, they administer justice by the same rules, their independence is secured by the same guarantees, for the judges of Ireland, like those of England, are irremovable.

As in England, the Irish judges go circuit to assizes twice a year; the juries are impanelled, and the verdict given strictly in the English form. In Ireland as in

---

36. One of the supporters of the Union being asked, "Will you sell your country?" replied, "Yes, and thank God I have a country to sell!"

37. Twenty-eight peers chosen for life.

38. One hundred and five commoners.

39. Forty-shilling freeholders have been deprived of the elective franchise in Ireland.

England, besides the periodical administration of justice, there is a daily kind which may be called local, though administered by justices of the peace who derive their authority in England from the sovereign, and in Ireland from the viceroy.

But though the most perfect similarity exists between the magistracy charged with the administration of justice in the two countries, still the execution of this justice is very different in the two countries.

Criminal law in England is doubtless not free from faults; it has even preserved some feudal traditions which might be deemed barbarous by a superficial observer. Thus, in certain cases, the prisoner cannot be defended by counsel;[40] and he cannot, even by payment, obtain copies of the informations, which the crown-lawyers may use at their pleasure. Finally, the evidence of approvers is admitted against the accomplices of their guilt. These laws are certainly rigorous, and yet, in England, the administration of criminal law displays nothing painful to the friend of humanity; in that country, mild habits correct severe laws; every accused finds in the magistrates, if not benevolence, at least unalterable impartiality. Feelings of equity, and sometimes of indulgence, animate all those who are engaged in the administration of English law; they guide the justices of peace when taking informations; they guide the sheriff in his selection of a jury; they inspire the depositions of the witness, the verdict of the jury, the sentence of the judge, the pardon of the sovereign.

See, on the other hand, the condition of the accused in Ireland. Suppose an unfortunate Irish Catholic arrested, not for a political crime which might provoke magisterial indignation, but for some ordinary offence,—theft for instance. He is brought before the nearest Protestant magistrate,[41] a man of English descent, full of contempt and hatred for the poorer classes of Irish. Now can you suppose that this justice of peace, before whom the poor Irishman is dragged, will examine the proofs of innocence as carefully as the indications of guilt? Do you think, that if the prisoner offers bail, the justice will be as ready to accept it as if the accused were a Protestant? Still the investigation is continued; it depends on the justice of peace whether it shall be fast or slow; but how can he show any anxiety to accelerate it, when he is influenced by no sympathy; when, performing gratuitous functions, he is not interested in displaying zeal; when, on the other hand, not being subject to the superintendence of a superior, he has neither praise to hope, nor censure to fear, for his conduct? It may be conceived, that in such a situation, not stimulated by the consciousness of public duties, and surrounded by absorbing private interests, he will forget what is due to *the Papist*, who, after all, will be safer under lock and key. In truth, the inquiry, re-

---

40. This law has been greatly modified.
41. This description of the Irish magistracy is greatly exaggerated.—*Tr.*

tarded by this negligence, will not be ready at the assizes or quarter-sessions; the affair will be put off for three, or perhaps six months, and the accused must remain all that time in prison, awaiting his trial.[42]

That day at length comes. A hundred or a hundred and fifty jurors have been summoned by the sheriff; but, in the first place, with very few exceptions, the Protestant sheriff has chosen Protestant jurymen. Out of the hundred, twelve are to be chosen to administer the law—the panel is called—scarcely is the name of a Catholic juror pronounced when he is peremptorily set aside by the clerk of the crown.[43] The accused is given in charge to twelve Protestant jurors, for the most part rich persons, equally the enemies of his class and his creed. Now what impartiality can he expect, who perceives in every one of his judges a religious or political adversary? Who can believe that such judges would be animated by the pure love of truth, which is the very first condition of justice? And moreover, how many strange obstacles beset the judge in the trial over which he presides! Frequently in Ireland the accused, being of Celtic race, speaks a language which neither the judge nor the jury, being of English race, can comprehend; hence the necessity of employing an interpreter, who translates to the judge the words of the prisoner, and to the prisoner those of the judge; here consequently is a prime source of confusion. This is not all—as every accused person in Ireland is looked upon as a victim by the people of his class, that is to say, the lower orders, false witnesses abound, and hence a new source of error is opened to the judge and jury. In the midst of this darkness it would be difficult, even with the best inclinations, to be strictly just. How then will matters stand when love of justice is not the predominant passion? For my part, I have been present at many criminal trials in Ireland, and it is impossible to describe the painful feelings with which such a spectacle filled my mind.

It is a sad truth, that, in every Irish court of justice, there are, as it were, two hostile encampments within sight of each other; the accused on one side, the judge and jury on the other. Amongst the spectators, the people is for the accused; the tribunal is supported by the soldiers, the constables, and the wealthy. As, in Ireland, the aristocracy is engaged in an open contest with the people, all that depends on the aristocracy, or sympathises with it, comes to support it on this terrible field of battle, where the strong exterminate the weak in the name of justice and the laws. The prejudices and malevolent passions of which the accused is the object, are displayed on every side; they may be heard in the accent of the judge, seen in the emotions as well as the passiveness of the jury; the very language of the counsel for the defence reveals them. It is difficult to form an

---

42. In this respect the administration of justice has been recently improved.

43. The abominable system of packing juries was abandoned under Lord Normanby's administration; but recent efforts have been made to revive it by Lords Brougham and Roden.

idea of the tone of contempt and insolence in which the members of the Irish bar speak of the people and the lower classes. Thus, in spite of the formalities of procedure—in spite of all the legal solemnities which surround the accused in the presence of his judge, there is an inward feeling, that this is not a deliberation of judgment, but a preparation of vengeance; this lie of forms, promising equitable chastisement, but concealing a kind of vengeance, is endured; but, when the judge pronounces the terrible sentence of death, it might be deemed the signal for a fierce engagement between the party of the judge and the party of the accused, were not the court filled with armed policemen, whose presence prevents the parties from coming to blows.

In England, the magistrate sees in every accused person an unfortunate fellow-citizen, a person charged with a crime of which he may be innocent, an Englishman invoking the sacred rights of the constitution. In Ireland, the justices of the peace, the judges, and the jury, treat the accused as a kind of idolatrous savage, whose violence must be subdued, as an enemy that must be destroyed, as a guilty man destined beforehand to punishment. In England, the penal laws are sanguinary, the forms of proceedings are in some respects barbarous, but the manners of the people are humane, the jury is clement, and the judge merciful. In Ireland the penal code is more sanguinary than that of England; all the bad principles of English legislation are practised, and the magistrate is as severe as the law.[44]

Hatred of Law by the People

Who now will be astonished to learn that the Irish population, which hates and despises its magistrates, hates and despises the laws of which they are the organs,[45] that in Ireland this hatred of the law is universal? Who will be astonished at the horror with which any share in its administration inspires the community?[46]

Sentence of death was once pronounced at Waterford, the culprit was ordered for execution, but even in that country of paupers no one could be found, at any price, to perform the revolting office, and the first officer of the crown was obliged himself to hang the criminal.[47]

Who now will be astonished at the public abhorrence which pursues not only every complainant and informer, but also every witness in a criminal trial? Who does not see, that hence results the impossibility of obtaining witnesses without buying them? Who does not comprehend that this contempt and hatred for criminal law produces the most anti-social disposition that can exist amongst

44. The criminal law is more penal in Ireland than in England.
45. Confidence in the magistracy has greatly increased of late.
46. Law is more respected than it used to be.
47. Sir Richard Musgrave, the libeller of the Irish Catholics, was the sheriff.

any people, the habit of having recourse to violence? Who does not foresee that this consequence of social evil might, if combined with political passions or circumstances, produce a violent revolution?

Will anybody be now astonished at the sympathy which every criminal excites in Ireland? And if matters have reached such a height that murders are committed in the noonday, persons looking on from their windows, and allowing the murderers quietly to escape; if, when the constables have arrested the guilty, the crowd will pounce upon the officers of justice and rescue their prey; if everybody believes that he will sanctify his dwelling by offering a refuge to the malefactor; and if a universal confederation exist in the land, to save from the penalty of law all those pursued by justice; who, I say, can be astonished?

The Office of Public Accuser is Wanting in Ireland

The social evil whose influence is observed in the execution of justice, is not only manifested by the passions that it raises in the magistrates and those subject to their jurisdiction; it attacks also judicial institutions in the first principle of their organization, and where it does not make them fatal, renders them unavailing. Thus, for instance, the theory or custom which generally leaves to private interest the care of prosecuting for crime or misdemeanour, is the same in England and Ireland. But who cannot comprehend, that though this system or mode is exempt from peril in England, it is full of danger for Ireland?

It may be conceived, that in a society like that of England, where the sovereignty of the law, the omnipotence of the judges, and the impartiality of the magistrates, are established in all the manners and customs; amongst a people, where all is life, activity, movement,—it may be conceived, I say, that in such a country it would be possible to dispense with permanent functionaries connected with judicial bodies, to enforce the suppression of all infractions of the public peace; in such a society it might be safe to trust private interest with the care of avenging violations of the law. The citizens, accustomed to exercise their civil and political rights, habituated also to the equity of their magistrates, will doubtless be prompt to claim spontaneously the justice which is their right, and will prosecute every attempt on property, liberty, and life, with as much zeal as they assert their right to vote at an election. Thus, society will find a sure defence in the sentiment which will impel everybody to seek his own private redress. In such a country, probably, the citizens will become more skilful in protecting themselves when they will not expect official protection from any authority. Perhaps from this abandonment of private interests to themselves, a new element of power and action will cause a more imperious necessity for a knowledge of the laws, a greater skill in their application; in every heart a more profound sense of its rights, a more enlightened love of its liberty, and thus a principle of social and political power may be derived from that which was at first an imperfection, if not a glaring omission, in the law.

But what will be the consequence if no such public amnesty exists in such a country as Ireland, where private individuals, long deprived of all political rights, and almost all poor, have besides an invincible repugnance to invoke the authority of the judge; where the law as well as the judge is hated; where the feeling of right is extinct; where no confidence is reposed in justice or its organs? It must happen, that private zeal will not supply the want of public activity, and that the greater number of the crimes committed will remain unpunished from not being brought under cognizance of the magistrates. It is not merely through pity for the criminal or distrust of the judge that complaint will be hushed, it will be omitted through ignorance of the right. No prosecutions will then be witnessed but such as are instituted through passion rather than interest. Hate alone will instigate prosecutions in a country where it is too often by the same sentiment that they are tried. Recourse must then be had to the most immoral means to effect the discovery of crime. Not only will public rewards be occasionally offered to informers, but the law will be found formally consecrating the right of every indigent person to a pecuniary reward for discovering a crime, or aiding in the conviction of a criminal.[48] How strange a means of inculcating justice, which violates the most simple laws of morality!

Another Example: Unanimity of the Jury in Ireland

It is in England a fundamental law of the institution of a jury, that the unanimity of its members is necessary to a verdict. Although at first sight it seems difficult to imagine any subject on which twelve reasoning men could perfectly agree without a single dissentient, still we find the principle of the jury work in England without much embarrassment; and all collisions between contrary and violent opinions end in the triumph of the sentiment which is mildest and most humane.

In Ireland the same principle exists, but how is it to be put in practice? Will you compose the jury exclusively of Protestants? Then, doubtless, unanimity will be established as easily as in an English jury. But if an Irish Catholic be at the bar, there is reason to fear that this unanimity, sometimes so difficult, may be rather too prompt in returning a verdict of guilty.

Will you, instead of Protestants, place none but Catholics on the jury? Then it is intelligible that unanimity will be easy; but this time it is for the accused Protestant that fears must be entertained. Perhaps you will compose the jury of

---

48. Grand Jury Act, sect. 105.

Protestants and Catholics indifferently, the only just course in such a case. But then, how are men, separated far more by political passions and prejudices of caste than by difference of creed, to arrive at unanimity of opinion?

This is a difficulty which seems to increase the more it is investigated. Does the judge refuse to deliver the jury, and lock them up until they agree upon their verdict? Such a proceeding is a sentence of death upon those jurors whose health is not so sound as their conscience. Perhaps, seeing that there is no chance of agreement, the judge will dismiss them without requiring a verdict; in such a case, the trial not being completed, must be adjourned to the next assizes, and the accused must remain three or four months in prison waiting for a second jury, which will perhaps be no less discordant than the first.

Thus one of two things almost always happens; either the unanimity obtained is marked by passion and party spirit, or it is not obtained at all. Justice is not possible when its source is thus tainted.[49]

It is thus that political and social circumstances may render a principle of civil legislation evil in one country, which has been proved beneficial in another.

How and Why It Has Been Found Necessary to Create in Ireland a Certain Number of Official Functionaries Which Do Not Exist in England

Of all the cares which an aristocracy really anxious to govern takes charge, there is doubtless none which demands more knowledge, more zeal, and more constant efforts, than the administration of justice; and when we consider the variety of duties that devolve on justices of peace in England and Ireland,—all the usages that they must know, all the statutes that they must apply, all the objects of police entrusted to their vigilance,—the multitude of judgments that they pronounce in civil matters,—the gravity of the sentences which they have sometimes to pronounce with all the severity of judicial forms,—finally, all the responsibilities that result from each of their actions,—we can scarcely conceive it possible for large proprietors, men of business, occupied with their own affairs, and not versed in the study of the law, could discharge such complicated functions with any success. In England, nevertheless, the difficulty, if not overcome, has been fairly combated; and although English justices of the peace are neither exempt from errors nor faults, justice is never wanting in the country, and magistrates are rarely wanting at the petty sessions, where ordinary business is transacted. The spectacle presented by a court of quarter sessions in England is often worthy of admiration.

But the task of administering the law was too severe for the justices of peace in Ireland; it could not be executed by an incapable and indifferent aristocracy. It constantly happened that, on the day of the week fixed for granting summonses

---

49. See Parliamentary Inquiry into the Administration of Justice in Ireland.

and other magisterial duties, two justices were not found in attendance, and the course of law was suspended for want of magistrates. Often also, when the justices of peace assembled at quarter sessions, there was not one of them qualified to act as chairman: and here it was not the absence, but the incapacity of the judge, which rendered justice impossible.

The evil long remained without remedy; the Irish continued loaded with a burden which it had neither spirit nor strength to bear, until at length the central government, taking pity on its weakness and inefficiency, came to its assistance. A law was passed in 1796, authorising the executive power to employ stipendiary magistrates, and place them in all the localities where gratuitous justices of the peace were not sufficient for the administration of justice. And to aid the justices of peace at the quarter sessions, the same law commanded the executive power to send to these assemblies a member of the bar to guide and direct their deliberations, and to assist in their judicial functions, whence he is called the assistant barrister. Although, according to law, the justices of peace are not bound to choose this barrister as their chairman, they very rarely elect any other person, so deep is their sense of their own weakness and their own incapacity.

Finally, as this aristocracy, destitute of all moral influence over the minds of the people, required the aid of physical force to produce obedience, the law has created a large corps of agents, half civil and half military, analogous to the *gendarmerie* of France, called the constabulary force; these are placed under the control of justices of the peace, charged with executing the mandates of the magistrates, and protecting them in their functions; and government has conferred on the chief constables the power of executing, themselves, all the functions of judicial police, which in England can only be performed by justices of the peace.

It is a sad and perilous condition for an aristocracy to be under the necessity of invoking and receiving the aid of the central government. In fact, which of the powers created for its support may not be employed to attack it? An aristocracy can only remain masters of its powers by personally exercising them; it has no real existence, and no true power, but when it brings to its functions of government knowledge and virtue. Now, how can it be skilful when it does not impose upon itself the cares of government? How can it be generous when, for both the country and the people, it neither feels affection nor sympathy?

SUBSECTION II

Influence of the Same Principle on the Institutions of the County

In Ireland, as in England, the state is divided into counties. As in both countries, the central power neither directly nor by agents occupies itself with the details of government; it is naturally in the county, which is the principal division of the state, that the administration of public affairs, properly so called, is made. Though the state cannot properly be said to administer the affairs of the county over which it is in principle the sovereign administrator, the state nevertheless has its own officers in the county, the chief of which are the sheriff, the lord lieutenant, and the justices of the peace.

These officers of the central government discharge in the county two sets of functions; the first may be called *general,* as they interest the entire country, the most important of which, the administration of justice, has been explained in the preceding chapter; the second may be named *local,* because they are specially directed to the affairs of the county in which they reside.

There are many things connected with the administration of an Irish county which in England belong to other bodies. For instance, it is the county that in Ireland undertakes most of the public labours undertaken in England by parliamentary boards of trust and commissioners, such as canals, &c. The county also regulates all the roads small and great, which in England are either turnpike trusts, or managed by the parish.⁵⁰ There was little public charity in Ireland previous to the introduction of the New Poor Law; but the few charitable institutions, infirmaries, and dispensaries belonged to the counties, whilst in England all public charity belongs to the parish.

In England, the special interests of the county are regulated at the quarter sessions; in Ireland, the magistrates at quarter sessions are limited to the administration of justice. At special sessions and road sessions they discuss county interests: but their examination of them is merely preparatory: they recommend rather than decide. The final decision must be controlled and sanctioned by the grand jury, a body which in Ireland plays the chief part in the administration of the county.

The grand jury in Ireland is at once a judicial and administrative body; it assembles twice a year, and then administers those affairs which in England are managed at the quarter sessions. The body that regulates the affairs of an English county deliberates, decides, and acts in perfect independence; whilst the administrative functions of an Irish grand jury are to a certain extent under the control of the judge, whose *fiat* is necessary to the execution of their presentments.⁵¹

Though the grand jury ceases to exist with the assizes, yet the same persons are generally summoned by the sheriff at the ensuing assizes. The judge might certainly oppose obstacles to an Irish grand jury which are not encountered by the English court of quarter sessions; but the central power has been so closely connected with the aristocracy, that few sheriffs or judges have been chosen in

---

50. The country has also the care of public canals, bridges, &c.
51. This *fiat* is often refused.

opposition to its will; practically, therefore, the Irish grand jury may be deemed as free in its actions as the English court of quarter sessions.

A moment's reflection will sufficiently show that the same moral causes, which render the same judicial institution beneficial in one country and pernicious in the other, are, for much stronger reasons, capable of exercising the same influence over the administrative functions.

The rich Protestant, who, as a justice of peace, acts in the capacity of judge, is doubtless subject to passions that bias his judgment; but still in his sympathies for the Protestant, and in his enmity to the Catholic, he is fettered by judicial forms, and obliged to cover his most iniquitous proceedings by a mantle of equity, which sometimes fails him, and from want of which he must either stop short, or compromise his character. His administrative functions are not thus embarrassed; he has no need to prove the same equity in his acts, and he is more easily unjust, because his injustice is less subject to publicity. Thus the arbitrary decisions arising from favour or hatred, and the oppression resulting from selfishness, are more easily practised by the administrator than by the judge: consequently we must not be astonished if the great landlords of Ireland, who as justices of the peace give such sad specimens of justices, should exhibit in general the most barefaced selfishness in their administration, and if it be difficult to find in their acts any views of public interest, or any trace of generous sentiment.

Invested with the exorbitant right of taxing the county, they bear heavily on the poor, and lightly on the rich. When these rates are levied, to what purpose are they applied? They are spent to promote the interests of the rich, and they are never applied to the profit of the poor. If they have any assistance to bestow, it is given to the Protestant, and not to the Catholic, though the former be rich and the latter poor. Does any one suppose that, when they create an office, it is for the general interest? Not at all; it is instituted to provide for some favourite. Authority is, in their hands, only a means of advancing their own affairs. If a road is to be made, they consider their own personal convenience, not the wants of the country; and the county will pay a heavy tax, not to join some important centres of population, but to make an easy and agreeable communication between the houses of two rich proprietors. But at least, in this country of misery and ignorance, will they not found schools and hospitals? No. What then will they do for the people? They will provide barracks and prisons, almost the only splendid buildings in Ireland. Finally, they will commit such enormous abuses, such gross frauds, and such monstrous excesses, as to render "Irish grand jury jobs" proverbial in England.

The rich in Ireland, masters of the entire administration, hold in their hands all the powers of society. How then shall they set bounds to their own authority? "It is," said Montesquieu, "proved by invariable experience, that every man in-

vested with power is tempted to abuse it; even virtue itself has need of limits."
If limits be wanting to virtue itself, how far will that selfishness advance which
has none?

If the best aristocracy is not exempt from faults, it may be fairly said that a
bad aristocracy is the worst of governments; and nowhere are its vices more
clearly displayed than in the daily administration of the laws. If an aristocracy
feels sympathy with the population, its members, dispersed among the people,
will be more inclined to protect the weak and succour the poor, as they will be
continually witnesses of the weakness of the one and the indigence of the other;
and the more powerful and rich they are, the more capable will they be, while
maintaining their own privileges, of defending the rights of their inferiors. But
when this aristocracy is the natural enemy of the people, its power no longer affords tutelary aid; should it be sufficiently strong and clever to preserve its own
prerogatives, it will not extend the benefits of its strength; all its members will
keep their privileges, but those beneath them will not have their rights. In such
a state, there will be all the subjection of inequality, with all the evils of servitude.

Nowhere will the oppression of the people be so easy and certain as in such a
society, for nowhere will the oppressed be so much within reach of the oppressor. In a country where every landlord is at once an enemy of the people and a
public functionary, it may be said that tyranny is everywhere.

If all things unite to render pernicious an aristocracy whose principle is vicious, it must be added that they equally tend to render it odious. When an aristocracy is not rejected by the national and religious sentiments, it has, in the
eyes of the people it governs, one singular merit, exaggerated perhaps, but still a
great glory and a great power,—that of exercising its functions gratuitously. It
doubtless finds in the social state by which it is supported, advantages and privileges which amply indemnify it for its labours; but then its members do not pos-
itively receive a salary; and there is in this apparent disinterestedness a something that singularly affects the mind of the multitude, and induces the many to
honour the character of those whose generosity they admire, at the same time
that they recognise the superiority of their intelligence. But this merit of an aristocracy is changed into a grievance, when, instead of being popular, it is odious
to the nation.

In fact, it seems as if oppression were more readily pardoned to a salaried
magistrate or judge, who, in practising it, seems only to perform the task by
which he gains his livelihood. It may be supposed that this functionary is only a
passive agent, who in his heart laments the evil that his hand produces; but
when he is an unpaid agent, it is naturally supposed that he takes a pleasure in
oppression, and that he practices with all his heart the tyranny of which society
does not defray the expenses.

SUBSECTION III

Influence of the Same Principle in the Municipal Corporations

Having examined the vicious principles of the Irish aristocracy on the powers of the state and the administration of the county, we are about to consider the influence of the same principles on the government of cities and towns, called municipal corporations.

Neither in Ireland nor England are all the towns incorporated, and also there are municipal corporations to which we could scarcely give the name of towns; for instance, the borough of Naas. A town is not a corporation because it contains a certain number of inhabitants, but because it possesses a charter: it is incorporated, not by right, but by privilege, the only universal and invariable privilege which existed in all societies of feudal origin.

The differences between the English and Irish corporations are not less striking than those between the English and Irish counties. In Ireland, the unchartered towns are the best governed. How, then, does it come to pass that in Ireland, where we have seen all public powers so open to abuse, municipal corporations should enjoy a bad pre-eminence for extravagance, jobbing, and tyranny? How happens it that we scarcely find in them a single one of the original principles on which their institution is based?

Thus the first and fundamental principle is, that the corporation should be composed of all persons contained within the precincts of the city, and that all should concur in the choice of the body by which the city is represented. Nevertheless, in most Irish municipalities, the great majority of the population is excluded from the right of citizenship. Who would believe that Belfast, that large and magnificent town, does not legally contain more than fifteen or twenty citizens? It is another fundamental condition of municipal institutions, that the body representing the city should be composed of those who are most identified with its interests, and most capable of comprehending them. Nevertheless, in most of the Irish cities, the representative body is in a great degree formed of persons destitute of fortune and education, and sometimes of non-residents. There are mendicants in the corporation of Dublin, while the most wealthy merchants are refused admission into that body. It is also an essential principle of corporations, that the body representing the city, the freemen, should be themselves represented by the officers who act in their name; nevertheless, corporate officers are not so elected in Ireland; by an incredible abuse, these officers have acquired the right of nominating each other. When an alderman's place is vacant, the other aldermen choose his successor; and these aldermen, whom the citizens have not elected, nominate the mayor, the sheriffs, and all the officers of the city. Thus not only is the city non-represented by the corporation, but, in addition, the corporation is not represented by its own officers. In these corporations several offices are grasped by the same functionary; the governing body multiplies sinecures for the profit of its members; the grossest acts of selfishness are perpetrated without shame; the corporations of Trim and Kells alienated their lands, that two or three of their members might purchase them at a nominal price; the corporation of Naas granted to a noble lord one of its members' lands, worth five hundred pounds, for twelve pounds; and at Drogheda, the corporation ruled that the charitable funds belonging to the city should be exclusively expended for the profit of members of the corporation and their families.[52]

And why all these contradictions?—why this violation of all principle?—why this assemblage of abuses? A principal cause supplies the explanation. It was necessary in the beginning to exclude the Irish from the cities in order to preserve the monopoly of commerce and wealth to the English settlers, and consequently laws and regulations were made, which excluded the *natives,* as Irish, from the corporate body. It was similarly necessary to exclude the Catholics from the right of citizenship, in order to maintain the Protestant ascendency in Irish towns.[53] Consequently the laws required that before a person should be admitted as a freeman, he should take the oaths of supremacy and abjuration. For cities where there were no Protestants worthy of representing the city, either from want of fortune or personal merit, it was necessary to invite to this representation either strangers devoted to the aristocracy, or poor persons sold to it. Finally, it was necessary to restrain as much as possible the number of freemen and corporate officers, in order that the aristocracy should have less trouble in their corruption, and less expense in their purchase.

Vainly have most of the laws which consecrated these exclusions been abolished: their spirit has survived their text. The emancipating law of 1793 opened the corporations to Irish Catholics, and rendered them eligible to the body of freemen; but this law is a dead letter. Catholics are admissible; but the admission depending on the body of freemen, these, being Protestants, refuse to receive Catholics. Thus in Dublin, where more than one half of the population is Catholic, there is not a single Catholic in the corporation.

The emancipation act of 1829 declared that, for the future, Catholics might not only be admitted as freemen into the municipalities, but moreover that they should be eligible to all the civil and judicial offices at the disposal of the corporation. But how can Protestant bodies, refusing to recognise Catholics as their fellow-citizens, elect one of them a magistrate?

---

52. First Report of the Municipal Corporations Inquiry.
53. Protestants, however, are excluded as well as Catholics.

There are certain radical vices in institutions against which the laws are powerless, when they are protected by usage and custom.

Formerly, in England, the municipal corporations presented in their government a portion of the vices and abuses which we have pointed out in those of Ireland. These vices and abuses were less pernicious in England than in Ireland, because, in the former country, they were subservient to an aristocracy which, after all, is not unpopular; whilst, in the latter, they only exist for the profit of an aristocracy odious to the nation. A recent law has thoroughly reformed the English corporations, and re-established them on a new and popular base. In Ireland, on the contrary, the old feudal and Anglican system of corporations has been left standing as the inviolable sanctuary of aristocratic privilege and Protestant monopoly.[54]

SUBSECTION IV

Influence of the Same Principle on the Parish

It only remains to examine the effects of the same principle on the parish, where it exercises perhaps a still more potent influence than over all the other powers.

Irish parishes are, in theory, constituted on the very same principles as those of England; the parish in both countries has a democratic foundation, and forms an equal anomaly amidst institutions derived from feudality.

The powers mentioned above, that of the state, that of the counties, that of the municipal corporations, have all the same origin: they all proceed from the sovereign, the only source of power in a feudal society: the municipal corporations themselves have a free and democratic constitution, only because they have received from the sovereign the privilege of thus constituting themselves. The parish has a principle absolutely opposite: it proceeds from the people.

This double source of political institutions in England explains better, perhaps better than anything else, the perpetual conflict between two adverse principles which we encounter in English society, and which we find in perpetual war; the one authority, the other liberty; the former drawing all power to a centre, the latter diffusing it amongst the people: the first supported, sometimes by the sovereign, sometimes by the parliament; the second taking its root in the parish: one a Norman principle, the other a Saxon principle.[55]

When William the Conqueror and his Norman knights succeeded in the conquest of England, they found the Saxon parish established there, the free principle of which was then in perfect harmony with that of all the other powers. William and his successors destroyed those institutions which placed power

---

54. This abuse cannot continue another year.
55. The Saxon institutions were more free than those of the other Germanic tribes.

in the hands of the people, and seized on all authority themselves; still, in this general destruction, one power was spared, that of the parish, which was, perhaps, respected on account of its semi-religious character, and became, under the tyranny of the Normans and the Tudors, the only asylum where the old Saxon liberties found a shelter.

When the Anglo-Normans conquered Ireland they brought with them the Saxon parish as well as the Norman county; there is not a single constituent principle of an English parish which may not be equally found in an Irish parish. How comes it to pass that the Irish parish, so similar in theory, should in practice be so different from one in England?

In England, the parish is full of movement and life; it is the centre of a multitude of great interests; it gives life and vigour to the principles of popular liberty, which are shaded by the aristocratic edifice.

A great social inequality doubtless reigns in England; but it is necessary to be present at a vestry meeting in that country to judge to what extraordinary liberty this inequality is allied. There may be seen with what independence of language and thought an obscure English citizen opposes a lord to whom he bowed down a moment before. He is not his equal:—but within the limits of his right he is equally free, and he is conscious of the fact. His right is to discuss the interests of the parish, and this right he exercises not only with liberty, but with a prudence and skill which it is astonishing to find in an orator whose stained hands and coarse habits prove him to be an artisan, or a man of the lowest class. The English institutions, collectively, form no doubt an aristocratic government, but there is not a parish in England which does not constitute a free republic.

In Ireland, on the contrary, the parish, which presents to the eyes the same external appearance as the English parish, has nothing of its life: possessing the same organs, it is languishing and inert, if not quite dead. Whence is this difference? One principal cause explains it.

Without doubt, the Irish parish did not, at its origin, find the same favourable circumstances which cradled the parish in England. When once the tempest of the Norman conquest was passed, the English parish raised its head, and continued to grow and develope itself in a country where it had taken root. The institution of a parish was introduced into Ireland by the Anglo-Normans, who carried with them the body rather than the spirit of the Saxon institutions; it necessarily suffered from transplantation into a land which had not given it birth: it wanted the Saxon soil, and it may be doubted whether, under the most propitious circumstances, it would have acquired the vigorous existence possessed only by institutions that sprang from a country and its habits.[56] But a per-

---

56. The translator does not share in the author's doubt; parochial self-government is well suited to the Irish character.—*Tr.*

nicious influence was superadded, which at once blighted its growth,—that of the Protestant principle, violently introduced into the centre of the Catholic population.

The first attribute of the parish, the very essence of its institution, is the support of public worship, the building and repairing of the church, providing salaries for its officers, &c. Now, what took place in Ireland, a country profoundly Catholic, when the English, having turned Protestant, undertook to make their new creed predominant in that country? In the first place, they forbade those parishes in which there were no Protestants to assemble in vestry, and provide for the support of their religion, the exercise of which was declared a crime. By this single act, three-fourths of the parishes of Ireland were at once despoiled of their first interest. Their next proceeding was to order that every parish in which there were any Protestants should be bound to pay for the support of worship what had been formerly contributed to the Catholic church; so that not only the vestry of a parish composed exclusively of Catholics could not assemble to vote money for the support of their own church, but it was further obliged to assemble, deliberate, and vote the expenses necessary for the support of the Anglican faith, simply because it was the creed of two or three members. Such a requisition was palpably absurd. How, in fact, could men persecuted on account of their religion willingly tax themselves to support the creed of their persecutors? The Catholics refused a vote which it was sheer madness to ask.

What then was to be done? It was required that the entire parish should defray the expenses of the Protestant church; but the vestry, the majority of which was Catholic, refused the rate.

In such a state of things, as it was impossible to force the conscience of the Catholics, it was resolved to violate the essential principle on which the parochial institution rests; and a law was passed, depriving Catholics of the right of voting on all questions concerning the Anglican church, and giving the Protestants, however few in number, the exclusive right of forming the vestry, voting the sums necessary for the expenses of their church, and raising the amount by a rate levied equally on Catholics and Protestants. Thus, in the greater number of parishes, Catholics had nothing to do with providing for worship; and in the parishes where a few Protestants had been raised, a different religious interest, an almost imperceptible minority, gave laws to the majority. Thus, in the greater number of instances, the parish in Ireland was deprived of its proper functions; and in the others it only preserved them at the price of violating its fundamental principle, and perpetrating gross injustice.

Still the law which excluded Catholics from the vestry, where provision was made for the Protestant worship, left them access to those which were assembled for any other purpose. But when once religious interests were set aside, what remained to be done in an Irish parish?

One of the greatest interests under the management of the parish in England is public charity. It is in England a fixed principle, that every indigent person has a right to the assistance of society, and the aid thus claimed by the poor is for the most part given by the parish.[57] This is an abundant source of immense duties and endless cares; for this obligation of providing for the wants of the poor brings with it, in England, a multitude of accessory charges. After having given bread to the poor man, the English parish deems it necessary to provide a residence if he wants one, clothes if they be required, medicine if necessary: if the poor man has children, the parish not only offers them the same aid, but further believes that it is bound to support and educate them; so that, in England, parochial charity comprehends not only food for the hungry, but moreover houses of refuge, hospitals and schools.

Why is it that in Ireland we find the parishes undertaking no such charge? The reason is sufficiently plain, and it is found in the English and Protestant character of the aristocracy. The poor-law dates from the reign of Elizabeth. Now, at that period, the sentiment which induced the rich in England to aid the poor had no existence in Ireland, where the rich were English and Protestants; and the poor, Irish and Catholics. The long resistance of the vanquished had inspired the conquerors with too much rancour to leave them accessible to the ordinary feelings of humanity; and on the day when the conquerors became, as Protestants, the religious enemies of the Catholics, it may be said that the sources of charity were dried up in Ireland. This is the reason why, in this country of paupers, a poor-law is but of very recent introduction; why, until now, public charity has never been instituted in the face of the most excessive misery imaginable. Whilst in England it is a principle that every pauper has a right to legal support, in Ireland the principle is rather, that the rich owes nothing to the poor; and hence the management of public charity, which has so greatly extended the sphere of parochial business in England, has added nothing to it in Ireland, where it was already so destitute.

The Irish parish, which was deprived of its most natural functions to advance the Protestant interest, has recently been deprived of its principal and almost its only rights, as a boon to the opposite interest.

The injustice of subjecting the Catholic population of parishes to the vote of an exclusively Protestant vestry having been finally recognised, a law was passed in 1833, prohibiting the levying of church-rates, and the parish has consequently abandoned all care of religious interests. Thus, the Irish parish, possessing the same powers and invested with the same forms as the English parish, is, by the effect of one single principle, so essentially different, that whilst the one is the very heart of political society, the other is almost inanimate power. It is with

---

57. The new poor law limits the right of the English parish.

difficulty that any object can be found to engage the attention of an Irish parish; it is not power that is wanting, but functions; at present its only business is to elect its officers, the clerk, the churchwardens, the beadle, &c., and to provide for their salaries. But when these officers are elected and their stipends voted, they are no doubt legally instituted, but they have nothing to do.[58]

Influence of the Same Principle on an Institution Common to All Public Powers— Judicial Authority, the Only Supreme Administrative Power

The most striking feature in the political powers of society in England and France is the almost total absence of an organised system. It is true that the houses of parliament enact supreme laws destined for all parts of the empire, but no state-authority attends to their execution. The parish acts by its officers, the corporation by its magistrates, and though there are state-agents in the counties, such as the lord lieutenant, the sheriff, and the justices of peace, yet their functions are gratuitous, and it is difficult to establish any durable direction given by superior power to unsalaried agents. The trustees of roads and canals are only controlled by parliament, and a deliberative assembly is obviously unfit to superintend the execution of the laws. In England and in Ireland, the only authority that has really a right to exercise a direct control over all these various powers, is the judicial authority.

The tribunal which in this respect exercises the widest and most potent jurisdiction in the Court of Queen's Bench, which in both countries is considered the supreme representative of the executive power. But this court does not and cannot interfere, save on the requisition of the interested parties. Such a system of administration, though perhaps good for England, cannot but be defective in Ireland.

The object of a system which places the control over all administrative bodies and agents in the judicial authority, is to give inviolable guarantees to the liberty and property of the citizens. But, in the first place, what can be the protection of this authority in a country where it is so difficult for the judge to be just, and where the person in need of justice is so little capable of demanding it? Such a system, we must see, is singularly complicated; it requires not only the confidence of suitors and good feelings in the judge towards the suitor, but also that the latter should have sufficient intelligence to comprehend the wrongs they sustain from power, and sufficient fortune to defray the expenses of a suit. Now the justice that is open to all is expensive, its forms are tutelary, but singularly slow, and the abuses of authority must have become excessive before persons will apply to law for redress.

It is easy to conceive that such a system might be applicable to a country like

---

58. They regulate the economy of the church and churchyard.

England, where the law is sufficiently popular for the citizens to seek its protection, and where these citizens are sufficiently enlightened and sufficiently rich to have recourse to justice. It may happen that several frauds and abuses of power will be committed in such a country, without the injured parties making a formal complaint; but there will, nevertheless, be always a sufficiently large number of suits instituted by personal interest or passion to bind public functionaries to the observance of the law.

But what must be the effect of such a system in a country where law is hated as hostile to the people, where the citizens, unaccustomed to defend their rights, are nearly all indigent? Of what value to a nation of paupers, long kept under the yoke, is a principle which, to be put in practice, requires great wealth and old habits of freedom? How can the judge, who is often unable to preserve his impartiality in the trial of an ordinary crime, because the prosecutor and accused are of a different religion, or because he looks upon them as of distinct races,—how, I say, can he decide, without favour or affection, a quarrel between public authority and a private individual? The plaintiff is a Catholic! the defendant is a Protestant! and is not the Catholic population in a state of war, not only against the Protestants, but against all authority? The functionary inculpated is rich; the plaintiff is poor; and is not the poor man in Ireland at war with the rich? The Protestant and wealthy functionary must therefore be supported against the poor Catholic complainant. When once his part is taken, the magistrate will not be in want of legal excuses to justify it: even supposing that those obstacles which shut the heart of the judge against complainants did not exist, can it be supposed that this population, which, as we have seen above, is scarcely able to demand justice for ordinary crimes, would be better able to establish its grievances against the agents of public authority, and distinguish at a glance the limits, often so hard to be discovered, between the legitimate exercise of power and its abuse? Assuredly, if ever there was a country in which the administration ought to act alone,—without demanding any money from the people, or requiring from it any cognizance of its rights,—by agents all whose movements should be spontaneous,—that country is Ireland. The Irish functionary, menaced by the possibility of a judicial suit, is in general little restrained by this fear, when the abuse of his authority is directed against some unfortunate being with whose ignorance and poverty he is acquainted; and yet does he not easily persuade himself that his conduct has been irreproachable, since it has never been made the subject of a trial? Thus, at the same time that redress is offered in the sanctuary of the laws to all who have reason to complain of public functionaries, a thousand obstacles render its attainment almost impossible to the people. Judicial authority is the sovereign guarantee of all rights—he who is charged with its administration does not dispense it,—he who needs it does not demand it. This is the reason why, with a principle designed to protect the property of the rich and the liberty of all, we find in Ireland liberty without defence, property without guarantees, and security for nobody.

Section III: Religious Consequences

Legal and Official Establishment of Protestant Worship in the Midst of Catholic Ireland—The University and the Protestant Schools

We have seen the influence exercised by the English and Protestant origin of the Irish aristocracy on civil and political society; it only remains to examine the consequences of the same principle on religious society. Thus, having considered how this principle affected the mutual relations of the rich and the poor, governors and subjects, we are about to consider its influence on the reciprocal relations of Catholic and Protestant.

We have already noticed under what circumstances England became Protestant, and how, when she made the change, she was anxious that Ireland should do the same. This anxiety was not merely the consequence of a religious passion, it was also the result of a political principle. No one in the sixteenth century could comprehend the complete separation of the temporal from the spiritual power; but, perhaps, in no country was the union of secular government and religious authority more close than in England, because nowhere else was the head of the state also the head of the church. It is easy, then, to see why the English, having based their own government on Protestantism, should have laid a similar foundation for the government of Ireland. The church and state were then but one. At a later period, a race of kings was hurled from the throne on suspicion of Catholicism; it was then required not only to be Protestant, but Anglican, in order to reign. This is sufficient to show that the English must have wished not only to render Ireland Protestant, but Anglican.

In the same way, as it is generally impossible to comprehend the existence of a religion without a system of public worship, the aristocracy could not understand a church without wealth and privileges; it was resolved that the church of Ireland should be wealthy and splendid, and that the aristocracy of Ireland should have an aristocratic church.

In England, the Catholic church was deprived of its lands and rights, which were transferred to the Protestant church. This spoliation might have been unjust, but it was effected for the advantage of a creed accepted by the majority of the nation. In Ireland, the same means of endowing the new church were adopted. It obtained the confiscated church-lands, and a right to the tithe of all Irish produce; but whilst the aristocracy introduced and established the new creed in Ireland, the people of the country clung to the ancient faith; so that a

Protestant church was established at great expense in the midst of a Catholic population. Hence arose a forced alliance between the Anglican church and the aristocracy; the latter being naturally attached to the religious system it had founded, and by which it alone profited; the former being entirely devoted to the political power that had created it, and which could alone protect it from the common enemy. We shall hereafter see that the links which united them from their cradle were drawn closer together: although the king ceased not to be the head of the church and state, the aristocracy soon domineered over both; the rich managed the state, and the bishops the church. Perhaps we may be permitted to see, in this parity of origin and precocious confusion of church and state, the germ of a common destiny.

From the time of this union the invasion of Ireland was not simply political, it was also religious. Ireland was not only covered with an army of soldiers and greedy conquerors, but also with a spiritual militia of archbishops, bishops, and Protestant ministers, who came with the avowed intention of changing the national creed; and the people, from the very outset, saw their religion menaced by the pious auxiliaries of those who had taken away their country.

England, which had been, turn about, Catholic and Protestant at the caprice of Henry VIII., which returned to Catholicism under Mary, became Protestant under Elizabeth, Puritan under the republic, and Anglican after the restoration of Charles II.—England, I say, without doubt, believed it sufficient to establish a religious creed in Ireland, supported by the civil law, to effect the conversion of the country. The Anglican church was therefore instituted under the presumption that Ireland would shortly become Protestant. We have already seen the evils that were derived from this delusion; we have seen the persecutions, the massacres, and the cruelties perpetrated by the church and the civil government, in order to convert Ireland to Protestantism. All these rigours have been vain; Ireland has remained Catholic, and it is now a truth established by the irresistible evidence of statistical documents, that the Protestants of Ireland are fewer in proportion to the Catholics than they were two centuries ago. Their ratio to the Catholics in 1672 was as three to eight—at present it does not exceed three to twelve. Thus Ireland is more Catholic after the persecution than it was before; a consoling result to every one who is the enemy of violence, and superior to the efforts of tyranny.

The age of the religious wars is past; the throats of Papists are no longer cut in Ireland; banishments to Connaught are no longer in force; the penal laws against Catholics have been successively abolished. Persecution has disappeared, but the Anglican church remains. At the present day, as in the first age of the Reformation, there is in Ireland a Protestant militia spread over the whole surface of the country.

The Anglican church envelops Ireland in a vast administrative net; four provinces, thirty-two dioceses, thirteen hundred and eighty-seven benefices, two thousand four hundred and fifty parishes—such is the religious division of the country. The parish is only an administrative fraction of the benefice which constitutes the smallest ecclesiastical unity; the Protestant worship has establishments everywhere, even where there is no Protestant congregation. Thus, there are in Ireland eighty-two benefices and ninety-eight parishes in which there is not a single member of the Anglican church to be found. The services of the church are not dispensed in the ratio of the Protestant population, but a Catholic country is partitioned in reference to the Anglican church. There are entire dioceses where the population is almost exclusively Catholic, but this does not hinder them from possessing a complete establishment suited to Protestantism. To cite only one example, the diocese of Emly contains ninety-five thousand seven hundred inhabitants, of whom only twelve hundred belong to the Established Church; all the rest, to the amount of more than ninety-four thousand, are Catholics. Nevertheless, the Anglican form of worship has in this diocese fifteen churches, seventy-one benefices, and thirty-one salaried ministers.

The establishment of the Anglican church is naturally divided into the higher and lower clergy; four archbishops, twenty-two bishops, three hundred and twenty-six dignitaries, such as deans, prebendaries, archdeacons, &c., compose the higher clergy; the inferior or parochial clergy comprises thirteen hundred and thirty-three beneficed ministers, to which must be added seven hundred and fifty-two curates. A great number of the Anglican ministers possess benefices exclusively tenanted by Catholics, consequently they have nothing to do, and hence are frequently non-resident. It was calculated, in 1830, that out of thirteen hundred and five beneficed clergy, there were three hundred and seventy-seven absent from their posts, and in 1835 there were a hundred and fifty benefices without a resident rector or curate.

The clerical body in Ireland is nevertheless magnificently endowed. Besides its right to tithes, it possesses six hundred and seventy thousand acres of land. On the most moderate and authentic calculation its annual revenues amount to about a million sterling, and all these revenues go to the maintenance of the clergy. The higher clergy, most of whose employments are sinecure, possesses immense wealth,—it takes to itself alone more than 320,000*l.* annually. The Primate or Archbishop of Armagh has over fourteen thousand a year; the revenue of the Dean of Derry is three thousand seven hundred pounds.

Here, then, is a country where half of the population is annually famishing, and where a million of money is spent every year on the ministers of a creed which is not that of the people!

Whatever objections may be made to the great wealth of a clerical body, it may still be conceived that a church endowed with large property may be popular and beneficial, when the creed that it represents is that of the entire population.

A religious nation may derive pleasure from surrounding the priests of its faith with splendour and magnificence. The more elevated the notions of the sacerdotal office are, the more such a nation desires to aggrandise its ministers. Among a believing people, the priest is the sacred intermediate between God and man. Without him there is no public worship, no solemn devotion. The priest blesses man in his cradle, pronounces the benediction on his union when he takes a companion, stands by him in all the changes of life; he knows nothing of the joys of the rich, but he is never wanting in the hour of misery: the priest hears the first and the last cry of man. It is he who instructs the people in the duties of this life, and the requisites for that which is to come. The people receiving from the priest the knowledge of things human and divine, bestow on him in turn a merited and splendid support.

Besides, there is commonly in the fortunes of the church a principle of charity expressed or understood, which protects them against the apparent scandal of their enormity: this principle is, that the church has only the wardship and distribution of the property entrusted to it. The church is the natural patron of the indigent. It seems as if it could not be made too rich, because its riches are those of the poor. Whatever may be the liberality of political institutions, there is a multitude of individual miseries that escape them, and which charity alone can discover and relieve. A church is religious charity personified. Thus understood, the opulence of the church is easily comprehended, if it be not justified.

But how are we to explain the immense riches of a church which is not that of the people? How are we to understand the immense revenues of a clergy instituted for the cure of souls, as its canons declare, and placed in the midst of a population to which its spiritual aid is odious? What means this charge of instructing the people entrusted to men whose teaching the people rejects? What is the sense of entrusting public charity to a clergy which cannot feel sympathy for the temporal distress of its religious enemies?

The Established Church of Ireland is, in reality, useful only to the small number of Anglican Protestants whose religious wants it supplies, and who pay just so much less for the expense and support of their religion as they compel the entire population, hostile to their creed, to contribute. If the members of the Church of England in Ireland, who amount to about eight hundred thousand, were to support their own church themselves, it would cost each of them, on the average, one pound sterling annually; but, by distributing the charge over six millions and a half of Catholics, and six hundred thousand dissenters, the cost to each member of the Anglican church is only two shillings. What a singular foundation for a church is a system which plunders the poor in order to assist the rich!

A generous or wise aristocracy would endow a church out of its own property, in order that this church, its ally and its friend, might be an intermediate between it and the Pope, and alleviate to the people the injustice and rigours of an aristocracy; but here is an aristocracy seeking its support in a church, useful only to itself, and the burden of which is thrown upon the people.

Such, nevertheless, is the institution with which the fate of the Irish aristocracy is linked.

The bond that unites both, is not only moral, political, and religious, it is also judicial; the Protestant ministers have not only the same creed, the same interests, the same passions as the landlords, but they moreover discharge the same administrative and judicial functions.

A great many clergymen of the Church of England are justices of the peace; that is to say, in other words, the Catholics are placed under the civil jurisdiction of churchmen, whose religious jurisdiction they reject. Thus the Irish Catholic, who only knows the Protestant ministers by the tithes he pays them, finds them on the bench, as judges at petty sessions and quarter sessions, meets them at the assizes, sharing in every process, whether civil or criminal, where favour prevails over right, where the rich condemn the poor. It is bad, as a general principle, to unite temporal and spiritual power in the same hand; it is bad that the voice of the pious minister, which proclaims pardon in the name of the All-merciful, should be charged with the application of a law which does not pardon. And what will be the rule of the priest that is a magistrate? Will he judge crime as a sin, or sin as a crime? Whatever efforts his conscience may make, will he be able to separate one from the other? Will he not condemn, from pious motives, what the law will command him to absolve? and will not christian charity render him indulgent to faults, for which the law prescribes punishment? But, if it is bad to entrust a clergyman with the office of condemning or absolving those whom his religious conscience judges differently from his reason as a magistrate, what will be the result of this minister be the pious enemy of those whom he is to punish in the name of the laws,—that is to say, if counsels of severity be found at the very source of charity; if, even without his own knowledge, every legal severity he inflicts on a misdoer flatters the first passion of his heart; if this same man, who, as a Protestant minister, levies tithes on the Catholics, sends them to prison as a justice of the peace? It must follow, that a church so constituted will excite universal hatred, and will have the power of rendering not less odious than itself, every authority of which it is the auxiliary or the friend.

THE UNIVERSITY AND THE PROTESTANT SCHOOLS

In England, the Established Church not only distributes amongst the people spiritual succour for the soul, it believes also that it has a right to direct the faculties of the mind; it not only regulates the form by which prayers are to ascend to heaven, it aims at guiding man in the efforts he makes to perfect his intelligence, and thus raise himself towards the Divinity. The church believes that it is called to superintend instruction as well as worship.

In England, the church and the university are sisters, and this explains the strict union between the university and the aristocracy. The university is bound to the aristocracy by the same link which unites that to the church. In Ireland, the church and the university are joined by the same bonds, and consequently so are the university and the aristocracy. But it is easy to understand that the same causes which have rendered the establishment of the Anglican church in Ireland a grievance, must exercise the same influence on the university, which is an integral part of that church.

The university of Dublin was founded by Queen Elizabeth, on the same principles as the English universities, and endowed with the confiscated lands of Catholic monasteries, and has at present a revenue of about eighty thousand pounds annually. It is just, however, to state, that it is less intolerant than the English universities, and that its statutes not only admit students of every creed, but that it grants degrees in all the faculties, (except divinity,) without any distinction as to the religion of the candidates.

But is it now necessary to state what renders an institution vicious in Ireland, which, though more exclusive in England, presents there some advantages in the midst of monstrous abuses? Can we not discover, at the first glance, that this institution, which entrusts the highest degree of instruction to a Protestant church, can only excite in Ireland sentiments of repugnance and hatred? What Irish Catholic, supposing him wealthy, will be inclined to incur for his son the expenses of an education, of which Protestantism is the foundation? Who will tranquilly entrust his son to the bosom of an establishment which is regarded in Ireland as the very focus of Protestant proselytism? Who does not understand that the Irish university, which in principle is, perhaps, less defective than the universities of England, is in point of fact a thousand times worse?

The university of Dublin is open to persons of every denomination, but, from the nature of its institutions, it is only suited to a minority. On one side, the universities of Oxford and Cambridge attract, by their greater fashion and celebrity, all the young Irishmen of wealthy families; and on the other, the principles and passions which the Irish university conceals within its bosom, repel from it the children of the Irish Catholics; so that, in a country almost exclusively Catholic, the Protestants alone receive the higher instruction requisite for the discharge of public functions. Moreover, the Protestants, to whom this instruction is given, do not belong to the upper ranks of society. Thus, the University of Dublin does not correspond with the purpose of its foundation; it has never been national, and it has lost the aristocratic character which belongs to the English universities. It is, in fact, nothing but a seminary of candidates for

the ministry of the Church of England: in this respect it is far from being abandoned; all who aspire to enter the church flock to the university, enticed by the
numerous benefices and magnificent livings which it has at its disposal.

We see, then, that this institution has nothing of a university but the name; it
was, at the very outset, paralysed, as an instructing body, by its union with the
church. It was founded, like the Anglican church itself, on the presumption that
Ireland would cease to be Catholic. Nevertheless, Ireland has remained such,
and the university on its side has continued Protestant.

The fate of the Irish university, which is nothing more than a school for superior instruction directed by the upper classes, explains the nature and destiny
of the other schools which the church has founded in that country. Once the
Protestant church said to the poor Catholics of Ireland, "Entrust your children
to us, we will educate them in the principles of pure morality and the knowledge
of the true religion." The Catholic population gave credit to the offer, and sent
its children to the charter-schools founded by the Established Church, but they
were soon withdrawn with horror, when it was found that in these schools the
children were taught nothing but hatred of their own creed, and respect for the
hostile creed. A second experiment was made; several benevolent Protestants,
sincere in their intentions, instituted schools for the education of poor Catholics, from which it was professed that the spirit of proselytism would be rigorously excluded; the enterprise was noble, it was pursued with ardour, good faith,
and charity, but success was impossible. In spite of themselves, or rather in consequence of their living and ardent faith, these Protestants could not remain impartial between their own faith and that of the young Catholics entrusted to
their charge; and for such impartiality, even if it were possible, the people would
not give them credit.

Thus, the Anglican church in Ireland, by the operation of one single principle, finds insuperable obstacles to the execution of everything which it accom-
plishes in England. This principle renders even charity impossible; and the
benefits which the church dispenses in England, and which procure for it the
respect and sympathy of the lower classes, become in Ireland new causes of hostility from the people.

III

Tithes

Resistance of Catholics and Dissenters to the Payment of Tithes

We have seen, in the preceding subsection, that one of the sources of revenue in the Anglican church of Ireland is the right to tithes. This right has been recently exchanged for a rent-charge, levied on all properties without distinction, and the mode of payment has undergone important changes; but it still preserves its original character, which is also its radical vice—it is a tax levied on Catholics and Dissenters, for the exclusive advantage of the Anglican church.[1]

It is easy to conceive all the angry passions that must be produced among the Irish Catholics by this obligation to pay for the support of the clergy of a hostile faith: it is a tribute whose payment implies a sort of homage to the receiver, and to the superiority of the creed that he teaches; a tribute which the Catholics formerly paid to their own church, the church of the country, but which they are now obliged to offer to the ministers of a faith introduced by strangers. How could the Irish Catholics pay with any cheerfulness this debt to such creditors, which is not only an onerous tax in itself, but which wounds their dignity, and indeed can scarcely be paid without some remorse of conscience? This impost not only offends the Catholics; it also wounds those who, though Protestants, follow a different ritual from that of the Established Church, and who are indignant at honouring and supporting a form of worship which is not their own.

Finally, tithes are unpopular amongst the lay members of the Anglican church itself,[2] for in their eyes their own clergy are already sufficiently rich; and the payment of this tribute is deemed a heavy burden, which can only be sustained by raising the rent on their tenants, and thus augmenting their misery, and all the perils that such misery produces.

Need we be surprised if, in the midst of these almost unanimous sentiments of hostility to tithes, the Catholics, who are naturally the most hostile of all to

---

1. Tithes were, however, debated more for the mode in which they were levied, than the purpose to which they were applied.
2. The Irish parliament did not scruple to rob the church of the tithe of agistment.

this revenue of the Anglican church, refuse to pay it, and choose rather to submit to the legal consequences of their refusal, that is to say, to all the processes and expense of judicial enforcement, rather than, by voluntary payment, perform an act that disgusts and degrades them?

Need we be astonished that repeated demands on one side, and perseverance in refusal on the other, should lead to collisions which first produce lawsuits, then secret hatred, and finally open violence?

When a people suffers from several forms of oppression,—when a great mass of evil is accumulated amongst this people,—when the grievances that this people sustain from the government are infinitely multiplied,—it might seem that if the people revolted, it would be in the name of all its miseries, that it would collect all its grievances as a support for its insurrection, and attack not one cause, but all the causes of its sufferings. It is not thus, however, that nations are accustomed to proceed in their efforts for deliverance; however innumerable may be the evils by which a people is oppressed, we may be assured that every explosion of popular passion terminating in a revolt, will adopt one principal grievance as the summary of all their grievances, as the representative of all the popular sufferings, and as the rallying point of all the popular animosities. Such a banner of sedition is incessantly offered, and will long be offered, to the popular passions in Ireland, by the demand for tithe, and the resistance it provokes.

When once the spirit of resistance has seized on all, behold how it proceeds; on all sides meetings are convened, speeches made, and resolutions adopted; the refusal to pay tithes is decreed by the popular voice, nearly in the same words as the resolution adopted at a meeting in the Queen's County in 1831. "Resolved, That the tithe system is peculiarly obnoxious to the people of this county, being compelled to support in luxury and idleness a class of men from whom they receive nothing but their marked contempt and hatred."

Still, in despite of these hostile manifestations, the ministry of the Anglican church prepares to levy the tithes; it is the right of the clergy, the right must be enforced against all the debtors, but they unanimously refuse. The Anglican minister appeals to the law, at the same time that he claims the support of the public force. A process-server is sent to serve summonses on the recusants, and in order that he should not be impeded in the execution of his duty, he is escorted by twenty or thirty policemen in his perilous enterprise. This formality being accomplished, judgment is easily obtained against the defaulters. But they still refuse; they appeal against the sentence on some real or imaginary grounds; they plead, incur expense, gain time: the superior tribunal condemns them over again; still they do not obey, but continue to refuse payment. The Anglican minister, whose rights have been most solemnly sanctioned by law, sees that these rights will perish unless he has recourse to rigorous measures, and he resolves to employ them.

Preparations are made to seize the cattle of the debtor: they cannot be found; they have disappeared the preceding evening, and are concealed. Search is made for them—they are seized—a mob assembles, and beats off the distrainers. The police force is summoned; scarcely is it on the road, when signals are made from the mountains, rallying cries raised, horns blown, to announce to the population of the neighbourhood the arrival of the constabulary force. These sounds are repeated by a thousand echoes, the distant cabins are agitated, the whole county is in commotion, everybody knows his place of rendezvous—it is that of the projected seizure. Peasants crowd to it from all parts; they consult, they encourage, they mutually stimulate each other to resistance: the signal is given, the constables approach, they arrive. Universal hisses, followed by an ominous silence, receive them. Aided by this imposing force, the officers of justice at length seize their prey. But whilst they are making out the schedule of the distrained property, the popular passion is inflamed, the sufferers are pitied; the wretched families, the wife and children, cling to their means of support about to be taken away; it is loudly proclaimed that these rigours, these miseries, and this sorrow, are the work of a minister of the Protestant church, whose opulence is to be increased by the blood of the poor Catholics: cries of horror resound; indignation and anger increase; terrible murmurs are heard, the storm rapidly advances, announcing its approach by the formidable threatenings of popular vengeance. In an instant, the public officers are insulted, menaced, and assailed with blows. Then a Protestant minister, who is also a neighbouring justice of peace, appears, reads the Riot Act, and orders the police to fire on the people. He is obeyed. From this moment the fury of the people knows no bounds. This population, that was deemed humbled and crushed because it was deprived of its arms, finds on the earth it treads terrible weapons to overwhelm its enemies. Energy and despair supply the means of combat, and, after a short struggle, half of the policemen remain on the place slaughtered by stones; the rest effect a retreat, leaving the crowd intoxicated by its unexpected success and sanguinary victory.[3]

It sometimes happens that the judicial sentence does not encounter such obstacles in its execution; the seizure is effected, but he for whom it is made obtains no profit.

The property of the debtor being placed in the hands of justice, it must be sold for the benefit of the creditor. Now the difficulty is to find purchasers. An auction is held, but there are no bidders; woe to him that would venture to make an offer. Frightful menaces are placarded against those who purchase any goods that have been seized for tithes. These menaces need not be written; they are in the clamour of the multitudes that surround the auctioneer and the public of-

---

3. This is a pretty accurate picture of what occurred at Rathcormack in 1834.

ficers; and, written or vociferated, these menaces will not be vain; terrible examples to the contrary are within the memory of all.

An armed force may easily protect the legal functionaries in the seizure; it may resist, conquer, and exterminate the rebels, though subject itself to cruel reprisals; but what it cannot do is to make the mute crowd round the auction break silence, or make a sale to those who refuse to purchase. Often, after many efforts, the distrained cattle and unsold goods are removed to the house of the Protestant minister, who keeps them until he obtains their price.

All sorts of expedients are employed to escape from this difficult conjuncture. Hoping that a sale might more easily be effected in a large city, the seat of government, the distrained chattels are sent to Dublin; but they are stopped on the road, tumultuous mobs assemble here and there, and soon in some struggle between the populace and the drivers, the latter are beaten, and forced to abandon their prey. Without abandoning this plan, other means are sometimes adopted for its execution. Every convoy of distrained goods is escorted by an armed escort from one police station to another. But when the seizure is offered for sale in Dublin, purchasers are not to be found, any more than in the rest of Ireland. It is like some pestiferous matter, whose contact everybody avoids; and whoever bids for it, is stigmatised with infamy; the newspapers publish his name, and popular hatred retains the remembrance. What then is to be done with these goods brought to Dublin, which cannot be sold? A last effort is made, they are transported across the Irish Channel, and, after a passage of a hundred and odd miles, they reach the port of Liverpool: but here their origin is quickly known; when they are offered for sale, no Englishman will sully himself by the purchase; no one will offer a price which will go to pay Irish tithes.[4]

Let us acknowledge that, when public passion is exalted to this point, and is so unanimous in rejecting a legal right, this right may continue to exist, but its exercise is impossible. Rigour, violence, judicial decrees, distraints, sanguinary collisions between the army and the people,—all these means will be unprofitable and powerless. Much blood will be shed, but it will be utterly wasted; neither tithes nor their price will be paid. And what is still more remarkable is, that the power of the Irish people is not in open rebellion, but in passive resistance. The Irish insurgents of 1831 sometimes committed violent and sanguinary acts; there were riots against the police; Protestant ministers were murdered, and their properties burned; other cruel acts of vengeance were committed; but these isolated outrages, like those of the Whiteboys, produced no political effect. That which rendered the force of the revolt irresistible was its cold and calculating nature, its passive character, the universal agreement of an entire people to

---

4. Similar circumstances occurred in other English markets.

render the exercise of an iniquitous right impossible by the simple expedient of refusing to recognise it.

Often, in such extreme cases, the Protestant parson, daunted by these obstacles, abandoned his right. Sometimes he clung to it more closely, but then he encountered invincible difficulties; every step was impeded, everything around him hostile. As perils followed in his train, he soon found none to aid him in his suit; neither attorneys, lawyers, nor witnesses: the magistrates, at first friendly, grew lukewarm, and began to abandon him; all were repugnant to severities which did not attain their object, and were perilous to themselves. The ground was taken from under his feet. *Then,* inspired by his interests and the sanctity of his unacknowledged right, he turned to the government, his last and highest refuge. "During the last year," he said, "I have not received a penny of the five hundred pounds due to me for tithes. My wife and children, like myself, have fallen into distress. I have been obliged to sell my carriage and horses." He then bitterly accused fortune, society, justice, his friends themselves. The ordinary magistrates, if he was to be believed, were insufficient; stipendiary magistrates were wanting; the public force was too weak; the police fought faintly; the army was unwilling to interfere; it was necessary to re-organise the yeomanry, and create a militia specially designed to act against the people. That is to say, it was modestly proposed that, in order to aid ten or twelve hundred Protestant parsons in levying tithes on six millions and a half of Catholics, and six hundred thousand dissenters, the army of Ireland should be increased by forty or fifty thousand men! Such demands could not be satisfied, and they were therefore disregarded. The Anglican clergy of Ireland were then heard to declare that government betrayed the cause of the church, and that the English constitution was in danger. They proclaimed that society itself was attacked at its foundation; for what is a state in which law is disobeyed and property violated? Is not tithe as much the property of the minister as rent of the landlord? Does not the law command the payment of one as well as of the other? The church is accustomed as much as possible to mingle its cause with that of the laity, and to confound its rights with those of the community. "You refuse," said the clerical body, "the tithes to the minister, which are his right; how then will you complain if your tenant refuses to pay his rent?"

Assuredly this open resistance to law is a sad course of instruction for any people. But who, in the presence of the legal tyranny which we have described, will venture to maintain that a legal right is always just, and that every resistance to the law is criminal resistance? Who will contend that a nation, after having endured an enormous iniquity for centuries, has not a right to cast off the burthen? What is the use of discussing principles when the facts have invincible sway, and when rebellion itself bears the manifest character of morality and justice?

Is it not a sad and solemn spectacle, that of an entire people crushed by the double burthen of a social misery that knows no bounds, and a religious oppression that exceeds belief; driven by the excess of its physical sufferings to a continuity of individual outrages; and propelled by passion into an inevitable circle of general and periodic revolts; incessantly borne down by the yoke of the aristocracy and that of the church,—by the exactions of the one, and the persecutions of the other?

When a stranger sees this emulation between the aristocracy and the church, rivals in tyranny, he asks which of the two excites most hatred in Ireland, and cannot determine whether the aristocracy is the more injurious to the church, or the church the more fatal to the aristocracy.

Sometimes disputes arise between the clergy and the rich, on which it would be difficult to come to a decision. "The church," say the landlords, "would be less odious to the people, if all ecclesiastical sinecures, which exhaust the resources of the country, were suppressed." "The rich should be forced to reside on their estates," say the clergy; "there would then be at least one Protestant family in every parish, and the office of an Anglican minister would be no longer a sinecure." . . . . "All the misery of the people," say the aristocracy, "arises from the cupidity of the clergy." . . . . "No," replies the church, "it results from the selfishness of the landlords."[5]

We may conceive an evil aristocracy whose vices would be corrected by a charitable and generous church. It is, moreover, possible to comprehend the existence of a church defective and full of abuses, but which, by its union with a good aristocracy, might still appear beneficial. But what must be the situation of these two bodies amongst the people, when there is a rivalry between them which shall produce the most misery, and when each of them, hated for itself, is still more hated on account of the other?

---

5. See the Works of the late Bishop of Limerick.

IV

Some Remarks on the North of Ireland

In the preceding chapters I have confined myself to general facts and principles, without taking any note of the exceptions; but I must now observe, that what is true of Ireland, taken as a whole, may appear inexact, if only an isolated portion of the country is considered. Let us cite an example.

In speaking of the Irish aristocracy, its nature and its vices, I have not distinguished between that of the south and that of the north. Still, if a person reflects on the elements of which each is composed, it is easy to understand that one cannot be in all points similar to the other.

I have said elsewhere that the population, which in the south is almost exclusively Catholic, is in the north pretty equally divided between Protestant and Catholic. In the north, as in the south, the landlords are Protestant; but with this difference, the Protestant landlord in the south has under him a poor Protestant population; in the north, the landlord is in contact with inferiors, half of whom are Catholics, and the other half Protestants. The result is easily seen. As there is a moiety of the population with which the landlords have a community of religion, this part of the poor population suffers less in its relations with the rich, and endures less tyranny on the part of its governors. On one side, the landlords do not attempt to impose so severe a yoke; and if they did, their inferiors would probably not endure it, for they are the more enlightened and the more powerful. The rich Protestants of the north have also a motive to be less oppressive than those of the south; that is, their division into two sects, the one Anglican, the other Presbyterian. Now the same reason that induces rival sects to display a zeal for proselytism, is the cause that the rich man belonging to the Established Church, and he who professes the Presbyterian creed, endeavours, each in his sphere, to show himself a better landlord to his tenants, a more uncorrupt magistrate, and more impartial to those who appeal to his justice; and it may be remarked, that this favourable disposition towards Protestant brethren indirectly reaches the portion of the inhabitants that are Catholic; for they could not be witnesses of the progress made in the condition of the Protestants, without labouring to effect the same advancement for themselves. And it is more difficult for a Protestant to show himself rigid and merciless towards poor Catholics, at the very moment that he treats poor Protestants with humanity. This is sufficient to explain why Ulster is more rich and prosperous than the other provinces of Ireland. It contains fewer paupers, the inhabitants are better clothed, their food is of a superior quality, and the ground is better cultivated. It is true that the north is enriched by manufacturing industry; but we shall soon see that it is to the superiority of its social state that it is indebted for its industrial prosperity.

Besides, the north of Ireland is not quite so prosperous as always to have escaped the social miseries described in the preceding pages. It was disturbed by the Oakboys in 1764, and the Steelboys in 1772, whose insurrections were occasioned by precisely the same causes as those of the peasants in the south, and fully proved that the tyranny of Irish landlords is not confined to the south and west. "All the actors in this insurrection," says the biographer of Lord Charlemont, "were Protestants, either of the Established Church or Dissenters." But, after these violent insurrections, the social condition of the north was modified. As the oppressed were less unfortunate, they became less cruel in their vengeance, less fierce, because they were more civilised. "A revolt of slaves," says Lord Charlemont, "is always more sanguinary than an insurrection of freemen." But also these men, whose revolts were less cruel than those of the southern insurgents, took up arms for weaker causes than those which impelled the others to violence; being more enlightened, and less miserable, they suffered as much from a minor evil.

Purely social insurrections have long ceased in the north of Ireland; they have become purely political; and this may be easily understood. We have seen what in Ulster constantly operates to diminish social oppression, and what in the south, on the contrary, tends to increase it; but a portion of the causes that produce these effects must, in the north, favour the growth of political passions and dissensions: in the south and west, the war is principally between the rich and the poor; in the north, it is especially between Catholics and Protestants: in the south, the Catholics are in such majority, that the Protestants can only struggle against them by legal texts; in the north, the parties are so equally divided, that each dispute may lead to an open engagement of brute force. The war is agrarian in the south, religious in the north. Thus outrages connected with the occupation of ground, or the vengeance of a tenant against his landlord, are far less frequent in the north than in the south; but in the north we more often find the assassination of a Protestant by a Catholic on account of his religion, false witnesses inspired only by religion, hatred, and the violence of parties. Before the tribunals of the north there is perhaps a greater display of passions between Catholics and Protestants than in the south; but at bottom the law is less hated, justice less odious, the judge less detested, because there are always great numbers who can love and respect both the judge and the law.

We can now understand the exceptional condition of the north of Ireland, where there is more political than social misery; whereas, in the rest of Ireland, there is more social misery than political.

V

General Consequences from What Has Preceded— Character of the Irishman—Explanation of Its Faults

The misgovernment to which Ireland has been subjected not only gives the key to its miseries, it explains, besides, the moral character of its inhabitants.

There exists in our days a school of philosophers which seems disposed to apply to nations the phrenological system which they employ to judge of individuals. Personifying all nations, and taking their skulls in their hands, they say to one, "The shape of your cranium indicates the passions that presage grandeur;" to another, "Nature has made you religious;" to a third, "You have been created for philosophy;"—"You have the organ of liberty,"—"You, the organ of servitude." And when they have thus felt the heads of all nations, attributed to one the genius of war, to another that of commerce, when they have proclaimed a third to aristocracy, and a fourth to democracy, they stop short, almost terrified at their prophetic power, for they believe that they have announced to nations the solemn decrees of inflexible destiny.

It is in England especially that I have heard these theories professed; and I am not astonished at it; for the English, who are a great people, have the most singular pride of birth that ever existed; they readily believe that the happiness and power of a people depend more upon its nature than its institutions; like those heroes who place more confidence in their destiny than in their valour.

I have never spoken to Englishmen of Ireland and its miseries without almost immediately hearing this objection: "Ireland complains of being poor—but what is to be done? Labour alone gives wealth; and the natural laziness of the Irish is an invincible obstacle to his labour, and consequently to the termination of his misfortunes. We shall never see industry prosper in Ireland. England is accused of keeping Ireland under the yoke: what a senseless complaint! The fickle character of the Irish must ever prevent them from possessing free institutions. Unfit for liberty, could they meet a more fortunate lot than to fall under the empire of a more civilised nation, which shares with them its glory and its greatness? The Irish, subjected to the English, submit to the law of nature: they are an inferior race."

This language always appeared to me the result of prejudice or injustice. I readily admit that there exist among nations marked differences of character and manners. I do not dispute that every people is endowed with certain peculiar inclinations, and certain faculties, which collectively give it a peculiar physiognomy in the midst of other nations. I grant without difficulty that the Irishman and Englishman have very opposite characters, not only in their actions, but in their opinions and habits of thought. Let us take, for example, the most prominent trait in the English character,—that firmness of soul which presides over all its enterprises, that unalterable perseverance in overcoming obstacles, that steadiness which never abandons the task till it is completed. Assuredly we find nothing like this in the Irishman. He seems, on the contrary, naturally fickle and inconstant, ready to pass from despair to hope, from exertion to despondency. Full of ardour, imagination, and spirit, he wants entirely that consistency which predominates with the Englishman, and supplies the place of those qualities in which he is deficient. All that can be done at once, and by sudden effort, the Irishman will execute better than anybody else, because no one is more enthusiastic than he is; he rushes to encounter an obstacle without measuring the difficulties; but if he fails in the first attempt, he turns back and renounces the enterprise. It is assuredly difficult to find two nations subject to the influence of more opposite dispositions; and I am tempted to believe that there is something in the hereditary character of the one race which leads to boldness of enterprise, whilst the disposition of the other is, from its very origin, more cold and less expansive.

But still, may not what we attribute to descent arise from some other cause? Even if this opposition of inclinations actually arose from diversity of race, what inference should we deduce from it? Ought we to conclude that the Englishman will never cease to be steady and persevering, and that the Irishman will always continue enthusiastic and fickle? Perhaps it is with nations as with individuals; the latter derive from nature diverse propensities, whose influence cannot be denied, but which, nevertheless, may be so powerfully combated by means of education, according as it is directed to good or evil, that the man naturally vicious may be rendered virtuous, and that the best natural inclinations may be depraved. Thus, after having demonstrated that any certain evil disposition is peculiar to a nation, it is further necessary, before pronouncing an anathema, to prove that this evil inclination might not be checked by some contrary influence. And when different faculties have been recognised in two nations, who is to decide which of these faculties gives the one a moral superiority over the other? Are the qualities of the head and heart to be weighed in a balance?

To deny the vices of the Irish people would be assuredly to contradict all evi-

dence. The Irishman is lazy, mendacious, intemperate, prompt to acts of violence. He has notoriously a sort of invincible aversion to truth. If it is necessary
to make a disinterested choice between truth and falsehood, he will tell the lie.
Thus, he scarcely makes an assertion without supporting it by an oath; he ac-
companies every statement with *"upon my honour," "upon my word,"*—phrases familiar to those who habitually violate truth.

His repugnance to work is no less singular; he performs generally without
pleasure, care, or zeal, whatever he undertakes to execute, and for the most part
he is idle. Many miserable Irishmen add much to their misery by their indolence; a little industry and a little activity are alone wanting to alleviate their distress; but nothing can withdraw them from their apathy and carelessness; they
seem contented with the mere display of their wretchedness, and to be almost
insensible of their wants.

These are deplorable vices, but still more terrible remain. Violent and vindictive, the Irishman displays the most ferocious cruelty in his acts of vengeance.
We have seen how the Irish tenant, who has been ejected from his farm, or
whose stock has been seized for non-payment of rent, is led by revenge to reprisals tainted with the most atrocious barbarity. The punishments which he in-
vents in his savage fury cannot be contemplated without horror.[1] Sometimes in-
cendiarism and assassination are not sufficient; he inflicts lingering tortures on
his victim.[2] He is often as unjust as he is cruel in his rage, and wreaks vengeance
for the wrongs he has suffered on persons totally innocent.[3] He not only attacks
the landlord or the clergyman on account of the harshness for which they alone
are responsible, but his violence extends to the agent of the proprietor, to the
new tenant, to the minister's proctor; he sometimes goes further, and carries off
the wives and daughters of individuals, to punish husbands and fathers who are
not themselves culpable.

These vices, these crimes,—I know them; I see them amongst the Irish, and I
do not find them amongst the English. Whence come these vices and crimes?
From birth? NO! I reject as a monstrous impiety the doctrine which makes vice
and crime depend on birth or nature. I never can believe that a nation has been
predestined by the fatality of its origin to vice, and linked by its nature with
crime. I never will be persuaded that God, who made man in his own image,
and fashioned him in his own likeness, has created a people deprived of the
power of becoming just and honest. I will never admit that he has refused moral
liberty to this people; that is to say, that, in giving it life, he has deprived it of the
conditions of virtue. Such an enormous injustice should be so irrefragably dem-

---

1. See Historical Introduction respecting Whiteboys.
2. See ditto.
3. The new tenant, not the landlord, is the usual object of Whiteboy vengeance.

onstrated, as not to be less certain than the existence of Deity, before I could believe it. But why should I admit it when it rests on no proof? Through what strange disposition should I attribute to the presumed injustice of Heaven an evil, of which I can clearly discover the causes upon earth?

Those who explain the immorality of the Irish by an original and hereditary taint, forget that during seven centuries this nation has been subjected to the most constant and the most merciless tyranny. We see every day the man possessing the greatest strength, and endowed with the highest moral energy, degrade himself, and fall into absolute physical weakness, under the influence of a few years of the rule of misery and corruption; and yet it seems we do not comprehend that six hundred years of hereditary slavery, physical suffering, and moral oppression, *must* have deteriorated a nation, vitiated its blood, and tainted its habits. Ireland has been subjected to the yoke of despotism; Ireland must of necessity have been demoralised; the despotism was long, the demoralisation must be immense. You are astonished to find the morals of slaves amongst the descendants of a people that has endured six centuries of slavery: for my part, I should be much more surprised to meet the habits and dignity of a freeman in him who has never known any rule save that of servitude. When I see a nation that has had the misfortune to fall beneath the yoke, and remain in subjection, I do not inquire what vices it has, but I ask what vices it has not, and what virtues it can have.

Consider attentively the character of the Irishman, analyse his virtues and his vices, and you will soon recognise that every one of his dispositions, good or bad, is directly derived from the state of Irish society since the Conquest, and that this social state has either originated his inclinations, or at least given them direction and development. Taking this as your starting-point, you will not be astonished, on comparing Ireland with England, to find them so dissimilar.

The fickleness that is sometimes remarked in the habits of a nation, is sometimes the result of misery; and such a nation, though now unstable and frivolous, only wants to acquire wealth and freedom in order to become grave and steady. I know not whether the seriousness of the English belongs more to their institutions or their race. There is neither a nation nor an individual so devoted to pleasure as that one of them which does not work; the Englishman spends little time in amusement, because he is engrossed by business. He has his rights and liberties to defend, whilst, at the same time, he has the wealth of the world to conquer. Would the character of the Englishman be the same, if he were deprived of his political privileges and the empire of the sea? I question it. I readily believe that under his cloudy skies he would never feel those soft sensations of languor, those invitations to repose and effeminacy, produced by the bright sun of Naples. But if it be true that the humid atmosphere in which he lives excites him more to action than the clear skies of Italy would, must we not acknowledge that his dispositions favourable to toil, produced by his stern climate, might be combated by political institutions which, instead of seconding his industrial inclinations, would restrain them?

See how his character is modified, despite of his race, according as he is subjected to different influences. Who in the cold, calculating, steady Scotchman of the present day, could recognise the poetical child of Caledonia, haughty, undisciplined, a rebel to all authority, descending from his mountains at the summons of his bards and his minstrels? Who in the midst of American democracy can recognise the Englishman, a friend to aristocracy? The Englishman in England wishes for liberty above all things; in America his darling object is equality. Who in the indolent planter of Carolina or Louisiana can recognise the Englishman unwearied in industrial toil? Look at France in the present day; do you deem that the character of its inhabitants is the same as it was before 1789? Whence do these differences of habit arise, unless from the difference of laws and institutions?

If you do not lose sight of this dominion of institutions over the morals of nations, you will no longer be astonished that the English people labour, and that the Irish people do not. We find in the ancient chronicles of Ireland that steadiness at work was once one of the distinctive traits of the Irish people, of whom instability is now the principal character.[4] Is it not natural that the spirit of industry should be prevalent in a society where the profits of toil, secured by law, have always been a fruitless source of honour and comfort, sometimes of power and glory? And, for the same reason, is it not a logical consequence, that a nation in which industry has never been honoured, rewarded, or free, should be lazy and idle?

During centuries Ireland was declared incapacitated from becoming rich; positive laws bound her to poverty. What inclination, then, could be felt for labour from which no property could be derived?

Stripped of the rights of property, the Irish were dispersed over the soil, and condemned to till the ground for the profit of their masters. They obeyed the necessity—they did toil; but, like all slaves, they conceived an invincible hatred and disgust for labour; the Irishman hates his task, as every man does who works without pay.

Such sentiments, the natural offspring of evil institutions, cannot disappear on the very day that better laws are established. Whatever you may do now, you cannot produce the deep instincts of property, nor the consequent love of exertion, amongst men who fifty years ago could neither purchase land, nor possess a horse worth more than five pounds.[5]

---

4. See Sir John Davis's Inquiry.
5. See Historical Introduction—Penal laws.

If the misery of the Irishman belongs not to his race, we may say the same of all the consequences which this misery has produced. Thus, this deplorable negligence, this absolute want of steadiness and care, perceptible in everything that he does, this recklessness, this total absence of self-respect, are the direct effects of his social condition. He feels that he counts for nothing in society, and that there are no means by which he may become somebody. If he wishes for work, he cannot obtain it without great difficulty; if any is offered, it is wretchedly remunerated; there is no order or arrangement in his mode of life, because all his means of existence are uncertain. He never attempts to look beyond the present moment, because his foresight enables him only to see evil in the future prospect. The question is not for him to choose between an unfortunate existence, the result of his indolence, and a comfortable life procured by his industry; he is sure to remain miserable; the only doubt is, whether he shall be more or less so: now this misery is so great, that the advantage of diminishing it by a degree is not worth the trouble necessary for his success. "We are so poor!" is the reply of the Irish peasants, when they are reproached with increasing their[6] misery by neglect; and they continue in the filth that chokes their hovels, without the slightest wish to keep them clean.[7]

Irish intemperance and love of whisky, one of the most deplorable of the national vices, arise from the same source.[8] As he believes it impossible ever to establish any durable accordance between his income and his expenses, he dissipates without scruple the moderate wages of his temporary employment.— Scarcely has he received his wages, when he runs to the whisky-shop, and, for some moments at least, drowns his misery in drunkenness and brutalization.

Thus, by the very condition of the people, all the vices usually produced by extreme misery are naturally explained. Thus also the secondary vices, which are the usual accompaniments of those I have mentioned, may also be explained; thus, the Irishman, precisely because he does nothing, boats and blusters; as he has a master, he is a flatterer, and full of insolence when he is not cringing. These vices, indeed, add to his misery, but they were first derived from it. From the same source that his other pernicious inclinations flow, is derived that sad habit of falsehood, and that frightful predisposition to the most cruel and the most iniquitous outrages.

There is no need of a very deep study of the character and habits of the Irish people to discover that they are often deficient in the most simple notions of good and evil, of right and wrong.

In the midst of the terrible catastrophes of which this country has been the

---

6. The translator has often been thus answered.
7. A perceptible improvement has recently taken place.
8. Temperance societies are now patronised by many of the Catholic priests.

theatre since the twelfth century, in the tumult of the awful revolutions which have transferred the property of the soil into the hands of all parties in their turn, led to the triumph of the most opposite political principles, elevated temples and altars for the most varied forms of worship; there has been formed amongst the Irish the most strange medley of ideas and opinions in morals, religion, and politics? Ascend to the origin of the tyranny, and what will you see?—men robbed of their property by confiscation, and reduced to the condition of labourers. Is this primitive act of violence one likely to confirm a people in the feelings of rectitude and justice?

Why has this spoliation been committed? Why were the estates confiscated from the original possessors? Because the owners adhered firmly to their religious faith, and preferred the loss of property to the abandonment of their creed. Is it a moral instruction to witness the injury of the upright man, whose probity entails his ruin, and to see this ruin profit a violent and sacrilegious usurper?

This lucky usurper, attached by no sympathy to the Irish, whose race he abhors and whose creed he contemns, treats them with merciless severity; after having robbed them, forbids them to become rich; absolutely closes political society against them, hampers them in civil society, establishes a regular system of religious persecution, and thus organises the most anti-social system that ever existed. Can any one find lessons of justice in this frightful oppression, weighing for more than a century on unfortunate men, whose only crime was to be vanquished, and who suffered because they would not abandon their conscience to their victors as well as their country?

The principal and most cruel tyranny that Ireland has had to endure, was that brought upon it by its creed. Does any one suppose that a man will derive sound notions of rectitude and equity from a government which he sees proscribing the religion which, according to his faith, is the only true mode of adoring God;—when he sees his mode of worshipping his Creator, in his view the first of all duties, raised into a crime; or when he sees his priests, that is to say, the men he venerates as the representatives of God on earth, driven into banishment—when, to hear the last words and the adieus of these proscribed holy men, he is obliged to shroud himself in secrecy and mystery under the most terrible penalties? Thus, in order to practise what is honourable and lawful, it is sometimes necessary to hide from human eyes; these duties are crimes punished by human law. There exist just actions which the law calls crimes, but which are not crimes!—Behold notions of morality which you may be well assured will bear their fruit.

Still this cruel tyranny runs its course; it crushes the people incessantly; all support it with equal energy: at length some despond and embrace the only means to assuage their misfortunes and alleviate their sufferings; they take oaths that their conscience rejects, they become renegades, and at once enter on the possession of the rights and privileges of which they have been deprived. Thus, apostasy, the greatest of crimes in the sight of the Irish peasant, is recompensed by the law. Thus, as there exist virtues of which human law makes crimes, there are also crimes which men agree to call virtues. . . . A second rule of morality, which will doubtless greatly aid the Irish peasant to distinguish between right and wrong.

Troubled by all these contradictions, which pass the limits of his understanding; constantly seeing what he regards as justice, truth, and rectitude, falling under physical force; the Irishman takes the part of submission, and seizes on the only weapons which belong to the feeble—cunning, falsehood, violence.

"Why," said he, sometimes, "should I not slay the man who has caused my brother's death? Why am I not master of the lands which my ancestors enjoyed? By what right does this man, who calls himself proprietor of an estate that ought to belong to me, eject me from the farm where I spin out a miserable existence?"—And sometimes a frightful act of violence is the conclusion of his reasoning.

But this violence is at once repressed by assemblies of his enemies that call themselves courts of justice, and where the organs of the law proclaim those deeds crimes, which a depraved conscience declares to be acts of substantial justice. Brought before the tribunal of his master, the accused generally defends himself by falsehood. His fellows are summoned to bear witness against him, they are sworn to tell the truth, the whole truth, and nothing but the truth. Will they observe the oath? No, without doubt. In this case, perjury is honourable, and telling truth would be infamous; they give false evidence in favour of a man oppressed like themselves, and their conscience testifies that they have acted right. This false evidence is, in its turn, declared a crime by those who derive their rules of morality from a different principle.

Sometimes a single individual opposes open resistance to the law; it is the powerless revolt of isolated misery: often several are associated in insurrection as they are united in wretchedness; it is not the vulgar war of a banditti against society which it still believes just,—it is a war waged against iniquitous laws, by men who think that they are so; it is the war of the Whiteboys. Finally, there are sometimes insurrections of the popular masses, as in 1641 and in 1798; then the ground itself quivers, and the entire social structure is shaken.

In every case, when the effort for freedom comes from one or from all, its moral effect, when it fails, is always of the same nature. Hence there is a terrible abyss for those minds which aspired to their own deliverance, and having made a vain effort, behold human justice in which they were ready to believe vanishing before their eyes; the chains of tyranny then fall with all their weight upon the people, as always happens when the slave who attempts to break his fetters falls again into the power of his master: this is the moment when the most fatal and depraving effect is produced upon the conscience; it is the hour that corruption chooses to penetrate the soul, and blight all that remains of virtue. Some who hitherto held out courageously against persecution and their interests, feel themselves falling; without doubt, they contracted many vices in this unequal contest, where it was necessary to oppose force with all the petty means that are at the disposal of weakness; but still, while resistance lasted, the moral sentiment of duty survived all the efforts of corruption. This struggle ended, no tie any longer bound the Irish renegade to what was just and honourable; his degradation was consummated.

This total depravity only reached a small number; but perhaps there was not one who, even whilst adhering to his religious creed, was not tainted by similar corruption. All lost the love of truth, because frankness and veracity brought down certain persecution on their heads; almost all contracted the habit of lying, because falsehood during a century was a legitimate and necessary weapon. They assumed habits of outrage and insurrection under the influence of a tyranny which drove them into open opposition to the law. Now do not complain, if you find amongst the Irish a general aversion to truth, and an absolute love of falsehood. Can the Irishman, gross and ignorant as you have made him, draw with any discretion in his mind the line between the cases in which conscience may pardon a lie, and those in which it cannot be justified? How is he to distinguish, amongst the crimes established by law, those which are not crimes and those which he should regard as such? How is he to distinguish among the virtues which his enemies honour, those that are real virtues from those dependent on convention and form?—Grant that he honestly attempts to make these distinctions, which are often so difficult, do you think, after the brutalisation he has undergone, that he will have the delicate tact to distinguish in the midst of all these incoherences, truth from falsehood, justice from iniquity? Be assured, that after some efforts he will fail in such an attempt; though intending to reform his vices, he will keep them; he will be sometimes just and honest, but he will never be certain of being so, for he will have lost the standard of justice and honesty. In a given particular case, he will be tempted to tell the truth; still in the midst of the uncertainties of his conscience, deprived of every moral guide, and open to the suggestions of interest, he will end by adopting the lie; he will lie because he will not be assured that in this particular instance falsehood is less lawful than in other cases, where he has no doubt that falsehood is permitted. He will, perhaps, hesitate to commit some particular murderous outrage; but he will banish remorse, if he feels the temptation, by representing to himself the analogy between the projected vengeance and other sanguinary acts of vengeance, which he has been accustomed to consider as lawful deeds.

In the uncertainty into which he is thrown by this confusion of principles, he also contracts certain habits of violence, and his mind carries into this violence a certain methodical arrangement which he afterwards applies in all cases. Who does not see in the brutal practices of the Whiteboys, in their principle of doing justice to themselves, in their system of intimidation, the source of the outrages recently committed in Ireland by the trades unions?[9] A manufacturer takes four apprentices: "It is too much," say the operatives employed in the trade, and whom the apprentices injure by their gratuitous labour; "if you do not turn off two of them, we will have your life:" and when the menace was despised, the crime was committed. Dublin, in the year 1837, was the theatre of a thousand atrocities of this nature, committed by wretches who looked upon violence as their only resource, and thus destroyed the industry of the country, by which alone they could hope to be supported.

It is thus that persecution and tyranny corrupt nations; cease then to attribute to degeneracy of race the moral degradation of a people depraved only by bad laws.

This depravity, moreover, is not confined to the man of pure Irish descent; it has corrupted all those subjected to its influence, whatever may have been their original descent. The complaints of England against the Irish are generally known, because that two or three centuries after the conquest the English settlers in Ireland had adopted the manners of the natives, and become more alien than the mere Irish *(hibernis ipsis hiberniores)*. The reproach was addressed to those of English as well as those of Irish descent, on whom the despotism of England fell with equal weight: they were corrupt, because they were equally bowed down by tyranny.

Sir John Davis, whose testimony will not be rejected by the partial friends of England, estimated that in his time, about three centuries and a half after the conquest, there were already in Ireland more English settlers than natives, whence he inferred the absurdity of those who attributed the calamities of Ireland to inferiority of race.[10] Let Ireland be carefully studied, and it will be seen that the misery and corruption of the people are everywhere spread in the same proportion as the tyranny which oppresses each district. Ulster is less unhappy and less vicious, because it has been less persecuted.

There is another common error in estimating the Irish character, which renders all just appreciation of it quite impossible. The Irishman is usually compared with the Englishman, his superior in rank and fortune, his political master, his religious enemy. This is a certain source of error. To estimate the morality of a man, he must be viewed in reference to his equals. On this account, in

---

9. See the last Parliamentary Report on Combinations.
10. "Inquiry into the causes why Ireland was imperfectly conquered."

order to comprehend the morals of an Irishman, you must not merely examine him in his relations with the superior Protestant class, but still more in his conduct to the Catholics, poor like himself.

See now to what an extent this Irishman, crafty and cruel towards the rich, is sincere and faithful to the man of his own class.[11] I have often heard the question asked, in all simplicity, how does it happen that the Irishman, often so treacherous and barbarous, exhibits on other occasions the most touching examples of humanity and charity? The answer is easy. He is inhuman to the enemies of his creed and race, and charitable to his brethren, humble and oppressed like himself. If you do not take this distinction as a guide to your observations, you will never comprehend the character of this people.

I have already said that in his blind vengeance the Irishman sometimes dishonours the wife or daughter of the person who incurs his resentment: it is, nevertheless, certain, that the Irish are remarkable for chastity; natural children are rare, adultery almost unknown. Whence arises this contradiction? Simply because the outrage is not dictated by lust, but is a means of vengeance employed against his enemies.

There is not, perhaps, one crime in Ireland which is not more or less tinged by the spirit and passions of party. Even the robberies that are committed partake of this character; even when dictated by cupidity, vengeance is never a stranger to their execution. Far different from the Spanish bandit, who, in the choice of victims, always prefers the traveller and stranger to whom he is unknown, the Irishman most readily attempts the life and property of those whom he knows. In no part of the world can a stranger travel with more safety than in Ireland.

From the foregoing, it appears that the Irishman is a complex character: he is composed of two distinct elements, which must be kept in view when his character is justly estimated; he is at once the man whom tyranny has endeavoured to corrupt during seven centuries, and whom, during the same period, religion has laboured to preserve pure.

All the faculties of his soul that despotism has touched are blighted; the wounds there are large and deep. All of this part of him is vice, whether it be cowardice, indolence, knavery, or cruelty; half of the Irishman is a slave.

But there are recesses where tyranny has vainly endeavoured to force an entrance, and which has thus remained free from every stain; they are the parts that hold his religious faith. Attacked in all his rights, he has yielded them to force, all save one, that of worshipping God according to his conscience; at the very moment when he yielded himself wholly to the tyranny of his masters, he

---

11. The charity of the poor Irish to each other is without a parallel.

reserved his soul, and thus kept an asylum for virtue. He did more than refuse submission. His conscience was roused, and maintained itself for centuries in a state of revolt. This rebellion of the slave is liberty itself; hence came persecution with all its miseries, but hence also sublime devotion and sacrifice, the source of all moral greatness and resignation, the eternal power of the feeble. Thus, religion has never deserted his soul, nor ceased to defend its sound parts against the enterprises of despotism. It is by the aid of religion that the Irishman, in the midst of the greatest oppression, has never ceased to be a freeman.

VI

Summary of the Preceding Chapters—
Illusions of the Irish Aristocracy

We have seen how a political cause and a religious principle have corrupted the aristocracy and its institutions in Ireland.

The Irish aristocracy, for the most part, does not govern at all, and when it governs, it governs badly. It wants the first condition necessary to the existence of a beneficent government, which is, to feel sympathy instead of contempt for its subjects. It is detested when absent; it is cursed when present; it possesses all the land in a country where the people have nothing but the land for their support, and immense revenues of which it never returns one farthing to the wretches from whom those revenues are raised. It possesses immense civil powers, and it makes such use of these powers, that neither government nor subjects recognise any proceeding but force, the one to impose the law, and the other to evade it. It has great religious privileges, which it has so strangely abused, that it has rendered its creed hateful among a thousand other objects of hate. Here are vices so great and enormous, that it may be said to possess nothing of aristocracy but the name.

But there is in this aristocracy something more surprising and extraordinary than its vices; I mean the delusions by which it imposes on itself, the faith that it has in the holiness of its rights and the legitimacy of its titles, the indignation which it displays when the least of its privileges is disputed.

I will grant, if they wish, that after the conquest of Ireland, there were great obstacles to the fusion of the English conquerors with the natives; I will concede, if required, that after the reformation, the English, having become Protestants, felt a legitimate repugnance to unite themselves closely with Irish Catholics; I will go further, and taking into account the genius of the age and of revolutions, I will concede that the Protestant conquerors laboured sincerely for the conversion of the Irish to Protestantism, and that they practised, from pure conscientious motives, a persecution which is often attributed to interest. These premises being established, I will easily give up the consequences. I will, without difficulty, acknowledge that the great English lord who possesses estates both in England and Ireland, ought to prefer a residence in England to one in Ireland. I will go still further, and concede that he who is a proprietor in poor Ireland only, is so near happy England that he is strongly tempted to dwell in it. I can readily conceive his abandoning Ireland, such as it is in our days, a prey to a thousand intestine commotions, and devoured by a thousand evils which he found in the land at his birth: I will also admit, that being far from his estate and his tenants, it must be difficult for him to know the sufferings which it is his duty to alleviate: nay, I will go so far as to concede, that the landlord who is kept at home in Ireland by mediocrity of fortune or any other cause, is less culpable in his oppression of a population that he despises and detests, in consequence of traditions received from his ancestors, than an oppressor would be who was exempt from these prejudices.

But what I cannot conceive is, that after two or three ages of useless persecutions to convert Ireland to the reformed faith, the Irish aristocracy does not clearly see that Ireland is destined to remain Catholic, and that persecution, exercised in vain, must have rooted in the hearts of the people the most profound hatred of their persecutors; further, what I cannot conceive is, that the great English or Irish landlord, who is merely a proprietor in Ireland, should pretend there to all the powers of aristocracy, should believe that he has a right to command his tenants to vote according to his pleasure, and when he sees them give an independent suffrage, should exclaim with profound grief, that the sacred bonds between landlord and tenant are broken;—it is impossible for me to comprehend how one man who does not reside on his estates, where he is wholly unknown,—or another who announces his presence only by rigour and exaction —the Irish justice of peace who resides habitually in London, but who comes on an occasional trip to sit on the bench of magistrates, and who, after having received his rents, will not depart without pronouncing sentence upon some Irish malefactors,—this justice of peace, whose decrees excite no feeling among the people but hatred and indignation, whose incapacity is so great that he could not administer the law without the aid of the central power, and whose authority is so feeble that without British artillery he would not be obeyed,—this minister of the Anglican church, to whom the poor pay taxes, and from whom the poor receive nothing,—who has come to Ireland as a missionary, and is nothing more than an annuitant, and who, finding himself surrounded in Ireland by hatred and peril, goes to expend the five or six hundred a year derived from his Irish benefice at Bath or Cheltenham,—it is, I say, impossible for me to conceive how such persons, proprietors, magistrates, or clergymen, who do nothing for the people, should claim the privileges of an actually governing aristocracy— should, after having abandoned the people to themselves, be surprised to see them ignorant and famishing—should, after having treated the peasants as slaves, be astonished to find them vile and degraded,—and, after having been the voluntary or involuntary cause of these evils, should wonder at being hated. What passes my powers of understanding is, that, after having degraded their country to a degree of wretchedness unknown to any other people, at a time when England surpassed in prosperity all the nations of the world, these lords of the soil are indignant, because they do not enjoy in Ireland the popularity which the aristocracy possesses in England,—that, deprived of all conditions of existence, this nominal aristocracy should declare itself legitimate, regard its rights as sacred, and its titles as inviolable; should rigorously claim the honour and respect with difficulty obtained by an enlightened, just, and beneficent aristocracy, and should raise the cry of impiety when the least of its privileges is attacked.

I am mistaken: these passions of the Irish aristocracy ought not to surprise me—they are natural;—does not he who is born a proprietor of slaves believe in the sanctity of slavery?

· PART II ·

How Ireland, Aided by the Liberties She Received or Acquired, Has Resisted Oppression

[For the 1839 edition, the translator omitted some material from Part II and numbered the remaining chapters consecutively with Part I.]

The Irish, brought under the yoke, had received from their masters too many means of defence not to resist oppression. Let the political organisation of Ireland, from the time of the conquest to the present day, be investigated, and there will be found in it all the forms, and nearly all the principles, of a free government.

Doubtless there was more than one error in this liberal organisation, in the very midst of which might be heard the clank of the fetters of servitude; yet would it be quite just to assert, that in all the constitutional laws given to Ireland, there was nothing but odious hypocrisy on the part of the legislator? Assuredly not. We have already seen that these institutions were honest at least to the English Protestants settled in Ireland, who obtained from England rights which she could not refuse them; and it was a great advantage to the Irish, bowed beneath the yoke, to have in the midst of them a society of freemen; for it is one of the sublime characters of liberty that it cannot be seen without being loved, and that, in order to be desired, it needs only to be known.

Let us add, in strict justice, that the Protestants, who doubtless at first desired their free constitution for themselves alone, could scarcely venture to refuse it entirely to the people entrusted to their charge, and that they conferred on this people certain political guarantees at the very time that they cruelly persecuted them on account of their religious belief. There was more good faith than is usually imagined in this assemblage of written laws and real oppression.

It is a phenomenon worthy of observation, that at the very height of his tyranny, an Englishman never departs from certain free principles inherent in his manners, habits, and even prejudices, which the logic of self-interest cannot always destroy. He enacts penal laws against the Irish Catholic, of unparalleled iniquity; but he deems that, in attacking Catholicism, he attacks absolute power, and that, while persecuting popery, he defends the sacred cause of liberty. Be well assured, then, that the same law which strikes the Catholic will respect the man, and that the citizen will preserve the rights of which the dissenter is deprived. The laws of the English Protestant place the Irish Catholic in a condition of social inferiority; but this is because an Englishman does not recognise an intimate connexion between liberty and equality. Social inequality appears to him the natural state of things; he sees it established in his own country; but he does not believe it just to deprive those over whom he is placed of their liberty, accustomed as he is to exercise his own rights against those who possess a greater extent of privileges. Though he places himself in superiority over millions of Irishmen, he still leaves them considerable liberties: at the moment that he subjects franchise, eligibility, civil magistracy, &c., to an oath which the conscience of the Irish Catholics rejects, he does not deprive them of those general rights which education has taught him to regard as not less necessary to existence than the air he breathes, and the ground he treads.

Turn to the press; from the time that it became free in England, it has not ceased to be so in Ireland. Swift published his most virulent pamphlets against the tyrants of Ireland at the period when that tyranny was most terrible.[1] In 1797, amid the symptoms of approaching civil war, journals bitterly opposed to England appeared every morning; and a Protestant historian, the Rev. Mr. Gordon, who approves of the penal laws, is indignant at the thought of violating the sacred principle of the liberty of the press.[2]

Under the penal laws, the Catholics of Ireland could not assemble in their chapels to worship God according to their conscience; but they were free to hold public assemblies, and discuss the rigours to which they were subjected. The exercise of this right, nevertheless, depended on the chief magistrate of the county, the sheriff, or, in case of his refusal, on a certain number of justices of the peace; but neither the sheriff, the representative of the central power, nor the justice of the peace, who belonged to the aristocracy, ever deemed it their duty to prohibit a meeting, because it was convoked for purposes hostile to their interests and their political passions. The rare examples of impediments offered to this right of holding meetings are considered as scandalous abuses, and stigmatised as acts of gross oppression.[3]

In 1792, at the moment when French democracy convulsed the world, Catholic Ireland was moved. Wearied of suffering in silence, the Irish people resolved to carry their sense of their wrongs and their desire for redress to the foot of the throne. In order that their wants should be clearly established, a general assembly was formed, in Dublin, of delegates from all the counties in Ireland; so that at the very moment when the constitutional parliament of Ireland, composed of lords and commons, held its sittings, and made laws for the country, another assembly, a kind of second parliament, was established in the same city, discussed all political questions, deliberated, adopted resolutions, published them, and was in fact the only national parliament.

What should the government do under such circumstances? Should it command a squadron of dragoons and a piece of artillery to disperse so dangerous an

---

1. The government, however, prosecuted Swift's printer.
2. Gordon's History of Ireland, vol. ii.
3. Interference on the part of the government is now rare.

assembly? No: this assembly, though dangerous, was not illegal; before forming it, those by whom it was convoked, investigated their right, and eminent lawyers declared that such a meeting was not contrary to the laws of the kingdom. And this was enough in a country distracted by party; those who had the law on their side tranquilly confided in their right, and though this right disquieted the government, it was respected.[4]

Who would believe it? At no period in Ireland has the principle of responsibility in the agents of power been set aside; and we find it remaining in full force in the midst of the most destructive troubles and revolutions. During the terrible crisis of 1798, a sheriff, grossly abusing his authority, caused a schoolmaster, named Wright, to be ignominiously flogged in Clonmell;[5] when the revolutionary tempest was passed, the sufferer brought his action in the ordinary courts of justice, and the sheriff's culpability having been recognised by the jury, he was condemned to pay five hundred pounds damages, and the costs of suit.[6]

The principle of a jury has never been contested in Ireland. Strafford, the greatest of tyrants, did not attempt to confiscate lands as forfeitures to the crown, without having recourse to the verdict of a jury, which he was not always able to obtain.[7]

In the breast of an English judge, notwithstanding political and religious prejudices, there are traditions of independence and respect for right, which are generally more powerful than his passions. Let us glance at the admirable scene in which Lord Kilwarden, chief justice of the King's Bench in Dublin, disputed with the government the custody of a political criminal condemned to death. In 1798, Wolfe Tone, the leader and creator of the united Irishmen, was taken in Lough Swilly, on board a French fleet conveying an army to invade Ireland: his crime was flagrant; he was taken with arms in his hand; he was bringing a foreign enemy into Ireland with the avowed object of breaking the English yoke, and proclaiming the country an independent republic. Dragged before a court-martial, he was condemned to death, and according to the rapid forms of military justice, was about to be executed on the spot. The remainder of the impressive narrative will be best told in the words of Tone's son and biographer.

"On the next day, 12th November, the scene in the court of King's Bench was awful and impressive in the highest degree. As soon as it opened, Curran advanced, leading the aged father of Tone, who produced his affidavit that his son had been brought before a bench of officers calling itself a court-martial, and sentenced to death."

---

4. Delegation was, however, prohibited by an act of parliament.
5. Wright had a note in his possession written in French; the sheriff was ignorant of the language, but he concluded that everything written in French must be treasonable.
6. He was subsequently reimbursed.
7. See Irish State Trials.

"I do not pretend," said Curran, "that Mr. Tone is not guilty of the charges of which he is accused. I presume the officers were honourable men. But it is stated in this affidavit, as a solemn fact, that Mr. Tone had no commission under his Majesty; and therefore no court-martial could have cognizance of any crime imputed to him, whilst the Court of King's Bench sat in the capacity of the great criminal court of the land. In time when war was raging, when man was opposed to man in the field, courts-martial might be endured; but every law authority is with me, whilst I stand upon this sacred and immutable principle of the constitution, that martial law and civil law are incompatible, and the former must cease with the existence of the latter. This is not, however, the time for arguing this momentous question. My client must appear in this court. He is cast for death this very day. He may be ordered for execution whilst I address you. I call on the court to support the law, and move for a habeas corpus, to be directed to the provost-marshal of the barracks of Dublin, and Major Sandys, to bring up the body of Tone."

Chief Justice—"Have a writ instantly prepared."

Curran—"My client may die, whilst the writ is preparing."

Chief Justice—"Mr. Sheriff, proceed to the barracks, and acquaint the provost-marshal that a writ is preparing to suspend Mr. Tone's execution, and see that he be not executed."

The court awaited, in a state of the utmost agitation and suspense, the return of the sheriff. He speedily appeared, and said, "My lord, I have been to the barracks in pursuance of your order. The provost-marshal says he must obey Major Sandys; Major Sandys says he must obey Lord Cornwallis."

Mr. Curran announced, at the same time, that Mr. Tone, the father, was just returned after serving the habeas corpus, and that General Craig would not obey it. The chief justice exclaimed, "Mr. Sheriff, take the body of Tone into custody; take the provost-marshal and Major Sandys into custody, and show the order of the court to General Craig."

The general impression was now, that the prisoner would be led out to execution in defiance of the court. This apprehension was legible in the countenance of Lord Kilwarden: a man who, in the worst of times, preserved a religious respect for the laws; and who, besides, I may add, felt every personal feeling of pity and respect for the prisoner, whom he had formerly contributed to shield from the vengeance of government on an occasion almost as perilous. His agitation, according to the expression of an eye-witness, was "magnificent."

The sheriff returned at length with the fatal news. He had been refused admittance into the barracks; but was informed that Mr. Tone, who had wounded himself dangerously the night before, was not in a condition to be removed. A French emigrant surgeon, who had closed the wound, was called in, and declared there was no saying, for four days, whether it was mortal. His head was to be kept in one position, and a sentinel was set over him to prevent his speaking. Removal would kill him at once. The chief justice instantly ordered a rule for suspending the execution."

Can any one say that all liberty is extinguished in a country where a judge, in spite of his passions, addresses such language to the agents of the executive power?

In times nearer our own, has not England been disquieted by storms gathering in Ireland, menaced by the political and religious associations formed in that country; and have we not seen the right to associate constantly respected?

Parliament, on certain occasions, has suppressed this or that association, but it has never attacked the principle of right to associate. When the Whiteboys covered Ireland with their terrible confederation, a law was passed, defining their association, and inflicting upon it the severest penalties: in the same way the parliament treated all the societies that succeeded the Whiteboys; and when the association, without being actually criminal, appeared dangerous, parliament was contented with enjoining its dissolution. But never has the English government been seen, under the pretext that criminal associations might be formed, attacking in its principle the right of subjects to associate, interdicting the use, through real or pretended fear, of the abuse, or, what is still worse, pretending to regulate the right by making its exercise depend on official authorisation, as if the imposition of a necessity for authorisation was not a virtual denial of the right.

But what is the use of liberty, if it does not prevent tyranny? Be assured that it is still of the highest use: though it does not prevent oppression, it fixes its limits; it is a weapon in the hands of the feeble, and if you see a people unhappy, though in possession of liberty, you may well believe that without such liberty it would be more unhappy still.

There is one circumstance which is too often forgotten. The miseries endured by a free people are known, because freedom publishes them: whilst in the countries of pure despotism, nothing is known of the sufferings of the people, for the tyrant conceals them with the more care, as they are the more frightful.

We should reject the most authentic evidence of history, were we not to recognise how much English domination in Ireland has been fettered and controlled by the free institutions given to that country. Perhaps there will be some persons who, seeing the English embarrassed in their persecutions by the rights given to the oppressed, will be of opinion that the persecutors were ill advised to create such obstacles for themselves. It is sad, I grant, for the friends of despotism to encounter liberties even amongst an enslaved people; there is doubtless cause for their surprise and chagrin. For my part, I deem this voluntary or instinctive sentiment noble, which disposes the oppressor to give his victim guarantees beforehand, and thus affix limits to his own tyranny.

These free forms, not useless for the present, will also be the source of safety for the future. The Great Charter, it is true, did not prevent the Tudors from establishing despotism in England; but when at length the English people, wearied of their despots, aspired to deliver themselves, they found all the resources of a free government ready prepared to their hands. It is thus that under the yoke of tyranny everything may be made ready for liberty, in the same way as it may happen that under a mild and free government everything may be prepared for servitude.

The jury, the press, the right of associating, responsibility of the agents of government, and the *habeas corpus*, are found in Ireland amid many arbitrary and oppressive acts; but is it not to these rights, always preserved, that Ireland is indebted for her daily conquest of the rights which are still wanting?

Ireland is doubtless very miserable, but she is farther advanced than is generally supposed in constitutional knowledge. There are many political questions still doubtful to many in France, which in Ireland would embarrass nobody. Never, for instance, in that country, would a person have a notion of demanding a political right without claiming a guarantee. Other countries more fortunate are less enlightened. Ireland resembles some invaded country, which, after a dreadful national struggle, has succeeded in expelling the strangers from its soil: it has learned all the arts of war and victory, but the land is covered with devastation and ruin: it is independent, but it is poor.

The poverty of Ireland did not vanish as its liberties were consolidated and increased. On the contrary, it would seem that, as the Irishman acquired political rights, his social misery was increased in the same proportion. It is certain that Irishmen have never been so free as at the present moment, and it is equally certain that they have never been so miserable.

It is a terrible truth, the proofs of which are abundant, that Irish landlords have never been so severe to the tenants and labourers on their estates as they are at the present moment. This is easily explained: when the Irish peasants were placed by law in an inferior condition, the rich treated them nearly as a master does his slaves, whom he oppresses sufficiently to let them feel the yoke, but to whom he allows so much liberty as will enable them to enrich him by their toil. But this calculation, formerly made by the Irish landlord, is at present overcome by passion. Since his power has been contested, and the slave presents himself as a free man, the desire of again abasing him prevails over the interest of profiting by him. The small farmer, formerly deprived of political rights, is now an elector; he has been recently allowed to send Catholics to parliament; he votes at elections against his landlord; it is his right; but on his side, the landlord has a right to eject the tenant from his farm, and of this right he makes the most rigorous use.[8]

---

8. See Lord Lorton's Letters.

We do not now see two or three Protestants assemble in vestry to tax the Catholic population for the support of a form of worship which, as it only interests them, they should maintain themselves; but these two or three Protestants, the chief landed proprietors of the parish, wishing to lighten the burden which must henceforth fall upon them, eject Catholic tenants, and put Protestants in their place, who may support with them the expenses of public worship.

We have seen that there is a war between the rich and the poor, the governors and the governed; now, the more strength the poor acquire, the greater are the fear and irritation of the rich. Oppressive laws are abolished, but the oppressor still remains; and in his rage for being despoiled, after having been so long the spoiler, he makes a terrible use of the powers which he derives from common rights. The situation of the rich is quite extraordinary,—no longer making the laws with whose administration they are charged; and this is one of the causes of their continually increasing rigour. Every new law conceived in a spirit more tolerant towards the Catholics, and more liberal towards the poor, appears to them an attack upon their authority as well as upon their creed, and therefore they make a more rigid use of the powers which they still retain. This disposition explains how it is that, with more liberty, the poor Irishman suffers perhaps more persecution; and how, whilst the country becomes richer, the cultivator becomes poorer. The land produces twice as much as it did fifty years ago, and the agriculturist is twice as miserable. Are we to conclude that the present condition of the Irish is worse than what it was fifty years ago? No. The miseries they experience are those which war brings in its train; they suffer, because they are in actual combat; but the struggle displays their strength, and I cannot bestow much pity on the slave wounded in the action that establishes his freedom.

And if, after having escaped political oppression, Ireland ever succeeds in rescuing itself from social misery, is it not to its liberties that it will primarily owe its success? Who can dispute the benefits which Ireland derives at this moment from the freedom of the press alone? What but the press has brought into open day the vices of its social and political condition,—the press, whose voice, powerful even to deceive, is so strong when it is the organ of justice and of truth? Is it not the press that has unveiled in the Irish government and the Irish aristocracy excesses and iniquities which could only be perpetrated in darkness, but which its brilliant light has doomed to perish? Every day it reveals the evils of Ireland, which were not less unknown to England than the rest of the world; every day its merciless publicity proclaims them; and after having displayed in the eyes of the master the hideous wounds of the slave, it demands a reckoning for the still more hideous wounds of the freeman; and now that they are exposed, they must be cured. How is this to be done? I know not; but the attempt must be made, for their enormity demands a remedy.

VII

An Examination of the Causes by Which Ireland, at Present a Free Country, Tends to Become a Democratic Country

In their resistance to political oppression, the Irish have triumphed. Now that they have learned the secret of their strength, will they limit themselves to defence? Will they not become assailants in their turn? Hitherto they have struggled that the guarantees of the English constitution should be honestly granted them; but if it be true that the aristocratic institutions which content England cannot satisfy Ireland, will not the latter use the liberties belonging to the aristocracy to attack the aristocracy itself? That is to say, by the aid of institutions which were wanting, and which Ireland has conquered, she will have the power to reject institutions which she possesses, but which she does not wish to keep. The future is veiled from our eyes, but the past and the present are before us, which exhibit to us the most terrific storms gathering over the head of this aristocracy, the source of all the miseries of Ireland. And the perils that menace the Irish aristocracy do not arise simply from the fact that Ireland has reconquered its liberties, but that a certain assemblage of facts, principles, and accidents, combines to render this free society a democratic society. What are these facts, principles, and accidents? Some present themselves of their own accord.

The first is the great national association; the second, the authority of one great chief, O'Connell; the third, the power of the Catholic clergy; the fourth, the character of the Presbyterian sect; the fifth is the growth of the middle classes; and sixth and last, the nature of political parties.

Section I. The Association

For every nation, as for every individual, held in slavery, there are two possible moral states,—discouragement or hope, despondency or energy, submission or revolt. So long as the slave is not brutalised, he ardently aspires to break his chains; if he does not make the effort, it is because he is crushed by the weight of his fetters, and rendered incapable of effort; but from the day when his loosened bonds permit him to move, we may be assured that he struggles for freedom. The happiness of slaves has always appeared to me an odious lie and a cruel mockery. I esteem my fellow men too highly to believe in the happiness of the nation, or individual, that is tranquil in fetters.

Until 1775, Ireland was in the situation of the motionless slave beaten down or degraded; at this moment, "a voice from America shouted to liberty," which stirred the captive in his chains, and the master in his tyranny. I have already described the circumstances of this popular awakening, and especially the great assembly of the volunteers in 1778, the first association that was formed in Ireland. The struggle in which the volunteers engaged, and which produced the parliamentary independence of 1782, was not, however, national; it was a quarrel between the Irish aristocracy and the English government. The Irish aristocracy, which, during a century, had been at the same time a slave and a tyrant, had habituated itself to tyranny without becoming accustomed to servitude, and, whilst continuing to oppress Ireland, it wished to throw off the yoke of England. Its triumph was at first brilliant; but it saw not that, in enfranchising itself, it set a pernicious example to its own subjects; it did not understand that, in employing them to fight its master, it taught them to turn their arms against itself. America instructed Protestant Ireland; that in its turn taught Catholic Ireland; besides, it was the time when revolutionary France proclaimed liberty to the world with a voice of thunder.

In 1792, the Irish people for the first time appeared on the stage in opposition to its two tyrants,—the Anglican faction established in Ireland, and England the support of that faction. This was the movement of the *United Irishmen,* the Catholics of the south, and the Presbyterians of the north, *united* more in their designs than their principle: more honest than rational in their alliance; it was the first truly national association, though still very imperfect; composed of the most heterogeneous elements, a medley of Puritan and of Popish passions, of Utopian philosophy and religious fanaticism, of American liberalism and French jacobinism; resting only on one common base, hatred of the English yoke, and desire for national independence,—a noble association, but ill defined, unsteady in its plans, vacillating in its progress, torn by a thousand intestine divisions, ready to make false estimates of its strength, and cherishing the illusions which terminated in the fatal insurrection of 1798.

Warned by this terrible effort for freedom, and arming itself against their rebellious subjects by the excesses which they had committed while wandering in the unknown, the two masters of Ireland forgot their mutual quarrel, and united, to separate no more. The Irish union of 1800 was far less a union between England and Ireland, than an alliance between the English party and the Protestant faction, which, being no longer able to govern Ireland, threw itself into the arms of the master whose detested yoke it had shaken off twenty years before, and abandoned all the instruments of power and persecution, on condition of being allowed to retain its tyranny as in times past.

Twenty years of silent oppression were the price of this reciprocal engagement. But, during the struggle between its masters, Ireland had conquered too many rights, and in its unfortunate efforts for deliverance it had gained too many useful lessons, to remain for ever passive and mute in slavery.

It was a second time in association that Ireland found the secret of its strength, and the hope of its freedom. About the year 1823, the Catholic Association was established in Dublin on a new plan, and according to new principles.[1] The volunteers of 1782, the United Irishmen of 1792, were armed bodies ready to fight a battle, rather than associations formed by citizens for the defence of their rights. The first of these bodies, almost exclusively Protestant, could not represent Catholic Ireland; the second, in which persons of every religious denomination were mingled, had ended in terrifying everybody by its revolutionary tendencies and manifestos. The new association, established for the purpose of effecting progress without violence, agitation without war, resistance without revolution, attracted into its bosom all the instincts and all the desires of independence that Ireland still possessed.

When the government of a country is rooted in a nation, if popular storms are raised against it, we may be assured of seeing it supported by a part of the nation, more or less considerable. Thus, when the aristocracy is attacked in England, finding amongst the people ardent and numerous auxiliaries, it doubts if it does not govern according to the wishes of the greater number; there are, to be sure, still powerful oppositions, but these are only parties in the presence of a government which is, or seems to be, the true representative of the country. It is far different amongst a people subject to an antinational authority. Thus, in Ireland, where the aristocracy is the enemy of the people, nobody resists whilst the government is strong: but the moment when opposition is free to declare itself, the hostility is universal, and the governing power, abandoned on all sides, falls into complete isolation. The opposition is then the nation, and the government a party or a faction. Such an opposition in the present day is the great Irish association.

But how can the government maintain its influence over an entire nation leagued against it? The difficulty is great, and, to comprehend its full extent, it is necessary to know all the democratic elements in the national association of Ireland. I therefore deem it necessary in this place to explain its plan, and indicate its character.

I am not sure that I have exactly caught its spirit and purport, but, in case of

---

1. By O'Connell and Shiel.

error, I cannot have recourse to the secrets and mysteries of this association, for all its operations were transacted in the face of day, and thus open to the judgment of all.

A central committee sitting in Dublin, and composed of members whose mode of election varied according to circumstances, represents the association, and adopts the measures deemed useful to the common cause.[2] This committee assembles regularly, examines the laws proposed to parliament, discusses them, censures the acts of power and its agents, adopts resolutions, publishes them,— in a word, acts like a real parliament, wanting only the regular power of making laws obligatory on all. The association has a journal, which publishes its acts and decrees.[3]

Like all established governments, the association receives a tribute in return for the protection it affords; the amount varies; it is levied in different forms, but it is always sure to be paid. In 1825, the tax paid by each member of the association (the Catholic rent) was a penny per month, a trifling sum, but sufficient to establish a contract of authority and obedience between those who received and those who paid. The association had collectors to receive the rent, which was the more regularly paid as it was voluntary. At present, the association does not send round collectors, the contributions are paid in the form of individual subscriptions; a mere change of form, rendered necessary by the laws with which government from time to time has assailed the association. Thus, for instance, at first the members of the central committee were elected by the entire people; every barony sent to the capital of the county a certain number of electors, who named one or more deputies to represent the county in the central committee; so that the leaders of the association were in substance and form delegated by the country. This form of electors was practised in 1792, but was prohibited by an act of parliament *(the Convention Act.)* This, however, did not prevent the association, in 1811 and 1825, from employing the same mode in the choice of representatives. But the decision of a jury in 1811, and a new act of parliament in 1825, (called the *Algerine Act,*) having dissolved the committee of the association, and the association itself as illegal;[4] it was necessary to have recourse to a different form of organisation: at present, the association has no chiefs regularly constituted. Every assembly of the association is a separate meeting, which everybody may attend, the chairman of which is chosen every time by the majority of votes, and in which every person has a right to declare his sentiments.

But whatever may be the form, the substance is always the same; the name of the association varies, but there is no alteration in the elements of which it is

---

2. The proceedings of the committee are not always recognised by the general body.
3. The Pilot.
4. This was deemed an essential part of the measure of emancipation, which it was supposed would have passed at the same time.

composed. In 1823, it was called the Catholic Association, not because Protestants were excluded,—on the contrary, a great number belonged to it,—but because then the great object was to obtain from England the emancipation of the Irish Catholics. When the association was dissolved by parliament in 1825, it was soon re-formed under another name; in 1837 and 1838, it was called the General Association of Ireland; whilst I write it has taken the name of the Precursors' Society; and in a recent speech, O'Connell announces that it will soon be called the National Association.5 Under these various denominations it is always the same, that is to say, the real representative of the great body of the nation.

It is under this title that it commands Ireland, and is obeyed. At its summons, all the parishes of Ireland assemble; societies are formed in baronies and counties, in every place where the citizens are required to move: at the same day, and the same hour, all Ireland is up, occupied by the same object, influenced by the same passions, pursuing the same end. The purpose is to prepare a petition to parliament, but what would be the result if, instead of asking for petitions, the association demanded bayonets?

The association, formed by popular sympathies, has become every day more powerful by its victories. The famous election of Clare, emancipation in 1829, the revolt against tithes in 1831, the triumphs of the popular candidates at elections, are its undisputed works. Every one is more obedient in proportion as it gives proof of its strength and skill.

The association has made itself the patron of all the citizens; it stimulates and receives the complaints of every one who has a grievance against the public authority, against the ministers of the Church of England, and especially against magistrates belonging to the aristocracy. Since the association has covered the country with its shield, there is not in Ireland a poor peasant so weak or so isolated who has not the support of the entire body of the nation against the most rich and the most powerful oppression. Is the cupidity of any Protestant minister harsh and rigid in the collection of his tithes represented to this body,—the association stigmatises him with public censure; and the fate of those marked out in Ireland for public hatred is sufficiently known. Has the poor man who owed the tithe been thrown into prison for non-payment,—the association raises the funds necessary to obtain his liberty. Whoever resists the payment of tithe, receives from it a moral and physical support. Once, in 1837, it received with loud acclamations a man sufficiently rich to pay his tithes, but who allowed himself to be dragged to prison rather than obey the law.6

But it is especially at the approach of an election that the association displays

---

5. This measure may, however, be abandoned; its relinquishment is very desirable.
6. It also honoured freeholders who voted against their landlords.

its power. Its first care is bestowed on the registries, and it defrays the expenses of registration when the electors are poor; and it objects to orangemen who have been unduly registered. When the day of election arrives, it issues proclamations to the people, to teach them their duties and their rights; it declares the reforms necessary to the safety of the country, and the pledges that should be demanded from every candidate for their suffrages; it loudly proclaims the names of those who alone have a right to popular confidence, tells each locality the representative that it ought to elect, his singular merits, his rare talents, his uncommon virtues; and not less openly declares the vices, servility, and incapacity of his rival. When the election is over, the association celebrates its victories, if it has triumphed, and, in case of a reverse, palliates its defeat. But its electoral labours have not yet terminated; it publicly decrees praise to the citizens, formerly enemies, who have become friends in the late contest; and at the same time it mercilessly stigmatises unexpected desertions. It particularly applies itself to watch the conduct of the aristocracy: if a poor tenant is ejected for having voted against his landlord, the association comes to his aid, gives him an indemnity, and holds up the name of the landlord to general censure. It sometimes does more: at the Longford election in 1836, an unfortunate elector, who was in prison for debt, received from his landlord, who was also his creditor, the promise of being set at liberty if he would vote for the Tory candidate. The poor peasant, brought from his prison to the hustings, was, perhaps, about to yield to the seduction, when, at the moment he was about to vote, his wife exclaimed, "Remember your soul and liberty!" The poor peasant having voted according to his conscience, returned to prison. In a solemn sitting the association voted a silver medal to this heroic female, on which her noble address was inscribed, *"Remember your soul and liberty!"*

It is one of the peculiar characters of the association, that it not only keeps a watch upon the government, but exercises the functions of government itself. It founds schools and charitable establishments, levies taxes for their support, protects commerce, aids industry, and performs a thousand other acts; for as its powers are nowhere defined, its limits are not marked.

In truth, the association is a government within a government; a young and robust authority, springing up within the breast of an authority aged, feeble, and decrepit: a centralised national power which grinds to powder all the scattered and petty power of an antinational aristocracy. It is not exact to say, that the association annihilates the aristocratic government of Ireland; for how can the name of government be given to the domination of a faction which can only maintain itself by the aid of foreign and physical force?

In a country where legitimate and regular powers existed, the establishment of such an association, if it could be formed, would be the very organisation of anarchy. In Ireland this association may become the principle and means of a political revolution, but in the mean time it is the most powerful social element that exists in the country.

Before the Irish association was constituted, the Irish sincerely thought that no temporal power merited obedience and respect, because it believed all human authority wicked and tyrannical. The association, which, be it remembered, governs Ireland, while subjecting the country to its power, and granting it protection, has taught that authority may be beneficent.

It is to the association that the Irish people owes its abandonment of the traditions of savage independence, and the adoption of social and regular habits. What a strange circumstance! The association which leads Ireland is the most factious of all powers; a day does not pass without its stimulating the people to violate some law; it prescribes to them as a civil duty the refusal of tithes, which are demanded by the constitution; it devotes to public contempt and hatred the municipal corporations, which, nevertheless, are legally constituted bodies; it similarly assails the Anglican church, which is the principal institution of the country, and the aristocracy, the actual depository of the administrative authority; and, nevertheless, I repeat that the association gave the Irish people their first notions of right and legality. Before the association existed, and, consequently, before its counsels were heard, the people felt the same sentiments of hate against all that they are now recommended to hate; but the people were then blind and cruel in their resentments. The association did not change the inmost feelings of the popular mind; it left there all the hates which it deemed legitimate, and this has been the cause of its strength; it has enlightened those passions, it has taught the people not to stifle but to restrain them. The association has softened the popular propensities, and pointed out mild, peaceful, and strictly legal means to the popular passions, instead of the violent and criminal means to which the lower orders were accustomed to have recourse. It has taught the people to receive superior direction, and accept the empire of an authority entirely moral, in place of the gibbet, the only social power in which it formerly had faith. The association has not subjected the people to the rules of the law, but to a rule; and thus an element of order has arisen from disorder itself.

"I have been struck," exclaimed a stout peasant, who could have annihilated his adversary with a blow, at the Waterford election.—"Why didn't you return the blow," said some one. "I thought that the association had forbidden it, or else—." Just before the Clare election, the association forbade the use of whisky during the contest, and not a drop of intoxicating liquor was tasted by any of the people.

The association has not the power to prevent Whiteboyism, which is connected with social rather than political causes; but though it does not destroy it limits the system, combats it openly, disavows it, and prevents political passions from taking its direction and seeking such an auxiliary.

Before the association came into existence, twenty Irishmen could not get together without some quarrel or outrage arising from their meeting: at the voice of the association tens and hundreds of thousands assembled peaceably on the same spot, and with the perfect order of a disciplined army, without the least dispute, or the slightest excess; and by these solemn demonstrations of a tranquil but menacing force taught England what she ought to think of barbarous Ireland.

But what appears to me most grave and worthy of attention in the Irish association, is the deep democratic character in this government of a people by one central power emanating from the universal will, expressed or understood; collecting within itself all the national elements; omnipotent by popular assent; absolute in every one of its actions, though constantly subjected to the control of all; levelling all above it, summoning to its bar all the aristocratic powers of the nation; thus accustoming the people to social and political equality; a power fluctuating and varying, though perpetual, incessantly changing its name, form, and agents, though always the same; that is to say, a democracy organised in a country supposed to be governed by aristocratic institutions.

Section II. O'Connell

The movement of the association is that of all Ireland; but this great work of the nation has special agents, and it possesses one so eminent and so celebrated, that I cannot pass him over in silence: I mean O'Connell. If the association guides Ireland, O'Connell rules the association. O'Connell exercises so extraordinary an influence over his country, and over England itself, that to omit him would be to neglect something more than a man, and almost a principle. It seems necessary, therefore, in order to give some details respecting him, that I should digress for an instant from the regular course of ideas with which I am engaged, but to which I shall be naturally brought back by this subject.

Every day, in our age, great men become more scarce; not because less great things are effected than of old time; but whatever great deed is now effected by the people, is the work not of one man, but of several, and in proportion as many agents contribute to a work, the glory of each individual agent is diminished. When in any country I do not find any single man elevated above his fellows, I do not conclude that all the men of this country are mean; I should rather infer, that they have all a certain degree of greatness. Nowhere are great individualities more rare than in a country of general equality. Look at the United States; where will you find the common level so high with so few individual prominences? Ireland, with its immense miseries, its contrasts of luxury and indigence, with its large masses animated by homogeneous passions, was perhaps the soil best prepared to nurture the glory of a single man.

Is not the power of O'Connell one of the most extraordinary that can be conceived? Here is a man who exercises a sort of dictatorship over seven millions; he directs the affairs of his country almost alone; he gives advice which is obeyed as a command, and this man has never been invested with any civil authority or military power. I do not know if, in the history of nations, a single example of such a destiny could be found: examine, from Cæsar to Napoleon, the men who have ruled over nations by their genius or their virtue, how many will you find who, to establish their power, did not first possess the majesty of civil station, or the glory of arms? Would the name of Washington have reached us if that great man had not been a warrior before he became a legislator? What would Mirabeau have been without the *tribune* of the constituent assembly; or Burke, Pitt, and Fox, without their seat in the British parliament? O'Connell is, indeed, a member of the British parliament, but his great power goes back to a time when he was not so—it dates from the famous election of Clare; it is not parliament that has given him strength; it is on account of his strength that he is in parliament.

What, then, is the secret of this power obtained without any of the means which are usually its only source? To comprehend the singular fortune of this man, it is necessary to go back to the political situation which was its starting point, and which is still its foundation.

After the fatal catastrophe of 1798, Ireland, cloven down, expiring under the feet of England, who crushed her without mercy, believed that henceforward she should renounce all hope of obtaining by arms the blessings, for the conquest of which she had so fatally revolted. She was then in the strange position of a nation, which, possessing some political rights, is menaced with their loss for having attempted to obtain by force those rights which were wanting; which, by an imprudent zeal to obtain complete independence, risks falling into complete slavery, and which, for the future, had no chance of obtaining new liberties, save contenting itself with those it possessed, and no longer disputing the rights of its master. Finally, after the union in 1800, it was more closely linked to England, which, holding Ireland as a rebellious slave, was greatly tempted to punish her, but could not do so without violating the engagements and guarantees, respect for which is so strongly inculcated by the British constitution.

In this conjuncture, what was necessary to Ireland? It wanted not a general fit to lead an army, but a citizen capable of directing a people; it wanted a man whose ascendency could be established by peaceable means, fit to gain the confidence of Ireland, without, in the first instance, giving alarm to England; who, deeply impressed with the state of the country, comprehending equally its necessities and its perils, would have the great art of devoting himself entirely to the one, and incessantly avoid the other; a lawyer sufficiently skilful to distinguish what had been repealed in the code of tyranny, and what still remained in force—an orator sufficiently powerful to excite the ardent passions of the people against, and sufficiently wise to check their zeal when it verged on insurrection—a clever pleader, as well as a fiery tribune, employed in keeping awake at the same time the anger and the prudence of the people; impetuous enough to excite, strong enough to restrain, capable of managing at will a public assembly, stimulating or soothing popular passion; and who, having taught the people to hate the laws without violating them, was also able, when excesses were committed, to defend them at law, to excuse the authors, and to fascinate a jury as if it were a popular assembly. Ireland wanted a man who, while he bestowed his whole heart on her, did not cease to keep his eyes fixed on England, knew how to behave with the master as well as the slave, to stimulate the one without alarming the other, to press forward the progress of the former without troubling the security of the latter; who, strong in existing institutions, made them his shield for defence, and his sword for attack; showed how one right summoned another right, one liberty another liberty; imprinted on the heart of every Irishman the deep conviction, that his want of independence exposed him to the severest tyranny, but was sufficient to conquer his complete emancipation; and after having thus disciplined Ireland, could one day present her to England as a nation *constitutionally insurgent*, agitated but not rebellious, standing up as one man, resolved not to sit down again until justice had been done. This man, for whom Ireland called, was revealed to her in 1810; it was Daniel O'Connell.[7] He could not appear sooner or later; for his production a country was required already free, and yet still a slave: there was wanting sufficient oppression to render authority odious, and sufficient liberty for the tribune of the people to be heard; there was wanting that singular accident of a tyranny supported by law, to give such empire to a man familiar with the laws, and who, from their skilful interpretation, could derive the liberty of the people and the independence of his country. Had O'Connell come fifty years before, he would probably have perished on the scaffold; half a century later, his voice would not be listened to in a country that had become more free and more prosperous.

Doubtless a providential interference assured to Ireland some great interpreter for her great misfortunes; but it was a fortunate accident for her that she met one so extraordinary as O'Connell. I am not one of those who believe that Ireland owes her being roused from slavery to O'Connell alone. No; the passions, the inclinations, the destiny of an entire people, do not belong to a single man. No; it is not granted to a single individual, whatever may be his genius and his power, to be everything for his country. The great men who seem to conduct

---

7. O'Connell succeeded Keogh.

the age very often only give it expression; it is believed that they lead the world, they only comprehend it; they have perceived the necessities of which they constitute themselves the defenders, and divined the passions of which they make themselves the organs. We are astonished, when they speak, that their voice sounds so loud, and do not reflect that their voice is not that of a man, but of a people. If O'Connell and the secret of his power be studied closely, it will be seen that his principal merit is having undertaken the defence of seven millions who were suffering, and whose misery was an injustice. It is pleasant to think that resistance to iniquity is so noble a source of glory. But if O'Connell has not created emancipated Catholic Ireland, what other person could so well have represented it? If he has not alone imprinted on Ireland the great movement which has stirred it so deeply, and still agitates it, how can it be denied that he has prodigiously hastened and developed it? He has not, it is true, forged the weapons of liberty that Ireland possesses, but who could have wielded them so well as he has done? Who, in the presence of the necessities of Ireland, would have studied them so wisely, embraced with such profound intelligence, and employed in their service such vast powers of mind?

I have said that the interests of Ireland required a *constitutional war*, a peace incessantly agitated, an intermediate state between the rule of the laws and insurrection.

Consider with what art O'Connell organised the plan of this association, which was to become the mistress of Ireland, and had to be formed in the midst of laws designed to prevent its birth. It is at present confessed by all, that the Irish association owed its life and its daily preservation only to the sagacity of O'Connell, who having preserved it in the cradle from the attacks of the laws then in force, protected it subsequently from the new laws by which it was incessantly menaced, and finally extorted from his adversaries the confession, that "it was very easy to talk about arresting Mr. O'Connell, and bringing him to trial, but the difficulty was to catch him tripping, and to find a law which he could be formally accused of violating."[8] Finally, the association triumphed over all attacks; it was predominant; O'Connell became its leader; and what a leader! —what zeal!—what prudence!—what impetuous wisdom!—what fertility of expedients!—what variety of means!

Look at O'Connell when he appeared in 1825 before a committee of the House of Commons for investigating the state of Ireland; you must admire the lucid simplicity, the ingenuous candour, with which he explained the rigours that then pressed upon Catholic Ireland; not mingling a single word of bitterness with his recitals, speaking only of peace, union, and harmony, assuring his hearers that when once parliamentary emancipation had been granted, Protes-

---

8. This was said by Mr. Plunkett, then Attorney-General, now Lord Plunkett.

tants and Catholics, hitherto divided amongst themselves, but not enemies, would love each other like brethren; answering all objections, declaring all grievances, indicating a remedy for all evils, not leaving a single one of the miseries of Ireland in obscurity, nor one of its persecutions, and pronouncing, in the midst of a thousand designed snares and a thousand inevitable interruptions, if not the finest, at least the most useful appeal that was ever made on the part of an oppressed people.[9]

But this timid and modest man, who held such conciliating language before a committee of the English parliament, was the same whose formidable voice echoed through the county of Clare, and said to the people,[10] "The law forbids you to send a Catholic to parliament! Well, I am a Catholic—nominate me." This man, so recently moderate and calm, appeals to all the passions of the people, rouses all their sympathies, excites their most ardent enthusiasm, breaks with one blow the bonds by which the aristocracy held their dependents in subjection, separates Catholic from Protestant, tenant from landlord, servant from master, procures every vote, and leaves in profound and unforeseen isolation this aristocracy, quite stupified by the audacity and success of its enemy.[11]

The principal arms used by O'Connell in this constitutional war, of which he is the leader, are his speeches in parliament, the association, and meetings, his election addresses, and his letters in the newspapers. His parliamentary labours engage him half of the year; he speaks on almost every occasion of public importance; when parliament is closed, he opens the sessions of the association, and supports the principal toil of debate; and yet these are not sufficient aliment for his inconceivable activity. Meetings, which, in Ireland as in England, are held for almost every purpose, and in which O'Connell rules, because he excels there, cannot satiate the thirst for action by which he is consumed. He never allows an opportunity to escape of declaring his opinion to the people, and exercising his power. Is there a general election? O'Connell directs it almost as a sovereign. He says to a constituency, "Vote for such a candidate;" to another, "Do not return such a one," and he is always obeyed. Informed that an election is doubtful in the north, he hastes thither, raises his voice, all-powerful with the Irish multitude, and ensures the triumph of the candidate he has supported; thence, without a moment's repose, he speeds to the south, where he has learned that another election is perilled; he fascinates and binds his hearers with a spell, procures the election of his son, his son-in-law, or some of his friends, and, resuming his journey as he steps down from the hustings, he arrives in Dublin

---

9. See Parliamentary Report on the State of Ireland, 1825.

10. This step was suggested by the late Mr. Leader.

11. The representation of the Irish counties has been almost wholly wrested from the landlords.

precisely at the hour the association is sitting, in the midst of which his voice is heard more fresh and sonorous than ever. O'Connell is endowed with indefatigable ardour; when he has not occasion to act, he speaks; if he does not speak, he writes; his acts, words, and writings, are all directed to one common object—the people, and attain their end by the same way—publicity. There is scarcely a single day in the whole year that the press does not publish a resolution, a speech, or a letter, from O'Connell.

What distinguishes O'Connell is not the splendour of any particular quality; it is rather the assemblage of several common qualities, whose union is singularly rare. It would not be difficult to find a more eloquent orator, a more skilful man of business, or a more distinguished writer; but the more brilliant orator could not manage public affairs; the man of business could not write; the superior writer could neither speak nor act. O'Connell, who probably would never have become distinguished by his writings, his speeches, or his political actions, taken separately, is at present the most illustrious of his contemporaries, because he is capable, though in a secondary degree, of all three at the same time. It is, however, only just to say that O'Connell was superior at the bar, and that in popular assemblies he is without a rival.

There is in O'Connell's fortune something still more surprising than its origin, and the means by which it was established,—that is, the duration of his power, a power entirely founded on the frail base of popular favour. Men may be seen who are great for a day, the heroes of a brilliant deed, the expression of some considerable event accomplished by them, or by the nation whose efforts they direct, and whose power usually vanishes with the great circumstance of which they are the representative; but what we find nowhere else is the continued empire of a single man, who during twenty years has reigned over his country without any title, save popular assent, every day required, and every day given. This is, perhaps, the greatest and most glorious of all existences, but it is also the most laborious. The life of O'Connell is one perpetual enterprise, a never ending combat. Were he to abstain from writing, speaking, or acting, for a single day, his power would instantly crumble into dust. The man, whom his country has invested with the supreme magistracy, continues strong, and is obeyed; after he has become president or king, he may remain so in complete inactivity. But O'Connell at rest is nothing; his power is only maintained on the condition of incessant action; hence that feverish agitation by which he is distinguished, and which, it must be said, is the source of his happiness as well as his glory, for repose is inconsistent with his indefatigable nature.

If it be easy to conceive how continuous efforts are necessary to perpetuate this power, which dies and is born again every day, it is far less easy to comprehend how the person, to whom the necessity of incessant action is imperatively prescribed, should always find abundant elements of action ready to his hand.

O'Connell excels as much in their discovery as in their management. Scarcely is one grievance of Ireland removed, when his vigilant eye discovers a new grievance, which is to become the text of his complaints; his tact in divining and anticipating the popular passions is quite marvellous; it is not that he forms thought differently from the rest of the world, but he thinks quicker, and he says what everybody was going to say. Of all his faculties, the most eminent, no doubt, is the good sense with which he is endowed, by the aid of which he measures a difficulty at a glance, sees at once the best course to adopt, and judges so surely of the present, that no one is so close to the future. Such profound intelligence is clearly genius, and, of all forms of genius, the most beneficial to the people, when selfishness does not corrupt it at its source.

Many represent O'Connell in the character of an ardent and devout Catholic, excited by fanaticism to the defence of liberty. To judge how far this opinion is true, we should be able to read the interior of hearts, a power that belongs to God alone. Still, if it were permitted to hazard a judgment on the most impenetrable secrets of the soul, I would say that in this respect O'Connell displays more good sense than passion, more intelligence than faith. O'Connell speaks to Ireland the only language that Ireland comprehends; he judges Ireland too well not to know that nothing can be done except by the influence of Catholicism; and he would probably be an ardent Catholic from calculation, were he not so from religious faith.

Others, who only regard O'Connell in his political life, ask whether he plays a part, or acts from conviction. It is a doubt that seems very difficult to be admitted. There is not a mere hired advocate who, after having pleaded for some hours, well or ill, the worst of causes for the worst of clients, does not become almost convinced of the sanctity of his cause, and is roused to zeal, and sometimes even to disinterestedness; and is it asked, if there be good faith and sincere devotedness in a man who for thirty years has defended the same cause—the cause of an entire people of a country which is his own,—a cause to which he has devoted all his life, and to which he owes all his glory,—the most equitable cause that has ever existed, and which he would believe just, even if it were not really so?

O'Connell is exposed to attacks which, if not better merited, are more easily understood. The declared partisans of passive obedience cannot pardon his liberal proceedings and his revolutionary tendencies; and those who regard an armed insurrection as the only remedy for the misery of the people, impute to him all the evils of Ireland, which suffers without revolting. It is plain that O'Connell's conduct cannot satisfy these classes. There is in the political principle which serves him as a guide in that intermediate doctrine between respect for the laws and aggression, a mixture that renders his character difficult of explanation, making O'Connell at one time a loyal subject, at another a factious partisan; one day humbled before the sovereign, the next, sovereign himself in some public meeting, half demagogue, half priest. To understand O'Connell, his character must be examined in this double point of view at the same time. O'Connell is neither a member of a pure parliamentary opposition, nor a revolutionist; he is one or the other in turn, according to circumstances. His principle in this matter is formed by events; all consists in obeying or resisting with discernment. O'Connell, whose good sense always masters his passions, never aims but at that which is possible. Does he find public opinion cold on the subject of reform, he will pursue parliamentary reform with no weapons but those of pure logic and reason. On the contrary, if a subject be agitated which excites popular passions, and in which the nation feels a deep interest, O'Connell no longer limits himself to a reasoning; he acts. He no longer simply invokes a principle; he makes an appeal to physical strength. Thus, in the time preceding emancipation in 1829, he had all Ireland on foot; thus, in 1831, he raised the entire country against the payment of tithes; observe, he raised, but did not arm it; he displayed menacing preparations, and waited until irritated power, by attacking him, would give him the privileges and advantages of defence. O'Connell knows wondrously the advantage to be derived from the shelter of law, and how far violence may be pushed without passing its limits; he deems it a folly for a people possessing liberties to abandon those potent arms, whose usage is legal and exempt from danger, to have recourse to insurrection, whose employment is so dangerous, and whose result is so uncertain. If O'Connell thought that a fair, open revolt would succeed, and render Ireland free and happy, he would assuredly become a revolutionist. He would have applauded the movement of the volunteers in 1778; but I doubt whether, in 1792, he would have engaged in the more national movement of the United Irishmen. O'Connell has his soul and his memory stored with all the miseries that violent efforts for independence have brought upon Ireland; hence his constant effort to create what he calls *constitutional agitation;* that undecided system between peace and war, between submission and revolt, between legal opposition and revolt,—a system which, without doubt, does not confer on the people the benefits of a sudden and prosperous revolution, but which also does not expose the country to the awful responsibilities of an unsuccessful insurrection.

But whether O'Connell be considered as an ardent sectary or as the great leader of a party, a politician or an enthusiast, a parliamentary orator or a revolutionist, in every case we are obliged to recognise his extraordinary power; and what is especially remarkable in this power is, that it is essentially democratic. O'Connell is naturally, and by the mere fact of his political position in Ireland, the enemy of the aristocracy; he could not be the man of the Irish and Catholic people without being the adversary of the Anglican oligarchy. Perhaps in no country is the representative of popular interests and passions so necessarily the fierce enemy of the upper classes as O'Connell, because there is not perhaps a country in the world where the separation between the aristocracy and the people is so open and complete as in Ireland.

We must not then be astonished if O'Connell wages an eternal war against the aristocracy of Ireland. Nothing can restrain him in those attacks which his passions suggest, and which his interests do not forbid. Nor must we be astonished if O'Connell, the idol of the people, provokes the bitter hostility of the higher ranks of society. There is not perhaps another man so much loved and so much hated. The resentment of the aristocracy against him is very natural; but woe to the Irish nobleman who, unable to disguise his hatred, provokes this formidable enemy!

Once at a public dinner, a noble lord, alluding to the tribute which O'Connell receives from Ireland, called him "the big beggarman;" the next day O'Connell, at the association spoke to the following effect: 'I have to tell you of a new attack made upon me by the Marquis of ——, who has dared to call me a mendicant. I should like to know what right he has to treat me in this way? Is it because I have sacrificed an income equal at least to the best of his estates, in order to devote myself more completely to the defence of my countrymen, and defend them better against an aristocracy whose only desire is to trample them in the dust? My fortune, perhaps, is different from that of any other man, and Ireland has done for me what no other nation has ever done for a private individual. Yes, it is true that I receive a tribute and high wages for my feeble services. I am proud of it. I reject with disdain, as I hear with contempt, the insults of this cowardly aristocracy, which would march over the body of the people, if it did not find me on the road. What are the claims of the Marquis of —— to public consideration? How did he get the large estates he possesses in Scotland? I will tell you. His ancestor was Lord ——, abbot of ——, in the time of Knox. Betraying the trust reposed in him, he surrendered the vast possessions dependent on his abbey, after having first secured for himself a grant of two-thirds. Let us look at the origin of his estates in Ireland. How did they get into his family? Why, by the usual way in those times—by perjury, robbery, and murder. And here is a man, inheriting the fruit of such crimes, who dares to attack a person whose only crime is, that he has been chosen the defender of his country against the monsters who have crushed it for ages beneath the weight of their tyranny."

It is not merely by bitter sarcasms, invectives, and violent declamations, that O'Connell attacks the upper classes in Ireland, and upsets their authority; he overthrows their empire by the ascendency he has acquired over those who owe them obedience; he destroys their power by the dominion that he personally ex-

ercises over Ireland. By placing the people under a single central influence, derived from the assent of each, O'Connell has taught them to count as nothing
the legal and traditional privileges which in an aristocratic government are supposed to be attached to name, birth, and social condition.

Section III. The Catholic Clergy

But of all the social elements existing in Ireland, and which, favourable to liberty, contain also the germs of democracy, there is perhaps none more fruitful, at
least in the present day, than the Catholic clergy. If O'Connell is the summit of
the association, the Catholic clergy may be called its base. But O'Connell is a
man whose power must end with his life, if indeed the decline of his influence
does not commence before his death. The clergy is a body that never dies.

The Catholic clergy is the most national body in Ireland; it belongs to the
very heart of the country. We have elsewhere seen that Ireland, having been attacked at the same time in its religion and its liberties, his creed and his country
were mingled in the heart of every Irishman, and became to him one and the
same thing. Having been forced to struggle for his religion against the Englishman, and for his country against the Protestant, he is accustomed to see partisans of his faith only amongst the defenders of his independence, and to find
devotion to independence only amongst the friends of his religion.

In the midst of the agitations of which his country and his soul have been the
theatre, the Irishman who has seen so much ruin consummated within him and
around him, believes that there is nothing permanent or certain in the world but
his religion,—that religion which is coeval with old Ireland,—a religion superior
to men, ages, and revolutions,—a religion which has survived the most terrible
tempests and the most dreadful tyrannies, against which Henry VIII. was powerless, which braved Elizabeth, over which the bloody hand of Cromwell passed
without destroying it, and which even a hundred and fifty years of continued
persecution have failed to overthrow. To an Irishman there is nothing supremely
true but his creed.

In defending his religion, the Irishman has been a hundred times invaded,
conquered, driven from his native soil; he kept his faith, and lost his country.
But, after the confusion made between these two things in his mind, his rescued
religion became his all, and its influence on his heart was further extended by its
taking there the place of independence. The altar at which he prayed was his
country.

Traverse Ireland, observe its inhabitants, study their manners, passions, and
habits, and you will find that even in the present day, when Ireland is politically
free, its inhabitants are full of the prejudices and recollections of their ancient
servitude. Look at their external appearance; they walk with their heads bowed

down to the heart, their attitude is humble, their language timid; they receive as a favour what they ought to demand as a right; and they do not believe in the equality which the law ensures to them, and of which it gives them proofs. But go from the streets into the chapels. Here the humbled countenances are raised, the most lowly heads are lifted, and the most noble looks directed to heaven; man reappears in all his dignity. The Irish people exists in its church; there alone it is free; there alone it is sure of its rights; there it occupies the only ground that has never given way beneath its feet.

When the altar is thus national, why should not the priest be so likewise? Hence arises the great power of the Catholic clergy in Ireland. When it attempted to overthrow Catholicism, the English government could not destroy the creed without extirpating the clergy. We have already seen how it tried to ruin that body. Still, in spite of the penal laws, which besides sometimes slumbered, there have been always priests in Ireland. The Catholic worship, it is true, had for a long time only a mysterious and clandestine existence; it was supposed to have no legal existence, and the same fiction was extended to its clergy. Even when the Catholic worship was tolerated, it was not authorised; it was only indirectly recognised when the parliament, in 1798, voted funds to endow a college at Maynooth for the education of Catholic priests. But now the Catholic faith exists publicly in Ireland; it has built its churches, it has organised its clergy, and it celebrates its ceremonies in open day; it counts four archbishops, twenty-one bishops, two thousand one hundred places of worship, and two thousand and seventy-four parish priests or coadjutors. The law does not thus constitute it, but the law allows it to form itself; the constitution affords it express toleration; and now the Catholic clergy, the depository of the chief national power of Ireland, exercises that power under the shield of the constitution. To comprehend this power, it is not sufficient to understand what their religion is to the Irish people, but also what their priest is to them.

Survey those immense lower classes in Ireland who bear at once all the charges and all the miseries of society, oppressed by the landlord, exhausted by taxation, plundered by the Protestant minister, their ruin consummated by the agents of law. Who or what is their only support in such suffering?—The priest. —Who is it that gives them advice in their enterprises, help in their reverses, relief in their distress?—The Priest.—Who is it that bestows on them, what is perhaps still more precious, that consoling sympathy, that sustaining voice of sympathy, that tear of humanity, so dear to the unfortunate? There is but one man in Ireland that mourns with the poor man who has so much to mourn, and that man is the priest. Vainly have political liberties been obtained and rights consecrated, the people still suffers. There are old social wounds, to which the remedy provided by law affords only slow and tedious cure. From these deep and hideous wounds the Catholic priests alone do not turn their eyes; they are the only persons that attempt their relief. In Ireland, the priest is the only person in perpetual relation with the people who is honoured by them.

Those in Ireland who do not oppress the people, are accustomed to despise them. I found that the Catholic clergy were the only persons in Ireland who loved the lower classes, and spoke of them in terms of esteem and affection. This fact alone would explain the power of the priests in Ireland.

The mission of the Catholic clergy in Ireland is the most magnificent that can be imagined. It is an accident, for to produce it there was required an aggregation of miseries which fortunately are peculiar to that country. But the Irish clergy have not neglected their opportunities; an admirable career was opened to the priests; they comprehended its grandeur, and entered upon it with sublime devotion: there is no longer any doubt on the continent respecting the life led in Ireland by the Catholic priest, who, in the terrible war waged by the rich against the poor, is the sole refuge of the latter, and who displays, in combating the misfortunes of his fellow man, a zeal, an ardour, and a constancy, which the most violent and selfish ambition rarely exhibits in the construction of its own fortune. It appears, besides, that everything in Ireland conspires to exhibit the virtues of the clergy in broad relief.

What must be the feelings of the people when it compares its church, humble and poor like itself, and like itself persecuted, with the haughty and splendid Anglican church, supported by the state, whose power it shares; when a severe law compels them to pay that church an enormous tribute for which it receives not a farthing's value, whilst the little that it bestows upon its own clergy is fully paid back, with an addition of care and devotedness which cannot be remunerated; when, before the peasant's eyes, a Protestant minister, a stranger whom he knows not, occupies a benefice where he only takes care of his family, his pleasures, and his interests; whilst the Catholic priest, who has no family, no fortune, and no estate, who is the child of Ireland, and has sprung from the popular ranks, lives only for the people, and devotes himself entirely to its service?

What must he think in the midst of his vast and deep miseries, when every day he hears the rich, almost all of them members of the Anglican church, proclaim charitable almsgiving the greatest of all evils, and a source of demoralisation to the people, whilst the Catholic priest from the pulpit denounces those "who have this world's good, and seeing their brethren in need, shut up their bowels of compassion," and cease not to proclaim those words of charity, "Blessed are the merciful, for they shall obtain mercy!"

I do not here inquire whether the rich Protestant or the Catholic priest is better acquainted with political economy; but I am well assured that the mass of the people will take the language of the rich for that of an adversary, whilst the words of the priest, like the voice of a friend, will penetrate to the bottom of the heart. Who now can be astonished at the power of the Catholic priesthood in

Ireland? This power has, besides, another foundation more solid than all the rest: in the same way as the Irish people has no prop but its clergy, the clergy has no support but the people. It is the people alone that pays the priesthood, and hence the double bond by which they are mutually linked together—by the bond of mutual dependence, the strongest of all possible ties. Let us add, that in this country, where all the superior and privileged classes are unpopular, the Catholic clergy is the only body more enlightened than the people, whose intelligence and power it gladly accepts. And this power is not purely social; it is furthermore essentially political. The free existence of the Catholic church in Ireland is, perhaps, the matter most directly hostile to the principle of government which has prevailed there for centuries. It is not only a church raised by the side of another church; it is not merely a corps of curates, priests, and bishops organised in rivalry to another clergy, raising altar against altar, and preaching sermon against sermon. There is, in the present free development of the Catholic church in Ireland, the mark of a new principle, victorious over the old Anglican principle, which was once the very soul of the English government; the Protestant ascendency is vanquished; it is a political, far more than a religious principle, that has triumphed.

Thus, the Irish priest does not limit himself to aiding the people in its social miseries, he also protects them against the political oppressor; he is not content to be a man and a priest, but he is furthermore a citizen, and is not less attentive to liberty than to religion.

During a long period, the Catholic clergy, subjected like their flocks to persecution, had no other care but to withdraw themselves from it, and was humbled too much to preserve any power for protection; it concealed itself from the penal laws, labouring to procure for the people the spiritual succours of religion, and when it had succeeded in this object, its task was accomplished. Thus, when oppression was at the worst, the Catholic clergy kept themselves strictly within the pale of its church, and continued to shelter itself there when Ireland fought its first battles, and gained its first victories. The priests naturally remained strangers to the agitation of 1778, which was a Protestant movement; and shortly afterwards, when the Irish Association made an appeal to the nation—they were at first deaf to its voice, and only lent it feeble aid, which was withdrawn when the clouds began to gather that presaged the storm of 1798.

When this dreadful tempest was passed, when the Irish ceased to be revolutionary and became constitutional, when ingenious modes of aggression were discovered, by which the fruits of rebellion could be obtained without encountering its perils,—immense perils, which the priest, anxious both for himself and his flock, keeps constantly in view—the Catholic priesthood in these conjunctures ended by warmly espousing the cause of the people; and from that day has been its most efficacious defender and the most formidable enemy of power.

There has not been since a political crisis in Ireland, in which the Catholic clergy has not played an important part. It was the constant auxiliary of the association, whose acts and decrees it explained to the people. There has not been an election in Ireland without the Catholic priests giving their advice, not to say their commands, to the people. The priests take part in all the affairs of the country; they attend and speak at all public meetings. The priest is often changed into a tribune of the people, and the same voice that recommends, "to render unto Cæsar the things that are Cæsar's," loudly proclaims, that it is the duty of every good Catholic to vote against the Protestant candidate, and that the most humble tenant should brave the severities of his landlord rather than not give his vote according to his conscience. No one is now ignorant, that the success of the liberal elections in Ireland is almost entirely due to the influence which the priest possesses over the hearts of the people, and to his opposing the menaces of the rich and powerful, by the promises of heaven and the terrors of hell. It was on the proposal of the clergy that the association resolved to give an indemnity to poor tenants, ejected from their farms for an independent vote; and thus the Catholic clergy of Ireland introduced charity into politics.

There is nothing, assuredly, in the traditions and principles of the Catholic clergy which would lead them to become enemies of established governments; and when difference of religious principle prevents an alliance, they in general abstain from hostility. Look at Prussia and Belgium. But what do we see in Ireland? Not only a Catholic clergy in presence of a government with which alliance was impossible, but a clergy against which that government waged a merciless war for three centuries, whose laws proscribed its worship and exiled its members; on which fell the most cruel persecutions, the memory of which is still alive in Ireland: a clergy, irritated not only by the evils which it endured, but perhaps still more so by the protection which the state granted to its most mortal enemy, the Anglican church; a clergy, in fine, which, always at war with the state, has never had any friend but the people, the poor people of Ireland, who, after having paid the landlord, the Anglican minister, the taxes levied by the state, the county, and the parish, found still a trifle for the proper support of its priesthood. Could any one desire, that when a struggle began, and continued during half a century, between the government and the people;—when, on a law, a tax, or an election, might depend the life, fortune, or liberty of all citizens; —when everything national was ranged on one side, and everything inimical to Ireland on the other;—when alternation of success and defeat invited every combatant into the lists;—could any one wish, I say, that the clergy, placed between this detested government and this affectionate people, should remain indifferent spectators of the combat?

No. Even if the Catholic clergy wished to remain neutral, it could not; but it has no need of doing violence to itself, to embrace the popular cause. The Irish

priest of the present day is far removed from those doctrines of passive obedience with which the Catholic church has been often reproached, and according
to which the people, bowed down under the most oppressive tyranny, has
not the right to raise their head. We may judge of the spirit that animates the
national clergy of Ireland, by the answer which Dr. Doyle, titular bishop of
Kildare, made before the House of Commons in 1832, for there is no prelate
whose name is more venerated by the clergy and people of Ireland.

Dr. Doyle had published a letter, addressed to all the Irish Catholics, exhort-
ing them not to pay tithes to the Protestant clergy, and to maintain their resistance by all legal means.

Thus, said the members of parliament, before whom he appeared, you establish the right to resist law as a principle; and what is to be the foundation of this
resistance? The individual judgment of each private man is to decide expressly,
whether law shall be obeyed or not. Can there be more complete anarchy?

"I think," replied the Catholic bishop, "that when abuses exist in a state, if individuals were forced to submit their judgment to the authority that protects
these abuses, no kind of reform would be possible; and not only would the principle of passive obedience be established on the widest base, but a doctrine even
worse than the divine right of kings,—the divine right of abuses. What progress
was ever made in this country that was not the work of men pursuing justice in
opposition to law? For my part, I know of none. The despotism of James II. was
strictly legal. Even on the question of tonnage and poundage, the courts of law
decided in favour of the crown. The revolution of 1688 was, beyond doubt, a violation of the British constitution, and yet it was the commencement of national
prosperity. Consider Catholic emancipation. During fifty years, it was eagerly
sought by Catholics, and many Protestants, and what a multitude of crimes has
accompanied the opposition it has met; how many collisions, hatreds, and sanguinary fights? To speak of something still more recent, is not the present organisation of the House of Commons constitutional? No one, doubtless, will
deny that it is so. Nevertheless, the king and the government are endeavouring
to modify this institution which the law protects, and their plan of reform has
been the cause of riots at Bristol and Nottingham. Who will impute these riots,
and the consequent bloodshed, to the government? If a right must be renounced
because the establishment of that right involves danger, it would be better to
submit to despotism at once; you can never succeed in chaining down my intelligence to the letter of the law, so as to prevent me from pursuing the truth and
justice pointed out by my conscience. Let us then take the principle of justice for
our guide, and resist abuses as best we may; but let us not, because these abuses
are mingled with a principle, sacrifice the principle itself. If we did so, it would
be better for us to cease to live in society, and we should assuredly be unworthy
of the free constitution which Providence has bestowed on these countries."

Such is at present the language of the priest in Ireland. Thus, an element favourable by its nature to established governments is derived from a principle pregnant with liberty to the people,—the principle of political resistance which has become so formidable in Ireland, that it is asked what authority can maintain itself against it; but yet it is a principle which its adversaries dare not touch, because it is the only social safeguard of those whose political power is attacked. The Catholic priesthood is almost the only moral authority that the people of Ireland can consult: it alone teaches the people those rules of conduct in private life, which are the surest guarantees of honesty in public life; and even where its political passions are engaged with its interests, when it adopts the cause of the people, it endeavours, while it follows, to direct the popular cause, and often succeeds. The priests have always condemned the principles and acts of the Whiteboys, and Dr. Doyle excommunicated them more than once. If, in the midst of its democratic agitation, the association succeeded in diffusing ideas of order and obedience to law amongst the people, it was because the Catholic priests were its immediate agents. If the rich landlord and the justice whom the people resist by the counsel of the priest are not robbed or murdered, it is to the priest they owe their safety. What a strange situation for an aristocracy, which, in order to preserve life and property, is in some degree obliged to abandon political power! What a singular destiny for a clergy, which, inclined towards authority by its instincts and its doctrines, has become the most formidable opponent of authority!

When the Irish priesthood, whose Catholic doctrine is not hostile to temporal power, goes beyond its first principle, it is naturally, and by an inclination peculiar to itself, the enemy of the aristocracy.

Christianity is democratic in its essence; it is the great source of the equality perpetually flowing and deluging the world. Christianity does not cease to be democratic except where it is directed from its natural course.

If the christian principle is the most democratic of all religious principles, it must be added, that of all the forms under which the christian principle is manifested to mankind, the Catholic form is also the most democratic. It alone passes the same level over all men and all nations which it subjects to the empire of one single chief, the supreme arbiter of the human race. How then does it happen that the Catholic religion is sometimes the ally and friend of aristocracy? The reason is, that the body which represents the religion, the clergy, may be so organised as to lose its original character, and to assume another which does not belong to it.

Suppose a Catholic clergy endowed with great privileges; hence will at once result, the instincts, the passions, and the interests of all privileged corporations. Suppose that, coexisting with nobility in the state, it possesses rights and advantages analogous to those of the nobility; that, like the aristocracy, it possesses great political powers, immense estates, great wealth; a natural sympathy will be established between the two bodies; a constant tendency will lead them to approximate and form a close alliance, to league for defence, to unite for attack. Then also its instincts, passions, and interests as a privileged body, will remove it as far from the people, that is to say, the great masses, as its principles of Christian and Catholic equality brought it near to them before they were adulterated: and its distance from the people will increase proportionably as the other privileged body, its equal and its ally, holds itself more aloof; so that if the aristocracy should go to war with the people, the clergy, the primitive and natural friend of the masses, will become their adversary.

But it is easy to see that nothing like this can happen in a country where the Christian and Catholic clergy possess no privilege and occupy no recognised rank in the state. Where, indeed, an aristocracy exists, but a Protestant aristocracy in the presence of a Catholic people; an aristocracy which, instead of attracting the national clergy towards it by parity of position, and thus inviting it to an alliance, on the contrary, rejects it with all the violence resulting from an assemblage of hostile passions, opposite principles, and contrary interests; in a country, finally, where all the principles, all the interests, and all the passions which sever the clergy from the aristocracy unite it to the people.

Thus, in Ireland, the clergy has complete authority over a people which recognises no authority but the clerical,—a situation very different from the case in which the clergy, united to an absolute monarch, is strictly kept within the limits of its spiritual influence, and from that where united to an aristocracy it has no political strength, but divided and unpopular. Here the Catholic clergy possesses a double authority over the priesthood, and exercises it alone. It is thus that a religious body, which we sometimes see the supporter of princes or the ally of privileged corporations, is in Ireland one of the most potent elements of liberty and democracy.

Section IV. The Presbyterians

There is another element of democracy, which, though not Irish either by its origin or its nature, is nevertheless found in Ireland, and exercises there a very marked influence. I mean the Scotch Presbyterians who came to Ireland in the time of James I., Cromwell, and William III., and settled for the most part in the province of Ulster.

The Presbyterian and the Catholic creeds, two religious adversaries, proceed from two principles directly opposed to each other, the first from liberty, the second from authority; the one subjecting every will and every conscience to a single conscience and a single will; the other leaving to each the care of forming his individual conviction by free examination. But these two principles, so directly contrary, have a common democratic effect, and by two different roads lead men to equality. According to the Catholic principle, all men are equal under a single master who levels all beneath him: in the Presbyterian church all are equal, because all are sovereigns. If a political and a religious institution could be compared, I should say that there is a very great analogy between the Presbyterian church and the constitution of the United States. In both, the authority is derived from the people and the majority, and ascends by degrees; the presbytery is the electoral district, the synod is the state, the general assembly is the congress. This is directly the opposite of the Catholic church, in which the authority springs from the head and descends to the people.

Assuredly the simultaneous encounter and development in the same country of these two democratic elements, so different in their nature, and yet united together to effect the same work, are a very remarkable phenomenon. The Catholic and the Presbyterian religions in Ireland were equally separated by so many passions and prejudices, that a mere analogy between the political effects of these doctrines would certainly not have brought them together, if there had not elsewhere existed from the beginning another cause of union between them, and that cause was the presence, in the midst of them, of a common enemy, the Anglican church, the ally of the English government.

For a long time the religious rancour which animated one party against the other, was too powerful for political interest to unite them; and of this, history affords us a memorable example. In 1703, a bill was proposed in the Irish parliament, imposing the sacramental test as a necessary qualification for office. Now this bill, primarily directed against the Catholics, was framed in such general terms as to exclude not only Catholics but Presbyterians and all other classes of Protestant dissenters; nevertheless, the Presbyterians did not reject it: and by accepting it they showed that they preferred sacrificing their own rights to sharing them with Catholics. In this instance, political interest yielded to religious passion.

At a later period, religious passions yielded to political passions: and those whom religion had separated were seen to unite in the common interest of national independence; this change dates from 1789. Already, before this period, the Irish Presbyterians had more than once manifested their republican and democratic inclinations. The great movements of 1778 and 1782, in which half of the nation appeared in arms, the popular conventions in which resolutions were carried by the plurality of votes, had as their central point the province of Ulster, and as their base the Presbyterian population. But a sectarian spirit then impeded the spirit of liberty; and, satisfied with obtaining rights and guarantees for Protestant Ireland, the Presbyterians of that day paid little regard to Catholic servitude. The French revolution imprinted on their minds wider and more generous tendencies. France spread over the world ideas of general liberty and universal emancipation, which found nowhere a greater echo than in Ireland, the most oppressed country of all. Still it was not amongst the most wretched, that is to say, the Catholics, that French liberty found the loudest echo; those most ready to adopt its counsels and instigations were the Presbyterians,—most attentive to its voice because they understood it best.

Thus, the whole Irish movement of this period was imprinted with the French character and the passions of France. They spoke in Ireland only of the rights of man and the sovereignty of the people; at Dublin and Belfast, on every 14th of July, they celebrated the capture of the Bastille; every victory that France gained over monarchical Europe, was to Ireland a subject of joy and an occasion for a national festival.—"Right or wrong," exclaimed the Irish people, "may France triumph! It is our cause that she defends, it is for ourselves that she fights; her cause is that of human liberty."

Acting under this generous impulse, Protestants who had hitherto shown themselves the most implacable enemies of the cause, became its most devoted champions, and displayed for Catholic emancipation more zeal and impatience than the Catholics exhibited themselves. All, or nearly all, the Protestants who then placed themselves at the head of the national movement, and by their junction with the Catholics formed the celebrated association of the United Irishmen, were Presbyterians.

Hence dates the first alliance formed between those mortal enemies the Catholics and the Puritans; hence, also, the first political schism in the Irish Presbyterian body; for whilst some hushed their religious passions, in order to listen to their political sympathies; others, stopping their ears against the voice of liberty which summoned them, clung obstinately to the yoke of their old hatred against Papists.

This division is still presented to us by the Presbyterians of our own day. Out of about seven hundred thousand, the number of the sect, there is nearly one half favourable to the democratic movement which the other half opposes. The latter have more hatred of the Catholic religion than love of liberty, and prefer rather to remain allies of the Anglican church, their political enemy, than unite with the Catholics, their religious enemies: the former, on the contrary, enter into a treaty with the Catholics, whose creed they dislike, through love of those political principles associated with the triumph of the Irish Catholic cause.

Whatever may be their apparent harmony, the liberal Presbyterians and the Irish Catholics agree completely only in the war for which they are leagued; enemies at bottom, they have ceased to hate each other, for the purpose of hating together a common enemy: it is a union of passions far more than of doctrines. Both, it is true, oppose the government of the aristocracy, but the Presbyterians detest their power because it is linked with that of the Anglican church—the Catholics, because it is Protestant and anti-national. The Presbyterians are likewise Protestants and foreigners, and for both reasons ought to be odious to the Catholics; but the latter, at least for the present, forget the origin and creed of their Presbyterian allies, and see in them only useful and generous auxiliaries.

These auxiliaries afford considerable assistance to the democratic movement in Ireland. They are, it is true, but a small part of the great national association, but they are the most enlightened and active section of it. It is worthy of remark, that never has any great event, any social or political crisis, any rebellion, prosperous or fatal, occurred in Ireland without the Presbyterians of Ulster taking the greatest share. They doubtless derive from their doctrines certain intellectual habits, which influence their political dispositions, render them unquiet and excitable, and impel them to take the lead in all agitations and changes.

Circumstances, besides, have rendered them peculiarly fit for the constitutional war which the national association, under the protection of the laws, wages against the aristocracy. The natural tendency of their doctrine is, without doubt, republican. What, in fact, were the independents, the levellers, the "fifth monarchy men" of England, but Puritans who applied their religious system to politics? But the Presbyterians of Ireland, in whose souls the first accents of the French republic had given birth to so many hopes and sympathies, lost these illusions when they saw the republic in France sully itself with excesses for its preservation, and Ireland have recourse to violence for its establishment. Since 1798, the idea of an Irish republic has been quite abandoned by the most democratic Presbyterians, who, by this change, have become the best soldiers that modern Ireland could have for the legal warfare in which she is engaged. They bring to this contest all their spirit of liberty and progress; and it may be remarked, that while they have renounced pushing their doctrine to its extreme consequences in politics, they are more ardent than ever to apply the less extreme principles, and manifest more incessantly the spirit of liberty, progress, and democracy, belonging to their character.

It may be set down as certain, that this portion of the Irish Presbyterians who make common cause with the Catholics, is on the increase, whilst the hostile party is diminishing. Besides the political division existing among the Presbyterians of Ireland, there is in their church a more ancient cause of schism, which is purely religious. Those called orthodox, though physically separated from the church of Scotland, always maintain a moral union with that body; now the Scottish church, though originally Puritan, has retained to some extent the principle of authority, since it requires from its members subscription to a profession of faith. The orthodox Presbyterians of Ireland are those who, according to this principle of the Scottish church, establish a system of doctrine which every member of their community must profess. It is, in general, amongst the orthodox Presbyterians, that opponents of the Catholics and their cause are found. The others, named Dissenters or Seceders, are those who, tracing the

Protestant or Puritan sentiment to its origin, recognise no authority but the Bible, which everybody is at liberty to interpret as he pleases, provided he believes in its inspiration. These Presbyterian dissenters are sometimes called Arians, and have a great resemblance to the Unitarians of the United States, who are so numerous at Boston. It is these dissenters that we find zealous partisans of the democratic movement which every moment gains ground.

I do not examine here what there may be salutary or fatal in this development of the democratic principle of the Presbyterian church: there the great question of human liberty and authority is fairly mooted,—the two powers that dispute the world,—which it seems equally impossible to unite or to separate; which wage a continual war, as if the first could not succeed without the destruction of the second, and which yet are so necessary to each other, that each only finds its safety in the mutual opposition of both. I confine myself to showing, that in the struggle that exists in the bosom of the Irish Presbyterian church, it is the principle of liberty that has the advantage over the principle of authority, and that the success of the dissenters over the orthodox adds to the number of the Presbyterians who are united with the Catholics of Ireland.

But is not this alliance between the Presbyterians and Catholics factitious and transitory? I am tempted to believe so. Take away the accidental causes of union, and I doubt if harmony would long subsist between such dissimilar elements.

In truth, there is every day in the two creeds a tendency to approximate both in ideas and manners. The Catholics of Ireland have long since rejected and daily disavow the superstitious doctrines and practices for which they have been most reproached by the Puritans. There is in the habits and preaching of the clergy of both a singular toleration, which is a fact if it is not a principle; Presbyterians and Catholic priests cultivate friendly intimacies: marriages take place between Catholics and Presbyterians, and the celebration of marriage, performed alternately by the ministers of the two communions, brings with it an exchange of courtesy and compliments. The spirit of toleration also diffuses itself with the march of time; a common warfare and common victories draw these first bands closer; and if this state of things continued for any length of time, it is conceivable that for the Catholics and Presbyterians united, there might result more than a momentary alliance of passions and interests: each creed, in the long run, might be so modified, that a durable agreement between them would not be impossible.

Still the Catholic principle and the Presbyterian principle are as much opposed to each other as the two eternal adversaries, liberty and authority. How then could they establish a sincere and durable union? I doubt whether this fusion can ever be accomplished, for nothing is so implacable as a principle. The Arians of Ireland, like the Unitarians of America, are the real adversaries of Catholicism. They are the philosophers of the Protestant church; happy philosophers beyond doubt, who have been able to graft their philosophy on a christian branch; surprising philosophers, by a singular mixture of passion and toleration, of intellectual boldness and faith; primitive Christians and modern philosophers; believing in the divinity of Jesus Christ, like Bossuet, and in other respects sceptics, like Voltaire; fervent as the Puritans of Cromwell, mild and tolerant as the disciples of Fenelon. Which of these two principles that dispute their soul will finally prevail? Will it be faith? Will it be doubt? How far will doubt lead them? Will it always stop at the divine origin of the Bible, a limit which it has not passed as yet? But whatever may be the amount of Christianity that they will retain, it is certain that their principle is examination, and their method doubt. Now this is precisely the principle most opposed to that of the Catholic church.

It is, then, probable, that when the Presbyterians and Catholics of Ireland will be no longer kept united by the presence of an enemy, they will divide and renew the war.

These views of the future are merely conjectural; but what is at present certain, is the immense power that Irish democracy derives from the existing union.

Section V. The Middle Classes

There exists in Ireland another principle of democracy, and in which the two last noticed seem to be contained, that is, the growth of middle classes. To this middle class belong all the remarkable men of the great national association that has been formed against the aristocracy and against the government. O'Connell is a lawyer who derived his first power from the bar; the Catholic clergy recruits its members among the farmers and tradesmen, and that part of the Presbyterians of Ulster which we find at the head of the intellectual and liberal movement in their sect, is composed for the most part of small landholders and fundholders, recently enriched by commerce.

The absence of a middle class in Ireland has been, and is still, one of the greatest misfortunes of the country. When a people has the misfortune to be subjected to an aristocracy anti-national and radically vicious, what chance has it of escaping, or at least of alleviating oppression, if it remains motionless in its ignorance and its misery; and if men do not arise from its own proper bosom, who, superior by their education, their talent, or their fortune, are capable of taking its cause in hand, and guiding the popular efforts for deliverance?

Whence comes it, that during nearly the whole of the eighteenth century Ireland, sinking under the most oppressive tyranny, presents only a long succession of individual rebellions and partial insurrections, destitute of plan, union, or morality? It is because the people, in the midst of its sufferings, was abandoned to itself, and that, having no friendly superior class to enlighten and lead it, in its wrath it committed outrages which could not but entail new rigours.

The impossibility of a people, however oppressed, raising itself when it has not the support of a superior class, was never shown more clearly than during the insurrection of 1798, when there were as many revolts as there were villages, —soldiers in abundance, but no officers. Everything aristocratic that then existed in Ireland was hostile to this national movement; the people could find no assistance but in a middle class, and such a class did not exist in Ireland. There were some individuals fit to make a part of this class, but not enough to constitute it. We may say, that there was no middle class in Ireland so long as the penal laws were in force, which, striking the Catholics even in civil life, forbade them the possession of estates, injured them in trade, and excluded them from the bar.

There were, it is true, at the same time in Ireland, lawyers, merchants, bankers, and tradesmen; but we should be strangely deceived, were we to believe that the members of these several professions formed necessarily, and wherever they were met, a middle class. In a country where no privileged aristocracy existed, they would naturally be the upper class, and we should have to search for a middle class in a social state, intermediate between them and the mass of the people. And even in a society whose summit was occupied by an hereditary aristocracy, they might, by closely uniting to it, so identify themselves with that body, that in order to find a middle class, we should still go a step below them. Look at England, where the titled and untitled aristocracy are confounded and blended in one upper class, to which every person that is rich and powerful may aspire: in that country, commerce and banking, on account of their large fortunes,—law and medicine, in consequence of their privileges, connect themselves so intimately with the aristocracy, that they are absorbed in it, and, aided by its malleable nature, form with it but one and the same body. Thus, perhaps, the middle class in England begins only with the farmers, the shopkeepers, the moderate fundholders, and ends with the ten-pound householders. Such was not the middle class in France before 1789. Then, all that was not noble, being inferior in right to the nobility, of which there were manifest proofs, the most eminent in commerce, manufactures, and the liberal professions, belonged by force to the middle class, that is to say, to that which, not being the vulgar herd, is just as little the superior class.

The condition of the middle classes in Ireland is neither what it was in France before 1789, nor what it is in our days in England. In truth, during all the time that the civil incapacities of the Catholics lasted, the higher industrial and liberal professions, being almost a monopoly of the Protestants, were in Ireland, still more than in England, associated with the aristocracy, towards which they were inevitably attracted by the sympathy of the same creed, the source of their common privileges. It was, then, truly impossible that everything which was Protestant in Ireland, the great lords, the merchants, or the lawyers, should not form a close and single phalanx against the Catholics, who were equally enemies to the Protestant monopoly of wealth, and the Protestant monopoly of power. There might be various ranks amongst the Protestants, but when opposed to the Catholics, that is to say, to the people, they seemed to form one single upper class, between which and the people there was no intermediate.

But when the industrial and liberal professions became equally accessible to Protestants and Catholics, the scene changed, and presented two different aspects, of which we must not lose sight. When the professions were filled by Protestants, these professions continued to furnish their tribute to the Protestant aristocracy, with which they allied themselves the more closely, as they found their enemies, the Catholics, becoming their rivals in industry, when they became free citizens. On the contrary, when occupied by Catholics, they stood aloof from the aristocracy, from which they were separated both by political interest and religious passion. So that from the same social element there issued as it were two streams running in opposite directions, one of which flowed into the aristocracy, with which it mingled and disappeared; whilst the other held its own proper course, and maintained itself between the people from which it issued, and the aristocracy with which it could not be blended. The second is the real source of the middle class in Ireland; it is that which, when there was no middle class in Ireland, contained its germs, and laboured for their development.

It was only in 1776 that agricultural industry was rendered free to Catholics, by the law which permitted them to become proprietors: the bar was not opened to them until 1793, and the end of the commercial monopoly of the Protestants must be dated from the same epoch. Still it would be an error to suppose that in Ireland before this time there existed absolutely no element of a middle class.

I have said that the Catholics were then trammelled in commerce and industry, but commerce and industry were not prohibited. We have already seen, in the account of the penal laws, how the Protestants, being masters of the municipal and commercial corporations, paralysed the industry of Catholics. Still, though they injured, they did not wholly destroy it; they alone occupied the summits of commerce from which they excluded the Catholics, but in the more humble regions the latter still made way. In case of rivalry, the Catholic, loaded with taxes from which the Protestant was exempt, sustained an unequal struggle; but still he did struggle; he worked with ardour; and this labour, the only refuge of a people to whom civil and political life was forbidden, could not be altogether fruitless. In this was really the future of enslaved Ireland; for in the long run labour creates wealth; wealth, strength; and strength, liberty.

It is manifest, that in a country where Protestant commerce was itself restrained, Catholic industry, loaded with such chains, could not easily produce a middle class. It, however, laboured to do so. And it is a very remarkable fact, that when, about the year 1757, three illustrious patriots, Dr. Curry, O'Connor, and Wyse of Waterford, undertook to regenerate enslaved Ireland, and conceived the first plan of a national association, they made an appeal to all Catholics which found an echo nowhere but in trade. The Catholic clergy, then timid and humbled, remained mute; the small remnant of the Irish Catholic aristocracy was equally silent; the merchants and traders alone responded to the summons. It was thus from trade that the first germ was derived of the great national association which embraces all Ireland: it was thus that trade produced a man too little known, who, for twenty years, alone managed Catholic Ireland; John Keogh, the predecessor of O'Connell, and who would be renowned if he had not been eclipsed by O'Connell, was a tradesman. And when the law opened the bar to Catholics, it was still industry which, raising them above poverty, enabled them to defray the great expenses that precede the exercise of the privileged profession. Thus, at the worst of the social and political oppression of Ireland, there already issued from the industry of the Catholics, though half enchained, a principle of independence and emancipation. At present this principle is developed in all its freedom. Catholic industry is liberated from every trammel, and the merchant of that religion has not only acquired wealth, but he has also gained all the rights which belong to fortune. In 1793 he obtained the elective franchise; in 1829 admission to parliament. Before these concessions were made, the Catholic merchants of Ireland might have formed a rich class, but they could not form a powerful class. Now, delivered from its fetters, strong in its rights, this class incessantly adds both to its power and its wealth; and it cannot be too watchful of its fortune, for everything unites to promise it in Ireland a glorious destiny.

In England, where the aristocracy is national, the middle class, in whatever rank it may be taken, can only play a secondary part, whether it unites itself to the higher class, and is eclipsed, or separates itself from it, and, in the attempt to balance its power, risks the destruction of its own. In Ireland, on the contrary, where the aristocracy is at open war with the people, the middle class, from the very moment of its existence, is quite naturally the first and only national power.

It is a great advantage for it to be the only superior class accepted by the people without being an aristocracy. It would have a far less favourable position, if there were no aristocracy in Ireland: for then it might, perhaps, aspire to become an aristocracy itself; and though it might not have such a pretension, it would be open to the accusation. But the existing aristocracy saves it from all peril; it would seem as if that aristocracy had resolved to oppose the perpetual contrast of a hostile power to the national power of the middle class, in order that the people should love the one as much as it detests the other; and in order that the middle class, incessantly beholding what it is that excites the hate of the country, should the better avoid the passions and errors that would deprive it of popular confidence and favour.

A vast and magnificent career is offered to the middle class in Ireland. There is one rock only in its course; it may, in spite of all that keeps it on the side of the people, sometimes incline towards the aristocracy, whether in an endeavour to approximate towards it, or merely to imitate it. The mere possibility of such a deviation from its natural course appears at first sight absolutely irrational; still one should be unacquainted with the English element that exists in Ireland, even amongst the people, and ignorant also of the germs of inequality in that element, not to feel that the middle class in Ireland will have to sustain a struggle in order to remain democratic;—a struggle against its prejudices and its instincts;—a struggle against the habits of the country itself, which is accustomed to see power only in the midst of aristocratic privileges, and which nevertheless, when it sees them there, prepares to combat, and aspires to destroy it.

We must not be astonished if aristocratic inclinations display themselves in the middling properties which are gradually being formed in Ireland; there is not a middling proprietor who, at the sight of the privileges attached to the possession of land, is not tempted to enjoy them himself: he is delighted at possessing in his condition some analogy to a noble lord, his country neighbour, whom he hates as his political and religious enemy, but from whom, to convert his hate into love, he probably waits only for a kind smile, or a complimentary recognition. The old soil of Ireland, like that of England, is impregnated with a sort of feudal contagion from which every possessor finds it difficult to escape. Up to this day, however, the middling Catholic properties have remained on the popular side, but perhaps more from accidental and transitory circumstances than from principle. When, in 1776, the Catholics obtained the right of acquiring real estate, they still continued subject to civil and political incapacities, the last of which, exclusion from parliament, only terminated in 1829; so that whilst they acquired lands, they obtained none of the rights derived from the possession of land; and this contradiction necessarily maintained in full force their hatred against the aristocracy, which derived from its estates benefits from which their estates were excluded. Will they persist in their hostile feelings to the privileged, now that their property gives them, besides all political rights, the chance of being named justices of the peace, being summoned on grand juries, sitting on the bench with the aristocracy in petty and quarter sessions? It is a question that cannot be solved. Besides, the obstacles that impede the transfer of land in Ireland, which will be discussed elsewhere, prevent real estate, at least for the present, from being a considerable element of the middle class; and this checks their aristocratic tendencies.

The bar has also its aristocratic tendencies, which are not without danger in the future destinies of the middle class. It is a privileged corporation, and has already shown the tastes and passions proper to its origin; and when, in 1793, the bar became free, the first Catholics who became lawyers associated themselves with the Protestant aristocracy. But the spirit of social privilege could not long resist the spirit of political party and religious passion. Barristers at present are the natural combatants in a constitutional and legal strife; and whilst the war lasts, which offers them peaceful and brilliant reputation, it cannot be doubted, that in their intermediate position between the aristocracy and the people they will adhere to the latter.

But of all the sources of a middle class existing in Ireland, that whose principle agrees best with the democratic movement working in the country, and that which is least likely to display aristocratic sympathies, is Catholic commerce; the primary source of a middle class in Ireland; a fruitful source which remained for centuries compressed as it were in the bosom of the earth, under the feet of the Protestant aristocracy, which at present may flow freely, supplied by the labours of several millions of men. A drop from its waves may be tainted, but the current will always remain pure. Party interests, sectarian feelings, present passions, vindictive remembrance of the past, all conspire to animate Catholic commerce against the aristocracy. Still we are sure, that in its resentments it will never pass certain bounds; the constitutional war which satisfies the others is a necessity to the middle class, for it cannot do without peace. "I begin to see," says Tone in 1793, at a time when he endeavoured to bring the commercial class over to his projects of republican independence, "—I begin to see that merchants are bad instruments of revolution. Commerce is adverse to violent revolutions, and yet it contains an eternal principle of movement; the principle of labour always creating by the side of the principle of indolence, which leaves property to decay: it is the principle of progress without privilege, of the perpetual increase of some without the fixed inequality of others. Here, especially, is the future of Ireland. I say the future, for a middle class in Ireland is as yet little beyond infancy.

It is not that it does not already possess great wealth; on the contrary, its advances have been singularly rapid. In 1778 there were only eighty Catholics in Ireland recognised as landed proprietors; at present, Catholic landed property may be taken as at least one-tenth; and many Catholics who do not possess land have heavy claims on it by mortgage. Forty years ago Catholics were excluded from the bar, where they are now the majority. Catholic commerce flourishing in all Ireland, but especially in the large towns, such as Belfast, Dublin, Cork, Limerick, and Galway, has already produced immense capitals. One single fact may suffice to show its importance and prosperity, namely, that in 1829 nine-tenths of the funds of the bank of Ireland belonged to Catholic proprietors.

Here, assuredly, are prosperous conditions for a rising middle class. Still it is a strange phenomenon in Ireland, and peculiar to the country, that whilst new fortunes are created, the number of new rich men is not increased in the same proportion. The reason is, that after the fortune is created, the rich man departs, and this is explained by the social and political state of Ireland.

The manufacturer, the merchant, and the banker, enriched by their industry in Ireland, would be doubtless tempted to choose that country as their resting place; but, besides the difficulty of obtaining land in Ireland, and finding a secure investment, there are in this country numberless obstacles to quiet possession. The state of Ireland is such that complete security over the land belongs only to the petty occupant, who covers his entire property with his person, and from his cabin extends his hands over all the wealth of which his field is the repository.

And it is not merely the country that is agitated; in the cities and towns, which indeed are less so, parties are so violent, contentions so fierce, the spectacle of the miseries of the people so terrific, that a dwelling in them cannot satisfy the man who, after having laboured, wishes to enjoy the fruits of his labours. It often happens, then, that finding no secure asylum in Ireland, those who have acquired wealth, go to seek it in some of the towns of England. We see, then, how it is, that while many make their fortune in Ireland, an equal number does not reside there; and nevertheless, it is the residence, not the fortune made, that must be taken into account. We have not, in fact, to consider whether Catholics gain more or less at the bar or in trade, and purchase estates or rent-charges in Ireland with the fruit of their labours; but whether they live on these estates in Ireland, or spend their income in an Irish town: and if, after having issued from the people by their industry and talents, they take an intermediate place between the aristocracy and the people, and maintain their station.

This evil, which regards the progress of the middle class in Ireland, diminishes every day. It decreases in proportion as large gaps made in the aristocracy open new social positions to the people. Thus, for example, the new poor law will help to detain many members of the middle class in Ireland, for it may be presumed, that from their body the greater number of guardians will be chosen.

It is not merely number that is wanting to the middle class in Ireland; it also wants, what it does not yet possess, knowledge, experience, and education. Issuing suddenly from the most profound obscurity to open day; raised from the general incapacity which sometimes excluded it from the management of its own private affairs, to be suddenly summoned to the direction of public affairs, the middle class of Ireland seems almost dazzled by its own splendour. It scarcely believes in so magnificent an elevation succeeding so rapidly to so great degradation; and in the intoxication of its sudden fortune, it with difficulty holds a proper position between the aristocracy, its enemy, which it does not always combat with dignity, and the people, which it does not always estimate sufficiently. It has a remnant of the vices belonging to the slave, who always desires to act the tyrant when he becomes free. To confirm its power, of which it still doubts, it might easily be led to extend it to abuse. But the middle class must watch its own conduct with very great care, for on its present wisdom or folly, its future destiny mainly depends.

If we are allowed to regret the obstacles that retard the increase of the elements of which it is composed, we may perhaps also regard it as a piece of good fortune, that this middle class has not been at once put into possession of all its powers. Before it can govern well, it must learn the science of government. It is in this respect that the labours of the national association are still of such immense importance: it is a school of government where instruction is every day afforded to the class that is destined to govern.

This class, which is beyond contradiction the most fertile in producing democracy, is also the most precious. Take away the middle class from Ireland, and you will at once have a country, the best possibly prepared for the reception of an absolute government. Every tyranny would be easy, and, I might almost say, agreeable to the people, provided it declared and waged war against the aristocracy. From this, indeed, democracy might result, but of the kind which despotism produces. There is in Ireland one chance for absolute power, which the rising middle class may dispute with it, and on the success or failure of this class depends the question, whether Ireland shall have the equality of despotism, or of a free democracy.

Section VI. On the State of Parties in Ireland

If the true character of parties in England be investigated, it will be found that there does not exist, at least in the present day, a party that can properly be called democratic. Tories, Conservatives, Whigs, are only different shades of the aristocracy, and the same thing may almost be said of the radicals themselves. Not that there do not exist great and deep differences between the parties; they assuredly aim at very different ends, and the controversies that lead them into the lists are real and substantial. But if it be true, that some aim at maintaining aristocratic privileges, and others at modifying them; it may, perhaps, be added that no party wishes to destroy them altogether. There is in the habits, the laws, and the constitution of the English people, an old feudal basis, on which each wishes to erect a different edifice, but which none are anxious to destroy. I will elsewhere attempt to show by what devious paths these aristocratic tendencies may lead England herself to democracy; here I merely take for granted, a character common to all English parties, which is nowhere found in Ireland. In the latter country, quite a different spectacle is presented to our view; two parties alone present themselves, between which there is no intermediate. There are no moderate Conservatives, no Whigs; there are only Tories and Radicals, and here the radicals are not aristocratic, for in Ireland the issue is staked between the aristocracy and the people. This extreme character of Irish parties is a fact singularly favourable to democracy.

Such was not always the state of things in Ireland. When the Catholic population in that country counted for nothing, the Protestants, sole masters of society and the government, divided and formed almost as many parties as we now find in England. It is thus that, at the close of the last century, we find these shades of difference very strongly marked amongst the Protestants of Ireland; those, who servilely devoted to the English government, sacrificed to it completely their own independence and that of their country: they were the Tories of the time. Then came the Protestants, who, without taking any account of Catholic Ireland, were anxious to have liberties, rights, and guarantees, for themselves; they were the Whigs of the day: for instance, Lord Charlemont. Finally, there were Protestants who, adopting more elevated principles, and more generous theories, demanded that the benefits of reform should be extended to all without reserve, at the risk of the advantage shared by the Catholic population; these were the radicals of the epoch; and such were Grattan and Curran. Finally, for some time, at the epoch of the French revolution, there was a fourth party, composed of Protestants and Catholics, which would not be called either Tory, Whig, or Radical, but simply revolutionary, anxious to shake off the English yoke, and establish a republic in Ireland; it was the party which, amongst the Catholics of Dublin, had at its head Theobald Wolfe Tone, and amongst the Protestants of the north, Samuel Neilson of Belfast.

All these elements of party are overthrown in Ireland, and their condition changed. The nation which counted as nothing has now become almost everything; the divisions between the Protestants could not remain the same, and when they separated it was no longer to form a distinct Protestant party, but either to join the popular cause, or organise an opposition against it. From that moment it was no longer different systems and opinions that were opposed to each other, but two implacable enemies which had sown each other's ruin, between which compromise was no longer possible, and which, even when they did not fight, retained their arms in their hands. Hence the necessity imposed upon every person in Ireland of ranging himself under one of the two banners that is presented to his view; hence the two parties which alone at the present day show themselves in the country.

The first is the old Anglican party, which takes for its motto the maintenance of the Protestant church, and for its rallying cry hatred of popery; its great principle is the intimate union of church and state, that is to say, of the Anglican worship and the English aristocracy. Whilst everything around this party advances and changes, it remains motionless, and would maintain, amidst the ruins of the universe, that a political society could not exist unless it was exclusively Protestant.

This party cannot conceive a Protestant society unless with a Protestant government, a Protestant king, a Protestant parliament, Protestant judges and functionaries, Protestant citizens and soldiers. Whatever in the country is not Protestant is in its eyes as if it never existed, and had only a fictitious life. This party considers everything that has been done contrary to its exclusive principle an evil. It believes that the constitution was violated when any single one of the laws enacted against the Catholics was repealed. These laws, in the opinion of the party, did not oppress the Catholics; it only depended on themselves to become free under the protection of the laws; for this purpose, it was only necessary that they should turn Protestants; and of course it was necessary to demand this condition, since Protestantism was the law of the state, the law of the country, the law of the land. This party is still at 1688.

According to this party, the constitution was violated when Scotland was permitted to have a Presbyterian church; and a sort of sacrilege was committed when the English parliament voted funds for a seminary destined to educate Catholic priests; the constitution was also violated when the elective franchise was conceded to the Irish Catholics, and again when they were allowed to sit in parliament; in the eyes of the party these concessions are as if they never were granted; and he who believes that they cannot be resumed deplores them. Every time that similar concessions are made to the Catholics, the Tory party sees, or pretends to see, a rabid monster about to escape from the cage in which it is chained, to pounce upon the Protestants, and swallow them alive. This monster is popery.

This party has a singular veneration for the name of William III., Prince of Orange, the conqueror at the Boyne, and the last founder of the Anglican church in Ireland; it displays his portraits and emblems, toasts at public meetings his "pious, glorious, and immortal memory," and endeavours to maintain in all its vigour the religious passions on which the fortune of that prince was raised. It is hence called the Orange party.

This party, which for more than a century trampled the Catholic people under foot, has still more contempt than hatred for this people; when it speaks of "good society," it always means a society of Protestants; in its mouth everything that is Protestant is called *respectable*, in opposition to everything Catholic.

This party believes that all the evils of the country have arisen from the weakness of government, which did not, when it had the opportunity, sufficiently repress rebels. After having shown that on the suppression of the insurrection of 1798, sixty-six persons accused of rebellion were executed in Wexford alone, the historian, Sir Richard Musgrave, who deemed this too lenient, says, "Hence we may judge of the lenity of the government.". . . . Here is the true orangeman. Under the ardent religious or political passions of the Orange or Tory party, some interested feelings may be found lurking,—amongst others a wish to preserve the enormous privileges of an aristocracy which performs no function of government, and the splendid revenues of a church that has nothing to do.

The Radical party is composed of all that do not belong to the Tory party; as it is supported on the foundation of the Catholic population entirely devoted to it, we find it sometimes called the Catholic or national party; it has for its root old Ireland, Celtic and free; and for its head, young Ireland enfranchised; for its soul, the Catholic religion; for its banner, liberty. Its grievances and its hatreds rest on six hundred years of oppression; its hopes on half a century of victories; the sanctity of its cause on a series of oppression surpassing all belief.

Although profoundly Catholic, many Protestants belong to this party, whilst there is not a single Catholic in the Protestant Tory party.

Thus in Ireland the Catholic party is the liberal party; and the reason is plain: the Catholics, of whom it is in a great measure composed, having been long oppressed, have naturally demanded reforms, which the Tories, for whose profit the tyranny was instituted, resisted with all their might. Those who reject such reforms under the pretext that they are inconsistent with the constitution, take, in opposition to the liberal party, the name of the constitutional party.

It is the National, Catholic, Liberal or Radical party which, during fifty years in Ireland, was compelled to hide its head, but now raises it, supported by seven millions of men. It is this party, which is more than a party, for it is the nation itself, which in 1792, raising its first cry, shouted that in order to be powerful it was only necessary for it to come into existence, and then obtained the first political emancipation of the Catholics. It is this party which, after having received a happy impulse from the French revolution, was afterwards crushed by it; it was accused of sympathies for a republic, for the outrages as well as the principles of liberty: it was aided by '89, and it was killed by '93.

It is this party over whose dead body the union of 1800 passed, which, after being annihilated for twenty years, revived in the association formed by O'Connell, took, in 1825, Catholic emancipation for its rallying cry; in 1831, abolition of tithes; in 1833, repeal of the union; and in 1838, reform of the church and of the municipal corporations.

When I say that there are only two parties in Ireland, I am far from maintaining that all who serve under the same banner think alike. There are Protestants in the Tory party who are far from sharing all its passions and principles. Survey that entire portion of the Presbyterians, which I have called orthodox, and who are for the most part firm supporters of the Orange or Tory party; it is not sympathy which unites them to that party, for they detest from the bottom of their hearts the Anglican church, which serves it for a base. But to make war on the Catholics, whom they hate still more, they are obliged to unite with the main body of the army, which is composed of Anglican Tories. Other Protestants contend for radical reform; but yet they proceed on principles in politics and religion very different from those of the Catholics with whom they are allied; thus the Presbyterian dissidents, or Unitarians, on many points far removed from the Catholic party, are nevertheless its valuable auxiliaries.

Shades of difference are particularly found amongst those Protestants who, though belonging to the Anglican church, separate themselves from the Orange and Anglican party to support the Catholic or national party; some, in embracing the liberal cause, only obey a deep sense of conscience and equity; others do the same from calculation: when the Anglican party was strong they supported it; they abandon it when it is weak, and go over to the Catholic party to which the strength was passed; the former act from prudence, the latter from fear. When the popular cause is ready to triumph, and its success becomes every day more probable, many, who before condemned this cause as absurd and seditious, begin to suspect its good sense and equity; they see on the side of the people approaching triumphs in which it will be pleasant to take a share, and in the opposite camp defeats and dangers which it is wise to avoid.

But whatever may be the operating motive, and whatever the differences which separate the main armies from their auxiliaries,—whatever repugnance those may feel to an intimate union whom political motives draw together, whilst they are divided by moral and religious causes,—so long as they are enrolled under the same banner,—so long as the Presbyterian is united to the Anglican, or the Anglican to the Catholics,—there is a close union, and a necessity of fighting together; for only two armies exist in Ireland, and it is absolutely necessary to belong to one or the other. In short, we may say, that nowhere are parties more rigidly marked, and yet that in no country is there a greater variety of passions, sentiments, ideas, and interests.

It would likewise be an error to suppose, because there are only two parties, that whoever has joined one is necessarily chained to it: there exists certainly in each an immovable and unchangeable main body; in the Tory party, it is the Anglican church and aristocracy; in the Radical party, it is the whole Catholic population. The Protestant middle class and the Presbyterians form what may be called the variable and fluctuating population, which furnishes turnabout materials to the Radicals and to the Tories. A Protestant, who in 1825 ardently demanded the emancipation of the Catholics, now votes against them at the elections. Another, who joined them to abolish church-rates and tithes, becomes their adversary when, instead of attacking the abuses of the Protestant church, they assail the principle itself. Far from being eternal, these alliances in Ireland are singularly frail. In the first movement of enthusiasm, acting under a generous impulse, they join, make a treaty of perpetual amity, and believe sincerely in the strength of this friendly alliance. But the union is more at the surface than at the bottom. Protestants and Catholics embraced when they won the great victory in 1829, due to their common efforts; the effusion of feeling was real, the harmony touching; nevertheless, the germs of division existed in the bottom of their hearts. The Protestant said in his heart, "Here is what will content the Catholics;" the Catholic, on the other hand, whispered to himself, "Here is a great conquest, by the aid of which I will obtain others." And on the following day the two friends were opposed as adversaries face to face. But the members who compose this variable element of Irish parties cannot quit one camp without passing immediately into the other; and often in the conflict of grave motives, which nearly balance each other, the slightest circumstance sends the Radical to-day over to the Tories, and will drive him back the next to restore him to the Radicals.

It would be difficult to tell how long this state of things will last. However, it appears to me, that if a third party should be formed in Ireland, it will not be amongst the Protestant aristocracy that it will have its birth, but rather amongst the Catholic population, which, confident in its strength, and prompt to forget, will be disposed to divide. But the course hitherto adopted by the leaders of the popular party has singularly tended to the maintenance of party union. The system of constitutional agitation nearly satisfies both those who, fond of peaceful discussion, reject the use of sanguinary violence as a means of success, and those who, believing the arms of logic insufficient, think that the aid of physical force should not be wholly neglected. Now this system, which very ingeniously combines the two powers of law and force, has hitherto succeeded in preventing amongst the people the formation either of a moderate Whig party or a revolutionary party.

Still it is probable that if, during a long course of years, England should refuse the reforms demanded by the Radical party existing in that country, there would be formed beneath that Radical party one still more radical, and which could not be so without becoming revolutionary; and, on the other hand, if great concessions were made to Ireland, her worst wounds would be healed, and a Whig party might be formed intermediate between the present Radicals and Tories.

Whatever may be the cause hereafter, the only party in which divisions could arise is now united and compact; and in Ireland a choice must necessarily be made between it and its antagonist.

Such are the principal features of the two parties, which in our day divide Ireland.

I do not know if these two parties were ever more opposed to each other than they are at present; but it would be difficult at any time to have exhibited greater hatred. Perhaps this may be a result of the greater liberty which they enjoy, and which permits them to express weaker enmity with greater energy; perhaps they are more vehement, without being more hostile. Within the last twenty years considerable changes have been wrought in the social and political condition of Ireland; the themes of triumph for one party, and of humiliation for the other: the recent recollection of these excites insolent joy with the former, and bitter regret with the latter. What cannot be denied is, that the spirit of party mingles with everything in Ireland. It poisons the social relations. The Irish Tories and Radicals not only form two parties, but two very distinct classes, which have no point of contact; far different from English parties, whose opposite leaders, after a violent struggle in parliament, may be met the same day in the same social circle, which they enter, after having laid aside every remembrance of quarrel and resentment. In Ireland, the separation of the two parties is, in some degree, physical; in every town there are the Protestant hotel, and the Catholic hotel: meetings, balls, dinners, are similarly distinguished; the same distinction extends even to roads and rivers: it is not very long since an Irish nobleman claimed the intervention of government to prevent the erection of a Popish bridge.

But the spirit of party does not stop there in Ireland; and who would believe it? Party enters so deeply into the soul, that in a christian country it has corrupted charity at its very source. "What use is there," exclaims a Protestant Tory, "in attending to the poor and their miseries? Are there not poor in all countries? Has not Ireland always overflowed with them?" . . . . "Accursed be the landlords of Ireland!" exclaims the Irish Radical; "they see without pity the misery that covers their estates." The poor, whose charity is to love the rich, owe them nothing but hatred.

But it is particularly in the north of Ireland that these hateful passions show themselves, and rage in all their violence; there the parties are not different, but they are in a different position. In the south, where, taking the average, there are about twenty Catholics to one Protestant; the Tory party is numerically too weak to measure itself against its adversary; there a single combat would be fatal to it; and it never acts on the offensive; when attacked by open force, instead of defending itself with arms, it calls to its aid the government and the law, the police and the army.

In the north, on the contrary, as the two parties are nearly equal, each may hope for success in a violent contest; and hence the two parties seem always ready to enter the lists, and might be supposed constantly on the eve of a civil war. The outrages, so common in the south, the attempts of the Whiteboys, and their fearful confederations, belong far less to the spirit of party, than to the vices of social organisation. On the contrary, it is the spirit of party that predominates in the north.

Wolfe Tone relates in his Memoirs, that, having visited the county of Derry in 1792, with one of his friends, on a political mission, the Protestant innkeepers at Rathfriland, knowing that they were Catholics, refused to supply them with breakfast for their money.

In the month of July, 1837, I traversed the province of Ulster; it is at this season that the Orange party is accustomed to celebrate the glorious memory of the Boyne and William III. My quality of stranger did not preserve me from the insults to which, at such a juncture, every Catholic is subject; and more than once I was assailed with the popular cry of *No Popery.* A sad event was then the topic of conversation. On the 28th of June, 1837, a holiday amongst the Catholics of Ireland, some Catholic women and children were assembled round a bonfire in the county of Monaghan, where a sportive gaiety was mingled with the sentiments of piety. Suddenly three musket shots were heard, and four children fell lifeless to the earth. The murderers remained unknown, but every one said that the hatred of the Orangemen for Papists had produced the crime, and nobody doubted it.

The Orange party, of which Ulster is the focus, manifests every day a greater desire to use violence than it displayed before. Formerly, the threats of physical force came rather from the Catholic and Radical party, from the popular masses, to which leaders and chiefs were alone wanting for an insurrection. For a long time the Irish nation believed that its deliverance and regeneration could only be obtained by a political revolution, which, bestowing on the government the disposal of rights and properties, would restore power and estates to the original possessors, or their heirs. These traditions, formerly familiar to the national party, were first weakened by long and useless efforts, and afterwards the success obtained by exertion and free institutions have completely dissipated the dreams of sudden and violent prosperity. But it seems that, at the moment the principle of force was abandoned by the Catholic party, it was adopted by the Orangemen. Nothing is more common than to hear members of that party express their ardent desire for actual civil war. "No union," they say, "is possible between Papists and Protestants: it is a mere chimera to wish that they should dwell in the same land; one must absolutely expel the other, as truth drives away falsehood; it is a quarrel of life or death. Let a decisive engagement, let a war of extermination, settle the debate." This language is not openly avowed by the Tory party, but many Tories use it. In fact, they think that, eventually, matters must come to this issue, and that it is better to have the fight at once; they feel power slipping from their hands every day, and they deem it wiser to commence the battle while they are still strong.

It would seem that there must naturally exist some mediator between the two parties, able, if not to bring them together, at least of calming their mutual animosity: this mediator is the government. In every country the government is the natural moderator of parties. To interpose between them, to hold the balance even, to temper one by the other, to force a concession from the one, an abandonment of a demand from the other, to protect all, to succumb to none such in Ireland is the path pointed out to the English government; an admirable task, but very difficult, not to say impossible, to be executed. There are in the two parties ancient spites, implacable passions, exclusive interests, which repulse every intervention of a mediator; and conciliation is impossible between parties so widely separated. In fact, there is no alternative for the English government but to side with one or the other; and such is the violence of those between whom it must choose, that the moment it chooses one party, it must abandon itself to the party altogether, follow instead of direct it; and thus the government is soon led by the passions which it ought to guide.

The English government in Ireland never takes the position it ought to take, until the two parties, arms in hand, are ready to cut each others throats, when it places between them its police and its soldiers. The government is allowed to suppose that without it the two parties would commence civil war; and this is sufficient to sweeten the task, otherwise so difficult, which it has to execute in this country; but with this exception, it exercises in truth no individual or spontaneous action over the parties, from which it receives impulse, instead of taking, as it ought, the initiative.

If it adopts the Tory party, it must necessarily take up all its religious prejudices, all its political resentments and hatreds; and acting thus, it must increase the national sentiment which rejects this detested party. Should it declare for the liberal or Catholic party, it does not less receive the yoke; and then, instead of restraining the popular torrent, it serves only to precipitate its course.

It is thus that the state of parties in Ireland is an additional and fruitful source of democracy.

· PART III ·

I

The Three Principal Remedies That
Have Been Proposed for Irish Evils

We have seen the evils that Ireland endures; we have seen that all these evils proceed from a primary and continued cause; finally, we have seen the kind of resistance that the excess of its miseries has produced amongst the people. The situation of Ireland may be thus summarily described—PROFOUND INDIGENCE AMONGST THE PEOPLE, PERMANENT ANARCHY IN THE STATE.

Now that all the social and political sufferings are known, how are they to be cured? How are we to alleviate the cruel sufferings of a starving people? How came the formidable revolts of irritated anguish? How give sustenance to the people, and peace to the country?

When we see millions of paupers in a population, the first sentiment felt is that of deep pity; and before engaging in reforms, which belong to the political organisation of society, is not the mind at once disposed to inquire by what means it can alleviate the physical condition of so many necessitous persons? We ask of ourselves, if, independent of all forms of government, the poor people of Ireland may not at once be raised from its profound indigence by some procedure, sudden, extraordinary, extreme, like the misery it is designed to cure? The Irish people are dying of hunger. . . . They must be aided. Is it by laws or constitutional reforms? No; there is urgent need; bread, not theories, is wanted. Employment and means of working are wanted. Miserable Ireland is surcharged with population; it is necessary to lighten the load that crushes her; and such aid must be given to Ireland immediately. And this misery, which calls so loudly for immediate assistance, is it not increasing every day? Each day this population of paupers becomes more numerous, and in proportion as its increasing misery excites more pity, the menaces of its despair inspires more terror. It is, in fact, a phenomenon worthy of meditation, that the population of Ireland, although so miserable, multiplies more rapidly than that of England and Scotland, which are so prosperous; and what is more remarkable is, that in Ireland itself the population is multiplied in direct proportion to its misery. It is in Connaught that famine rages most severely, and it is there that the population multiplies most rapidly. Why, then, should we not attempt at once to arrest this frightful misery, the progress of which reveals so much of suffering, and so much of danger?

Three systems are offered which promise to lead to the end that we wish to attain. I. To procure employment for the unoccupied paupers. II. Diminishing the population by furnishing the indigent with the means of emigrating. III. Supporting at the public expense those who are neither employed in Ireland, nor removed to another country. In other words, three means are offered for the salvation of Ireland,—industrial employment, emigration, and poor laws. Let us examine these three systems separately. They have been, and are now, amongst the best statemen, objects of study and labour, which demand our serious attention.

Section I. Increase of Industrial Employment

Of the three means proposed, the first would undoubtedly be the best, if it were practicable; for assuredly it is better to draw an idle population to useful labour than to feed it with alms, or send it into exile.

The statement, that there are four millions of persons unemployed in Ireland is doubtless an exaggeration. Official documents prove that, out of 7,763,000 inhabitants, there are 4,863,000 engaged in agriculture, and 1,419,000 employed in trade or manufactures; whence it would follow that about one million were destitute of all employment. But in Ireland the greatest number of paupers consists not of those who have no work but of those who have not regular work. Half of the Irish farmers are paupers for a part of the year; and if account were taken only of the agricultural labourers and manufacturing operatives who have employment all the year round, the amount of such labourers would be next to nothing. We may then, without risk of error, affirm that, out of the eight millions in Ireland, half have either no employment, or employment insufficient for acquiring the means of subsistence.

The same statistical documents, which show that in Ireland nearly five millions of individuals are employed on the land, show that in England and Scotland, out of a population of 16,205,000, not more than five millions are engaged in agriculture; that is to say, nearly the same number that is so employed in Ireland; nevertheless, England and Scotland have an extent of 54,000,000 of acres, whilst Ireland has only 19,000,000. So that in Ireland the land absorbs two-thirds of the population, whilst in the other two countries it does not engage quite one third; and that Ireland employs as many labourers to cultivate her soil as England and Scotland, which are double her size. Finally, it appears certain that by the Irish system of tillage the ground produces one half less than it does under the management of an English or Scotch farmer; whence it follows that three Irish agricultural labourers do rather less work than an Englishman or Scotchman. Even supposing that the number of English and Scotch labourers is too small, that of the Irish agriculturists is clearly excessive. And the defective cultivation of the ground depends precisely on their quantity.

The employment in tillage of more hands than are necessary, and who injure each other from the mere effect of their numbers, is an absolute evil in an economic point of view; but this evil may be a relative good in politics. Thus, if it were true that every one in Ireland not engaged in the cultivation of land is absolutely without employment, and that every unoccupied individual is an enemy of the public peace, we should be compelled to acknowledge that, even for the general advantage, it would be better that the land were covered with the greater number of cultivators, even though the produce were less. Thus, whilst the principles of political economy would advise the ejection from the land of half of those who occupy it, the political state of the country would require that the number of cultivators should be still further increased.

What, then, is to be done? Must we, by tearing away a portion of those who derive from it some means of subsistence, increase the number of Irishmen who have neither resource nor employment? Or must we increase the sum of misery that crushes the country, by breaking up the portions of the present occupants, and distributing the fragments to those who have none?

Assuredly, if there is any country to which the establishment of manufactures would be a blessing, Ireland is that country. Employment to its half-occupied or idle hands would be to Ireland not only an element of happiness, but a means of safety. There is in Ireland a productive force of several millions of hands which is inert or ill-directed. It is an instrument which manufacturing industry would set at work where it is now idle, and render fruitful where it is barren.

All causes unite to render the development of industry in Ireland desirable: if the physical existence of the lower classes is interested in it, so also is the future of the middle classes, whom we have seen invited to so high a destiny; industry alone can feed the one, and enrich the other.

There are countries where the progress of manufacturing industry is not viewed without a kind of disquietude and terror; they are those where the peasants seem to desert tillage in multitudes for the factories, and where the large manufacturers, by their number and system, seem to contain germs of corruption for the people, and danger for the state. But what reason is there to fear that the land would be abandoned in a country where the people knows and loves nothing but it? What we have to dread in Ireland is not the excess that would drive too large a portion of the population from the country into the manufacturing towns, but the very contrary extreme. We should fear that the people chained to the soil should not be sufficiently detached from it to support manufacturers. Even supposing that a factory life exercises a pernicious influence on the physical and moral conditions of the operatives; supposing that the factory corrupts women and children, and attacks the habits of domestic life, and the future prospects of society;—were it true that the aggregation of large masses of operatives, in particular parts of the country, becomes too considerable a power in the state, and too dangerous an instrument in the hands of parties;—were it no less firmly established that these great operative masses which manufacturers employ, are subject, from their oscillations, to fall suddenly and without transition, from labour into idleness—that is to say, from comfort to destitution; these evils, admitting them in their fullest extent, would be a thousand times less than those which exist in Ireland; where idleness corrupts far more than the labour in factories,—where misery depraves all those whom idleness does not corrupt, and where millions of starving paupers are a more formidable cause of disorder and anarchy, than a like number of individuals could be in any case, who found in their labour numerous means of existence. Whence, then, comes it, that Ireland so much required, and is at the same time so destitute of, manufacturing industry?

It is not because the protection of government is wanting to industry in Ireland, but that protection is almost barren. The system of prizes to encourage certain fabrics has been tried, some efforts of production followed, which ceased so soon as the prizes were withdrawn. In order to open a free scope for Irish industry, government is anxious to open immense lines of communication by canals and railways; assuredly such means of transport are admirable aids to industry, but they must first find the industry existing; they might aid its birth, but they could not create it. In 1780, Ireland had fine roads. Arthur Young, whose testimony has great weight, declares that at that period they were far superior to the roads of England. Ireland was then not the less destitute of commerce and manufactures; whilst England had already entered on her era of commercial wealth and industrial prosperity.

In its desire to promote Irish industry and trade, government has proposed to execute itself the great lines of communication which it deems proper to be made. But this is a perilous means. Is it fit that government should be a speculator in public works? Can private industry securely advance in a country where it may at every step find a rival so powerful as the state?

The government of Ireland might perhaps see in this system of works executed by the state, the advantages of at once giving employment to those not employed by private industry; but such work would only afford partial and transitory relief. And it would be so especially in every British country, where the intervention of government in public works is considered, and not perhaps without reason, a fraud on private enterprise. Now this accidental employment of idle hands would be an evil rather than a good, if the labourer, after his temporary engagement with the government, found afterwards no employment in the factories of private speculators. It is a great misfortune for a country to believe that the protection of government is necessary to the prosperity of its industry. Industry and industrial employments are not created by imperial decrees or acts of parliament; governments have been led to believe that they can create them, by the facility with which they can destroy them, or prevent their birth.

There were formerly flourishing manufactures in Ireland; the English government, then, to effect this purpose, had only to fetter them, for liberty is the vital air to industry: it loaded with trammels half the operatives of Ireland, and interdicted its ports and those of the entire world to the products of Irish labour.

England's oppression of Ireland is nowhere shown so clearly as in its commercial policy. England wished to sell everything to Ireland, and purchase nothing, which was just as absurd as it was unjust: for Ireland could not traffic with England, and how could those buy which did not sell? This commercial selfishness of England was sometimes pushed to downright insanity. In the reign of Charles II., England having resolved to extend its exclusion of the products of Irish industry, a bill passed the Commons, by which the importation of Irish cattle was declared *a nuisance;* in the Lords some objection was made to the word *nuisance,* and one member proposed that it should be a *felony;* the chancellor, with more wit and as much reason, said that it might as well be called *adultery.*

The unjust trammels which fettered Irish industry are now broken: all Irish operatives are free; Ireland may send her produce to every part of the world; and the ports of England are open to her. The commercial liberty which unites Ireland to England is not merely that which is established between nation and nation, but that which naturally exists between different portions of the same nation, between two territories subject to the same empire; Ireland and England are in the same commercial relation to each other as any two English cities; Dublin trades with Liverpool, just as Liverpool does with London.

But the industrial employment which despotism so easily destroys, does not so easily revive with liberty; for though it cannot exist without freedom, yet freedom is not its creator; far different conditions are required both for its birth and development.

The commercial liberty of which the conquest was begun in 1782, but not completed until 1820, has hitherto produced only one salutary effect in Ireland. It has opened an immense market to its agricultural produce, and secured a kind of privilege for its corn in the English ports from which the grain of other countries is excluded. But it has conferred no advantages on Irish manufacture; Ireland still continues to use the products of English industry.

There are some who believe it impossible for Ireland to establish manufactures whilst England is allowed to import the produce of hers; those who are of this opinion propose, that in order to protect the rising manufactures of Ireland, a duty should be imposed on the import of English goods. But then, in retaliation, the agricultural produce of Ireland would be similarly taxed in England. So that she possesses and would compromise a certain advantage for a future and very dubious good. Besides, is it true that the competition of English industry is the principal obstacle to the growth of manufactures in Ireland? Certainly not: the greatest obstacle is elsewhere; it arises less from England than from Ireland herself.

Without doubt, the English operative is on the whole superior to the Irish operative: he is more skilful and steady; he works longer and better; but the immense use made of Irish operatives in England, proves that the objection is not caused by themselves. Manchester and Liverpool employ myriads of Irishmen in their factories. Assuredly, when we see the two greatest industrial and commercial cities of Britain, I may say of the whole world, prosper by the labour of Irish operatives, it cannot be said that the defective labour in Ireland depends on the very nature of the workman.

It must be added, that if the labour of the Irishman is inferior to that of the Englishman, the defect has a compensating advantage, which is, that it is cheaper. A journeyman's wages are very low in Ireland, because there is little work and an immense competition of workmen: should an Irishman in a factory do only half the work of an Englishman, it will be still more profitable to employ him, for the Englishman gets more than double his wages.

It seems, then, that Ireland is in the most prosperous condition for the establishment of manufactures. But it is not sufficient that industry should be free; it is not sufficient to have instruments of execution; the prime mover is still wanting, that is to say, capital. Now in Ireland there is absolutely no capital. And why? Because this country has been long subject to the persecutions of an arbitrary government, and capitals only show themselves under the auspices of justice and guarantees; because this country possessing in the present day considerable liberties, whilst at the same time it remains subject to institutions radically vicious, is kept by the inevitable struggle in a constant state of agitation. Capital is wanting to develope industry in Ireland, but capital flies from agitation; and as capital withdraws, misery is augmented. This increase of misery multiplies the chances of trouble and disorder, and renders capital still more scarce. Once involved in this vicious circle, escape is scarcely possible.

Capital is not only wanting to manufacturing industry in Ireland, we find a similar deficiency in agricultural industry. Because there are in Ireland nearly five millions occupied with the ground, it is supposed that there is not a supply of land for the population, and that the insufficiency of the soil is the cause of all the evils. But this opinion must yield to a physical fact. Out of nineteen millions of acres, forming the surface of Ireland, there are five millions of land on which the industry of man has never been tried, and which, nevertheless, might be profitably tilled or employed in pasturage. And why do these lands, which seem to invite labour, remain naked and deserted? Because, in order that they should be fertilised, advances of capital are required, which the poor man cannot make, and the rich will not. And why will not the rich man invest capital in the culture of the Irish soil, without which that culture cannot increase? Because the state of the country prevents him. It is not land, then, which is wanting to the population in Ireland; it is capital that is required for agricultural labour as well as manufacturing industry.

This want of capital is not the only impediment to the improvement of the Irish workman. I have already said, that the Irish workman is not unfitted by nature for manufacturing industry, and the example of all the Irishmen profitably employed in England and Scotland attests the fact. But we must confess that so long as the Irishman remains in Ireland, he has certain grievous faults which belong not to his nature but to the country, and which render him a bad servant.

Accustomed to endure every sort of oppression in Ireland, he has, when employed, one fixed idea, which is, that his employer will either give him no wages, or that he will pay him a less sum than is justly his due. Thus, what happens when a manufacture is established in Ireland? Scarcely are the operatives, who at first consented to work for moderate wages, masters of the field, when they combine to obtain higher wages, and applying the Whiteboy principle to manufactures, they arbitrarily fix the price of a day's work; they enact terrible penalties against the master who should pay, and the journeyman who should consent to receive, less wages; and this barbarous code does not contain idle menaces; punishment follows close on the offence; and not long since, Dublin was the theatre of horrid murders committed on poor operatives, whose only crime was that they worked for a lower price than that fixed by the "Union of Trades;" unfortunate beings, who were murdered because they were satisfied with moderate wages, and who must have starved for want of work, if they asked higher! And what is the infallible result of these outrages? If the manufacturer yields, he is ruined; if he resists, the operatives refuse to work. In either case industrial enterprise is destroyed, and the operative who complains, and perhaps not without reason, that he receives too little wages for his work, is deprived both of work and wages.

Here and there in England we see examples of such combinations, called sticks and strikes, but they have always been partial and transitory; they have frequently ruined one branch of industry, but never every branch of industry. In the place of the continual dread that an Irishman has of never being paid for his work, the Englishman has in general great confidence in his employers, because he is accustomed to find them careful of his rights and faithful to their engagements. The English operative, besides, generally possesses sufficient knowledge to comprehend that a temporary increase of wages may be pernicious to himself, if that increase destroys the branch of industry on which his wages depend.

This explains why the Irishmen are good workmen in English factories. When they leave Ireland, they abandon these savage traditions, and whilst they bring their physical and intellectual faculties to England, they acquire there the morality in which they were deficient, and they acquire it the more readily, when they learn that in England the rights of the journeyman are as sacred as those of the master.

The same reason explains why it is that manufacturing industry, languishing or destroyed in almost the entire country, is rather prosperous in the north of the island, where the higher and the working classes are not, as in the south, in a state of mutual suspicion; where there is war between political and religious parties, but not between the rich and the poor, the master and the workman.

Thus, on one side the agitated state of Ireland prevents the introduction of capital, and when capital is introduced by persons sufficiently bold to brave this agitation, these brutal and violent passions, which the working class seem almost to breathe in the atmosphere that surrounds them, raise an almost insurmountable obstacle to the success of their enterprise.

Without these two causes which have been just explained, capital, instead of flying from Ireland, would resort to it, and we shall soon see the source from which it would flow.

England is overflowing with capital; she sends her money over the entire world; she invests it on her continent, in America, in Asia; she speculates on land in the United States, on mines in Mexico; she establishes steam-boats in India. Why then, instead of sending her capital eight or ten thousand miles, should she not invest it in a country under her hand, where there is such a fund of labour, only requiring to be set to work? "England," say some, "wishes to keep to herself the monopoly of industry." I should be glad if her policy tended to this object—but what matters it, whether or no? Capital has no national spirit; wherever there is most profit and security, it makes its home. Besides, Ireland is English; it forms a part of the British empire. We should assign very extravagant national passions to English capitalists, if Belfast and Dublin differed in their eyes from Manchester and Glasgow. Let us state the matter fairly: the obstacle clearly arises from Ireland being the most miserable and agitated country in the whole world; hence an Englishman will invest his capital anywhere rather than in Ireland, and precisely because the country is directly before his eyes, he sees more clearly the danger to which his capital would be exposed if he sent it thither.

What must we conclude from the preceding statements? In the first place, so long as the causes exist which oppose the spontaneous development of Irish industry, it is not from manufactures that we must ask work for those who have it not, and a remedy for the evils of which the idleness of the people is the real or supposed cause: and in the second place, that to render the development of Irish industry possible, it is necessary to begin by removing the causes by which it is now paralysed. These causes are notorious; they are the anarchy of the country, and the spirit that animates the working classes.

But whose business is it to combat these obstacles, so ruinous to Irish industry? The establishment of manufactures is, doubtless, no business of the government; but assuredly its natural task is to prevent or dissipate the political causes which prevent the rise and growth of manufactures.

Now, by what means can the government restore peace to the country, and bestow upon the people the dispositions which are necessary to the establishment of industrial employment in Ireland? This is a question of a different nature from that which we are discussing, and which goes beyond the scope of the present chapter. I have limited myself to showing, that manufacturing industry, under present circumstances, cannot be a means of safety for Ireland, since it must encounter immense obstacles in the country itself. These obstacles arise from the inherent vice of its institutions, so that to inquire the means of developing industry in Ireland, leads us to search what sort of reforms ought to be made in the institutions of the country. The question is stated, but the arrangement of the work requires that the discussion should be placed elsewhere.

Section II. Emigration

If it is impossible to find employment in Ireland for all those who are wholly or partly unoccupied, we must, say some, diminish the number of labourers, and what better means is there of attaining this end than emigration?

Of all the systems which during the last twenty years have been proposed for the safety of Ireland, there is not perhaps one which has met more favour in England than emigration conducted on a large scale. It is a violent remedy, it is true, but it is one which rests on a fact apparently simple, and suited to catch the imagination. There are some millions of people whose situation in Ireland is truly deplorable; let them be transported to another country, less crowded with inhabitants; they will there find a happy lot, and those who remain, delivered from a superabundant population, will be comfortable and prosperous. This theory is supported by the authority of economists; it has several times received the sanction of parliament itself, and many would believe the wounds of Ireland incurable if emigration could not heal them.

Are not the political doctrines by which nations are governed subject to strange variations? We are still close to a period when the theories of statesmen and the science of government had in view no object more constant or more dear than the increase of population. Severe on celibacy, the laws favoured early marriages, and public rewards were decreed to prolific mothers, and the emigration of children from their country was forbidden as a public curse. Now, amongst one of the most civilised nations of the earth, an opinion is established that the increase of population is the greatest danger with which a nation can be menaced; we are taught that to avert this peril, it is necessary not only to check the tendency to increase, but also to diminish the existing number: and emigration is not only permitted, but solemnly encouraged as a means of safety, both for those who emigrate, and for the country relieved from the surplus population.

It was down to our days a doctrine universally consecrated, that a dense population is the source of strength and national wealth to a country, and that though it may injure it from being badly directed, yet it is always capable of being converted into an instrument of power and prosperity; a very different theory from that which now prevails, when the population seems excessive, and one-half must be banished to ensure the prosperity of the other.

What must Ireland think of her governors? The time is not very distant when her inhabitants were rigorously prohibited from emigrating by the very English government which now offers every encouragement to emigration.

Without dwelling further on the contradictions between these different systems, and without examining to what extent the successive employment of each was justified by a difference of circumstances, let us inquire if emigration could at this moment be of any benefit to Ireland.

And in the first place, is it true, that if the population of Ireland was diminished by a third, or even by a half, the miseries of the country would cease? This is a first point which I may be permitted to doubt. The population of Ireland is, in truth, reduced to miserable expedients for subsistence. It imposes on itself the most cruel privations, which do not save it every year from enduring a famine more or less severe. It is fed on the worst of food, in spite of which it is exposed to periodical starvation. It has adopted the system best adapted to sustain the greatest number of inhabitants on the smallest possible territory. For it is a well-established economic truth, that the same extent of land which planted with potatoes would support twenty persons, would not grow corn sufficient for more than four or five, and would, if employed as pasturage for cattle, not feed more than one individual. Ireland has absolutely renounced the use of bread and meat, to live entirely on potatoes. She has done more; as amongst potatoes there are some which multiply faster than others, she has taken as her food the *lumpers,* the least agreeable to the taste, but which are redeemed in the eyes of the Irishman by their prodigious abundance.

It seems, at the first glance, that for a population which derives subsistence from the soil with so much difficulty, every diminution of number would be an immense benefit; still if the question be investigated, it will be found that the emigration of four or five millions of Irishmen would not necessarily produce for the four or five remaining millions better or more certain means of subsistence. In fact, whence does it arise, that the agricultural produce of Ireland does not appear sufficient for the support of the population? It is not because the country does not supply sufficient food for eight millions of men; everybody knows that this fertile country could easily support twenty-five millions of inhabitants. Why then does the third of that number live so wretchedly? Because, before asking from the land and its produce what is necessary for his subsistence, the Irishman must first take what is necessary to pay the rent to his landlord. This explains why, in a land capable of giving bread to twenty-five millions of persons, eight millions with difficulty find support from the cultivation of the worst kind of potatoes. If these eight millions of Irishmen wished to feed on corn, nothing would be more easy, for the land furnishes far more than their necessities require, but then they could not pay their rents to the lords of the soil. Now see how the Irish cultivator is obliged to act; he sows a part of his land in corn to sell the harvest, and he plants a small spot in potatoes, on the produce of which he lives. In the first case he hopes to derive from the land the best kind of harvest, with the price of which he will pay his rent; and in the second, to obtain the more abundant produce capable of supplying his more imperious wants; and as the rent which the landlord requires from him is constantly raised, he constantly enlarges the space on which he raises the articles that he sells, whilst he as constantly narrows the space on which he produces the potatoes that support him. Now suppose that the landlords of Ireland see nothing but what is natural and regular in this distress of the agricultural population; suppose it one of their familiar principles that the tenant should derive no profit from the culture of the soil, but just so much as is absolutely necessary to his support; finally, suppose that this principle should be so rigorously applied by Irish landlords, that every more economical mode of life discovered by the tenants necessarily leads to the augmentation of their rents. In this hypothesis, which to everybody who knows Ireland is a sad reality, what would be the consequence of a diminution of population?

The soil of Ireland having to feed a less number of inhabitants, would they hereafter be maintained in a better position? Not at all. For if, instead of continuing to eat potatoes, they began to feed on bread, the landlord would see in this change an increase of prosperity and a sign of fortune which would at once induce him to raise the rent. In order to pay this larger sum, the poor tenant should at once revert to his former system; if he delayed, he would be soon ejected for non-payment of rent, and his miseries would begin again as before. Thus, after millions of Irishmen were removed from Ireland, the condition of the remaining population would not, perhaps, be at all changed, but would remain equally miserable. Hence we can understand why Ireland a century ago, with only a third of the present inhabitants, was just as indigent as she is now, and subject to the same causes of misery, independent of number.

Now, if it were true that the Irish population might be considerably diminished without any amelioration of its condition, it would follow that a system of emigration which rests entirely on the efficacy of this diminution must vanish completely.

Still, suppose that the primary basis of the system has not been overthrown; that the utility of diminishing the population of Ireland were, on the contrary, well established, and that the emigration of some millions offered an efficacious and undisputed remedy for the evils of Ireland. We may admit this hypothesis, because, though the depopulation of Ireland might not produce the expected advantages, it might lead to other salutary effects which would give it value. Would it not, in the first place, be profitable to the emigrants? It seems that to whatever other part of the world they were transferred, they would be more comfortable, at least less miserable, than in Ireland. Would not the remaining population, at least in the first instance, be reduced by the departure of some millions of labourers, its competitors? Delivered at once from its most idle and turbulent population, the country would become more calm; this repose would profit England herself, who always feels the rebound of the agitation in Ireland; and if it were true that the absence of three or four millions of Irishmen from Ireland, only for a few years, would spare her the trouble caused by that country, would not this be sufficient inducement to adopt a system of emigration?

Admitting, then, that the emigration of a portion of the Irish people would be sufficiently profitable to Ireland and to England to merit examination, let us inquire if it would be possible. This examination will not appear unprofitable, if we reflect on the multitude of persons in England prejudiced in favour of a vast system of emigration.

And let us first remark, that this emigration must be on an immense scale, or it will be absolutely fruitless, at least in an economical point of view. To judge what it must be in order to be efficacious, let us consider what takes place at present in Ireland. There is not, perhaps, one county in Ireland from which thousands of the inhabitants do not emigrate every year. Nevertheless, it has been established by official inquiries, that this emigration, more or less advantageous to those who depart, produces no sensible effect on the condition of those who remain. It has been found that in the parishes from whence there was the greatest emigration, the wages of day labourers have not been raised one farthing, and the employment of the labourers who remained in the country has not been increased by a single day's work. In certain counties it would be necessary to remove nine-tenths before the inhabitants would derive any sensible benefit from emigration. It is astonishing to see how quickly the void created by emigration is filled, and it is not easy to discover by what enchantment the paupers who depart have their places supplied by other paupers. Millions of Irishmen must, therefore, be removed from Ireland, or the effects of emigration will be imperceptible. But such an emigration is at once singularly difficult and expensive.

Whither are three millions of emigrants to be conveyed? Assuredly, of all countries England is that to which this difficulty would be the slightest, for she has colonial establishments in all parts of the globe, and her navies give her free access to the countries which she does not possess. But all vacant territories would not be equally suited to Irish emigration.

The largest and most fertile would be Australia. But how could the poor population of Ireland be sent to a place designed to receive the criminals of England? Ireland, perhaps not without reason, would regard the proceeding as an insult; and this impression, right or wrong, would render the enterprise impossible. Would the United States of America be their destination? This country would certainly be the best and most prosperous for the emigrants that could be chosen; but is it to be believed, if the United States were menaced with the invasion of three or four millions of Irishmen, that the government of the country would leave the American ports open to these swarms of paupers? I may be allowed to doubt it. Ireland sends some thousands of poor emigrants every year already to the United States, and this moderate current of emigration has already raised so much clamour in the country, that it has been several times debated, whether the ports of the United States ought not to be closed against Irish emigrants, either by a formal interdiction, or a tax sufficiently high to serve as a prohibition.

Canada remains. It is, in truth, the natural asylum of Irish emigrants. Canada is of all the British colonies the least distant from Ireland; it is a country that has become English, thanks to the cowardice of Louis XV. and his court. Many Irish are settled there already who would receive the new-comers; and though the best lands of this colony are already occupied, a sufficiently large extent still remains to receive for a long time the surplus of English population. Still it is matter for inquiry, whether, when the English power is tottering in Canada, it would be prudent to reinforce that country with some millions of men, who, as Irishmen, instinctively detest the English yoke, and as Catholics would be the natural allies of that part of the Canadian population most hostile to England.

Still let us further suppose, that these different objections against Australia, Canada, and the United States, have been obviated—suppose that a place for emigrants has been found, the first difficulty is overcome; but how many others instantly present themselves!

It is by no means a trifling enterprise to transport several millions of men eight or ten thousand miles across the ocean. Experience shows us, that for a long voyage a vessel ought, in general, to carry less than a thousand passengers; let us, however, take a thousand as the average. Adopting this base, a hundred voyages out and home would be required to the emigration of one hundred thousand persons, that is to say, only a small fraction of the population that it would be necessary to remove. How many years would be necessary for such transport, even if England were to devote all her navy to it, though her fleets have plenty of occupation elsewhere? Nevertheless, to obtain the proposed end, a sudden and complete emigration of all the population deemed superabundant is required; every slow and partial emigration would afford no remedy for an evil so prompt to renew itself as fast as it is cured.

But let us go further: suppose that the transport of the emigrants, which appears impossible, could be effected, the expenses of this transport would be so great as to present a new obstacle. In fact, it has never entered into the heads of the warmest advocates of Irish emigration to limit themselves to shipping off some hundreds of the poor Irish, and setting them ashore, naked or covered with rags, in a new country. To treat the poor Irish thus, would be to serve them worse than the malefactors transported to Australia, and settled there at great expense. Even if this course of conduct were adopted at the request of the emigrants themselves, it would still be without excuse. No one is ignorant of the extreme distress to which poor families are consigned, who, flying from misery in their own country, and destitute of capital, go in search of better fortunes to a distant land, where they only find trials still more frightful. We can understand why a government may leave such acts of imprudence free; but, assuredly, it should never become an agent in them. In England it has been always considered an essential feature in every system of emigration, that the government should make provision for the passage and all the expenses of the emigrant from his first starting to his arrival at his destination, and all the expenses of his first establishment. Now the total amount of these expenses is enormous. In 1826, they were estimated at 60*l.* for every family of five, or 12*l.* a head. But if we turn from estimates to actual experiments, we shall see that the expenses absolutely necessary exceed this amount, and that the emigration of a family of five involves an outlay of 100*l.*, or 20*l.* a head. Consequently, the emigration of four millions of persons would cost 80,000,000*l.*! Taking the smaller amount, 12*l.* a head, it would come to 48,000,000*l.* And supposing that only two millions emigrated, the expense would be 40,000,000*l.*, according to the estimate derived from direct experiment. However interested England may be in removing the evils of Ireland, it is very doubtful whether she will ever have recourse to such an expensive remedy.

Let us further admit, for a moment, that all the preceding objections and improbabilities have been obviated; another obstacle would remain, more difficult to be overcome than all the others. It would not be sufficient that three or four millions should have the physical possibility of leaving Ireland; it would be further necessary that they should be willing to do so. "It would be their interest to emigrate, and they would be wrong to refuse the means;"—such is our feeling. But would their judgment be in accordance with ours? Their refusal to emigrate would render the system impossible, for forced emigration is a penal exile. And on what would be founded the right of treating the poor Irish as malefactors? It would be first necessary to proclaim poverty a crime. Now, though in English habits poverty is, doubtless, a great misfortune, and sometimes almost a misdemeanour, it has not yet become a crime.

If voluntary emigration is the only possible system, we must conclude, that a system on such a scale as that which we have examined, can never be executed.

There exists in Ireland, as has been already stated, a free and spontaneous current of emigration. But we must remark, that in general it is not the poorest who emigrate. The emigrants belong chiefly to the middle classes; they are comfortable tradesmen, or small farmers, who, though already possessing some comforts, are anxious to better their condition; who, possessing small capital, are anxious to find a country where a capital may be more safely invested than in Ireland. They are in a large proportion Protestants; that is to say, persons of a condition above the common. In a word, all those who depart, are the persons whom the country is most interested to keep. And if the poor Irishman does not emigrate as well as the rich, it is not merely because he has physical means inferior to the rich, but because he has not the same inclination. In spite of all his miseries, the Irishman passionately loves his country, and seems attached to her by closer ties the more miserable he is. Perhaps it would be just to say, that attachment to country is in the inverse proportion of the comforts enjoyed in it. The English, whose physical comforts surpass those of any other people, understand less than any the links that bind man to his natal soil. He has tasted certain comforts which are absolutely necessary to him, and without which he cannot exist; when these comforts begin to fail in his native land, he seeks them elsewhere; and even when not deprived of them, he constantly seeks their increase; his country is the land where he can obtain the greatest amount of happiness. The poor Irishman, on the contrary, does not seek after enjoyments of which he has never formed a notion; having never known of anything but a miserable existence, he does not suspect that any other is possible in this world; a great enterprise, undertaken to procure happiness of which he is incredulous, has no charms for him. He remains on the spot of his present misery, little anxious to search for fresh misfortune at a distance; and it is some consolation for him to bear the load of life in the country where he was born, where his father and mother lived and died, and where his children will have to live and die.

If, then, emigration were offered to those millions of Irishmen whose absence is so desired, the greater number would not accept it. We may add, that many who are desirous to emigrate would cease to have the wish, if the plan of emigration should be formed and executed by the English government. The Irishman with difficulty believes that *he* can derive any benefit from such a source: and in this case, are not his fears natural? Setting aside every cause of political distrust what terrible risks must the unfortunate beings run, whose emigration becomes an official function of the government? Who is to guarantee to the poor emigrants that they will receive the care and attention designed for them? Are not they justified in fearing everything? Are they very sure that once embarked, and the ocean interposed between them and their country, they will not be cast on some unknown and desolate shore, to die of famine, cold, and misery? A terrible responsibility weighs on the head of a family who engages his wife and children in this perilous path. People may persist in believing that he is wrong not to emigrate, if the means are afforded him, but everything shows that, guided by his own judgment, interests, and passions, the poor Irishman will not emigrate.

These difficulties are so great and obvious, that the most ardent partisans of emigration cannot mistake them. Still they do not abandon their favourite theme, they modify it, and, restricting their system in the hope of rendering it more easy, they still believe it the best means of safety for Ireland. Let us, then, examine their subsidiary plan.

The reader has already seen the extreme division of the soil: its being portioned into small farms of one, two, or three acres, has infinitely multiplied the number of agriculturists in Ireland. This multitude of occupants, surcharging the land, is, as some people say, one of the principal causes of Irish misery: and the natural remedy, they say, would be to destroy small, and establish large farms. But, in the first place, in order to abolish the small farms, you must remove the small farmers; and how can these expulsions be effected in a country where those who are ejected wreak the most terrible reprisals, and the most cruel revenge? To this the Englishman will answer, "The dispossessed tenants must emigrate." Let us examine, attentively, the different systems of emigration proposed for Ireland, and we shall find that, at the bottom of all, the predominant idea is the diminution of the agricultural population.

But, within such restricted limits, would a system of emigration be more practicable than that we have just examined? . . . No. It may be said that it would be less so. In fact, out of the five millions of agriculturists existing in Ireland, there are certainly more than two millions who, in the system of the English economists, must be regarded as superabundant, and who consequently should emigrate. Now we have already seen what enterprise and expense the emigration of such a number would involve; and if it be true that such obstacles are sufficiently grave to prevent England from effecting the emigration of millions of poor Irishmen, whose misery is to her a source of alarm; how are we to believe that she would be tempted to surmount the same difficulties for the mere purpose of diminishing the agricultural population of Ireland? It is evident, that if the emigration of the Irish farmers were possible, England would not undertake it, because their lot, compared with that of others infinitely more wretched, could only excite a secondary interest.

It may well be conceived, that a landlord would be more interested in the removal of an agriculturist who surcharges his estate, and whose weight is felt by him alone, than to clear Ireland of a pauper whose burthen is borne by the entire country. But what follows from this, except that the emigration of small farmers would be profitable to the rich? Another consequence would result, the Irish landlords, being the only persons interested in emigration, ought to bear the entire expense. Now, supposing that the Irish landlords had the power to effect this emigration, have they the will? . . Not they truly. . . It would be first necessary that they should feel that a diminution of the number of farmers would be useful to their interests; now, on the contrary, it is certain that the excessive number of cultivators, so far from being regarded as an absolute evil by the greater part of Irish landlords, is considered by them, in some respects, as a real advantage. We have seen above, that the emigration of 2,000,000 of souls would cost 40,000,000*l.*; now the entire rental of Ireland is estimated at about 6,000,000*l.*; so that the expenses of such an emigration would consume seven years of their revenues. We may then, without rashness, affirm that such sacrifices will not be made by an aristocracy that not only lives up to its income, but almost, as we may say, "from hand to mouth."

We must add, that the execution of a task so delicate and so extensive, would not only require the stimulus of private interest, but also the incentive of generous sentiment. The idea of emigration should be enforced with ardour and charity by the Irish landlords, as a means of relieving great sufferings, and establishing comforts on their estates. Now, how are we to believe that they, who, by their carelessness or selfishness, have allowed immense miseries to accumulate in Ireland, will display extraordinary zeal in their diminution? How are we to believe that they will do from remorse what they have not done from conscience? Is it reasonable to expect from them lively sympathies for those whom emigration will remove six thousand miles from Ireland, when they are so often found without pity for the frightful distress of which they are the witnesses? If the Irish landlords were capable of the sacrifices demanded of them, emigration would not now be necessary. The remedy would be useless, because the evil would not exist.

As the emigration of the agricultural population can neither be obtained from the English government, nor from the interests or sympathies of Irish landlords, a third system has been recently tried, under the authority of the law. The counties are permitted to tax themselves for the purpose of facilitating emigration, and we may see, from the discussions on this enactment, that its principal object was to provide for the emigration of small tenants ejected from their farms.

It would be easy here to demonstrate the perils of such a system, fitted to encourage the selfishness of the rich, who, seeing for the future, in the gratuitous emigration of the ejected tenantry, a means of escape from the vengeance of the poor, will no longer be restrained by any check in their oppression of the agricultural population; and on the faith of this emigration, which, perhaps, will not take place, they will show themselves more severe than before, so as to provoke reprisals, the more formidable as they will be suspended over their heads, at the very moment that they believe them most distant. But, salutary or fatal, emigration restricted by such limits can only have a very partial effect. Reduced to these terms, it may protect or compromise some private interests; but the plan is not sufficiently extensive to produce a sensible influence on the social and political condition of Ireland.

Thus, everything in these various systems of emigration is defective: an efficacious emigration is impossible; that which is practicable would be vain and incomplete. One set of difficulties only gives birth to another: the discovery of a proper country for the emigrants, the length of the voyage, the vast amount of expense, the complication of the enterprise, all prevent it; and when these objections are removed, a thousand others instantly appear. Emigration being rendered possible, it is not determined who are to emigrate; and the choice of emigrants being made, they will reject emigration. Finally, passing from one obstacle to another, from one impossibility to another, we at last lose sight of the point from which we started, and having in vain sought the means of clearing away the wretched and demoralised portion of the population, we at last come to applaud the discovery of a plan for exiling those who, in the present state of the country, are the most valuable to preserve. Even if all these impossible plans of emigration could be effected, would the slightest good result to Ireland?

Consult the animals of the country, and see what little influence all the violent enterprises and extraordinary accidents of depopulation have had on its social and political condition. Calculate all who perished in Ireland during the wars of religion;—count the thousands slaughtered by Cromwell, and the thousands he transported to the colonies;—consider the hundreds of thousands carried off by famine, whose number in one year (1740) surpassed forty thousand;—forget not the thousands destroyed by the plague and national wars at various times;—take into account those who are constantly wasted away by disease and misery;—omit not the estimate, formerly very large, of those who perished by the hand of the executioner;—finally, attend to the twenty-five or thirty thousand Irishmen taken away every year by the natural course of emigration: and when these facts have been verified, investigate the consequences: when, in the midst of these various changes, you will find Ireland the same at all epochs, always miserable in the same degree, always overstocked with paupers, displaying the same deep and hideous wounds; you will then confess that the evils of Ireland do not arise from a surplus population; you will see that it is the nature of its social state to produce profound indigence and infinite distress; that if, by some magic spell, millions of paupers could be at once transported from Ireland, their place would soon be filled by the overflowing of that well-spring of misery which is never dried up; consequently, our attention must be bestowed, not upon the amount of the population, but upon the institutions of the country.

Here, again, we are brought back to the first cause of the evil, and to the question of determining what reforms should be made in institutions whose vices continually reappear as the source of all evils; but the time is not yet come for discussing that question. At present, it is sufficient to have shown that a remedy for the evils of Ireland would be vainly sought in emigration.

Section III. Poor Laws

The English parliament, within a short interval, has passed two laws which alone would enable us to judge between the English aristocracy and that of Ireland.

In England, public charity had been practised for centuries so generously and imprudently by the upper classes, the poor rates consequently pressed so heavily on property, that it was at length necessary to check the abuses of indiscriminate relief, and to force the rich to be less benevolent to the poor. Such was one of the principal objects of the New Poor Law enacted in 1834.

In Ireland, on the contrary, the absolute want of public charity, or individual sympathy of the rich for the poor, produced from year to year, and from age to age, so enormous an accumulation of extreme misery, that it became necessary to introduce into that country a part of the principle which was reformed in

England, and to constrain the rich in Ireland to give some relief to the poor, whilst in England they were restrained from giving too much: this was the object of the statute enacted by parliament in 1837.

This law commands the erection of a certain number of workhouses, to be supported at the expense of the landlords of the county. And this poor law, say some, in the absence of manufactures and emigration, will save Ireland.

Numerous benefits are expected from it: regarded in an economic point of view, it will support millions of unemployed labourers: considered in its political bearing, it will extinguish the anarchical passions which have their source in extreme indigence; and examined in its social aspect, it will serve to reconcile the rich and the poor, as the sufferings of the latter will be greatly alleviated; such are the promises made by the new law, but which seem difficult for it to perform.

Doubtless it appears rash to pronounce judgment on an experiment now in progress, which has only just commenced its trial, and the issue of which cannot be known. Still, recognising all that in such an enterprise the future veils from our eyes, are there not parts of it which human intelligence can penetrate? If we cannot tell all the consequences of the New Poor Law in Ireland, can we not at least foresee with some certainty the effects which it will not produce? and without predicting the entire fate of this measure, may we not affirm that it will not realise the great hopes that are reposed in it? Will not one of these two things necessarily happen; either the law will be enforced extensively enough to render it efficacious, and then it will become an impossibility—or it will only be executed as far as it is practicable, and then it will become powerless, if not pernicious?

Its influence would doubtless be felt if, through its means, the two or three millions of paupers in Ireland receive at once public and legal aid from society. It would be, it is true, a great question to determine how far such influence would be salutary; all, perhaps, would not be beneficial in an institution which, while it gave to millions of individuals the privileges of pauperism, inflicted on them also its disgraces and its vices. We may doubt whether the supplying with food these two millions would sensibly change the condition of four or five millions more, who are scarcely less miserable; and we may be allowed to fear that a measure, destined to relieve the misery of the country, may render it more incurable by reducing it to a regular system. But supposing that such a measure could have a favourable result, is it practicable? Is there a possibility of supporting two or three millions of individuals on public charity? No; the simplest calculation will prove it.

Suppose that society takes charge of the two millions of paupers—the lowest estimate that can be admitted. Humanity, doubtless, would admit a less, but the estimate cannot be reduced, if it is intended that the relief given the Irish poor should produce a social and political effect. Now, suppose the very cheapest food to be given to these two millions of paupers, barely as much water and potatoes as will be sufficient to support life. The expense for each person will doubtless be very little; take it at two-pence a day for each individual; nevertheless, the sum-total would amount to more than 6,000,000*l*. annually.

What poor law will be established in Ireland at such a price? Who will pay the expenses? It is not to be supposed that England will add millions to her debt, to bestow them in alms on the Irish; and if such a tax should be levied on the Irish landlords, it would absorb their entire rental, so that it would be better at once to pass an agrarian law. And even if these 6,000,000*l*. were obtained, and ever so wisely applied to the profit of the two millions of paupers, could it be said that a legal system of public charity existed in Ireland?

Is a cheap ration of potatoes flung to the indigent in the public street, assistance worthy of the state? Must not a house be prepared for the pauper when he requires shelter? Is it enough to appease his hunger when he is famishing? Must he not be clothed when he is naked? Must he not receive medical aid in sickness, and be buried when he dies? Food, clothing, lodging, an hospital, a grave, are the primary necessities of every christian and civilised society, and cannot be omitted in any system of public charity.

When a government dispenses charity, it cannot administer it like a private individual. The private person, who from his limited means offers incomplete succour to his fellow man, seems always to go beyond what he can afford, because in reality he always does more than he ought. A similar judgment is not formed of society, which, when it takes up the burden of public charity, is always supposed sufficiently strong to bear it, and people are inclined to accuse it of parsimony, even when it shows itself generous beyond its means.

Must we now investigate how many millions should be added to the six millions to procure Ireland a system of charity, I will not say equal to England, but simply such a one as public authority could recognise? Such calculations would evidently be superfluous; it would be like an attempt to carry the heavier burthen after a vain effort to lift the lighter.

Thus, to be perfectly complete, the public administration of charity in Ireland would require sums too enormous to be calculated; and reduced to almost contemptible proportions, its expenses, though less, would still infinitely exceed the will of England and the means of Ireland.

When the English legislators gave Ireland a poor law, they saw very clearly the extent of the difficulties just explained; and, seeing that it was impossible to offer even the coarsest relief to all the existing paupers, they deemed it necessary to direct their attention to restricting the number of persons relieved.

But how, when a system of public charity is established in a country where paupers are found in millions, can the object be attained of succouring only a small number of them? The new law has adopted two principal means to this end. First, it has not conferred on the Irish poor an express right to relief; and second, it has annexed conditions to the distribution of charitable relief which are not of a nature to render it desirable; so that the poor have neither a right to ask for charity, nor a great wish to obtain it.

It would be a great mistake to suppose that the principle of public charities, which has been recently introduced into Ireland, is the same as that which has prevailed in England since the reign of Elizabeth. Public charity, but not legal charity, has been established in Ireland; and this is a very important difference. The character of public charity is to have the agents of authority for its officers, as is the case in France. But what constitutes legal charity is, that the distributor, whether a public authority or a private individual, cannot refuse the pauper who demands it, and, in case of a groundless refusal, can judicially compel relief to be afforded. Such is the English system. In Ireland, charity will be public, since its management will be entrusted to public officers; but it will not be legal, for the poor who will receive it will not have the right to demand it; and all those to whom it may be refused will have no coercive means to enforce relief. This principle being established, it is at once seen how the administrators of the law will have a right to reduce as much as they please the number of persons to whom relief is to be granted. We see how, being armed with discretionary power, they will always be able to proportion the amount of relief granted to the amount of expense that is possible; and we can understand that if the resources of the country will not allow them to afford assistance to more than eighty or a hundred thousand individuals, they will be at perfect liberty not to assist a greater number.

But, at the same time that we see the means by which the law has been rendered practicable, we may also see how it will become absolutely inefficacious; in fact, we may ask of what consequence to the welfare or repose of the country will be relief given to a hundred thousand paupers; that is to say, less than one tenth of the paupers of Ireland?

Besides, is it deemed an easy task to choose out of the two or three millions of paupers that Ireland contains, these eighty or a hundred thousand privileged paupers, to whom alone public relief will be given? I can clearly see the right of making the choice, but I cannot comprehend on what principle the selection will be made.

Will an effort be made to afford relief only to the most extreme destitution? But, in the first place, it will be necessary to determine it. Now, how is a distinction to be made amongst the millions of voices which will raise the same cry of distress? Who will possess the magic secret for divining the different degrees of suffering in conditions perfectly similar. There is an excessive misery in which the degrees, if any exist, cannot be marked. Who can tell which is the most hun-

gry in the midst of famishing millions? In no country, perhaps, is there so uniform a type of misery as in Ireland. See what incredible efforts every one of
these millions of paupers makes to appear the poorest of all; what an emulation
in indigence!—what a rivalry in rags, in real or feigned diseases, in true or simulated sores!—what a prize offered to imposture! Observe that if all these paupers
were themselves willing in good faith to tell which of them are most wretched,
they would be sorely puzzled to do so: how then are you to succeed in discovering the truth amid so many efforts made to lead you astray?

The distribution of public charity is already a very difficult and delicate task
in a country where poverty is a rare case, and misery the exception. How then is
it to be accomplished in a nation where indigence is in some sort the common
lot, and the condition superior to poverty an accident? How is the pauper to be
discerned in a nation of paupers?

Evidently, whatever may be done in the absence of all legal rule and all moral
means of judgment, the execution of the law will be forcibly brought to the mere
simple procedure of arbitrary selection. But an arbitrary power is precisely the
most dangerous vice that can be found in any institution given to Ireland. This
country has been so long the sport of caprice and tyranny, that it with difficulty
believes in the impartiality of those who govern it; and supposing that the selection of Irish paupers should be made equitably, it would be sufficient that it was
made arbitrarily to persuade the people of its injustice. Thus, whilst the assistance given to the paupers relieved will only slightly ameliorate their condition,
we may reckon on the fact, that the paupers to whom public charity will be refused, will believe themselves the victims of the most iniquitous exclusion.

Seeing that it was not less difficult to make a selection of paupers than to
succour all, the English legislators have had recourse to a second expedient to
diminish the amount of relief. They considered that, as it was impossible to relieve all claimants, it was necessary to labour that all paupers should not make
claims; and in order to limit their number, they have surrounded the charity
with all circumstances fit to make it repulsive.

The poor law for Ireland consequently enjoins the erection of eighty or a
hundred workhouses, where relief will be granted. These establishments, each of
which will contain a thousand inmates, are to be subjected to a rigid discipline.
Every poor person will not of necessity be admitted, but no one will receive relief if he does not enter and remain within the precincts of the walls. There the
husband will be separated from his wife, the mother from her children. The
name of these asylums would seem to show that they are designed for places of
labour, but the impossibility of suddenly creating eighty or a hundred thousand
manufactories, and of finding employment for eighty or a hundred thousand
paupers in a country where the free labourers can scarcely find employment, sufficiently proves that they will be completely idle. Thus all the miseries, all the

sufferings, and all the corruptions of poverty, and all the vices of idleness, will be found jumbled and united on the same spot. It has been supposed that the necessity of entering these establishments, in order to obtain relief, will greatly diminish the number of claimants; and doubtless the calculation is very just, for it is impossible to see how the condition of the paupers will differ from that of persons imprisoned for crime.

Is it not necessary here to state frankly the true character of such a law? Whether does it contain a principle of charity or of severity? With one hand it offers alms to the Irish poor, with the other it opens to them a prison. This prison, it is true, will only receive those who wish to enter, and in truth also they will be at liberty to depart when they please. But if they do not enter, they will not receive relief, and the relief will cease when they depart. In fine, it is succour offered to the poor of Ireland on the condition that, in order to receive it, they must abandon their liberty, and throw themselves into the focus of corruption.

It has been supposed that this excessive severity might be justified by the example of England, in which, since the celebrated reform of 1834, similar establishments, subjected to like regulations, have had, they say, the salutary effect of diminishing the number of paupers who claimed relief, and at the same time of affording shelter to those whose distress was real. But is it not easy to see how different are both the principles and the facts of the two countries?

In England, the fundamental principle of the old poor law, that is to say, the legal right of the poor to charitable relief, still exists. The reform of 1834 did not abolish this principle, it only modified its execution. Formerly, the English pauper received parochial relief proportioned to his exigencies in his own house. Nothing, without doubt, could be more convenient to the indigent than this parochial assistance coming to him in his cottage, in the midst of his family, his domestic habits and ease; but also no form of charity was more productive of abuse. To remedy this evil, it has been ruled that, besides out-door relief, there should be relief given in the workhouse; and it has been established that the overseers may, at their discretion, grant or refuse out-door relief; and that they are bound to yield to the demand of the pauper only when, on claiming relief, he is ready, if required, to enter the workhouse before receiving it. Thus the English pauper has preserved the chance of being relieved according to the old form of English charity, and he has the certainty of being assisted according to the new. It is evident, therefore, that the condition of the English pauper is theoretically different from that of the Irish pauper, who can in no case obtain relief without losing his liberty, and who, though unable to obtain relief except in a kind of prison, has not the right, but merely the chance, of admission.

But the cases are even more different in fact than in theory. In England, there are paupers, but not a nation of paupers; the mass of the population is employed, and those who pretend that they want work would easily obtain it, if they did not take greater pleasure in idleness, and preferred living on public charity, rather than their own industry. It may be conceived that, in such a country, a discretionary power may be given without inhumanity to the dispensers of public charity, who, without forbidding the milder form of relief in favour of the irreproachable indigent, may adopt a more rigid system to distress those suspected of idleness. Such a power could not produce much severity in a country where the mode of assistance most agreeable to the poor man is deeply rooted in the habits and manners of the people; and there is much more reason to fear, that the power given by law to be less indulgent may never be exercised.

The institution of workhouses for the poor in England has a moral aim which is easily understood; it is a menace against voluntary idleness, pretending to be unfortunate: and when a pauper pretends that he is in want, it is a standard by which the reality of his distress may be tested.

But what can be the merit of such an institution in Ireland, where, if all doubtful cases of indigence were removed, there would still remain millions in undisputed destitution; where these millions of paupers are plunged into distress, absolutely independent of their will; where they do not work, not because they will not, but because they cannot; where this impossibility of obtaining any employment is not accidental and transitory, but continuous and permanent? To apply the English system to the Irish poor is cruel or absurd, or both.

To try by any moral influence to force people to work, who are physically incapacitated from working, is nonsense. And if, by this influence, those to whom succour has been promised, are kept from the place where relief is afforded—men to whom relief is absolutely necessary for existence—what can be said, except that a hypocritical engagement has been made, which must be violated at all hazards, and a way of escape opened from the obligations of impossible charity by the adoption of inhuman expedients?

We have shown how the conditions annexed to this charitable relief will prevent its being sought by those to whom it is most necessary. Still there is a case in which, according to all probability, a vast number will claim public aid in spite of the severities attached to it; I mean those epochs of general distress when famine rages amongst the people, and where the physical necessity of supporting life overcomes all moral repugnance. But then it is not by hundreds or thousands, or hundreds of thousands, it is by millions that the Irish will rush to the house of charity, for at these frightful seasons an awful level of misery is established in Ireland. Now, where are the means of satisfying these famishing multitudes? Thus, when relief will be possible, it will be so trammelled as not to be sought, and when extreme circumstances arise to give it some value, it will at once be claimed by so great a multitude as to render it impossible.

But the poor law granted to Ireland would be only half deficient, if it were merely powerless; does not everything seem to show that it will be pernicious?

The simple fact of its inutility would be a real evil. England is persuaded, that by founding this institution she has done much for Ireland, and believing that she has applied a remedy to the evils of the country, is tempted to remain quiet, at least for some time, in the satisfaction arising from the feelings of having accomplished a great duty.

And in Ireland will not this law at first excite amongst the people hopes that it cannot realise? When an institution of public charity was announced to Ireland, the people took no account of the limits by which it was to be restricted. They believed that henceforth the poor would be supported by the public; and this opinion was the more readily adopted, because Ireland, though she has never possessed the English system of charitable relief, is acquainted with its principles and traditions. But when, instead of seeing distress succoured, it will be found that only a coarse relief is given to a few select paupers, will not the disappointment be felt as a cruel deception? and will not suffering Ireland, having been led to expect a great alleviation of her evils, be irritated at comparing the wretched alms she receives with the immense benefits she expected to receive?

Though powerless to assist the people, this law will probably not be inefficacious in their further demoralisation. There are in Ireland numbers of paupers, who, though they can get no work, have an eager desire to work, and who make great efforts to create means of subsistence. Here now is an institution which suggests to them the fatal notion, that it is possible to live without work, and that the public will assist every one in need. How many, on the faith of this chimerical expectation, instead of looking for employment, so difficult to be found in Ireland, will wait inactively, resigned beforehand to the misfortune of never seeing it arrive. How many will prefer to ill-paid labour, the chances of charity bestowed on idle poverty?

But this institution not only risks depraving the people without aiding them; it will, perhaps, deprive the poor of the little charitable relief they receive at present. Hitherto there existed in Ireland no general system of public charity; still the poor were not wholly destitute of assistance; not that the rich succoured them, but that the poor gave to the poor. What must result when the law solemnly declares, that the burthen of supporting the poor will fall upon the rich? All the poor of Ireland, no doubt, will unanimously applaud the equity of such a principle; but will not the lower classes believe that they are not henceforth bound to the obligation of mutual charity? And when the poor mendicant will present himself, as of yore, at the house of the small farmer, will he not be repulsed by being told to go to the neighbouring town, where there is public relief for the poor? Should matters thus turn out, it will follow that the law which promises Ireland illusory aid, will deprive the poor Irish of the only real assistance they possess.

And how are we to find, in such a law, the means of drawing closer the rich and the poor in Ireland? The most zealous partisans of the institution admire, as they say, its power of inspiring the Irish landlords with salutary terror, as the poor rates will be levied on their estates. They suppose that henceforth the rich will feel more sensibly the misery of the poor; that he will be interested in preventing it, and checking its growth. But these menaces addressed to the strong are dangerous for the weak. It is designed to force the rich man to aid the pauper whom he sees dying of hunger; this is a violence very difficult to practise. Charity is not thus constrained. There is reason to fear, that after having bestowed charity on the poor, the landlord will discover the means of taking back from the poor what he has reluctantly given, and that setting a higher price on his land, already over-rented, he may indemnify himself for the alms thus extorted. The law risks the chance of rendering the rich more hostile to the poor by the very means taken to inspire them with more humane sentiments.

If this institution is not calculated to inspire the upper classes with better feelings towards the poor, we are equally at a loss to know how it will render the latter less hostile to the rich. Were the law efficacious and salutary, it is doubtful if the indigent population would take any notice of the landlords, whom it would regard as passive distributors of compulsory benevolence. What, then, must be the effect on a people of a law fraught with such perils; in which we can see the germ of so many evils, and which appears inoffensive only where it is found powerless? Does any one wish to know what the poor of Ireland will say, when the ephemeral illusions of unreflecting hope are dispelled? They will say that the law was good, but that its agents have made it bad; that the measure was charitable, but the execution of it inhuman; and people will still find the means of charging the rich with the faults of an institution, which is vicious in its very principles. Sometimes they will blame the commissioners for not admitting enough of paupers into the workhouse; sometimes they will blame them for receiving too many into those mansions of corruption and idleness. These contradictory reproaches, which, thus coarsely expressed by the people, may appear inconsistent, will, nevertheless, be both merited; for if it be a charity that is bestowed, those who receive it will have no stronger claim than the millions to whom aid is denied; and if, under the name of charity, it be a punishment that is inflicted on misfortune, though the rigour be voluntarily accepted, the number of those subjected to it will always be too great.

May we not, then, fear that this measure, designed to reconcile the rich and the poor, will only increase their mutual enmity and their reciprocal grievances against each other? How, then, can a remedy be found for the evils of Ireland in a measure which is likely to aggravate them still more?

II

Remedies Proposed by the Author—The Civil, Political, and Religious Privileges of the Aristocracy Must Be Abolished

We have seen how chimerical are the various extraordinary means of safety tried or proposed for Ireland; a multitude of other analogous plans might be discussed, whose total inutility may be shown by a very brief examination.

What, then, must be done in the painful and formidable condition of Ireland? How is she to be left without a remedy for such calamities and such perils? What is the advantage of trying useless remedies? What complicates the difficulty is, that it is not enough to find measures good in themselves; it is further required that their application should be practicable. It is not sufficient to discover the system of administration best suited to the state of Ireland; it must also be adapted to the taste of England.

Is it not better, then, first to consider, abstractedly, what the interests of Ireland, taken apart, and by herself, would require?—reserving for subsequent examination how far that which is desirable is practicable; if what ought to be done will be done; if the interests of England will allow that to be accomplished which the interests of Ireland demand.

We have seen in the preceding chapters, that all the evils of Ireland, and all its difficulties, arise from the same principal and permanent cause—a bad aristocracy, an aristocracy whose principle is radically vicious. What is the logical consequence to be deduced from these premises? Clearly, that in order to put an end to the misery of Ireland, it is necessary to do away with the aristocracy in that country; as, to abolish the effect, we must remove the cause.

Whence arises the inefficiency of all the measures tried or proposed? From this simple fact, that no one of these modes of cure applies to the primary cause of the disease.

Thus a means of alleviating the immense misery of the lower classes is sought in providing them industrial employment by the establishment of manufactories; but it is soon seen that the agitation of the country, and the passions of the people against the rich, render such establishments impossible: that is to say, the remedy for the evil is rendered impossible by the evil itself.

It is proposed to relieve the country by the emigration of some millions of paupers; but besides the enterprise being impracticable, we may soon see that if millions of paupers were removed from Ireland by enchantment, they would soon be reproduced by her institutions, always fertile in the production of miseries of every kind: to act thus would be to suppress the effects, and leave the cause in full force.

It has been thought that the most painful wounds of the country might be cured by forcing on the rich obligations of charity towards the poor; but here we are again brought back to the very principle of the evil—that is to say, to the heart of the aristocracy, which rejects charity. And we see, though some wound may be healed, and some pains alleviated, the sufferings of the poor would again spring in multitudes from the inexhaustible source of tyranny. This source must be dried up; it is this primary cause that must be attacked; the evil must be assailed at its root; every remedy applied to the surface will only afford transitory relief.

The social and political state of Ireland is not a regular state; everything shows that it is vitiated at the core. The disorder appears not only in the infinite miseries and perpetual sufferings of the population; it is even seen in the means adopted to effect deliverance from those evils.

What is this association, leading the people in defiance of government, but organised anarchy? What must a country be, where this anarchy is the sole principle of order? What is it, I say, but a society whose head is at enmity with its body,—which is in perpetual rebellion against itself?—in which every rich man is hated, every law detested, every act of vengeance legitimate, every act of justice suspected? Here is a violent and anomalous position, in which a nation cannot long continue.

We may conceive Ireland cloven down and trampled under foot by its aristocracy for centuries, but we cannot comprehend when Ireland has arisen, the aristocracy and the people facing each other, the former still eager to oppress, the latter sufficiently strong to resist oppression, without bringing it to a close.

Though the necessity of reforming the Irish aristocracy should not be proved by what has been already stated, perhaps one single argument will suffice to demonstrate it. In fact, look at the alternative: if allowed to subsist, one of two things must be done—the aristocracy must be supported against the people, or the people allowed to overthrow it.

In the first case, the sustaining power must become the mere instrument of all the passions of this aristocracy,—of its desires as well as its hatreds;—must place the artillery of Britain at the disposal of every landholder who cannot get his rents from his tenants,—must subject to arbitrary and terrible laws every county in which the poor make an attack on the rich and their properties:—can the Irish aristocracy, with any conscience, demand—can it even wish for such sanguinary protection?

In the second case,—that is to say, if the people be supported against the aristocracy; or, what is nearly the same thing, left to itself,—the aristocracy, deprived of a support without which it cannot exist, is delivered over, without defence, to the most cruel reprisals; it falls, bound hand and foot, into the hands of an enemy, full of resentment, subject to all the vengeance and all the madness of a victorious party; and, in this case, it may be asked, whether destruction is not more humane than such a state of existence?

This destruction, equally just and necessary, would be singularly easy in Ireland. In the first place, it would be aided by the whole strength of national feeling. In England, where the aristocracy is still so powerful, and, I might almost add, so popular, there is scarce a suspicion of the feelings with which Ireland regards her aristocracy.

Generally contented with their lot, the lower classes in England do not dispute the privileges of the rich; I might almost venture to say, they take pleasure in them: they see with a sort of pride these immense fortunes, large estates, parks, castles, and splendid abodes of the aristocracy; and they say that if there were no lower ranks, such glorious opulence and national splendour would not exist. People may laugh at this indigent enthusiasm in the happiness of the rich: I agree to it; but it is a proud thing for an aristocracy to have inspired such sentiments. In general, a poor Englishman regards the rich without envy, or at least without hatred. If he sometimes attacks him, it is without bitterness, and then he rather assails the principle than the man; the person most opposed to aristocracy shows a profound respect to aristocracy; whilst he blames the political privilege, he bows to the lord; and even when he affects to despise birth, he honours fortune. England, fondly attached to liberty, does not care about equality.

In Ireland, on the contrary, where the laws have never been anything but means of oppression for the rich, and resistance for the poor, liberty has less value, and equality greater. Doubtless there is too much of the English spirit in Ireland to allow of liberty being absolutely despised, or equality thoroughly comprehended; but the people is driven towards it by its most powerful instincts. In truth, there is nothing of philosophy or reason in its desire for equality. The feeling is still undefined in the soul, as the idea of it is still vague in the understanding; still it is the passion which seems destined to seize strongly on the heart, and which indeed is predominant there already. Equality is in all the Irishman's wants, though it be not in all his principles. He already loves equality in so far as inequality is odious, and established for the advantage of those whom he detests. I do not know that he has an enlightened taste for democracy; but most assuredly he hates aristocracy and its representatives. A remarkable fact! In England, in the midst of feudal institutions singularly mingled with democracy, a good government has produced respect, and sometimes even a passion for aristocracy. In Ireland, unmingled aristocratic institutions, under the influence of pernicious policy, have developed democratic sentiments, instincts, and wants unknown in England.

The overthrow of the aristocracy, which would be so popular in Ireland, would also be easy, for at the same time that democracy is rising in that country, aristocracy is perceptibly on the decline. This aristocracy never possessed any great organic force.

What renders the English aristocracy particularly powerful, is the strict union of all the elements that compose it: large estates, great capitals, the church, the universities, medicine, the bar, arts and professions, form a compact association in that country, whose members have one common interest, passion, and purpose, the conservation of their privileges.

Nothing like this exists in Ireland. If we except the university, which is so closely connected with the church that it may be regarded as its twin sister, all the aristocratic elements are held together in Ireland by the feeblest of ties.

There is, indeed, a great and natural sympathy between the landlords and the ministers of the Anglican church; the same religion, the same passions, the same political interests. Rejected by the same hatred, they are disposed to approximate like two transported criminals in their place of exile. But their mutual relations have not that regularity which can alone be derived from real and solid union; neither resides habitually in Ireland, they only meet there by accident, they regard each other as if they met in a strange land; it is a transitory union, which, however sincere it may be deemed while it lasts, leaves no traces behind.

The great wealth and possessions of the church are, besides, a subject of jealousy, and an occasion of discord to the landlords. We have already seen with what emulation churchmen and laymen press upon the people; and how the exactions of one are injurious to the other. The tenant used to pay his landlord badly on account of the tithe he owed to the minister; the parson found it difficult to recover his tithe, because the landlord charged too high a rent. These rivals in extortion are, nevertheless, political allies; and after having mutually imputed to each other the miseries, famine, crimes, and desolation of the country, they renew their friendly intercourse; but their union, sufficiently apparent for the tyranny of the one to injure the other, is not sufficiently close to afford mutual strength to both.

The support which the aristocracy receives from its other auxiliaries is still more feeble and uncertain.

The municipal corporations, its most faithful allies, have long fallen into a state of discredit and disgrace, which renders the advantage of their assistance very doubtful; and the scandalous abuses in which they are steeped, imprint disgrace on the power they sustain, more injurious than the zeal they display in its service. Besides, these corporations have not the strength which their great wealth gives the English corporations. Formerly, as Protestants, they had the monopoly of commerce, and all profitable industry; but, whilst this monopoly lasted, Irish industry was sacrificed to that of England. Their privileges, therefore, were worth little. To preserve them, they were, therefore, forced to place them at the mercy of England, whose yoke they endured for the sake of imposing their own. At present, they are delivered from the bonds of England, but we have already seen that since its enfranchisement, Irish industry creates more democratic properties than it does wealth in alliance with privilege.

We have seen that Catholics of the middle class have taken possession of the bar, formerly the ally of the Protestant aristocracy. Thus on all sides this aristocracy is feeble, divided and menaced in the small remnant of its strength. Aristocratic life, in fact, exists only in one body, the lords of the soil. There only can we find any accordance between the views of the members, any regular proceedings, any durability of union; but, even here, the most wealthy, that is, those who could give most power to their order, are out of the country.

Finally, the largest proportion of Irish landlords has recently fallen into a state of distress and degradation, which deserves to be considered. We have seen a description of the evils endured by the poor agriculturists of Ireland; the misery of the rich in that country would also furnish a very sad picture. It is an undisputed fact, that most of the landlords are greatly embarrassed in their fortunes; they are crushed by a weight of debt, their estates are loaded with mortgages. Many of them, bound to pay interests equal to the whole amount of their rents, and perhaps even more, are but nominally proprietors of their estates. I have seen an estate of fifty thousand acres, bringing a rent of 20,000*l.*, out of which the proprietor only enjoyed about 500*l.* a year. Nothing is more common than to see receivers appointed over large estates, charged with collecting rents due to the landlord for the benefit of the creditors, and appointed, either by a court of law, or in consequence of a special agreement.

This distress of the Irish landlords, which goes on continually increasing, arises from several causes; but the first and chief is their own recklessness. They have for centuries thrown all the trouble of their affairs upon agents or middlemen; and now they begin to perceive that their affairs have been badly conducted, and that their fortune, instead of increasing, has declined. Another cause is their blind cupidity, which, by rendering their tenants miserable, has become a source of impoverishment to themselves. And then, as they are actually in a state of war with the population, this incessantly causes them great loss, without any other advantage than the pleasure of injuring the people in their turn. It would be difficult to form an idea of the number of cattle maliciously killed or mutilated every year on the lands of the rich; the quantity of wood and houses burned, and of meadows dug or ploughed up. I find that in 1833 more outrages were committed in the province of Munster, for the mere purpose of injuring the landlords, than for the purpose of procuring any advantage to the perpetrators. Thus, in this catalogue of crimes I find only fifty-nine robberies, but I observe one hundred and seventy-eight outrages dictated by brutal and vindictive violence, which ruin the landlord without enriching the tenant. I have said that nothing can compensate the poorer classes for want of sympathy in the rich: it must be added, that the rich can never find an adequate substitute for the sympathy of the poor: and when the poor hate the rich, there is no severity of law, no court-martial, no punishment, which can prevent the poor from labouring to effect the destruction of those whom they detest.

Finally, the indigence of the rich arises from the following final cause, of a more recent date. During the war of France with Europe, and especially from 1800 to 1810, England having been almost entirely reduced for subsistence to the resources of its own territory, Ireland, which had always been its most abundant granary, became more so than ever. The demand for the agricultural produce of Ireland became, consequently, so great, that the prices were raised out of all proportion. This state of things continuing from year to year, the landlord, perceiving that the harvests of their tenants rose to double or triple their value, raised their rents in the same proportion; and not foreseeing that this increase of fortune, so agreeable to their pride, would cease with the accident which gave it birth, they established the expenses of their households on this fragile base.

So long as the continental blockade continued, the Irish aristocracy was splendid and prosperous, and the peasants themselves suffered less; but peace having been restored to the world, the Irish corn market was deprived of its monopoly, agricultural produce lost its exaggerated value, and the fortune of all the landlords was suddenly reduced. Still, in spite of the reverse, which took away one half of their revenues, the rich did not diminish their expenses.

It is in the nature of aristocracies not to be able to retrench; they are erected on a pedestal, of which vanity is the base: now, vanity would cease to be itself, if it submitted to restriction or abatement. Such resignation is especially impossible in an aristocracy of wealth, for when fortune is the measure of rank, who would wish to humiliate himself by acknowledging the diminution of his riches?

The Irish landlords could not, and would not, diminish their outward show on the scale of their declining fortunes: continuing to live at the old rate with decreased resources, some have been completely ruined, and others are rapidly hastening to the same consummation; and rather than reform in their household one horse or one servant, they are about to fall from the summit of their pride into extreme indigence. It is a common weakness of mankind not to be able to support the approach of a light evil whose hour is fixed, and to advance resolutely towards an immense inevitable misfortune, the date of which is uncertain. Aristocracy exaggerates all the vices, as well as all the virtues, which proceed from pride.

Whatever may be the fortunes of the Irish aristocracy, no tears will be shed over their fate. Why should any one be grieved to see the decrepitude of a body whose end is unavoidable? Left to itself, this aristocracy would probably perish. But ought it, infirm and impotent as it is, to be allowed to languish for years, perhaps for ages, and expire in slow agonies amidst the outrages it will excite, the miseries it will produce, and the curses it will bear to its very last hour? No; its weakness, instead of being its protection, should be its condemnation: it can never be anything to the Irish people, but the blood-stained phantom of a government; and, doubtless, it will never recover from the terrible attacks made upon it, when even its season of unresisted tyranny has sunk so low. It is, therefore, nothing better than a scourge and a nuisance, which should be removed as soon as possible.

III

It Would Be an Evil to Substitute a Catholic Aristocracy for the Protestant Aristocracy

It is not only the Protestant aristocracy that should be abolished in Ireland, but every kind of aristocracy. Nothing could be more pernicious than to erect a Catholic aristocracy on the ruins of a Protestant aristocracy. I have already shown that there is no greater peril to the middle classes in Ireland, than their inclination to seize the privileges of which the aristocracy will be despoiled. This danger, if it be not in the present, is certainly in the future. But it is not sufficient to state as a certain danger, the mere possibility of a Catholic aristocracy; we must also show why this chance is an evil.

Doubtless we may suppose, that if the upper classes, in possession of the soil, were Catholics, many of the oppressions which bear heavily on the Catholics would be removed or greatly alleviated; but then, what would be the fate of a million and a half of Protestants scattered over the surface of Ireland? Would not they risk encountering, from an aristocracy hostile to their creed, the same persecutions which Catholics endure at present? Would it not be, in truth, the substitution of one tyranny for another? and then, it would be just as well to leave the present one to continue.

Besides, how far could a Catholic aristocracy in Ireland be beneficial to the Catholics themselves? Does any one suppose that it would display generosity, sympathy, and liberality to the people? Might it not offer a dangerous lure to the Catholic priesthood, and risk, by bringing that body over to itself, depriving the clergy of more influence than it would have retained by adhering to the people? But before interrogating the future, let us consult the past.

We have already seen that, in the confusion of political confiscations, a small number of Catholic families saved their properties and titles. There has been, then, constantly in Ireland the fragment of a Catholic aristocracy. Now, what assistance has it afforded to the population, professing the same creed as itself?

During the entire period of Protestant persecutions, persecuted itself, it thought far more of its own safety, than of that of the people; and for this it is not very much to blame. As it was rich, it had everything to fear from Protestant tyranny, which was directed far more against property than against creeds. The Catholic aristocracy was cautious of giving umbrage to its political enemies, and, consequently, did not venture to offer its friends any protection. It lived without ostentation or noise on its estates, miraculously preserved, and abstained from showing any dangerous sympathy for the lower classes of Catholics. We should not require from men sacrifices beyond the reach of humanity. Was not the rich Catholic who adhered to his creed, in spite of the political disqualifications attached to its profession, performing a great duty?

But, if the Catholic aristocracy could not do more, did it sufficiently endeavour to establish between it and the poor those relations of benevolence on one side, and respect on the other, which form the aristocratic link between the poor and the rich? No. There was no close alliance formed between the rich and poor Catholics during the whole of the eighteenth century, at the time when it would seem that they ought to have been united by a common persecution. Besides the prudential motives which separated the rich from the poor, there was also a remnant of pride of race which prevented their intimate union; the few rich Catholics who escaped confiscation were of English descent, and accustomed to despise, as Irish, those with whom they were connected by religion.

But this old aristocracy of Ireland did not confine itself to refusing all political and social protection to the people. All the records of Irish history show that it oppressed those whom perhaps it might be excused for not defending. It did not escape the selfish passions that animated the Protestant proprietors, and showed itself to the full as severe and avaricious towards its tenants as they did, and in consequence provoked the same hatred. It is very difficult for a landlord to avoid endeavouring to get from his estates as much as he sees his neighbours get from theirs. However that may be, the rich Catholics inflicted on the lower classes a social oppression precisely the same as that exercised by Protestant landlords; the people could not distinguish one from the other; it mixed both in its hatred, and in the popular outbreaks of vengeance assailed rich Catholics equally with rich Protestants. This explains why the Whiteboys attacked the first, just as well as the second. These popular outrages completed the separation between the people and the Catholic aristocracy; and thus, during the whole course of savage reprisals between the poor and the rich, the Catholics had no aid from the nobility or gentry of their own creed.

However, when Catholic Ireland struggled against its chains, and loudly proclaimed its determination to be free, we see this aristocracy partially appear on the stage: not that it came of its own accord, it was sought. There was need of it; for how could any enterprise be formed if a lord did not preside? It then gave the support which it dared not refuse.[1] But this alliance was of brief duration. The Catholic population of Ireland assumed sufficient courage to desire to send an address to George III., expressing the wishes of the country: the petition was prepared, the people assembled, tried its voice and its strength. At the sight of these movements, the Catholic aristocracy of Ireland, fearing to be compromised by adhering to the popular cause, separated itself from the people. This occurred in 1791. Still the national movement continued; the retreat of the Catholic aristocracy taught the people to do without it; a plebeian[2] took the helm of affairs; victories were gained, checks experienced; and when the frightful crisis and the terrible storms had gone by,—when, after so many trials, the triumph of the people was finally assured, the Catholic aristocracy was seen to reappear; it returned to the popular cause, which it had abandoned in the hour of danger, and vainly aspired to direct it; and now, placed between the Protestant power which it detests, and the Catholic people whose alienations it dreads, it has no resource but to disappear entirely: it either dissembles or departs.

I doubt whether such antecedents could be the starting-point for a good aristocracy. Yet this starting-point will no doubt have great influence in its consequences. The aristocracy which may be established will, it is true, spring in a great part from a new source, as already shown; but the present cannot be thus separated from the past; and whether the rising aristocracy of the middle classes attaches itself to the old branch of the Catholic aristocracy, or to the rotten trunk of the Protestant aristocracy, it will assuredly receive pernicious traditions and a fatal heritage.

The kind of instinctive and hereditary contempt which the rich feel in Ireland for everything that is poor and beneath them,—the prejudice which even amongst Catholics makes this contempt a sign of fashion and elegance,—the opinion so generally diffused, that the rich man has a right to oppress the poor man, and trample him under foot with impunity,—such are the traditions from which a new aristocracy in Ireland cannot escape without great difficulty.

Were even these perils avoided, there are others from which this aristocracy could not escape; even though it would not merit, it would excite all the hatred shown to its predecessor: for the people of Ireland has also its tradition, which is to believe in the selfishness of the rich, and the right of the poor to detest them.

These mutual feelings of the poor and rich in Ireland are doubtless not graven for ever on the soul; if they were so, we might despair of the country and its future fate; for, whatever reforms may be made, rich persons will always be found amongst the people. But it is impossible that such sentiments, sealed in

---

1. The alliance was hollow and insincere.
2. John Keogh.

torrents of blood and ages of oppression, should not be long perpetuated; and they will be vivid in proportion as the new class of rich men retain the titles, privileges, and honours of the extinguished aristocracy. If the rich can ever be reconciled to the poor in Ireland, it must be by ceasing to appear before them surrounded by the same ensigns which, during centuries, were displayed by an odious aristocracy. It is also perhaps the only means for themselves to lose their pernicious habits of oppression and tyranny.

It will therefore not be enough to destroy the Protestant aristocracy; the very principle of aristocracy must be abolished in Ireland, in order that no other may take the place of that which must be suppressed. After the existing institution is humbled down, the ruins must be cleared away, and the ground prepared for the erection of a very different edifice.

IV

How and by What Means Aristocracy Should Be Abolished in Ireland

When I say that the Irish aristocracy must be destroyed, and its very roots extirpated, I am far from intending a violent and sanguinary destruction.

I do not agree with those who believe that, in order to establish order, prosperity, and union in a country, it is necessary to begin by massacring some thousands of persons, exiling those who are not murdered, seizing the property of the rich, and distributing it to the poor, &c. I at once reject all such measures as iniquitous, and I stop not to inquire if they be necessary. I believe, without any examination, that they are unnecessary, because they are not just, and because they are atrocious. It is in my eyes a vicious proceeding, when an injustice is about to be reformed, to begin by the perpetration of another, to commit a present and certain evil for the sake of a future and doubtful good. I distrust these criminal and doubtful means which the end must sanctify, and which, if the end fails, leave nothing but crime to those who use them; or rather, I do not believe that criminal means can ever become honest. Besides, I cannot admit that injustice and violence can ever profit either nations or individuals. I esteem the progress of humanity too highly to believe that it will be profited by excesses which dishonour it. Does that crime really hasten liberty, which gives it a powerful impulse that endures but a day, and then retards it for centuries? Were it even proved that iniquity would be advantageous to the present generation, I could not be persuaded that it has the right to burden future generations with the certain expiation.

By abolishing the Irish aristocracy, I merely mean that it should be deprived of the political power, which it has used only for the oppression of the people; that it should be stripped of its civil privileges, which have been only the means of satisfying its selfishness; and that its religious predominance should be abated, which, though it no longer generates persecutions, perpetuates the remembrance of them.

Section I

What Should Be Done in Order to Abolish the Privileges of the Aristocracy—
Necessity of Centralisation

To destroy the political power of the aristocracy, it would be necessary to deprive it of the daily administration of the laws, as it was formerly deprived of
legislation. Consequently, the whole administrative and judicial system must be
changed from top to bottom, in so far as it rests on justices of the peace and the
organisation of grand juries as at present constituted. In order to accomplish this
destruction, power must be centralised.

If it is, in general, difficult to conceive any foundation for a new government
without the aid of the central power, which commences with the destruction of
the existing system, the assistance of this central power seems especially necessary when, before laying the basis for a new system of society, an aristocracy is to
be overthrown. What means, in fact, are there of reaching the multitude of petty
powers scattered over the surface of the country, all these local existences, all
these individual influences peculiar to aristocracy, unless by concentrating the
whole public strength on one single point, from which it might be brought to
act against every condemned privilege and rebellious superiority?

In the countries where the best aristocracy exists, the central arm, when extended to strike them, is, in general, popular with the masses. This is sufficient
to show how popular in Ireland a powerful system of centralisation would be,
established on the ruins of a detested aristocracy, against which political hatred
is mingled with religious hatred.

The more the state of Ireland is considered, the more clearly will it appear
that, under all circumstances, a strong central government would be the best
which that country could possess, at least for the present. A bad aristocracy exists, which there is an urgent necessity for destroying. But to whom must the
power wrested from its hands be entrusted? Is it to the middle classes? They are
only beginning to exist in Ireland. The future belongs to them; but will they not
compromise that future, if the power of leading society at the present is entrusted to their unskilled hands and violent passions?

Such is the present state of parties in Ireland, that justice cannot be obtained
if the political powers are left in the hands of the Protestant aristocracy; and that
it cannot furthermore be expected, if these powers are at once transferred to the
rising middle classes of Catholics.

What Ireland wants is a strong administration, superior to parties, beneath
whose shadow the middle classes might grow up, develope themselves, and acquire instruction, whilst the aristocracy would crumble away, and its last remains

gradually disappear. Here is a great work to be accomplished, the execution of which is offered to the English government.

When I indicate centralisation as a means of reforming political society in Ireland, I hasten to explain my whole opinion on this head. I am assuredly very far from considering as salutary in itself the absolute principle of complete centralisation. There may be a central government of such a nature that it would be, in my opinion, worse than aristocracy itself. The principal vice of an aristocracy is, that it restricts by patronage the number of individual existences; but a single central power, which does everything and directs everything, not only diminishes but annihilates the political life of the citizens.

Although this power might not be tyrannical or oppressive, though it may restrain itself within the limits of law, and respect the popular passions and interests, still I should not find it the less bad; for it would still annihilate the political existence of individuals. Now, just as the best education is that which developes man's intelligence and multiplies his moral forces, so the best institutions give him the greatest number of civil rights and political powers. The greater number of people that there are in a state, competent to manage and guide their family, their parish, their county, or the state itself, the more political life will there be in that country, and the more the value of each individual will be increased.

Though it might be proved to me that this single central power, whether of a man or of an assembly, a minister or a commission, might execute, better than all the individuals together, the affairs of their parish, their province, or their entire country, I would not be less of the opinion, that it is bad to take from them the care of their private interests, because, in my view, it is of less importance to render their lives physically pleasant and comfortable, than to increase by political interests and domain offered in this world to their soul and understanding. It is not, then, as a final form of government that I recommend centralisation to Ireland.

Just so much as a central government appears to me necessary for this country, would its long continuance seem to me an evil. Extreme centralisation is rather a violent remedy than an institution. It is not a state, but an accident: it is a weapon potent in combat, which must be laid aside after the battle is over, under pain of being wounded by its edge, or borne down by its weight. It is a stage through which every nation must pass that is obliged, before erecting a new social edifice, to clear away the ruins of the old; and from which they must hasten to depart the instant that the work of transition is completed. Unfortunately it is not always easy to dismiss this auxiliary when its aid is no longer required; and society may find the seeds of destruction in the very cause by which it was saved. There is the danger. This danger is so great, that a people should not incur it, unless it were about to be exposed to a greater danger. There is a choice to make between the chance of not being able to destroy a bad government without the aid of centralisation, and the risk of not being able, after the destruction is accomplished, to get rid of the instrument by which it was effected. But it is because the overthrowing of the aristocracy is in Ireland the first and most urgent, that it is necessary to employ the most powerful though the most perilous instrument.

It accords neither with my wishes nor my purpose to explain the form and mechanism of the centralisation that would suit Ireland; I limit myself to recognising, as a principle, its transitory utility to that country. I will, however, venture to suggest one single practical idea. In order to organise a powerful central government in Ireland, it would be necessary to draw closer the bonds that unite Ireland to England, to bring Dublin as close as possible to London, and to make Ireland an English county. Everything at the present day tends to make this an object of easy execution; we are no longer at the period when a voyage of weeks or even months separated Ireland from England.

Once, in the reign of Henry VIII., the Irish parliament, long deprived of all news from England, on the arrival of a long-delayed courier passed an act recognising the king's marriage with Anna Boleyn; and on the following day, having received a second and a speedier courier, solemnly voted the nullity of the marriage.[1] If an Irish parliament existed in our day, and if a tyrant asked from it a similar act of baseness, it would not run the same risk of displeasing its master by its very servility.

Thanks to the improvement of navigation and the roads, London is now within twenty-one hours of Dublin. Ireland is nearer the English parliament than Scotland or Wales. How strange! England is now nearer to the United States of America, though they are six thousand miles distant, than she was to Ireland half a century ago, though Ireland is separated from her only by a narrow strait. These wondrous creations of human science, which are destined to change the social relations, not only of men but of nations, will exercise their first influence on Ireland, for the route between London and Dublin is the first great distance by land and sea which has been greatly diminished by steam. Whence comes it, then, that Ireland continues to retain a government distinct from the English government, a special executive power, peculiar and local administrations? This distinct government separates Ireland from England, to which it could not be drawn too close. The English who come to Ireland to contend against the aristocracy, are less powerful than if they remained in England. Every administration in Dublin is in one or other of these two predicaments: it either submits to the influence of the aristocracy which it ought to at-

---

1. This occurred in 1525.—See Lingard's History.

tack; or, if it rejects the aristocracy, it is exposed to attacks which it is less able to resist in Dublin than it would be in London.

We do not dispute that Ireland has need of a special government; and if there be a necessity of governing it on a legislative system different from that of England, special agents are required to apply different rules of administration. But this being granted, we see no reason why the seat of Irish government should not be fixed in the first city of the British empire.

There are those who consider the vice-regal court of Dublin as necessary to temper the violence of parties, and keep them separate when it cannot extinguish them. But has this opinion any foundation?

The only way in which a court can be brilliant is, by calling around it the aristocracy of the country. Now this aristocracy, exclusive by its nature, being in possession of the ground, will not suffer the inferior classes to mingle in its ranks; and besides, of what fusion or what harmony can this court be the source? Suppose that the head of the court in Dublin has received orders to combat the Irish aristocracy, how can he invite its members to his parties, or how avoid the invitation? If he asks for their company, he deceives them—if he passes them over, he insults them. And even should he attempt to attract them, this aristocracy, mortally wounded in its pride, will hold itself apart, will affect to despise a court which it will call mercantile and vulgar, and will refuse to join in pleasures, of which, however, it will not hear the fame without regret. In fact, a court at Dublin would create parties, if they were not already in existence.

The reform of the viceroyalty, and the abolition of the local administrations of Ireland are, doubtless, mere changes of form. But they are practical means, indispensable for the execution of the political reforms of which the country is in want. It is absolutely necessary, that during the period of transition in which Ireland is placed, those who govern the country should be completely severed from it, from its habits, and its passions. The government must wholly cease to be Irish; it must be, if not entirely English, at least entrusted to Englishmen.

Section II

What Must Be Done to Abolish the Civil Privileges of the Aristocracy in Ireland
—Necessity of Rendering the People Landed Proprietors

It would be of little value to attack the Irish aristocracy in its political privileges only; it is its social power that must especially be assailed. Whatever revolution is effected in a country, society remains nearly the same, if its civil laws are not modified at the same time as its political institutions. Political laws change with the passions and fortunes of the parties that succeed to power. The civil laws, in which a multitude of interests are engaged, do not change. Consider the two greatest revolutions that have convulsed the world in modern ages, that of 1649 in England, and of 1789 in France. Popular clamours were equally loud in both countries; the same enthusiasm of reformers, the same passion of levelling; in the political order, every thing was overthrown, broken, and trampled under foot; here and there the existing world was demolished, to raise on its ruins a new world, an ideal world, where justice, reason, and truth would be the only sovereigns; both countries went nearly the same length astray, the one with its philosophy, the other with its religion; they seemed mutually to copy each other in excesses, illusions, and miseries; each sacrificed its holocaust of royal blood; each had its anarchy and its despotism; the one its Napoleon, the other its Cromwell; each returned to its ancient dynasty, England to the Stuarts, France to the Bourbons; the similitude seems perfect between the two epochs and the two nations, except that in France there was more glory and in England less blood. How then comes it to pass, that from the very outset, the first completely changed its appearance, whilst the second retained its likeness to itself?

Scarcely had Charles II. resumed the crown, when English society returned to its accustomed channels; nothing farther remained of the revolution; twelve years of reforms, acts of violence, despotic interference of the state, passed away like a tempest, the traces of which are effaced by a calm. In France, on the contrary, in spite of the political form that attempted to reproduce the ancient state of society, quite a new people is revealed to our view; no matter whether it be called republic, empire, or royalty, the monarchical France of 1789 has become democratic, and will never cease to be so.

Why is there so great a difference in the effects, when the causes appear so similar? Because in England, at the very height of political destruction, the reformers did not touch the civil laws. They abolished royalty, and left the right of primogeniture untouched; whilst in France the changes were made in civil and political order at the same time. Social reform even preceded the great revolutionary crisis; the laws that abolished feudal services, which substituted equality of inheritance for privilege, had been all enacted when the republic came into existence. These laws attacked the very heart of the old social system, that which is most immovable amongst a people, land, and family. The republic passed away, but the civil laws remained. They had at once reached the foundation, whilst the other had only run lightly over the country, not indeed like the breeze that passes away, but like the scythe, which, though it mows down, only affects the surface. It would then be an idle enterprise to deprive the Irish aristocracy of its political authority, if at the same time its civil privileges, which are the soul of its power, were not taken away. There are, in Ireland, social wounds which it is more important to cure than political evils. What is essential is the establishment of harmony, not only between the governing power and its subjects, but between the labouring and the wealthy classes. What must first be checked is the war waged against society by the peasant, whose profound misery merits so much pity, and whose passions menace so many dangers. There is a bad democracy, it is that which is hostile to the fortunes created by industry; but there exists also a good democracy, it is that which combats the fortunes maintained by privilege alone.

Now it is these laws of privilege, such as entails and the right of primogeniture, which both in England and Ireland concentrate the possession of all territorial wealth in the hands of the aristocracy. The monopoly established by these laws is doubly pernicious, by the evil it inflicts and the good it prevents; it chains down the land in indolent and selfish hands, to which it only lends a pernicious force, and it prevents the land from falling into the possession of those who, by improving it, would enrich themselves and benefit the entire community. It does not always save stupid or foolish landlords from ruin, and it forms an insurmountable obstacle to the acquisition of landed estates by the people. And yet can any one see Ireland and its immense agricultural population, without recognising that the true remedy for the misery of the people would be to render them proprietors instead of tenants?

England demonstrates better than any other country, how with a good aristocracy the agricultural population may be prosperous without ever acquiring property in the soil; whilst Ireland proves that there are countries where the people are absolutely miserable in the condition of tenants.

It is difficult to imagine a country in which property is worse distributed than Ireland. In England, large farms established on vast estates employ only a few cultivators, but these few live comfortably. In France, where property is infinitely divided, the agricultural labourer is for the most part the proprietor; and his farms, when he has any, are sufficiently large to render his condition far from deplorable. In Ireland, properties are as large as in England, and farms as much divided as properties in France; in other words, the country has all the abuses of large properties without any of the compensating advantages; with all the inconveniences of small farms, a system of which it possesses nothing but the vices.

English economists frequently quote the example of poor Ireland, to prove the great injury of the extreme division of land in France. Yet such a comparison can only be a source of error, for there is only an apparent similitude in the agrarian distribution of the two countries. The land in both is, I grant, equally loaded with agriculturists; but there the analogy begins and ends; since in France the petty agriculturists are owners of the parcels of land which they occupy, whilst in Ireland they are only tenants.

When people see the peasants of Ireland sunk in wretchedness on the miserable "lots of land" which they cultivate, they conclude that in France the same misery must be the lot of the person who occupies an equally small fraction of ground: no conclusion, however, can be less logical. It is for himself and for his own profit alone that the French agriculturist waters with the sweat of his brow the ground whose harvest is assured to him; whilst the Irish peasant sows for another, reaps a crop of which he never tastes, and has for the most part exhausted the soil, when he has raised from it the rent that he is bound to pay his landlord. Who does not see that the same spot of ground which amply supplies the wants of the one, must necessarily be insufficient to the other? Who does not comprehend that on his small farm one may be free and happy, for the same reasons that will render the other dependent and miserable?

It is a common objection against the division of land, that as the partition never ceases, estates will be cut up into such small fractions, that each parcel will only be a barren boon to its possessor, and a general source of impoverishment to a society composed of such proprietors; but are not such fears exaggerated or chimerical? Do we not see the partition of land in France halt at the point where it ceases to be useful; more restrained where land bears a less price, more developed where a less extent represents an equal value?[2] When a proprietor has no interest in preserving land too limited for his purposes he sometimes sells it, and sometimes farms it out to a neighbouring proprietor; most frequently he cultivates it himself, and in such case, however small it may be, he finds it his interest to keep it; but as the care of his farm does not occupy him the whole year, no more than its profits would afford him sufficient support, he joins some other branch of industry to his agricultural labours. Most of these French petty proprietors work for others; some as day-labourers, others as vine-dressers; some as small shopkeepers in the village, others as mechanics. But it may be asked, does not the land thus broken, divided, and delivered over to feeble resources for its cultivation, lose its value and fertility?

I will not here discuss the great controversy about small and large farms. I know it has been maintained that a large farm produces more proportionally, than several small farms of the same extent; because the large proprietor has the command of capital and processes which are not within the reach of the small proprietors; but I am not sure whether it might not be answered, that the petty occupants, in the absence of monied capital, expend on the parcels of which they are the proprietors an amount of activity and personal energy which could not be obtained from a hired labourer; that all labouring thus for themselves, and under the influence of a fruitful selfishness, may, by the force of zeal and industry, succeed in obtaining from the lands as much, if not more, than a single proprietor, compelled to hire the labour of others, could procure: that this employment of the greater force to produce the same result, is not to be regretted in a country where, if the people did not turn to the land, they would not engage in

2. See Mr. Leon Foucher's *brochure* on the Division of Land in France.

any other branch of industry; finally, that these petty cultivators, obliged to superior efforts in order to obtain an equal end, need not be pitied, because they find in the interest and passion of property an inexhaustible source of vigour, which renders their heavy burthen lighter. The experience of modern times has shown what a difference in value there is between the work of the free labourer and the slave; but we do not yet know how much the labour of the cultivating proprietor is better than that of the hired labourer.

However this matter may be, leaving the examination of this question to the economists, I limit myself to the assertion, that if the economical advantages of the division of land are doubtful, its social and political benefits are far from uncertain.

Ask all those in France, who have known anything of the condition of the people before 1789, and they will tell you that it is now infinitely more prosperous than it was formerly: and what has been the chief cause of this sudden change? simply, that the people have become proprietors. But we have no need of the traditions of the last century, to convince us of this truth. Let us only look at what is passing before our eyes: which of us is not struck by the revolution suddenly wrought in the entire existence of any one of the people who was not a proprietor, and has become so? Land is in France the supreme ambition of the working classes. The domestic servant, the day-labourer, the operative in the factory, labours only to purchase a small piece of ground; and he who attains the object so eagerly desired, not only becomes physically more comfortable, but morally a better man. At the same time that he wears better clothes, and uses more wholesome food, he conceives a higher idea of himself; he feels that henceforth he counts for somebody in his country; whilst wandering about from district to district, and from town to town, he was little interested in living honourably, and incurred few perils by an immoral course of life. Here nothing was known of the regular life he had previously led elsewhere; there, people were ignorant of the dishonesty that disgraced him in another place. But now that he is attached to the soil, he knows that everything will be taken into account; from this moment he keeps a watch over himself, for he will suffer all his life for an evil action, as he is sure always to derive advantage from his good deeds. He is thus more moral, because he is more independent. In general he takes a wife at the same time that he purchases his land; and soon, in the bosom of the domestic affections, he learns order, economy, and foresight: he is better both as a man and a citizen; his country is to him something tangible; is not his country the land? Henceforth he has a place on its bosom. In vain would economists prove to me that by the division of land less produce is obtained from the ground at greater expense; I would reply, that I know no means of covering the surface of the country with inhabitants more prosperous, more independent, more attached to their native land, and more interested in its defence.

If the acquisition of property in the soil has been such an advantage to France, with what great blessings would it be fraught to the poor people of Ireland! By becoming proprietors, the French have passed from an endurable condition to a much better state; the people of Ireland would clear at one bound the space which separates a prosperous lot from the most wretched condition imaginable.

The more we consider Ireland, its wants and its difficulties of every kind, the more we are convinced that such a change in the condition of its agricultural population would be a remedy for all the evils of the country. So long as the Irishman will be merely a tenant, you will find him always indolent and wretched. What energy can you expect from the agriculturist who knows that, if he improves his farm, his rent will be augmented?—that if he could augment its produce one hundred fold, his share would not be one whit greater? who takes his farm at so high a rent that even in the most prosperous year he cannot clear off arrears; who always sees "the hanging gale" suspended over his head, as a menace, the obvious purport of which is, that if at the next harvest he should collect a few more sheaves than was expected, the profit shall not belong to him! Suppose him, on the contrary, the proprietor of the two or three acres which he now rents; with what ardour will he till the soil which will recompense all his pains? Of what efforts will he not be capable, when he will see a reward attached to every toil, an advancement at the end of every furrow?

It may be fairly presumed that whenever Ireland shall have small proprietors, the greater part of the miseries of the country will cease. The fatal competition for small farms, which is not less injurious to the landlord than to the tenant, would soon disappear; for wherever the people possess a mere sufficiency of sustenance from their own ground, they will not farm the land of others, except on advantageous terms. The rich, ceasing to have the monopoly of the land, will no longer incur the curses of the poor; and besides, the petty occupant who covers with his body his field and his cabin, will have nothing to fear from the attacks of which land is the object in Ireland.

England is now making great efforts to raise Ireland from her frightful state of misery; all theories are invoked, all superior intelligences set to work, all means are tried, from the charity which gives bread to the poor, to the emigration which exiles him from the country. All these violent or factitious means must be ineffectual. Let people coolly reflect, and they will see that the land on which the poor live now so miserably, can alone render their condition better. It is in vain to attempt saving Ireland, by introducing manufactures: Ireland is essentially agricultural, and she is so, precisely because England is essentially manufacturing. The people must find a prosperous condition in the land, or resign itself to be eternally miserable: since the Irish peasants are profoundly wretched as tenants, is not their only remaining chance to become proprietors?

I could support my opinion by a thousand other arguments, but I forbear. If an English reader deems my reasons insufficient, I beg of him to consider that every one but an Englishman will find them superabundant.

But if it be true, that the Irish nation is doomed to languish in frightful distress so long as it will be excluded from property in the soil, how is this right of property to be attained?

Grave and distinguished publicists have given a solution of this difficulty which I cannot accept: admitting the necessity of the principle that I have established, they propose that the tenants now in possession should be simply and plainly declared proprietors.[3] This is not a question for discussion, but clearly a revolution. I have already given my sentiments on the nature of the proceedings by which social or political reforms are effected. In my opinion, to be good they must have one primary condition; that is, they must be conformable to justice and morality. Now, though it is less cruel to deprive a landlord of his property than of his life, the spoliation is quite as unjust as the murder, and therefore equally odious. It is very gratuitously supposed, that this agrarian revolution would be legitimised by a British act of parliament. But, in the first place, the dispossession of the rich for the profit of the poor would not be one whit more equitable because it was executed in the name of the law. Vainly would they allege that the actual possessors of the Irish soil having been usurpers, it is just to resume it. What present existing right would stand against an examination of the past? And which set of proprietors would be declared usurpers? Would they be merely the descendants of the companions of William III.? But then, only a small portion of the land would be resumed? Would they add to these the lands of Cromwell's soldiers and adventurers? But why not then go back to the settlers in the time of James I., or even of Elizabeth?

Since the sixteenth century, property in Ireland has changed hands a thousand times, not merely from the shock of revolutions, but by sales and transfers. Are all possessors to be shipped off their estates, by whatever title they hold them? even those who have purchased them with their money, under the protection of the laws? But then, Ireland must be thrown into frightful confusion, and the evil will strike without distinction the old proprietors and the new purchasers, the Catholic and the Protestant; the person who has purchased an estate from the fruits of his industry, as well as the person who inherits it from his ancestors; the merchant who has advanced money on mortgage, as well as the proprietor himself. Besides, though we may understand how, by such a system, the poor will cease to be indigent, we do not see what is to become of the rich, who, doubtless, will not remain cool and passive spectators of their own ruin, and who, if they do not kindle the flame of civil war in their country, will doubt-

---

3. This plan is proposed amongst others by Von Raumer.

less abandon it, so that all the proprietors having disappeared, there will only remain in Ireland rude peasants turned into masters. A singular means of advancing the civilisation of Ireland, of restoring peace to a country distracted by six centuries of civil discord, and of restoring the feelings of right and rectitude to a land where they have been lost!

For my part, it seems to me so important not to trouble the public conscience by any violation of rights, and not to agitate society by interference with property, that I equally reject the system of those who would wish to distribute the three millions of waste land in Ireland amongst the poor peasantry. In order to bestow such a gift, the lands must first be taken from their present proprietors. Now, in my view, every attempt on property is a bad measure of political economy.

Cannot the proposed end be attained by mild, equitable, and legal measures? —an end which would cease to be desirable, if it could only be reached by injustice and wrong.

What is it that is wanting to the lower orders in Ireland? To acquire property in the soil; but not to obtain it by iniquitous force: we must not make, but aid them to become, proprietors; and to attain this end, they must be supplied with the means. Now it is the means that is absolutely wanting at present. The Irishman finds it absolutely impossible to acquire property in the soil, not only because he is poor, but because, in both countries, civil laws made for the advantage of the aristocracy tend constantly to the concentration of the land in the smallest number of hands—because, in one word, these laws prevent land from being a marketable commodity. The inaccessibility of the land is the great obstacle to overcome; it is the most important of all aristocratic privileges to destroy; and its magnitude is so great, that I shall make it the subject of special examination in the next chapter.

SUBSECTION I

Feudal State of Landed Property in England

In order to comprehend the condition of landed property in Ireland, I must explain its state in England. In the latter country, land is still feudal. The hand of the cultivator has long been free; but he has not broken his old chains; and whilst all around him is agitated, changed, and modified, he alone is unchanged, an unalterable fragment detached from a state of society mutilated by time and by revolutions.

In spite of all the victories gained every day by the new principles of society over the old, the labour that creates over the privilege that preserves, eternal progress over eternal immobility, land is what it was seven centuries ago—the feudal base of a social system no longer in existence, a living emblem of an extinct world.

The art by which the English aristocracy has preserved its civil privileges entire, whilst it surrendered its political privileges, is a fact worthy of observation. The spirit by which it is animated is nowhere shown more clearly than in everything related to land. Assuredly it would be easier to extort universal suffrage from the English parliament than a change in the law of inheritance. The English aristocracy has only preserved the portion of the feudal system favourable to it as a body; it has abolished all that was inimical to its pretensions.

In truth, the sovereign is, by the present law, presumed to be the sole proprietor of the soil, of which the actual occupants are only proprietors in the second degree. But this is a legal fiction totally destitute of reality. The *suzeraineté* is purely nominal; and the inheritor of an estate in England enjoys as absolute right of property as that which is defined by the French law. The royal privileges in this matter have been all abolished; the laws which secured the privileges of the aristocracy have alone remained in force.

The principal object of these laws, extorted from feeble princes by powerful barons, was to preserve the vassal in full possession of his fief. What means were taken to attain this end? They tended to render lands unalienable and fixed in the hands of the possessors by the system of entails. They opposed the division of land among all the children, by the law of primogeniture. And now a fief purchased by a retired merchant may be protected, if he pleases, by the same laws which gave power to a vassal in the time of Edward I. The spirit of the feudal law has disappeared, but its consequences have remained. It, however, appears to me that very few in England think about these anomalies.

SUBSECTION II

Feudal Condition of Landed Property in Ireland—Necessity of a Change

The law relating to estates is the same in Ireland as in England. Thus, the same causes which tend to the conservation and indivisibility of the soil in the former country, exercises the same influence in Ireland.

The obscurity respecting the titles of property is not, however, so great as in England. In the reign of Queen Anne (A. D. 1708) a system of public registration for all deeds relating to land was established in Dublin, and since that time every deed of sale or mortgage is regularly registered. The principle of the institution was doubtless good, but, whether through original defects of form or subsequent abuse, the benefit is of little value. The expense of searching the registries is very considerable, and can only be borne by the rich.

Besides, this examination does not dispense with the necessity of consulting a lawyer, who possesses the same monopoly in Ireland as in England, and the same mystic authority in contracts. Though land in Ireland is not covered with so thick a veil as in England, it is, perhaps, loaded with more complications, embarrassments, and encumbrances. Independent of the feudal bonds that fetter it as in England, it has chains peculiar to itself.

In the first place, a great number of titles in Ireland are vitiated by defects belonging to the time when, according to law, the Catholics of Ireland could neither be proprietors nor tenants on long leases. As it sometimes happened that Catholics had money wherewith to purchase, and Protestants land to sell, a disposition to elude the law arose on both sides, and the land afforded an opportunity for a thousand clandestine transactions, the object of which was to bestow a right of property on those who could not legally possess it.

Every estate in Ireland, small or great, is, besides, infected with a kind of incurable leprosy. It is covered with an immense population of small tenants, whose burden must be borne by the person who becomes proprietor. And all these tenants do not occupy the ground on the same terms; some have a lease for twenty-one years, others for thirty-one, some for ninety-nine, and others for ever: there are some also who hold their farms not directly from the landlord, but from an intermediate tenant. How can a new purchaser recognise the rights he acquires in the midst of this crowd of occupants, middlemen and tenants, secured by anterior rights, and often mutually pledged to each other? Must he examine successively all the contracts between the occupants and the middlemen, to find which are obligatory on the lord of the soil, and which illegal? How can he purchase an estate entailing such investigations? And if he omits them, how can he purchase without any security?

But if it be true, that there are more physical obstacles to the transfer of land in Ireland than in England, we must at the same time confess that its indivisibility is not protected in the first country by the same moral and political laws that come to its aid in the second.

We have seen that there is in England a population which, so far from envying the land, has no desire to possess it, but rather regards it as a weighty charge imposed upon the wealthy. It is a superfluity of luxury and opulence; and in this country, where so many different roads are open to human exertion, it is not easy to see what interest the lower ranks would have in becoming proprietors; it is certain that they do not aspire to be so.

In Ireland, on the contrary, land, instead of being a luxury, is a necessity. It is the only good to which everybody aspires, it is the subject of all engagements; it is the passion which rouses every soul; it is the interest which stimulates every intelligence. Land in Ireland is the common refuge; it is not enough to say, that land is desired in Ireland; it is envied and coveted; it is torn to pieces, and the fragments are fiercely contested: when it cannot be occupied by fair means, it is seized by crime. I need not inquire if the Irish people are anxious to become proprietors of land, when I see them risk their own lives, and take those of others, to become tenants of half an acre of ground: though the peasant could not explain his passion, it would not the less exist; property is so far from him, that it appears to his mind as a chimera for which it would be folly to hope, and if he does not aim at its acquisition, it is not because he disdains it, but because he deems the price too high.

Feudal property in Ireland, besides, is not fenced by the popular sympathy which in England protects its indivisibility. Confiscated three or four times over, land in Ireland is associated only with recollections of violence, persecution, and blood. In some hands, it is the solemn testimony of an usurpation which does not go farther back than a century, and those who possess it in general excite nothing but hatred.

It must also be observed, that the economic advantages asserted to result from the concentration of land in a few hands in England, can in no way follow from a similar system applied to Ireland.

England prides itself on an agricultural theory, which, by employing few hands, sends into the factories all those who are not employed in the cultivation of the soil. Who does not see at the first glance that such a system is inapplicable to Ireland? It is not for keeping up large farms, that the indivisibility of the soil is maintained in Ireland; for all the farms are small, and an extensive system of culture is unknown: it is not for the sake of public wealth that a system is maintained by which the most fertile lands continue unproductive, or produce less than half of what is obtained from inferior soils in England.

In a country where there are eight millions of inhabitants, without any other resource than the land, what can be the advantage of this theory, the object of which is to employ on land the smallest number of labourers possible? If such a system suits a country where hands are wanting for manufactures, would it not be fatal to a people, where all not occupied upon the land are necessarily unemployed?

The English labourer, repulsed from the land, immediately becomes a producer of national wealth in the manufactory. But what will the Irish peasant do when removed from his little cabin? To what branch of industry will he apply himself in a country where no manufactures exist? Do you suppose that the land will produce more, when freed from the super-abundant labourers? Perhaps it might, but society will have to take charge of an unemployed labourer whose idleness will be dangerous. The day that the labourer quits the land, what can he become but a mendicant or a Whiteboy?

None of the moral and political reasons which, if they do not justify, at least explain the permanence of feudal land in England, exist in Ireland. In this latter country, to become proprietor is a question of life or death for the people; but, in spite of this necessity, they have the same obstacles to over-come as in England, where the people have neither the desire nor the want of land. The chief obstacles, as I have already stated, are the laws of entail and pri-mogeniture; these are of sufficient importance for us to resume their consider-ation.

SUBSECTION III

Entails in England and Ireland—Necessity of Abolishing Them in the Latter Country

The most striking feature in English entails is, that they are left by the legisla-ture to the caprice of individual will; they are weapons placed in the hands of proprietors for the protection of their estates, which they may use or not at their discretion.

There are in England no perpetual entails; that is to say, none, by the mere force of law, annexed to the inheritance, so as to fix its descent by invariable principles which cannot be set aside.

The longest entail terminates at the second degree; that is to say, if the child of the person for whose profit the entail was made, does not renew it, the entail is at an end; he may dispose of the estate, which becomes essentially alienable. Besides, by the present regulations of English jurisprudence, the proprietor of an entailed estate may always, by the aid of certain judicial forms, dock the en-tail, and acquire a full right of selling the land.

Are we then to conclude, that the aristocratic principle of entail has disap-peared from English institutions? It would be a great mistake. The lands of the rich are not, it is true, necessary unalienable, but it depends on his pleasure that they should become and remain such. Does he wish to secure his property by an entail? He has only to speak, and it is done. Does he deem it less advantageous to keep his estates than to sell them? The law, again, comes to his aid, and ren-ders that alienable which a moment before was not so.

A law, leaving so much in the power of an individual, would be ill suited to a pure monarchy. There, the entails which preserve large properties in certain no-ble families are established for the benefit of the throne, of which these families are the support. It is not inquired whether it suits the nobility to keep their lands or not; the monarch sees that it is his interest, and that is sufficient. It is differ-ent in an aristocracy where the lords of the soil are rich and powerful of them-selves.

It would, therefore, be an error to suppose, that the law of entail in England and Ireland has lost its efficacy, because we see it yield to the pleasure of the lords of the soil: its modifications are for their profit. In Ireland, the system, instead of protecting aristocratic fortunes, would have proved their greatest enemy, if the country had not possessed the secret of making entails yield to the will of the proprietors.

We can easily understand the assistance which a wise and enlightened aristocracy might derive from a system of absolute and inflexible entails. Accustomed to regularity, it would be protected in occasional extravagance, by a system which declared its estates inalienable; it would be always sufficiently rich to keep its credit, and if by chance it incurred debts, it would be saved from selling its property to pay them.

But, in place of this enlightened and powerful aristocracy, imagine an aristocracy destitute of prudence, talent, and conduct, degraded in public opinion, impoverished as much by its vices as its errors. In a word, put the Irish aristocracy in place of the English aristocracy; then the law framed to perpetuate its wealth will only accelerate its ruin.

Sinking under the weight of its debts, and destitute of all credit, the aristocracy of Ireland can only raise money on mortgage; but who will lend money on an entailed estate? The embarrassment of the landed proprietor is very great, and he often curses the law which was instituted for his protection. He has then recourse to legal proceedings. I need not explain the process of "common recovery;" I need only mention that it is attended with greater facilities in Ireland than in England.

What obstacle is there, then, to the abolition of entails in Ireland? The landlords, it is true, would lose the advantage of being able to render their estates inalienable; but, in their present state of distress, would not the advantage be more than compensated by the credit which would result from the right of sale?

We are not here inquiring into the means of strengthening or enriching an aristocracy, the ruin of which is proved to be necessary; but ought not every process which would annihilate the body without individually injuring its members be the best that could be selected? Now, if entails were abolished, every Irish proprietor would be more completely master of his land; more rich, because he would have more credit. The land, delivered from these fetters, would become free; it would be the first step towards the division of the soil.

SUBSECTION IV

Primogeniture in England and Ireland—Necessity of Abolishing It in the Latter Country—General summary

Land must, doubtless, be rendered alienable, in order that the people should acquire it; it is a necessary condition, for that cannot be purchased which is not an article of commerce. The abolition of entails is the first thing to be done, but it will not be enough. The people cannot become proprietors if the lands to be sold are of great extent, and they will preserve this great extent in a country where primogeniture prevails.

If the English system of legislation respecting inheritance is open to any reproach, it is that of excessive freedom; the owner of an unentailed estate may leave it to whichever of his children he pleases, or he may disinherit his family altogether, and leave the property to an entire stranger. Hence, the English frequently fall into the error of supposing that their law of primogeniture has no force of itself, and that the system is maintained by the habits and inclinations of the country.

Englishmen who employ such language are right to a certain extent. It is very clear, that if the law of primogeniture was contrary to the opinions and habits of the country, it would cease to exist wherever it is not obligatory. Still it has its roots in the law. What is the legal principle?—Simply this: if the father does not make a will, the eldest son inherits all, to the exclusion of his brothers and sisters, who inherit absolutely nothing. Now what is the consequence?—When the father keeps silence, the law speaks, and its voice is always in favour of the eldest son. You may, if you please, say that the law is not tyrannical, since resistance is permitted, but do not say that it is powerless, for if a man dies intestate, it acts with absolute sway. . . . . . This right is indisputably the most important privilege of the English aristocracy; we may add, that it is also the most national. The beauty and richness of England, and the conservation of the splendid demesnes along every line of road, depend upon keeping estates together, and hence a sort of popularity is attached to the law of primogeniture, without which those splendid groves and plantations would fall beneath the axe, when the principle of equality divided and broke up inheritances.

Primogeniture is as strong a legal principle in England as in Ireland; but it does not find the same support there in the condition of the land, in the prejudices and the national passions. It is true that in Ireland, as in England, all those who possess large estates have the same aristocratic feelings for the conservation of their property as the English proprietors, and exhibit the same attachment to the principle which prevents their being divided. It is also true, that those who purchase estates with recently acquired wealth, are, as in England, at once seized with the same desire of founding a family and preserving the estate entire.

But, in Ireland, the respect and love for aristocracy end with those who are, or suppose themselves, members of the body; and this number is very limited. In England, by the side of every old fortune, there are a thousand new ones springing into existence. It is not the same in Ireland, where misery is almost as immovable as the land. Few hope to attain the object, and those who succeed are hated. I have never, in Ireland, heard the people evince for the vast possessions of the aristocracy the same indulgent and even enthusiastic sentiments with which I have been often surprised, in England, from the mouth of a poor man. Primogeniture may consequently be abolished in Ireland without at all offending the national feelings. On the contrary, it would be the best means of reconciling the law with public opinion. If the civil laws of a country are the expression of its habits, may it not be said, that so long as an antinational aristocracy will preserve its privileges, there will be in that country a flagrant opposition between the manners and the laws?

The abolition of primogeniture would not cause the same ruin in Ireland which it might produce in England. There are magnificent demesnes and splendid mansions in Ireland, but they are like oases in the desert. The rich Irish proprietor is accustomed to surround his residence with a certain extent of reserved land, on which he accumulates all his cares, all his luxury, and all his pride. Whilst our view is restricted to this narrow space, we must almost suppose ourselves in England; but when we look beyond, we are struck with the most lamentable spectacle; the land seems as poor as its inhabitants, and appears to reflect their misery: filthy hovels, unenclosed fields, naked land entirely destitute of trees, present a sad prospect of desolation.

In England the farm is so rich, that it may be confounded with the demesne of the landlord. In Ireland there is a sudden break where the demesne ends; it appears almost incredible that the hideous form which displays so much indigence and misery, should belong to the superb palace containing such enormous opulence.

Now, does any one suppose that there will be matter for much regret, when, by a new system of legislation, these immense estates so shocking to the sight will be divided? Would there be any cause to lament the mutilation of vast inheritances, if, instead of exhibiting barbarous hovels and filthy tenants, they were covered with neat houses and small proprietors? Here, then, we see that it is for the interest of Ireland, it is necessary, to subvert an institution which may be allowed to stand in England.

The abolition of the right of primogeniture in Ireland is absolutely necessary to the objects which must be attained. In the first instance, it would be sufficient to enact, that in case of a father's dying intestate, the property should be equally divided, and thus render an express declaration necessary to enrich the young son at the expense of the elder branches.

Doubtless, for a long time such a law would have little efficacy, because the habits and manners of the rich would struggle against it; but would it not be the surest and most equitable means to form new habits? In the first place, it would be imperative on every occasion that the father of a family died intestate; and how many are taken by surprise in their last hour! It would also remove from the selfishness of pride the excesses under which it finds shelter. Out of five children four are destitute, and one is rich;—this, at present, is the work of the law. But hereafter they might say to their father "This revolting inequality in the condition of those who had an equal right to your tenderness is your work: it results not from an omission on your part, but from a positive act of which you are the author."

I cannot believe but that in the long-run such a law would be fruitful in results, and would cause the division of a great number of estates. A glance at France will show with what rapidity such a division takes place, when once the principle of equal partition is admitted. When once primogeniture is abolished, the division of estates would afford the rising middle class in Ireland lands of an extent suited to their means, and, as it continued, would end by rendering landed property accessible to the lower classes themselves.

In fine, to attain the proposed end, the chains which fetter the feudal soil must be broken, entails abolished, the law of gavelkind substituted for that of primogeniture, landed property delivered from its trammels, the uncertainty of title removed, publicity given to all sales and transfers of land; the registry of mortgages and all engagements relative to land freely opened to the public, security and guarantees given to those who lend money on land; and the form of the deeds of sale must be simplified, so as to render the purchase of small and great estates equally possible.

I do not pretend to point out the legislative means by which the evils I have enumerated may be cured, and I limit myself to saying to those persons on whom the fate of Ireland depends, "Hasten to make laws which will render land a matter of easy traffic; divide and partition the soil as much as you can, for it is the only means, in overthrowing an aristocracy which must fall, of elevating the lower classes; it is the only means of placing the land within the reach of the people, and it is absolutely necessary that the Irish people should become landed proprietors."

Section III

What Must Be Done to Abolish the Religious Privileges of the Aristocracy

SUBSECTION I

Necessity of Destroying the Supremacy of the Anglican Church

Finally, it would not be sufficient to deprive the Irish aristocracy of their social and political privileges, unless they were at the same time stripped of their religious privileges. These are the supremacy and predominance of the worship, which, though followed only by a small minority, is the legal religion of all; and the great wealth with which that church has been endowed by the state.

How could the aristocracy, after the loss of its social and political privileges, retain its religious supremacy, which was only an accessory to its other privileges? It is with great difficulty that the Anglican church maintains itself while supported by the temporal powers of the aristocracy,—what would become of it when these are removed? Doubtless, in the midst of the ruins of the old edifice this church would not be preserved; for it is so great a scourge to Ireland, that were all the other privileges of the aristocracy spared, its destruction would be necessary; how then is it to be preserved if they fall?

In the midst of the vicious elements in Irish society, the supremacy of the Anglican church stands out in more prominent and revolting relief than the rest, not only because it is the most pernicious, but also because it is the most absurd. The obstinacy displayed in maintaining the legal principle and official existence of a Protestant church in Catholic Ireland proves that there are in human institutions degrees of selfishness and folly, to which it is impossible to assign limits.

We can understand the Anglican church in Ireland only at the moment of its birth; the religious zeal of the period explains it. In the sixteenth century, every sect believed that it exclusively possessed the absolute truth, and regarded it as a sacred duty to impose its creed, even by force, on those who were so unhappy as to have a different faith. The spirit of proselytism then reigned over all parties, and the Anglicans, who possessed the temporal power, would have shown at this period wondrous moderation if they had limited themselves, as at present, to placing before the Catholics of Ireland what they called the *model church, the type of the true faith;* and whilst offering to them *this only form of true devotion,* they had not forbidden every other mode of worshipping the Divinity.

It may further be conceived, that if such a religious passion existed in our days, it might have become obstinate in an enterprise, the inutility of which has been demonstrated by three centuries of fruitless efforts.

But has not toleration in our days replaced the spirit of proselytism even in England? In spite of its Anglican nature, the English government recognises all creeds; and the most different sects which formerly raved against each other, now live quietly under the protection of the laws. What, then, is the meaning of a church, erected in a country by religious fanaticism, and which, after three centuries of barren persecutions, continues to exist when the fanaticism is destroyed?

We find still, it is true, among some of the religious Protestants of England, Ireland, and Scotland, an enthusiastic zeal and religious ardour, which recal the early times of the Reformation; but we must render the Anglican church of Ireland this justice, that it is totally exempt from such passions, and that, condemned to live in the midst of a Catholic population, it appears quite resigned to its misfortune. The Anglican ministers do not seem much occupied with the care of making converts; and the best proof that they can give of their perfect toleration is, that they do not even reside amongst those whose conversion they ought to attempt. It is, besides, a common custom with the Anglican ministers of Ireland to reproach the Catholics with their spirit of proselytism. Assuredly this moderation is laudable, and must be highly approved. But if the Anglican ministers are not in Ireland to make proselytes, why are they there at all? Placed in the country to attain an object whose pursuit is abandoned, why do they remain? If not kept by passion, must it not be by interest? And though they have not converted Ireland to their creed, do they not, nevertheless, hold the privileges, lands, and revenues given them, on the condition of effecting this conversion?

What a sad condition for a church which, in order to avoid the reproach of selfishness, must either be intolerant, or perish! If, in spite of the lessons of the past, the Anglican church of Ireland still dreamed of the conversion of this country to Protestantism, it might excite more passion, but it would be less offensive to taste; it would be more irritating, but less absurd. Its first establishment was an act of violence, its present maintenance is sheer nonsense. In its recognised weakness to communicate its creed to those who pay it, it endeavours to render itself inoffensive, and does not see that the more it obtains indulgence the more it revolts reason.

Since the church has ceased to persecute the Catholics with the penal laws of the eighteenth century, it manifests singular surprise at the attacks of which it is the object. With what is it to be reproached? Do not its ministers live peaceably on their lands? Are they not found indulgent to their tenants, good neighbours, and good fathers of families? Do they not expend their revenues for the profit of the labouring population? And is it not a great benefit for a country still in a wild state, and where the upper classes are non-resident, to have here and there scattered over its surface a certain number of intellectual men, who, though they do not extend Protestantism, at least spread the germs of civilisation? Such is the language of the church of Ireland and its ardent supporters. Still, if the Anglican ministers, so often absent from their post, never quitted it, they would be powerless to effect the good required of them. Vainly will tithes be converted into rent-charges; the clergy will still be regarded by the people as the ministers of a hostile creed. Their fortune, however moderate, is a burthen to the poor, and a scandal to the Catholic. The violent and direct persecutions of the church have ceased, but the moral oppression which has succeeded them is still a heavy burthen; the mere existence of the church in Ireland, as at present constituted, is a constant tyranny.

So long as the Anglican creed remains the religion of the state in Ireland, the state will be odious to the country, and neither prosperity nor tranquillity will be possible.

Anglican supremacy is the principal and continued source of all the evils of

Ireland. To the Irishman it means confiscation, violence, caprice, cruelty; it is in his eyes the certain sign of injustice, falsehood, and spoliation. So long as the Anglican church shall be the established religion of Ireland, right or wrong, the country cannot be looked upon as free; it must always esteem itself treated as conquered and oppressed, because the bitterest recollections of the country are all mingled with Protestantism, and there is no recollection of Protestantism which is not mingled with tyranny.

This Anglican root of the aristocracy must therefore be extirpated, for, whilst it continues to remain in Ireland, it will throw up poisonous sprouts. Whatever government may be established in Ireland, woe unto it if it manifests any sympathy for the old Anglican privileges!

This principle of religious domination, in which all the grievances of Catholic Ireland are contained and perpetuated, will be, whilst it endures, an inexhaustible source of divisions, animosities, attacks, and resistances; it will render all authority impossible, even the most beneficent, if supported by it. Vainly would a government, however national, aim at establishing itself in Ireland; it would be powerless and weak if it rested on this vicious base. Vainly would internal reforms be effected in the Anglican church, its abuses corrected, its sinecures abolished, the wealth of its clergy diminished; the evil will always be the same, so long as the principle prevails which gives the Anglican worship a predominance over all other creeds; and this evil will always provoke the same resistance; the same deeds of violence, and the same popular rebellions, will appear again. In what form will the new resistance show itself? What will be the occasion? I cannot tell, but the event is certain.

It is a common error to believe, that a diminution in the revenues of the Anglican church would lessen the religious evil. In the first place, this reduction could not without injustice exceed certain limits. The higher ranks of the clergy are alone opulent in Ireland. The rectors have not, on an average, more than 500*l.* a year. This sum, enormous to those who pay it against their will, is barely sufficient for the ministers who receive it. These are almost all the younger sons of high families, to whom the church is an estate; their fortune, however large it may appear, is far inferior to their condition and their wants; they are married; they have children to educate and establish in the world; they have rich friends, relations, and connexions in the fashionable world; their charges are heavy, and their revenues below their wants. Perhaps, to be impartial and just, we should add, that the Irish clergy has never rigorously insisted on the whole of its claims. Tithe in Ireland is doubtless lighter than in England. In place of a tenth, the Irish parsons frequently receive only a twentieth; and this is not the mere result of the law; it has always been the case in Ireland, either from the moderation of those who claimed, or the resistance of those who paid. Nevertheless, the riches of the clergy excite complaints in Ireland, which they do not provoke in England. The high pay of the Irish church is indeed a mere pretext, and not the real cause of complaint.

Those who believe that reforms in the recognised vices of the church of Ireland would render it a beneficent institution, have only to cast a glance at the past. The hatred which this church excited, having in 1824 attracted the notice of the English parliament, it was imagined that the hatred of the institution arose from the mode in which tithes were levied, and that every grievance would be removed when the vicious form was corrected. The Tithe Composition Act was then passed, by which tithes were commuted for a fixed sum. Still, after this law was enacted and put into execution, tithes and the church were attacked as before.

It was then pretended that the hatred of the Irish to the Anglican church could only be attributed to the political incapacities with which the dissidents from its worship were punished, and that when Catholic emancipation was granted, the enmities of Irishmen would be at an end. Still, after the emancipation measure of 1829, was the Irish church less hated and attacked? In 1830, resistance to tithe commenced; in 1831, all Ireland was in open revolt against the rights of the church. Then it was supposed that these agrarian aggressions had their source in some forgotten grievances.

"Tithe is odious," it was said, "on account of the personal relations it produces between the Catholic payer and the Protestant minister; it was not enough to authorise commutation, it must be rendered obligatory." A new law was consequently passed, which, instead of permitting commutation, rendered it necessary. This reform was doubtless a step in advance; and assuredly, if the institution, which was its object, had not been radically vicious, the benefit of the change would have been felt and received with gratitude.

Still this law, designed to stifle, served only to irritate passions; the change was made in 1832, and during that very year Ireland was in open insurrection against tithes.

But misapprehension still prevailed; it was said that the insurrection was not directed against the institution, but against some abuse still undiscovered. An abuse in the church was sought; it was easily found; and in 1833 it was supposed that the clamour against the church would be quieted by the abolition of the most vexatious of its imposts, church-rates and vestry-cess; and that all attacks would be at an end when they reduced the number of Protestant bishops, diminished their revenues, and provided for the better administration of ecclesiastical property. This law, however, passed without the designed effect; resistance to tithe has continued; the church still excites the same passions, and is exposed to the same attacks.

Finally, after five years of anarchy and confusion, Ireland, say they, "is about to regain peace and order; tithes themselves will be reduced, the burthen will be transferred from the poor to the rich. This great innovation has been made; we are its witnesses." But are not those greatly deceived who expect considerable effects from this reform? The new Tithe Act reduces the tithes twenty-five per cent., and changes them into a rent-charge, which in future will be paid by the landlords, and not as heretofore by the petty farmers.

The intention of this law is generous; but people will be deceived who suppose, from the date of its passing, tithes in Ireland will cease to weigh upon the poor population, and to excite popular resistance. The situation and feelings of Irish landlords are sufficiently well known, to judge of the impatience with which they have received the burthen imposed upon them. How will these rich, already so poor, pay the new debt? Many will hardly have the power, the greater part will not have the inclination. In the first place, we may fairly reckon on all, or nearly all, endeavouring to throw the charge upon the people, and for this they will have the simple means of raising the rent in proportion to the new charge; thus they will indirectly obtain from the people what could not be raised directly. But what will be the consequence? The hatred of the tenant to his landlord will be increased, and the landlord will vainly attempt to throw upon the church the odium of an exaction from which alone it is the gainer; the unfortunate peasant, who toils from morning until night, will only understand that, before, he paid a sum to a church which he hated, and he now pays a landlord whom he scarcely hates less.

Every one must foresee the repugnance to tithes that must be produced even amongst the Protestant landlords in a charge which will not only add to their pecuniary embarrassment, but expose them to fresh popular resentments. But not only Protestant landlords, Catholic landlords also will be called upon to pay tithes. Is it to be supposed that these landlords, whose number is rapidly on the increase in Ireland, will be better disposed to pay tithes than their tenants? Will not their consciences as forcibly reject the tribute paid to a hostile creed? Does not their reason suggest the same objections? Does the rich feel less forcibly than the poor Catholic the wrong of being forced to pay a Protestant church? The same resistance will manifestly continue. The only difference will be in the modes of procedure. The resistance of the rich will be more skilful and enlightened; it will have chances for succeeding without violence, which it had not when allied to the lower classes. But if recourse to open force shall be necessary, it will still be more powerful, because better directed; it will rest on people interested in rejecting a burthen which in the end always falls on the labouring classes. There are, besides, in Ireland popular masses, suffering and irritated, which will not long be wanting to the support of violent parties.

But why should we speculate upon the future? Does not the present convey sufficient instruction? Months have elapsed since this expedient for the tranquillisation of Ireland became law, and we already see tithes, under their new name, excite the same resentment and the same fury amongst the people. Whence arises this inutility of all the efforts that have been made to reform the Anglican church in Ireland? It is simply because Ireland requires not the reform of the Anglican church, but its abolition. The radical vice of this church is, that it has been appointed the legal and official religion of a people which has a different religion. The abuse is the very fact of its establishment; its creation, in the midst of a Catholic people, is an outrage perpetuated so long as it endures. The great wrong of the church of Ireland is, that it is placed in the midst of a Catholic population which rejects it without examination. Its riches, its luxury, its idleness, are assuredly great defects; but the most enormous of all its vices is its existence. Its destruction must be the first step in Ireland towards good order and common sense.

When we speak of abolishing the Anglican church, our meaning is, not that the episcopal form of worship should be annihilated, but simply that it should be deprived of its supremacy over all other forms.

In abolishing the supremacy of the Anglican church, care should be taken that the domination of the Catholic hierarchy should not be established in its stead. Equality of creeds is what is necessary for Ireland. The popular masses in Ireland are indeed Catholic, as they are Anglican in England, and Presbyterian in Scotland; and it would be strictly logical that Ireland should have a Catholic establishment, as England has an Anglican, and Scotland a Presbyterian. But, in the first place, the expediency of connecting church and state is a great problem. How are the frail and fleeting institutions of man to be associated with the eternal institution of God? Besides, what would be the result of making Catholicity the established religion of Ireland, save to destroy the religious privileges of the Protestants, and transfer them to the Catholics? After having abolished the injurious supremacy of the Anglican church, which offends the majority of the people of Ireland, might we not see the Protestant faith oppressed by the creed over which it formerly tyrannised? One of the greatest perils to which Catholic Ireland is exposed is, that, after having been domineered over, it should attempt to exercise domination. It would be a fatal source of peril for England and for itself;—for England, which could not endure such a domination of a sect, which would revive all the old passions of the Reformation, and the ancient horrors of Popery; and for Ireland herself, which would be again crushed by England.

It is important, then, to both countries that Ireland should accustom herself to religious liberty. Now what better means can be devised to teach lessons of mutual tolerance than to place all religions on the same level? And it is precisely at the present moment, whilst England protects Ireland, that she ought to give the Catholics of the country a lesson of this kind. Equality of religion should come to the Irish as a benefit; at a later period, they will perhaps consider it an evil; and this will assuredly be the case, if equality is delayed until the Catholics become masters of political society; they will then believe that equality is introduced for the purpose of lowering their creed.

SUBSECTION II

Means of Establishing Equality of Creeds in Ireland—Expediency of Paying the Catholic Clergy

An English statesman has said, that there are two ways of putting creeds on the same level, paying the clergy of all, or of none. The system by which every religious community is left to provide for its own forms of worship, and its own ministers, is, assuredly, the most equitable of all; since nobody in this order of ideas is called to pay for another's religion, and bestows on his own only just what he pleases. Still there is equity, and perhaps more wisdom in the system which charges the state with providing equally for the expenses of all forms of worship, without giving pre-eminence to any. And if there were any doubt on this important question, it would be removed by the special condition of the Catholic clergy in Ireland.

I can well understand a system by which the members of each community sustain their church themselves, and contribute freely to defray the expenses of public worship; I can conceive such a system in a country, which, like the United States for instance, contains a multitude of different sects, none of which possess considerable power in the state. But who does not see, at a glance, all the perils that such a system offers to Ireland? where there are only two communions in presence of each other; where the Catholic church alone contains seven millions of souls; where the clergy of that church is the first power in the country; where the clergy is in intimate dependence upon the people, and the people upon the clergy; and where both clergy and people, political enemies of the government, increase their mutual force by a close alliance against it.

There is, doubtless, an excess in the popular power of the Catholic priesthood in Ireland, which seems to require that it should be moderated; a salary given by the state to all members of this priesthood would have such a moderating influence. This salary being proportioned to that given to the Anglican and Presbyterian ministers, would attest the political equality of creeds. The Irish clergy attached to the Irish people by the sympathy of a common creed, would not at the same time be emancipated from all connexion with public authority. Receiving a fixed income from the state, the priests would ask nothing from the poor and miserable people; it would be less popular, but more independent; less free, perhaps, in its relations to power, but less fettered by the passions of party. What could be the obstacle to this measure? Would it be, that a Protestant government cannot pay a Catholic church, or that a Catholic church could not consent to receive a salary from a Protestant state? These objections would have weight, if the state, by paying the Catholic clergy, recognised their religion as that of the country; or if the Catholic priests, by accepting a salary, were bound to recognise the supremacy of a Protestant state. After the legislative union, Mr. Pitt contrived a plan of Catholic emancipation, part of which was the payment of the Catholic clergy by the state; all seemed settled; parliament was contented to give, and the priesthood to receive. Contemporary history proves the assent given by the Catholic bishops to the project of the English premier: the Pope himself had agreed to it. But George III. believed Catholic emancipation contrary to his coronation oath, and before his obstinate will the payment of the Catholic clergy vanished, with the emancipation project of which it was an accessory.

At present, should the plan be resumed, the greatest obstacles would arise, not from the sovereign or the parliament, but from the Catholic priesthood itself. In the beginning of the year 1837, a report was spread that government intended to revive the project; the Catholic bishops of Ireland were roused, and unanimously declared that they would not consent to receive from the state the incomes they derived from the people. Is this declaration to be received as a final resolution? I may be allowed to doubt it. I have already shown that it is not in the nature of the Catholic hierarchy to be hostile to established powers. It cannot be denied, that in several respects the Catholic clergy of Ireland is driven from its ordinary course; its devotion to the people is, indeed, in accordance with its nature, but its hostility to temporal law is not so. From what passed in the time of Mr. Pitt we may conclude that an arrangement would have been easy between the government and the Irish priesthood: this transaction, at that time, pleased the greater part of the clergy; it assured them a fixed income, instead of uncertain support; a regular salary, in place of an uncertain revenue, paid in pence and halfpence. It delivered them from popular caprice, without rendering them dependent on power.

But since that time the social existence of the Catholic clergy has changed. The great struggle during twenty years between the government and the people, the solemn and national contests, in which the Catholic clergy has fought and conquered with the people; in which the priest, having become a tribune, has mingled in all the popular movements, become the defender of every violated right, the partisan of every reform; has enjoyed complete success, and drained the intoxicating cup of popularity;—these struggles, I say, have created for the Catholic clergy of Ireland the greatest political existence that any religious body ever possessed; and now that the Catholic clergy has tasted this mode of life, it can enjoy no other.

When the Catholic clergy declared that if government offered salaries it would refuse them, it was not merely to flatter the people, on whom they depend, that they used such language; they, doubtless, expressed their sincere sentiments; they had a consciousness of all they would sacrifice by accepting an income from the state, and they saw that whilst they gained a fixed and less casual income, they would sacrifice a part of their power and greatness.

Still if the conditions of strict union between the Catholic clergy and people of Ireland cannot be changed, they may be modified. Every circumstance, every event which tends to limit the political sphere of the Catholic priesthood will facilitate their accordance with the government. Let it also be considered, that such a measure should, as far as possible, be executed suddenly and secretly, and not discussed. Until the Irish priests are absolutely taken into pay, they must continue to declare that they take nothing, except from the people on whom they depend at present. As in all affairs where the church is interested, this measure requires to be managed with great tact and prudence, and, like every measure affecting an entire people, it requires resolution. Many other difficulties present themselves: thus, if the English government paid the Catholic bishops, it would require to have at least some indirect control over their nomination; but the mere idea of a *veto* exercised by a Protestant sovereign over the election of a Catholic prelate would seem a monstrous impiety to the Irish priesthood, though the court of Rome, more wise and politic, recognises such transactions.

This is not the place for examining these objections in detail; it is enough to show the object that must be pursued. If I could point it out, others might attain it. What seems certain is, that the body of the Catholic clergy of Ireland is not in its proper state. Its present condition may serve a country involved in a revolution, but it will not suit other times. We must not forget that Ireland is English, and destined to remain such. Catholic Ireland must endeavour to become prosperous under Protestant England: the first condition of this prosperity is, that it should act with wisdom and skill, internally and externally: now, at present, the priests are the most enlightened of the national advisers; but they are kept in absolute dependence on the populace and its blind passions. How can they escape this species of servitude?—I see but one way, by ceasing to be paid by the people. Now, if the people do not pay their salaries, the state must.

SUBSECTION III

Equality of Creeds Could Not Be Established in Ireland, if the Anglican Church
Retained its Tithes and Estates—What Should Be Done with Both

The equality of creeds that must be established in Ireland could not be maintained, if, after having given a salary to the Catholic clergy, the state left the Anglican church its tithes and its estates. If these were retained, the Irish people would believe that religious predominance was kept likewise. Even if the produce of the tithes and estates did not amount to an equivalent of the salary paid by the state to the ministers of the Catholic church, they would still see privilege instead of equality, because these two sources of revenue have been for ages attached to the dominant church, and have been regarded by it as privileges.

We must not forget that in Ireland, above all other countries, any injustice imprinted on the soil is with difficulty effaced. Land is everything to the Irish people: it is the only book which they can read; the Irishman knows no other annals; and so long as he sees the Anglican church in possession of large estates obtained in the times of supremacy, he will regard it as still the dominant creed.

But here a question presents itself—namely, how far can the law, without interfering with the principles of property, deprive the church of its estates?

It is a principle admitted by all publicists, that the property of the church, of a corporation, or mortmain, is not of the same nature as private property, but is governed by very different rules. There are substantial differences between these two forms of property which theory cannot dispute. Every successive possessor of ecclesiastical property has only a life interest; he can neither sell nor bequeath; the property has to him no futurity. It is certain also that, the present being everything to him, it is his interest to derive from the land the greatest revenue possible, even at the risk of exhausting and rendering it barren: in a word, he has all the passions of an irresponsible life-tenant, and none of the sentiments which animate the father of a family. Thus necessarily subjected to selfishness and improvidence, mortmain property is subject to another vice; it has the defect of being inalienable, and removed from the market. Badly managed, it produces little, and it is chained to the hands that administer it badly.

Now it may be asked, what analogy in principle can there be between private property and that of a corporation,—between the right of a man who, inheriting from his father, transmits to his son, unless he likes to dispose of it otherwise,—and the right of an individual who is put into possession of an ecclesiastical domain because he has been named to an ecclesiastical dignity, an estate which he cannot alienate, for which his heirs have no hope, and which will cease to be his, I do not say on the day of his death, but at any time when, for some cause or other, he might cease to be a minister of the church. Land, consequently, to the religious minister, is merely a means of support, an element of his salary.

Consequently, if the same powers which created such or such an ecclesiastical dignity, suppressed the office, who would assert that such an abolition was an outrage against property? Property ceases when there is no proprietor, or rather when the precarious tenant has disappeared. The real proprietor still remains, that is to say, the nation, the society, the state, which had assigned those lands as a salary for a public duty, and to which, when the office is suppressed, the land naturally reverts. We can see that the office is abolished, but we cannot see that any individual is plundered. And if the legislator has a right to suppress the office, has he not also the power of changing the mode of payment? To support the assertion that it is an act of spoliation to take lands from the church, it would be necessary to go farther, and assert that any revenue, salary, or estate bestowed on a public establishment, becomes irrevocable property. Now, could such a theory be supported by plausible reasons? Suppose that an establishment, endowed when it was believed salutary, should become pernicious, or that it has ceased to answer the purpose for which it was formed, must society continue to bear the charges imposed to maintain an institution proved to be bad, which charges are only imposed in the hope of great benefits? It is difficult not to see that property, in the hands of ecclesiastical corporations, is *a trust* for which they are accountable to the country, and which may be resumed by the same power by which it was bestowed.

This principle is less disputable in England and Ireland than in any other country, because there the church and state are one, and consequently the property of the church is also the property of the state.

And how can doubt be maintained in presence of what has been done already? In Ireland, tithes were formerly paid to the Catholic church, which is now deprived of these revenues. How? By authority of the king and parliament. On what grounds? On the principle that it belonged to the government to regulate ecclesiastical property, and make the best use of it. Tithes were, consequently, transferred to the Anglican church. For what object? To render Ireland Protestant, which, nevertheless, has continued Catholic.

Are we to conclude that tithes should be restored to the Catholic church? The consequence does not follow; the state, disposing of its property at its pleasure, may do so, if it deems such a course advantageous; but, thus acting in a country where the notion of sacerdotal supremacy is attached to the payment of tithes, it would place all Ireland under the domination of the Catholic church, and we have seen that nothing could be more ruinous to Ireland itself.

What consequence, then, must we draw? If the state legitimately deprived the Catholic church of its tithes, and transferred them to the Protestant church, in the trust that Ireland would become Protestant, it might, *à fortiori*, after three centuries of expense, recognising the vanity of its efforts and the chimera of its expectations, resume the tithes, and dispose of them anew.

The right which belongs to the state of disposing of the property of the church does not depend on the use that will be made of the property after it is resumed. The right is absolute, and subject to no other conditions than those of morality or utility. If the power of the state to resume the property of the church be disputed, when the interests of the country and religion require it cannot be disputed, we must also confess that it may distribute this property in the way most useful to society. A recent law of the English parliament has recognised all these principles, by taking one-fourth from the revenues of the Irish clergy. The reduction is trifling, but the principle is everything; for, by adopting it, parliament has declared that the possessions of the church are a national property, the disposal of which belongs to the state. If parliament has a right to take from the church the property called *tithes*, it may also resume the property called *land.*

In truth, the greater part of the land possessed by the church of Ireland arose from gifts and bequests. May it not be said that the law cannot, without impiety, defeat the religious purposes of the donor? But see to what this principle will lead. Most of these foundations were made by Catholics for the interests of their church and the establishment of their religion. Still, at the Reformation, the state endowed the Protestant church with all the wealth it took from the Catholic church, and surely it could not perform an act more directly opposed to the will of the donors. Now, one of two consequences must follow; the state had a right to act thus, or it perpetrated injustice. If the latter, the wrong should be repaired, and the confiscated property restored to the Catholics, which I believe would be an evil. If it acted legitimately, it has a right to resume the gift, and dispose of it in another way.

It appears, then, that no considerations of morality or equity would oppose the resumption of ecclesiastical lands and tithes, if their revenues were secured to the actual possessors. It must not be understood that the ower of tithes should be freed from the debt, or the tenant of the church turned into a proprietor; tithes would become a tax due to the state, which would also become proprietor of the lands. It would be bad, in abolishing tithes, to remit the debt; for it is of evil example to a nation when debtors escape their obligations by a display of force. Landed property in Ireland is loaded with a *grievous* rent—grievous, because it is paid to a detested church. Let us haste to change its nature; let it, like other taxes, be paid to the state. Nothing is more dangerous and depraving to a people than to make money by revolutions. For the same reason, it would be bad to give the church lands to the occupying tenants. These lands belong to the state; if sold for the benefit of the people of Ireland, they would bring an immense profit. Badly cultivated at present, they only bring in one hundred and fifty thousand pounds a year; but it is calculated that they might produce seven hundred and thirty-two thousand pounds. Hence we may judge what a price would be paid in Ireland for these lands. A precious means would be offered to the government of obtaining the desirable object of rendering the people proprietors. There would be six hundred and seventy thousand acres of land to sell, scattered though all the parishes of Ireland; and if a law was made to divide it into small parcels of about ten acres, it would at once create a large number of small landed proprietors. On the day when there will be one hundred and fifty thousand small proprietors in Ireland, property will be more firm, and the security of landlords greater than it ever can be by any political measure.

Thus, the most indispensable of all religious reforms would lead to the most salutary of all social reforms.

· PART IV ·

I

What Will England Do?

We have just seen what must be done in Ireland to attack in their first principles the evils which desolate that country, and to restore to its social state, profoundly troubled, the conditions of order, harmony, and tranquillity. Now, is that which is desirable, likely to be accomplished? Will, or can, England effect the immense changes which the interest of Ireland demands? It is not easy to think so. What Ireland requires, is the abolition of its aristocracy, and England is still essentially aristocratic. She loves the institutions which Ireland detests, and is eager to maintain all that is necessary for Ireland to throw down. England, doubtless, is no stranger to the general movement of democracy which agitates the world. The great principle of equality, that fundamental principle of religious and political law, could not but make its way in a country of light, Christianity, and liberty. Besides, it finds a very powerful auxiliary in the everincreasing development of English industry, which, incessantly bringing the inhabitants of the country into the towns, unpeoples the places where inequality is best established, and increases the population least subject to aristocratic prejudices. Were we only to look at the surface, and the external aspect of things, we might be led to believe that the old constitution of England is menaced with approaching ruin.

Just survey the progress of democracy in that country since 1830. Parliamentary reform, agitated for more than half a century, suddenly arrested in 1793, and suspended for nearly forty years, suddenly resumes its course, and having become irresistible by the energetic demonstrations of the national will, developes itself, and becomes established on a large basis. From that time England, instead of four hundred thousand electors, reckons more than a million; the House of Commons has ceased to be the creature of the House of Lords, and, supported by the people from which it has emanated, has become the first power of the state.

When these great changes were executed, it seemed as if a new era was beginning for England. Tradition formerly presided over its councils; for the first time it took logic as its guide, and regulated its conduct, not by precedents, but by reason. This intellectual revolution was, perhaps, the most difficult that could be effected in a country attached, like England, to its old customs. When once it has entered on the rational course, it will traverse it completely, unless checked by some extraordinary circumstances.

It was absurd, they said, that a petty borough, containing only two or three houses, should send members to parliament, whilst towns like Manchester and Birmingham, containing from one to two hundred thousand inhabitants, should have no representatives. Doubtless. In consequence, the borough was deprived of its privilege, and rights were given to the large towns which they had not before.

It is absurd that the citizens, who pay the taxes, should not all be invited to elect the representatives who have the power of voting those taxes; and, in consequence of this just reasoning, an immense extension was given to the elective franchise. Very well; but is it not absurd, that the municipal towns should be represented by those whom they have not elected, and be governed by officers whom they have not instituted?—Assuredly; in consequence, the municipal corporations of England were reformed and re-organized on a rational plan of free government.

The same logical method assails all abuses, and does not confine itself to the political world; it embraces the entire circle of humanity: the penalty of death has been abolished in a multitude of cases as useless and barbarous: and because slavery is unjust the emancipation of the negro slaves has been purchased from the colonies at a vast expense.

When the democratic advance has proved its strength and morality by such conquests, when it has had the good fortune to mingle its cause with causes so holy; we cannot discover what is to check its course; every circumstance seems to lend it aid; every logical reform leads to another reform, every victory gained is the pledge of a new victory. The singular impulse that has been given to the public mind leads not to a change of institutions, but to their examination. It is inquired if it be reasonable to have justices of peace as magistrates, whose entire qualification is their wealth, and to have men as legislators whose only merit is, that they were born lords. It is inquired if it be reasonable that representatives, chosen by the people, should be trammelled and controlled by lords who are not so chosen. The church itself and its abuses are put on trial; the oldest prejudices are assailed; religious intolerance is attacked in its very citadel; old puritanism is vanquished, and the leader of the Irish Catholics is honoured with a popular oration in the capital of Scotland.[1] A farther advance is made; the boldness of

---

1. O'Connell's reception in Edinburgh was a triumph rather than an ovation.

the English spirit is carried so far, that the equity of primogeniture and entails begins to be suspected.

Thus, undeniably, democracy is making its way in England; its progress is manifest and constant, and it will perhaps be less difficult to destroy the privileges of the aristocracy, than to reach the length of discussing them.

But though this movement in England is continuous, and though the progress grows more rapid as it becomes more logical, we must also confess that the English democracy is as yet only at the beginning of its career; though it has already made great progress, it has not yet established its empire. Its adversary will not confess itself vanquished for one day's defeat; and by the side of the forces which urge forward the car of reform, there are considerable powers that resist, or at least endeavour to moderate, its progress.

All the splendid existences of the aristocracy, the influence of large fortunes, the splendour of illustrious names, the multitude of individual conditions that depend on the nobility, and those which have been regulated on the belief in its duration; the popularity of the old families invested with the privileges attached, the prodigious exertions of those, who having recently come into possession of these privileges, labour to guard so precious an advantage, and one obtained with so much difficulty; the ambition of those who aspire to the aristocratic ranks, and who, though they have not yet gained their object, are so near it, that they defend it before it is reached: the number of capitalists who abound in England, whose only thought is to increase their wealth, and who, having need of peace to pursue their designs, are alarmed at every agitation in the state, whether the movement is made backwards or forwards;—all this forms an extraordinary mass of influence, passions, and interests, which openly or secretly tend to retard, if not to impede, the advance of democratic reform.

One of the greatest obstacles to democracy in England is, that philosophic equality is almost unknown. Some superior minds comprehend it, a few perhaps love it, but no one has a passion for it; and among the people there is neither a taste for it, nor an idea of it. The habits of the country are so impregnated with aristocracy, that the very peasant feels its influence, and in his most laborious efforts it is not equality, but inequality, that he pursues. His stimulus to exertion is far less the condition of those whose equal he will be, than that of those whose superior he aspires to become. However, he pursues his object honourably. It is not by humbling others, but by elevating himself, that he aims at becoming great; and if he fails, he submits without a murmur to chances more prosperous than his own, that have gained the privileges to which he aspired. So long as this sentiment will prevail among the lower classes, the aristocracy will preserve a mighty power.

But democracy has a more formidable enemy in England, and one visible to every eye: the church.

We may, doubtless, perceive in England some signs of decline in religious faith. Philosophical scepticism has penetrated into the upper classes, where it is disguised under the mask of Unitarianism. Among the lower classes, mechanical labours, by materialising man, remove him farther from religion, which in truth is nothing more than the bond which unites the soul to that which is the most widely separated from matter, God.

Whether from philosophic tendencies, or from physical degradation, it is certain that there was never perhaps a period when there were so many in England belonging to no definite creed as at present.

But though these symptoms of irreligion and incredulity are more apparent every day, they are as yet rare accidents in England. Of grave importance for the future, they have but slight weight for the present. Taken in the mass, England is still profoundly religious, Christian and Protestant; and the English church, the official form of its worship, is singularly popular.

In truth, the Protestantism of England is not uniform; it is calculated, that the dissenters from the Established Church, Quakers, Methodists, &c., form one-half of the population; and these, though fervent believers, are not necessarily animated by the passions which belong to the church of England. It must be added, that as the dissenters belong principally to the lower classes, all that is not in accordance with the church may be regarded as imbued with democratic tendencies. But it would be a mistake to suppose that the dissenters, though nearly equal in number to the members of the establishment, form an equally powerful party. Ranged under the same banner, the members of the establishment form a close and compact phalanx, whose strength is increased by union; whilst the dissenters, who would be so strong if united, forming as many separate bodies as there are different sects, are weakened down by division.

There is, besides, in the long existence and in the recollections attached to the Anglican church, something very pleasing to the national spirit of the English. They see in it the living tradition of the Reformation, and the continued triumph of the Protestant faith over Catholicism. The church has all the passions of the people on its side; it knows this, and every time that the aristocracy is in danger, the church comes to its aid, denouncing its assailants as the secret enemies of the church. The clamours it raises retain a great number who would be well inclined to destroy aristocratic privileges, but who fear to touch an edifice in which the church is a column, lest the column should fall with the rest of the building. This religious fear is, perhaps, the circumstance which of late days has most tended to suspend the democratic movement. The English reformers having imprudently avowed their intention of reforming the church itself, reform has been stopped short. The rejection of the bill for the abolition of church-rates in England, may be regarded as the halting place of the movement that originated in the parliamentary reform of 1832. From a multitude of causes, which it is not within the scope of this work to examine, England is attached to aristocratic and religious institutions, and adverse to a change.

How, then, can we suppose that England will effect or permit the extensive reforms which Ireland requires? Will she not, in her attachment to her old constitution, believe that it cannot be destroyed in Ireland without being weakened in England? Will not every alteration of the tenure of property in one country be perilous to property in the other? If the privileges of birth and fortune be overthrown in Ireland, can they be maintained in England? And the church, that corner-stone of the British constitution, the *Established Church of England and Ireland,* can it be glorious and powerful in one country, after having been demolished in the other?

Such objections, even supposing them ill grounded, are so completely in accordance with the passions of the people of England, that it may be boldly foretold, that she will not make all the changes that are necessary in Ireland.

Perhaps England will be wrong not to abolish the institutions in Ireland that she wishes to maintain for herself; perhaps the destruction of these institutions in the country hostile to them would be a means of their preservation in the country that is content with them; perhaps it would be a proof of great wisdom on the part of the English legislator, to recognise and declare openly, that different forms of government are necessary for countries whose social condition is so dissimilar, and that other laws are necessary for other habits. This principle once established and understood, many of the difficulties connected with Ireland would vanish.

Ireland would no longer have reason to complain that she is treated differently from England; and the latter, on her part, would not dispute the necessity of a different form of government. At present, it is absurd, that laws fitted to consolidate the aristocracy and church of England should be enacted for Ireland. The latter rejects them, and with reason; and nevertheless England might say, "you ask for the same laws." It is also an error, when reforms, liberal rather than democratic, having been accomplished in England, are extended to Ireland. Aristocratic England has need of more liberty; Ireland requires more equality. The English government is then wise when it refuses to Ireland what it grants to England; and yet Ireland may say, since you impose upon me your social irregularity, give me also your political liberty.

These inextricable difficulties in a system of uniform government for two countries would disappear as soon as it was established that each people has need of its peculiar legislation, and that Ireland should be treated otherwise than England, not because it is inferior, but because it is different.

But whilst we admit that England would act wisely and justly in pursuing such a course, we may, nevertheless, foresee that it will not be possible for her to act in such a manner. A single obstacle will be sufficient to prevent her,—the prejudices of England, and her passions, which are more powerful than her interests.

Such a condition is, doubtless, sad and pregnant with grave consequences; but, before deducing them, ought we not first to explain more completely the conditions of the problem?

If it be true that England cannot, or rather will not, effect the reforms in Ireland, the necessity of which we have demonstrated, does it follow that she will reform nothing in that country? Assuredly not. Everything, indeed, proves that the aggregate of the proposed reforms would be repugnant to English feelings, but each of them separately would not encounter equal hostility. Should we not, consequently, among the reforms pointed out, distinguish those which England would absolutely, and those which would be partially, admitted? We believe that all the reforms we have mentioned are necessary to the peace and prosperity of Ireland; but if the accomplishing of all is impossible, would not the best, or rather the least defective, plan be that which would permit some of them to be executed?

Besides, how is it possible to pass an absolute judgment on the feelings of a whole nation? There are some features universally diffused through the general aspect of a country, which allow of our attributing certain tastes and distastes to the great mass of the population; but such common features are few. A great people, especially a free people, is not so uniform in all its parts; the difference of classes and ranks, the variety of political interests, religious divisions, give rise to a multitude of opposing sentiments and contradictory passions. It is not always the same sentiment that triumphs; sometimes one notion prevails, sometimes another: the one in possession of power to-day, destroys what the other erected the day before. When, then, we have examined what a people will or can do under given circumstances, we cannot carry the investigation very far, unless we distinguish the different elements of which this people is composed; and, after having made the distinction, we must carefully examine the nature and bearings of each. Consequently, after having examined what England, viewed as a whole, would do for Ireland, we must analyse the English people, and appreciate what it might effect under the successive influence of the different passions and opposite interests by which it is divided. In other words, we must examine what each of the great English parties would do for Ireland.

II

What Each of the English Parties
Could Accomplish for Ireland

There are three great parties in England—the Tories, the Radicals, and the Whigs: let us examine what Ireland may expect from each.

Section I

The Tory Party

The English Tories are the party that displays the most anxious desire and firm will to preserve the institutions of the country intact: in their love for what exists, they defend all privileges, protect all abuses, and stigmatise the partisans of every reform as enemies of the constitution. They are the most constant and devoted friends of the church; in a word, they offer the highest expression of the aristocratic and religious passions which England contains.

It is not enough to say, that it would be impossible for this party to make the changes in Ireland which the country requires. If England, with its various interests and opposite passions, would be generally adverse to such reforms, how can they be expected from the party in which all the passions most hostile to innovation are concentrated?

In truth, a new party has lately been formed under the banners of the old Tory party, less absolute than that is in its principles, and which, whilst it displays the same attachment to the ancient institutions of England, does not profess an equal respect for the abuses with which they are mingled. This new party, commonly called Conservative, and of which Sir R. Peel is the leader, is generally composed of the more moderate and enlightened Tories, who comprehend that the best means of rescuing the assailed aristocracy, would be to correct its most salient vices as fast as they are revealed by time, and whenever their reform is imperiously demanded by public opinion. This party is, perhaps, the most faithful image of England, considered by itself; everything leads to the belief, that it would have the majority; indeed it would already possess it in parliament, only that Scotland and Ireland return one hundred and fifty representatives, most of whom are Radicals or Whigs.

But it is easy to see that this second party would not be less incapable than the first of giving Ireland the satisfaction which she requires.

It is not merely abuses that must be corrected in Ireland; it is institutions that must be destroyed. Now, how could these institutions be destroyed by a party, whose very name indicates that its mission is conservative?

In order to effect great reforms in Ireland, it is absolutely necessary to engage in a struggle with the aristocratic and religious passions of England. This the conservative party would hardly do, for such passions are its main support: its moderation consists in not exciting them, and in striving to assuage them; but it could not combat them. This party might, doubtless, make useful innovations in the details of public administration, but it would not execute the reforms suited to changing the social and political economy of the country.

Still there are many who believe that the conservative party would be the best to reform the vicious institutions of Ireland; they found their opinion on the fact, that the greatest changes which have been made in Irish institutions were effected by moderate Tories, and they quote as an example the concession of Catholic emancipation, in 1829, by the Wellington administration. But we must not confound what has been done by a party, with what may be expected from its principles.

Catholic emancipation was not in its nature a Tory measure: Lord Wellington undertook it, not because it was conformable to his principles, but although it was adverse to them. He has himself declared that, in accomplishing it, he did not yield to feelings of justice, but to the necessity of tranquillising Ireland, which menaced England with insurrection. He did not freely execute reform; he made a necessary concession. Now we are examining whether, if the conservative party undertook the government of Ireland, it would be compelled to make concessions—we are examining whether it would be in the nature of its principles to effect reforms.

Even if the Conservative party had the power and will to execute certain reforms in Ireland, there is one absolutely impossible for it to undertake, and which would stop it at once—the reform of the church. As religious questions are those which excite the most lively passions in England, the most temperate of the Conservatives could not apply their principles of moderation in matters that concern the church. Here the abuse is quite as sacred as the principle. But we have already seen that no reform in Ireland could be salutary, which did not, in the first place, subvert the Anglican supremacy. Thus the very first reform required in Ireland—that without which every other would be vain and fruitless

—is precisely that which the Conservative party would be utterly unable to accomplish.

Section II

The Radical Party

If the Tory party is by its nature unfit for the great reforms that Ireland requires, is not the party most capable of these reforms *that* whose doctrines are most opposed to those of the Tories, and which represents in the English nation the opinions most favourable to movement and progress, as the Conservative party expresses the passions most friendly to immobility?

We may certainly grant that if the English Radical party were in power, it would effect great reforms in Ireland. Still it would not be a task exempt from difficulty to determine what acts should be expected from its principles. We clearly perceive its general tendency towards democracy, but it would be difficult to say how far it goes on this road. Its march is uncertain, its theories vague, its plans are not yet formed. Either because it does not itself know the object to which it advances, or that it fears to frighten England by showing it, it is certain that this object is not clearly perceived. In its largest and most explicit professions of faith, the Radical party claims annual parliaments, universal suffrage, and vote by ballot; important reforms, without doubt, but which are means, rather than ends. We may, it is true, foresee that if the Radicals were masters of parliament and power, they would abolish the political and civil privileges of the aristocracy, and thus remove one of the greatest obstacles to the abolition of the same privileges in Ireland. But who can tell when the Radical party will have the power of executing such reforms? The party is at present small; it has little influence with the English nation, for it is too far in advance of the people; it counts but few members in parliament, and power is so far from it, that we need not inquire how power would be used by the party. Even had the party sufficient strength to deprive the English and Irish aristocracy of their civil and political privileges, could it at the same time abolish their religious privileges,—that is to say, the reform which in Ireland must precede all others? We may doubt it. And the obstacle by which it would be checked would be found within itself.

These religious passions, which we have already seen as powerful in England, are, perhaps, nowhere more active than with the Radical party, where they are more violent and less enlightened than in any other. In truth, the Radical party being principally composed of dissenters from the established church, the fanaticism of religious party, which pushes it towards democracy, would, in this respect, appear favourable to Ireland; but at present its passions are Protestant, rather than democratic, and the Irish are Catholics. The English dissenters, most of whom are Radicals, are assuredly enemies of the supremacy of the church; still they would hesitate to overthrow it in Ireland, through fear of giving a triumph to the Catholics. These passions of the Radical party against Ireland grow weaker every day, and are combated by the leaders of the party with all their might; still they occasionally burst forth. To quote only one example; when, after various attempts, a plan was formed by the English government for paying the Catholic clergy of Ireland, a fierce opposition was kindled by the dissenters, who branded as an act of impiety the payment of Popish priests by a Protestant state. Thus the Radicals, like the Tory party, might be stopped short at its first step in Irish reform by a cause arising from religion; with this difference, that the Radicals, in forbearing to attack the supremacy of a church so essentially aristocratic as that of Ireland, would do violence to their political principles, whilst the Tories, by preserving it, would act consistently with their passions, their doctrines, and their interests.

Let us add, that the prejudices of the Englishman against the Irishman, the contempt which the first so commonly feels for the second, are nowhere so strong as amongst the lower classes, where the Radicals naturally look for support.

The preceding observations apply with still greater force to an extreme Radical party which quite recently has manifested itself in England, and which, collecting large assemblages, is distinguished by a singular violence of language, and a great exaggeration of theories. In direct opposition to the moderate Radicals, who, not to alarm England, doubtless announce less than they wish to effect, this new party seems anxious to terrify the Conservative interests as much as possible: not that its doctrines give a clear idea of its projects; it does not say precisely what it will do, but takes care to spread abroad that it will accomplish great and terrible things; it is not satisfied with reform, it demands revolution; its motto is, the employment of physical force; it collects multitudes at night by torch-light, and, to remove all doubt respecting its designs, it invokes the memory and proceedings of Danton. It is doubtful if the Radical party, composed principally of the most fanatic dissenters of England, would do more for Ireland than the moderate Radicals: but what is certain is, that it would have far less power, for it has gone so far in advance of the people that it has left the nation behind altogether.

Section III

The Whig Party

We have just seen why, from different reasons, the two parties, which represent the most contrary ideas and opposite passions in England, could not effect any important reform in Ireland; one, because it blindly supports the constitution; the other, because it is supposed to be the enemy of the constitution; the first, because it has not the will to make any innovation; the second, because it will not be entrusted with the power.

But between these two parties there is a third, composed of those whom Tory immobility disgusts, and whom Radicalism terrifies; who, sincerely attached to the institutions of the country, nevertheless believe that they may be modified, and who, by turns ardent in attack and zealous in defence, admit enough of reform to advance the onward progress of democracy, and at the same time are sufficiently moderate in change not to alarm the aristocratic influences of England. This middle party is that of the Whigs.

From the few preceding words, it will be at once evident that it would not be in the power of the Whigs to execute all the changes which we have shown to be necessary in Ireland; for a destruction is what is required in that country, and the natural inclinations of the Whigs do not lead them beyond reform. In fact, it is only on the condition of destroying nothing that they retain the power of reform; but we may also see that whilst the Whigs are interdicted from entirely abolishing the institutions of Ireland, they at least derive from their principles the faculty, and from their interests the desire, of effecting great innovations.

The Whigs, who have the will to execute reforms, of which the Tories are destitute, possess also the power in which the Radicals are deficient; for they are at present the ruling party in Great Britain. They have, besides, motives of a different nature to effect reforms in Ireland; innumerable evils have accumulated in that country during the period that the Tories, enemies of all change, possessed power; the Whigs, who, after fifty years of exclusion, are come back to power, must naturally apply their remedies where the most grievous wounds are to be healed.

This generous disposition is strengthened by personal feelings. They are so much the more inclined to carry on reforms in Ireland, as they are prevented from effecting them in England. In the latter country, political parties are so uncertain and so divided, and the passions most favourable to the Whigs so uncertain and variable, that they have a great difficulty in devising a reform which, while it satisfies one division of their supporters, will not offend others. Still they must continue to reform so long as they carry on the government; this was the sole object for which they were restored to power. If conservation alone were required from the rulers, the charge would be entrusted to the Tories, whose business and right are the maintenance of existing institutions. Thus, always compelled to advance, and not knowing how to take a step without stumbling, the Whigs willingly turn to Ireland, which opens to them a limitless career of reform, and gives them ground less difficult to hold, because the conservative passions of England are there less violent.

Since the Whigs have the power of doing many things for Ireland, and since, at the same time, they are limited in their sphere of action, it becomes necessary to inquire what acts are within their reach, and what beyond their power. It is important to know how far they can advance in the reform of Irish institutions; which of the wants of Ireland they will be able to satisfy, and which they will be able to supply, and what influence on the country and its future condition will be produced by the reforms within their power; in one word, we must investigate how far they can apply to the evils of Ireland the remedy already indicated; that is to say, the abolition of the civil, political, and religious privileges of the aristocracy.

SUBSECTION I

Reform of Religious Privileges

The first, and perhaps the greatest, advantage which the Whigs possess over the Tories in all questions relating to Ireland is, that they are not at once stopped short by the obstacle of the church.

The Whigs are assuredly attached to the Anglican church, and prove themselves its ardent partisans; but they do not, like the others, insist on its preservation at any price. The Tories say, "Let Ireland perish rather than the Anglican church." On the contrary, the Whigs say, "Let us save Ireland, and also endeavour to preserve the church." The former would consent to make some reforms in Ireland, provided the church could be maintained in all its privileges and monopolies; in other words, they would offer some partial remedies to the country on condition of leaving intact the primary cause of its evils. The Whigs, on the contrary, look first to the miseries of Ireland, and the necessity of effecting their cure. They would be anxious to establish peace and tranquillity in the country without touching the church; but if , in pursuing this object, they are impeded by any abuses of the church, without any regard to the Anglican principle that fetters them, they abolish the principle and the abuse.

We everywhere find in the acts of the Tories and Whigs the consequences of this difference at starting. Take for example the doctrines and proceedings of each respecting the religious instruction of the people.

For more than a century the lower classes of Ireland were deprived of every kind of instruction, simply because they were Catholics, and the only schools in Ireland were Protestant. The Tories were then in power; and when reproached with an institution which gave the poor Irish no choice between ignorance and apostasy, they replied, as they still maintain, that national education is a privilege of the church which ought not to be taken away.

The Whigs, on the contrary, believing that the instruction of the people is essential to the safety of Ireland, recognise primarily the necessity of education;

and as it has been clearly proved that Irish Catholics will not send their children to Protestant schools, the Whigs have been forced to attack the monopoly of the church; and, in spite of opposition, they have established new schools from which everything sectarian is banished, and where religious liberty is assured to all creeds. The establishment of these national schools was one of the first acts of the Whigs, and there is not one that does them greater honour.

The Tory party believes the rights of the church so sacred, that a violation of them appears the greatest of evils; and when Ireland contests one of the rights of the church, for instance when it resists the payment of tithes, the Tories believe that the church should, at all hazards, be maintained in the integrity of its privileges: if the whole nation resists, its resistance must be beaten down, and the last Irishman exterminated, rather than that tithes should remain unpaid. In similar circumstances, the Whigs act differently; like the Tories, they wish the debts due to the church should be paid; they even prescribe this duty as one of rigorous obligation; but when they find the whole population rebellious, they do not take the same means of quelling the rebellion; they try rigorous means, but they do not persevere in them; they stop short at the commencement of the sanguinary career which the Tories traverse completely; the general interests of the country appear to them superior to those of the church, which nevertheless touch them nearly. They then endeavour to appease the people without overthrowing the church. They do not abolish tithes, the suppression of which would be a great blow to the church; but they endeavour, by modifying the institution, to render it less odious, and, by calming the popular passions, to render the government of the country possible.

It was thus that, in 1832, the Whigs abolished the most unpopular ecclesiastical tax, church-rates. And thus, in 1838, judging from the experience of five years that the Irish were resolved to pay no more tithes, the Whigs reduced the tithes one fourth, and transferred the obligation of payment from the tenant to the landlord. Such changes do not attack the evil in its root, but they render it less painful.

It does not enter into Whig principles to abolish religious supremacy in Ireland, which would be the first condition of peace and prosperity in the country; but they can at least render the fatal principle, which they do not destroy, less offensive and less odious, and that is a great deal. The Anglican church is not the only wound of Ireland, but it is the most sensitive, and the cure of the others is impossible if it be not assuaged. This is the reason why, under present circumstances, the Whigs alone can govern Ireland.

If the Whigs were animated by mere vulgar ambition, it would be their interest, so long as they retain the government, to protract the reform of the Irish church; for, so long as that church shall be maintained with all its defects in the midst of the violent passions it excites, accession to power will be very difficult to the Tories, whose very name would drive Ireland into insurrection, and who could not make their peace with that country, unless they began by attacking the religious institution to whose support they are so firmly bound.

Still, when we see the Irish church attacked by the Whigs, we can understand that this is not the object to which they would choose to apply their reforming principles, for it is the battle-field on which they feel least at ease. If they struggle first against the church when they enter on the career of reform, it is because the church is the first adversary that they find before them, and which they must either overcome, or withdraw from the contest. The reform of the church, then, is not so much an object which they pursue, as an obstacle which they labour to remove.

SUBSECTION II

What Reforms the Whigs Can Make in the Civil Privileges of the Irish Aristocracy

Now that the religious obstacle is removed, what reforms may be made in the civil and political privileges of the aristocracy? This question presents difficulties whose importance will be understood in the sequel. The English Whigs are certainly very aristocratic in most of their passions and principles; a single fact will justify this assertion: they have governed England for about eight years.

On the other hand, we are forced to recognise that they have effected many reforms, the effect, if not the principle, of which is singularly democratic. Thus parliamentary reform, municipal reform, the withdrawal of certain powers from justices of peace by the New Poor Law, are the work of the Whigs. Thus many acts favourable to democracy have been passed by the aristocratic Whigs. Is there not here at least an apparent contradiction? In what, then, are they democrats? In what are they aristocrats?

This inconsistency in the character of the English Whigs will disappear, if we take care to distinguish between the principles by which they govern civil society, and those which they apply to political society.

If we study the doctrines of those Whigs who approximate most closely to Radicalism, we shall find that they go so far as to sacrifice a part of the political privileges which belong to large properties in England. Doubtless they deem it just that a certain number of men, by the mere chances of birth and fortune, should have a right to govern their fellows,—should be justices of the peace because they are rich, and legislators because they are lords. Still they do not consider the institution of justices of the peace or of lords as inviolable.

Thus they admit that if the House of Peers became an obstacle to innovations considered necessary, this body ought to be, not abolished, but reformed, and composed of persons who had acquired, either by great personal merit, or by fortune, the right of representing a principle or an interest in parliament; they would willingly invite a greater number of citizens to take a share in affairs of state; and whilst they extended the circle of electoral capacity, they would increase the number of functions conferred by popular election. Thus it would not be contrary to their principles to organise county-boards, where citizens, elected by the people, would perform the functions now exercised by justices of peace. Their tendency, then, would be, by enlarging popular representation, to give, by elections, that administration to the middle classes, of which the landed proprietors have the privilege and the monopoly. In this body of doctrines there is assuredly a very democratic leaning.

But these same men, who would allow equality to be established in political society, do not show the same tolerance when the question of regulating civil society is mooted. They do not obstinately adhere to the preservation of the hereditary right of sitting in parliament to the eldest son; but they obstinately defend the right of the eldest son to take the whole of his father's inheritance, to the exclusion of his brothers and sisters. They can understand that the government of society ought not to be placed in the hands of a narrow oligarchy; but when the political privilege is suppressed, they will consent that this oligarchy shall have the monopoly of half the land in England, and keep it for ever by means of entails and civil laws, which render land to some extent inalienable in its hands; that is to say, whilst they consent to introduce equality into political life, they are firmly resolved to maintain inequality in civil society.

The Whigs thus form in their minds, and strive to establish in the country, two distinct zones, as it were, in each of which they establish a different principle of government, as democratic in the one as it is aristocratic in the other; and, as if there existed no intimate link between the government of a people and its habits, they do not appear to suspect that the doctrine of equality admitted into the state can ever enter into the family; and they seem to believe that property will remain the monopoly of a few, after political rights have been shared between all. This is not the place for examining how far such a distinction is logical, and whether this artificial separation between the man and the citizen can be durable; but it is important to show that this theory is a summary of the principles of the most advanced Whigs, because it contains a primary solution of the important question mooted at the beginning of our inquiry.

In fact, cannot everybody see that, from the very nature of this doctrine, the English Whigs neither could nor would abolish the civil privileges of the Irish aristocracy; that is to say, reform the laws which keep nearly the whole soil of Ireland in the hands of that body? Does it not also follow that though the Whigs, according to their own principles, cannot reform the civil privileges of the Irish aristocracy, they may be led by the same principles to abolish its political privileges? The first of these consequences is simple, and requires no comment; it clearly shows what, in such a case, the Whigs cannot do. The second, not less manifest, is rather more complicated; for, while showing how the Whigs, in another case, may effect several things, it is necessary to inquire what those things are. Let us then see what changes the Whigs can introduce into the political society of Ireland, and what political privileges of the aristocracy it is in their power to reform.

SUBSECTION III

Reforms Which the Whigs Might Make in the Political Privileges of the Irish Aristocracy

The Whigs, when in power, may attack the Irish aristocracy in two ways easily distinguished from each other. 1. By general reforms in the constitution, equally applicable to England, Ireland, and Scotland. 2. By reforms special to Ireland.

General Reforms—Vote by Ballot

Among the number of Whig reforms which, extending over the three kingdoms, would of course affect Ireland, the most important is vote by ballot, because it has often been discussed in parliament, and has made such progress as to be now admitted as an open question.

It is an opinion generally diffused amongst the English Whigs and Radicals, that if the parliamentary reform of 1832, which more than doubled popular representation, has not produced all the democratic effects expected from it, this result must be attributed to the mode in which the electors give their suffrage; that is to say, by public vote, which places them under the influence of the aristocracy; and it is supposed that if the vote were secret, as in France, the electors, rendered more independent, would prove more friendly to the reforms demanded by the popular will.

Without examining this question here under its different aspects, it will be sufficient to observe, that were the principle of secret voting adopted at elections, the democratic advantage of the change would be, at the least, doubtful in Ireland.

It is easy to conceive the support which secret voting would give to the independence of democratic voters, where the aristocracy is not only an established power, but moreover a dominant power, whose empire is accepted. The vote by ballot is a weapon of the weak against the strong. But, for the very same reason, might it not have an opposite effect in Ireland, where democracy is the popular power, and aristocracy the power feeble and assailed?

The Irish elector has no absolute need of the ballot to be independent. In truth, we must allow that the resistance he makes to the efforts of corruption may bring evils on his head from which he would be sheltered by the secret vote;

—tenants are expelled from their farms for having voted against their landlords, and these might escape these cruel reprisals if protected by the ballot. But such acts of vengeance, which ruin some unfortunate beings, are also fatal to their authors; in the first place, they prove the powerlessness of corruption, which never loses temper save when it is inefficacious, and they excite in the highest degree popular resentment against the aristocracy.

Secrecy of voting, which is not in Ireland absolutely necessary to the independence of those who attack the aristocracy, might possibly injure the democracy by protecting those who oppose it. We must not forget, that besides the influence of the upper classes at an election, there is also the influence of the people: now this influence, powerful in public voting, wholly ceases under the ballot.

There is something solemn in England, but more especially in Ireland, when the electors openly name the representative they choose in the presence of a countless assembly, which presses round them, excites, conjures, supplicates, menaces them, blesses those who vote in accordance with popular feelings, reviles and execrates those who pronounce the name of an enemy, and causes to be heard the great and terrible voice of the people, which, though often unjust, is always sincere, and always imposing even to those who affect to despise it. In England, the eye of the rich is most feared by the voter; in Ireland, the observation of the poor man is the object of dread.

Thus, vote by ballot, though favourable to democracy in England, might in Ireland prove advantageous to the aristocracy.

Political Reforms Peculiar to Ireland, Which the Whigs Might Make in Parishes and Municipal Corporations

The reforms which the Whigs are making or may make in the political powers of the aristocracy, have necessarily for their object the powers belonging to that body, either in the state, the country, the corporate towns, or the parishes. When they abolished church-rates in 1833, they destroyed a privilege, at once religious and political, exercised by the Anglican aristocracy in the Irish parish. Here we may add, that they have no other reform to make, for the Irish parish, of which the whole life was an abuse, may be said no longer to exist, since the abuse has been abolished.

The Whigs would wish to affect a reform not less extensive in the municipal corporations of Ireland, and which would be more complete, for here they undertake not only to destroy but to rebuild. They are anxious to destroy the Anglican and aristocratic monopoly of these corporations, and to construct on their ruins a free and democratic municipal organisation. The abuses of the Irish municipalities were so gross and revolting, that their most zealous partisans were forced to abandon them; and the only question at issue between Whigs and Tories is the amount of qualification which shall determine the right of citizenship. (Even this difference has been so narrowed by the bill of the present year, that the question may be considered as settled. Corporation reform will probably pass this session, and certainly cannot be delayed longer than the next; it is therefore unnecessary to pursue the discussion.)

The reform of the political powers possessed by the Irish aristocracy in the municipal corporations, and of those which it formerly held in the parish, is doubtless important; but that which is of greatest weight, that without which all others would be nearly vain, is the reform of the privileges belonging to the aristocracy in the counties. It is in the county that the aristocracy must be attacked, if the blow is designed for its heart; there are the justices of the peace, there are the grand juries, and we must particularly know what reforms the Whigs can execute in the Irish counties, if we wish to have the exact measure of their ability to attack the Irish aristocracy in its political powers.

Reforms Which the Whigs May Effect in the County

We have already shown, that in order to overthrow the political powers of the Irish aristocracy, the first step should be to centralise the administration of the counties: the first question, then, is to know if the Whigs can execute this system of centralisation. Here it is especially necessary to distinguish between the principles which guide the Whigs in the government of England, and those which they apply to their administration in Ireland.

Since the Whigs have come into power, a certain tendency towards centralisation in the administration of public affairs is perceptible. This tendency is necessarily exhibited in every county, where either democracy or absolute power aim at establishing themselves; for, as both aspire to level ranks, they have need of an instrument of equality. As we see, then, democracy develope itself in England, we may be sure that its progress will be manifested by some effort at centralisation. Thus, the Reform Bill of 1832 was followed by three laws tending to centralise relief to the poor, prison discipline, and a system of civil registration: laws purely social in their object, but essentially political by the new forms of administration which they introduce into the state, and which perhaps, for this reason, may be regarded as the most marked expression of the democratic movement that England received from the revolution of 1830. Still a person would be deceived, who supposed that these laws had any analogy to the system of centralisation established in France, provincial or municipal.

With the French, when any local power, aristocratic or democratic, is abolished, the destruction tends to the profit of the central government, which takes to itself the entire suppressed authority, and exercises it easily by one of its innumerable agents.

When the central government in England attacks the aristocracy, it does not proceed so openly and so plainly; it advances on this course with extreme prudence and great reserve; it spares the very power that it wishes to despoil. Thus, when the Whigs deprived the aristocracy of the exclusive administration of the poor laws, they instituted a central commission in London, to maintain uniform principles of public charity throughout England; but, at the same time, they instituted local boards, composed partly of justices of peace, and partly of citizens elected under qualifications which tend to give the administration to the middle classes.

It is assuredly a phenomenon worthy of observation, that this system of semi-centralisation, by which power is secured at the centre, should at the same time extend it to the circumference; it seems as if the two principles which we have already seen disputing empire with each other, Norman centralisation and Saxon liberty, had made their peace, and were for the future united against the aristocracy as a common enemy, which is thus pressed upon both by the prince and the people.

This moderate centralisation, which inflicts very feeble blows on the aristocracy, satisfies almost all the friends of reform in England, where the desire of weakening the aristocracy does not prevent a fear of despotism in the central government; and this fear is more natural in England than any other country. If, in countries less free, it is perilous to establish an absolute system of centralisation, because it may at some future time produce an invincible obstacle to the development of liberty, how much more formidable is this danger to a people amongst whom liberty exists, and where, consequently, the danger is not to compromise the greatest of blessings in the future, but to lose it in the very moment of enjoyment? At this moment there is not a parish or municipality in England which does not form a true republic, a free democracy. Would the English people act wisely, if, in order to aid the central power in striking at the aristocracy, they would resign their rights and liberties to the government, at the risk of not being able to resume them when the enemy had been overthrown? Is not that country in a fortunate position, which, requiring certain reforms in its institutions, can confer on the central authority sufficient power to effect them, without bestowing so much as would render that authority tyrannical?

But though such attempts at centralisation might satisfy England, they would be utterly insufficient for Ireland, where the legitimate passions and interests of the people require that the aristocracy should be openly attacked. The condition of England allows of a doubt, whether it would be better to accomplish a rapid reform at the risk of liberty, or accept slower reforms with the certainty of remaining free. But such a question cannot exist for Ireland, where the destruction of the aristocracy is the first of all necessities. Thus, the Whigs employ more potent means of centralisation against the aristocracy in Ireland than in England.

We have already seen how, at the close of the last century, certain powers belonging to the aristocracy were, for the sake of its own interests, taken from it and given to the central government. A judge removable at the will of the vice-roy was appointed to preside at the quarter sessions; stipendiary magistrates were appointed to aid the ordinary functions of justices of peace; and, finally, a constabulary force was appointed to protect the properties of the rich. These were so many means taken by the central government to aid and defend the fee-ble and unskilful aristocracy of which it was the ally and friend.

Scarcely had the Whigs obtained possession of the government, when they turned on the aristocracy the centralisation which had been formerly established for its protection. The assistant-barrister, who formerly received from the cen-tral government the mission, tacit or implied, of sustaining the upper classes against the people, is now charged with the support of the people against the ar-istocracy. Formerly he employed all his art to conceal the injustice or the inca-pacity of the justice of peace, now he labours to throw a veil over the faults or er-rors of the people. The stipendiary magistrates are now appointed, not to aid, but to supply the place of justices of the peace. They amounted to eighty-one in 1837, fifty of whom had been nominated since 1835. These stipendiaries are pop-ular in Ireland; they generally act better than the aristocracy, and in all cases they have the merit of not being its agents. Finally, the constabulary force has been completely centralised since 1836, and its direction transferred from the aristoc-racy to the viceroy.

But not only do the Whigs turn against the aristocracy the old laws which were passed to give it strength; they also endeavour to create new instruments of centralisation, or to perfect those which already exist. Justices of peace, since the year 1831, have been subjected to a regular system of superintendence; the pow-ers of grand juries have been restrained, and their deliberations opened to the public: finally, three central administrations have been formed in Ireland, each of which has inflicted a blow, more or less grave, on the aristocracy. The first is the Board of Public Works; the second, the Board of National Education; and the third, the Board of Poor Law Commissioners. The first is the one which strikes most directly against the power of the aristocracy in the counties, since it gives the government means of accomplishing those objects of which the grand juries had formerly the exclusive direction: the other two attain the same end in-directly—the former, because the establishment of a system of public charity demonstrates the indifference of the rich for the poor; the second, because it be-stows knowledge on the people, and thus gives it new strength against its ene-mies.

We have now seen how far the Whigs have employed centralisation to re-form the institutions of Ireland. We see that they proceed less timidly in Ireland than in England; not that they transfer in a mass to the central government the powers of the humbled aristocracy; but that they centralise a part, confer new attributes on the government, and trammel the power of the aristocracy in the portion of authority which it still retains. They are, however, far from effecting all the political reforms required in Ireland. They reform rather than overthrow the aristocracy of the counties; they weaken, they mutilate, but they do not venture to destroy it. We also found among the Whigs, though not so prominently as in other parties, that eternal tendency of English governments to make reforms in Ireland similar to those in England, and the constant disposition, when they displace a power, rather to distribute it among all ranks of society, than to give it to the central government alone. Thus it may be looked upon as probable, that if the Whigs abolished grand juries in counties, their functions would not be transferred to the central government, but to bodies chosen by popular election; a liberal, but a complicated system, suited to a country where the different classes of society, whose concurrence is desired, live in perfect harmony, but which is, perhaps, ill suited to Ireland, where the middle class is still in its infancy, where the people want the habit of self-guidance, and where the aristocracy is so antinational, that it is requisite not to look to the regulation, but to the abolition of its powers; an insufficient system in a country where the central government, though backed by the popular will, is far from being too strong in its contest with the aristocracy.

Reforms Which the Whigs May Effect in the State

We have seen what political reforms the Whigs may effect in the parishes, the municipal corporations, and the counties; the state remains to be considered. During the entire time that the Tories governed Ireland, the aristocracy possessed an immense political privilege in the state, namely—the constant favour, or rather the partiality, of the executive power.

The principles established by law are doubtless important, but the spirit in which they are enforced is of still greater weight. Now, under the rule of the Tories, the laws theoretically designed to protect the Irish aristocracy were also administered so as to gratify the most ardent passions of that body. It was then a received tradition among the governors of Ireland, that the laws were made for the aristocracy against the people, with the sole object of keeping the latter in servitude, and protecting the former against resistance. If a Catholic complained to government against a Protestant, or a poor man against a rich, the appeal was received with indifference or contempt. Justice itself, from the way in which it was administered by the agents of government, was corrupted at its very source. To give only one example, it was a constant custom at criminal trials in Tory times for the clerk of the crown to set aside Catholic jurors, and endeavour to form a jury composed exclusively of Protestants.

At this period the Orange party in Ireland was so powerful from the support given it by the executive power, that it would with impunity trample the popular party under its feet. Every year the anniversary of the battle of the Boyne, the triumph of Protestants over Catholics, was celebrated with all the demonstrations most insulting to the vanquished. Not only did the government permit these insolent provocations of a faction to an entire people, but moreover if the humiliated people dared to raise its head, and struggle against its oppressors, the central power supported the latter in their tyranny, and placed the police and the army at their disposal.

The Whigs have introduced different maxims and proceedings into the government; they have prohibited Orange processions; they have endeavoured to render the administration of justice impartial, by leaving the jury-box accessible to citizens of every creed; they proclaim the principle, that public authority is instituted as much for the benefit of the people as of the upper classes, and if their balance inclined to one side more than the other, the scale would turn in favour of the poor, rather than of the rich.

In fact, it is sufficient to glance at Ireland, in order to discover that the Whig government not only withholds from the aristocracy the exorbitant protection which it received from the Tories, but also that it treats the aristocracy as a hostile body. The Whigs not only do not confer on that body the employments of which it formerly had the monopoly, they sometimes take away those which it still possesses. If a justice of peace, being a large landed proprietor, commits any fault, the government takes the opportunity of supplying his place by a stipendiary magistrate. If any public functionary takes a leading part as head of the Orange faction, he is dismissed very unceremoniously.

At the same time that the Whigs take away from the Irish aristocracy the favours and graces of the executive power, they also grant these favours and graces to the most violent enemies of that aristocracy: they appoint the most eminent men of the national party to public functions; they endeavour to increase the number of Catholics in the commission of the peace; from the lowest to the highest employments, from a seat on the bench to a place in the police, they select agents of the popular party. In truth, the Whig government of Ireland and the aristocracy of the country are at open war.

This proceeding of the government is not intelligible at first sight: though it is easy to comprehend why the Whigs in this country, as in England, should be the adversaries of the Tories, it is not so easy to understand why they should display a hostility to the entire aristocratic party which they do not manifest in England. In the latter country the most Radical law emanating from the Whigs is tempered in its execution, and even when directed against certain powers of the aristocracy, the government does not attack the aristocracy itself. In Ireland, on the contrary, the application of such a law by the Whigs is always more hostile to the aristocracy than the law itself. Whence does this difference arise?

The cause is to be found in the nature of the parties existing in the two countries. We have already seen that there are only two extreme parties in Ireland, the Tories and the Radicals; the Whig party is there unknown. We have also seen that the English government established in Ireland, is under the absolute necessity of making a choice between the two parties, and attaching itself to one or the other; and that when it has declared for one of the two, it must give itself up to that one, body and soul, and yield to all its impulses.

When the Tories had the power, their representatives in Ireland inevitably fell under the yoke of the Orange party, of which they were the slaves, when they only wished to be its allies. When the Whigs succeeded to power, they were inevitably at the mercy of the opposite party; they had not even an opportunity for deliberating whether they would join the popular party. They found themselves necessarily fixed on that side, by the simple fact that the aristocracy, of which the Tory party is the sole expression, immediately assumed an attitude of hostility.

Perhaps it would be just to say, that the executive power in Ireland is more completely annihilated by its fusion with the popular party, than by its alliance with the aristocratic party. In the latter case it only sides with a faction hated by the people; it is, therefore, better able to regulate the assistance it affords; indeed it may limit itself to defending the party when attacked, and may withdraw its aid when that party becomes the aggressor. On the contrary, when the executive power in Ireland adopts the national cause, it is more irresistibly dragged on with it, and more blindly hurried forward by the popular torrent on which it is embarked.

It is not without some degree of alarm and repugnance that the English Whigs form the alliances which they are forced to contract in Ireland. They cannot, doubtless, but be disposed to strike at the Tory or aristocratic party, which has been their merciless adversary; but they are troubled not by the fate of their enemies, whom they combat but by the strength of the friends whom they mistrust. They would gladly see the Orange party fall in Ireland, and feel no disquietude, if the formidable power of a democratic party did not rise on its ruins. They fear the triumphs of their allies almost as much as the success of their adversaries, and timidly inflict a blow which, whilst it overthrows a detested enemy, may exalt a formidable friend. Their favourite object would be the creation of a Whig party, but they have made the attempt in vain. When the government in Ireland takes the side of the people, it becomes the instrument of the popular party.

We now see why the English Whigs are forced to be Radicals in Ireland: and this explains the clamour which the English Tories incessantly raise against the Whig government of Ireland, which, say they, and not without reason, gives to the laws enacted by parliament a more democratic application than the legislature intended. Hence also, we can understand why the Radicals of Ireland are much better satisfied with a Whig administration than those of England.

Although the Whigs do not give Ireland the institutions which the country would wish, still they do much for her by executing the laws according to her interests and desires. This is the reason why O'Connell and all his friends have separated from the English Radicals in their late attacks on the Whigs. The Irish Radicals care little for what occurs in Canada, or even England itself, compared with what passes in Ireland. It is of little importance to them that parliament refuses to reform church-rates in England, after having abolished them in Ireland. They forgive the Whigs for being every day less radical in England, provided they do not retrograde in Ireland.

The attacks of the Whig government on the Irish aristocracy have not all the effect which might at the first glance be attributed to them. Almost all the reforms which are the work of an executive government are frail and transitory. When that changes, they disappear with it; if a Tory administration gained possession of power, it would soon put in force the old principles of government, and restore the aristocratic spirit to the execution of the laws. Most of the liberal institutions which seem the best established, such, for instance, as the system of national education, would receive a direction from the Tories which would change its principles. The public force, that is to say, the police and army, which the Whigs have placed at the service of the national party, would be soon restored to the disposal of the aristocratic party. These two bodies, blindly subject to the principle of passive obedience, would certainly sustain the popular party, so long as the government would require of them such support; but being for the most part composed of Englishmen and Protestants, they are at bottom friends to the Tory and Protestant party in Ireland; if another administration gave them different orders, they would much rather fire on the Catholics, whom they are now forced to protect, than injure the Anglicans, to whom they are now placed in opposition.

Still the administration of the Whigs is a great benefit to Ireland, not only in the present, but as regards the future. It has taught the Irish that there may exist among the English a party favourable to the people; and, consequently, that all governments coming from England need not necessarily be hateful.

The English Whigs have the advantage of being able to govern Ireland without having recourse to violent measures, with which the Tories could not dispense. For more than half a century, that is to say, from the time when oppressed Ireland awoke from its servitude, the English government has been unable to keep the country in obedience, without a certain number of exceptional laws, which, under the name of *insurrection acts,* or *coercion bills,* invested the central authority with extraordinary powers, to be used at its discretion. The chief of these powers consisted in proclaiming a county, and arbitrarily changing the jurisdiction in criminal matters; for instance, bringing before a court-martial crimes committed in a proclaimed county.

These extraordinary powers were exercised not merely for the suppression of political enterprises, such as seditions, rebellions, or conspiracies against the state. Their first object was rather to reach crimes of a social character; they had particularly in view the constant and terrible war waged by the people of Ireland against the persons and properties of the rich. When the aristocracy of Ireland had the executive power on its side, it employed its political influence to exercise greater social oppression. It maltreated the poor and feeble with less reserve; it crushed more resolutely the wretch who rebelled against its rigours, when the cry of the unhappy found no echo, and when fearful laws checked his projects of retaliation. Thus, protected by a sort of legal terror, the rich in Ireland were more at their ease, collected exorbitant rents with less trouble, and practised their tyranny more tranquilly. Now these laws have been almost wholly abolished by the Whigs. They have only preserved in the government of Ireland a mere shadow of the coercion bill, a legal phantom, of which they make no use.

There are two principal reasons which compel every Tory administration to enforce these exceptional laws in Ireland: the first is, that these laws are demanded from them by the aristocracy on which they depend; and the second is, that their attainment of power revolts Ireland, and they are thus driven to violent means of repression. This is what renders a return to power so difficult to the Tories, for they would be forced at the very outset to establish a cruel and sanguinary system of rule in Ireland. This, also, is the great merit of the Whigs, that they can govern Ireland without having recourse to those odious laws, which violate common right and common humanity.

It must not be supposed that the Whig government of Ireland does not repress the attacks made on the persons and properties of the rich. It represses them, but in a different way. In the first place, outrages are less frequent under Whig rule, because the rich, having less power and privilege, do not excite so much hatred; and then, when outrages are committed, the punishment of them is entrusted to the ordinary courts of justice.

This regular and moderate system of repression, the only one which the Whigs authorise, is, doubtless, unsatisfactory to the passions of the Irish aristocracy, accustomed to special protection, and which, through fear of a criminal being acquitted by a jury, exclaims that society is menaced with dissolution; that security of person and property no longer exists, that justice cannot have its course under the ordinary laws, and demands that the insurrection act should be immediately enforced.

Very lately the aristocracy of the county of Tipperary unanimously applied to the central government to have that county placed under the insurrection act, averring that such protection was necessary, in consequence of the systematic war waged by the poor against the person and the properties of the rich. But their request was refused, and the Whigs, justly persuaded that the outrages which desolate that country have been provoked by the selfishness and improvidence of the rich, had the courage to tell the aristocracy of Tipperary a great truth too long misunderstood in Ireland. They reminded the petitioners that property perils its rights when it neglects its duties.

Thus, the Whig government of Ireland, doubtless, does not destroy the political power of the aristocracy, but it combats that body; with the incomplete arms it possesses, it could not better sustain the struggle against so formidable an adversary as the aristocratic body; it could not more skilfully weaken the enemy which it is unable to destroy.

In fine, the Whigs are doubtless unable to effect all the reforms in Ireland which the safety of the country would require; they can only make political reforms, for which they are best adapted, of a partial and transitory nature; the religious reforms which they attempt are fundamentally wrong, since they leave untouched the base, the Anglican principle, which is the first grievance of Ireland; and they do not even attempt the reform of the civil privileges which are the soul of the aristocracy. But though the Whigs do not cure the evils of Ireland, they have at least the power of alleviating them; they gain time, they accustom England to attend to the country, and they expose to view its most hideous wounds.

Thus we may say, as a summary of all parties, the Radicals have never been tried, and Ireland knows not what to expect from them;—she has known the rule of the Tories, who can only drive her to revolt;—the Whigs do not give her satisfaction, but they keep her quiet.

III

General Survey of the State of Ireland—
Conclusion—A Glance at the Political
and Religious Future of the Country

The facts are now known. We have seen with what evils unfortunate Ireland is afflicted;—how a bad aristocracy is the primary and permanent source of all its misfortunes;—what symptoms of resistance, and what elements of democracy, this bad government has produced in the country. We have also examined the means necessary to produce order and peace. Finally, we have investigated what England ought to do, and what probably she will not do; and we have seen that the English party, which is least incapable of governing Ireland, is nevertheless unable to accomplish the fundamental reforms required by the state of the country.

Now that the conditions of the problem are stated, what is to be its solution? What will be the consequence of such a state of things to Ireland and to England herself? What are we to conclude for the present;—what to conjecture for the future? Let us pause for a moment, and then advance slowly on the road of speculation and conjecture.

The state of affairs which we have described, is, doubtless, extraordinary and singularly complicated, but it is still the clear result of circumstances. Ireland, convinced that her misery arises from her institutions, must wish to destroy them; England, who sees in her institutions the principal cause of prosperity and greatness, naturally desires to preserve them. The great difficulty then is, that the same political rule which is salutary to one people is pernicious to the other; and that one feels it must die of the government which is the very life of the other. If the laws which are dear to England are maintained, Ireland remains with all its sufferings and all its perils; if it is resolved that they should be cured, the only remedy that can be employed is painful to England. The difficulty, in fine, is, that two nations to whom a common system of rule is fatal, each requiring a different code of laws, are still obliged to live under the same constitution;

and that, forming one and the same empire, they are subjected to a single authority, whose acts are salutary to the one, and ruinous to the other.

If England and Ireland have such opposite interests, and if it is so injurious to both to form a single people, it would seem that the only remedy would be, that they should separate, and form a distinct state, having its own nationality and proper government. This expedient would, doubtless, remove all difficulties, but we may boldly predict that it will not be adopted. In fact, it is sufficient to consider the geographical position of Ireland and England, to see that the latter will never renounce her sovereignty over the former. Ireland is a vital member of the British empire,—a gangrened member, but one without which the empire could not exist. In truth, if any convulsion of the globe sank Ireland in the bottom of the seas, England might be strengthened by the loss; but whilst this country, holding the place of an arm to the body, keeps its present position in the ocean, England must assert supremacy over it.

In all times Ireland has been the aim of the enemies of England; she was so in the twelfth century; for history informs us, that the use which France might have made of her was one of the causes that induced the English kings to undertake her conquest. When, in the age of the Reformation, a plan was formed by Catholic Europe for striking at Protestantism in England, it was on Ireland that Spain cast her eyes, and it was on that country that the famous armada of Philip II. disembarked. It was to Ireland that Louis XIV. sent the army destined to aid the Catholic James II. in regaining the throne occupied by the Protestant William III. And when republican and democratic France struggled against the European coalition of which England was the soul, she could devise no surer means of success than to send an army to Ireland; and for this purpose she prepared three successive expeditions in less than two years. Assuredly these different attempts at invasion have not been prosperous, and Ireland has always so feebly seconded the efforts of strangers, that she cannot be reckoned as a certain ally to the enemies of England.

Still England sees Ireland too near her not to wish to retain its management; she cannot consent to see a country isolated from her, from which she is only separated by a narrow strait, and whence an Irish or foreign army within sight of her shores might invade her territories in a few hours. And it is precisely because Ireland is Catholic and democratic, that aristocratic and Protestant England cannot leave her independent, and abandon her to her sympathies for nations whose political and religious institutions are repugnant to England, from the same causes that render them agreeable to Ireland. Independent of these considerations, what nation would consent to its own dismemberment? Does not every power, whose territory is diminished, appear to be on the decline? England, who would not consent at any price to the loss of Canada, which is fifteen hundred leagues from her, will assuredly not abandon Ireland, which seems like a portion of herself.

But, though we may regard it as certain that Ireland will never form a state separate from England, may it not happen that the two countries, remaining still united by political ties, might be legislatively separated; that is to say, be under the same imperial government, but have each its own parliament,—obey the same sovereign, yet have special laws adapted to their different interests? This parliamentary separation was, in 1833, the wish of nearly all Ireland; and at this very moment O'Connell declares that it is the only certain salvation for Ireland, if she does not obtain the reforms she requires from the English parliament.

We cannot confidently affirm that no such legislative separation will ever take place; in the first place, the fact proves it to be possible since it existed for six centuries previous to the legislative union in 1800; and it would, perhaps, be wrong to deduce an absolute objection from the servility and baseness of the old Irish parliaments, for if the parliament of Ireland were restored, might it not be established on a basis calculated to secure its independence?

But there are so many other grave and weighty objections to the re-establishment of the Irish legislature, that we may take it as nearly certain that it will never take place: this may be shown in a few words. Why does the English parliament not give Ireland the political and religious laws that she claims? It is not that the English legislators deem the institutions of Ireland the best that the country can have, but because they believe it dangerous to abolish them. They fear that the blow which levelled these institutions in a neighbouring country, would shake them at home; and that the law which struck at the aristocracy in one island, might affect the other by contagion of principle. Now, England would have precisely the same subjects of alarm, if Ireland obtained the power of making laws for herself.

When two nations are so close as England and Ireland, there can be no commotion in one which will not agitate the other. Under the publicity essential to the free institutions of Great Britain, each of the two nations must know every day what passes in the other. Now, supposing that the physical interests of the two countries, such as commerce and manufactures, should not, as in former times, be a source of perpetual collisions between the two legislatures, would not the discussion of political questions alone produce great embarrassment, and serious disputes? What could England say or do, if, for instance, the Irish parliament, yielding to the wishes of the country, abolished the principle of the Anglican church; and, after having overturned the religious privileges of the aristocracy, destroyed its civil and political privileges, dismissed justices of the peace and grand juries, set aside the laws of entail and primogeniture, and removed all the impediments to a free trade in land? Does any one believe that the adoption of such measures in Ireland would not find a formidable echo in England, and rouse the conservative passions of that country? Would England, while she believes herself so interested in maintaining the aristocracy and established church at home, tamely view their abolition in a neighbouring country, and in a country too which forms part of her empire?

Evidently one of two things would happen; either the Irish parliament, through fear or corruption, would submit to the good pleasure of England; and whilst preserving the outward forms of an independent body, would only make such laws as would suit English taste; and in such a case we cannot see what advantage Ireland would derive from a legislature, the servile instrument of those from whose power she is anxious to escape. Or, the Irish parliament escaping such influences, would freely and boldly enter on an examination of Irish grievances, and then England, seeing her own institutions attacked, at least indirectly, would hasten to deprive Ireland of a legislature. An Irish parliament sold to England is not desirable; an independent parliament is impossible. Thus, the two countries cannot be governed by different legislatures, and their parliamentary union must be considered as necessary as their political union.

Thus, England and Ireland, separated by their prejudices, their passions, and their political interests, are united by their destiny. With such different habits and opposite wants, they must adhere together, simply because, on the same day they rose side by side from the depths of ocean; like those monstrous twins, which, condemned by nature to form only one body and the same flesh, have, nevertheless, contrary tastes, and which incessantly afflicted with the desire of parting, are forced to move together, to live and die externally united, but internally discordant.

But what follows from this fatal union? Simply, that the weaker must yield to the stronger; in other terms, Ireland must accept the laws which it pleases England to impose. This is the reason why an established church and an aristocracy exist in Ireland. But are we to conclude from the preceding statements, that Ireland, interested in the destruction of these pernicious institutions, must endure them as long as England is resolved on their maintenance? Shall Ireland be condemned to eternal suffering, because the remedy for her grievances would alarm England? No—there is no reason for coming to so desponding a conclusion.

We may, doubtless, foresee that England will endeavour to maintain her own constitution in Ireland. She believes it dangerous to govern that country otherwise than as she is governed herself; she will endeavour only to make such changes as will give her no cause of fear, and she will attempt to restrain the religious and democratic reform now running its course in that country. This is the system which she has pursued for centuries, and in which she is so deeply engaged, that we cannot see how she could abandon it. But whilst we foresee that she will aim at this object, we may be pretty sure that she will not attain it. For fifty years it has been the object of all her efforts, and they have all been fruitless.

When we consider what has been accomplished in Ireland within half a century, it is impossible not to discover that the institutions founded by the English in that country are attacked at the heart. These institutions breathed Protestantism only; it is undeniable, that the principle which animated them is in rapid decay. How will the destruction that has begun terminate? By what deeds and under what circumstances? Will it be slow or swift—peaceable or violent?—We cannot tell, but it is impossible not to see that it is in preparation, and will come to pass.

Ireland is a country essentially Catholic, and the legal lie which made it a Protestant country is now so shaken to its base, that it cannot long stand. We may, therefore, regard it as certain, that, in a given and no very distant time, the Anglican church will have ceased to be the official and public establishment of Ireland.

The question whether the Catholic religion will become the dominant creed in Ireland, like the Anglican in England, or the Presbyterian in Scotland, is a question of a different nature and of doubtful solution. We have already seen, that the predominance of Catholicism in Ireland would be an injury rather than a benefit to the country. Ireland already possesses religious liberty; what she wants to acquire, and what she doubtless will acquire, is equality of creeds. There are, however, some, who believe that the Anglican creed will long retain its supremacy in Ireland. The British constitution, say they, the fundamental principle of which is Anglican, would cease to exist if the church of Ireland were overthrown. The sovereigns of England, whose right to the throne is a Protestant right, could not consent to the destruction of the supremacy of the church in Ireland without a breach of their coronation oath. Finally, the Irish Catholics, who in 1829 obtained emancipation, on condition of respecting the church and its establishment, would be guilty of perjury if they demanded its ruin.

It would be a great mistake to suppose, that the powers which are working the overthrow of the established church in Ireland will be checked by any such obstacle. Even were the English constitution opposed to its ruin, I would not less believe in the fall of that church; but it is false to assert, that the existence of the British constitution depends on the maintenance of the established church in Ireland. It is one of the great advantages of this constitution, that, not being written, it can never be violated. All requisite changes demanded by opinions or habits may be made without injuring it. This is the reason why Scotland became Presbyterian, and Canada continued Catholic, under the sceptre of England, without any violation of the English constitution. Similar changes in the constitution, so far from destroying it, may be considered as means of its preservation.

And why should anybody dwell upon the charge of perjury urged against the Catholics of Ireland, as having obtained large reforms on the condition of asking for no further changes? If the Irish Catholics, in 1829, promised to be contented with parliamentary emancipation, they assuredly made the most insane engagement that can well be imagined; it would be as if they had sworn not to fight so soon as they should be supplied with weapons. And the legislators, who from necessity, not from justice, ceded emancipation on such conditions, would not have been less destitute of common sense: it would have been as if they had said to the Catholics of Ireland: you are already so strong, that we are obliged to cede what we would not give you freely; consequently, we are going to increase your power, on condition that you will never make use of it. These conditions, which it would have been as absurd to offer as to accept, had they been seriously stipulated and taken, would still be purely chimerical. The oaths which a man takes voluntarily, are of value sometimes; those imposed by a party never.

If nothing can stop the reform of the Irish church, the reform of the aristocracy advances not less surely. The members of this aristocracy are always strangers in Ireland; they act as at the time when the conquerors of Ireland had only barbarous hordes to contend against; and yet they are now in presence of a well-disciplined people, guided by a great leader, and conscious of their strength.

The aristocracy of Ireland has from the beginning united its cause to that of England, and its destiny seems to be to live and die with it. Will another aristocracy be constructed on the ruins of that which is crumbling into dust? It is very difficult to tell. The tendencies of the English spirit lead to such a result, but the passions produced and maintained by a detested aristocracy may be an obstacle. And the more this antinational aristocracy will resist the blows directed against it, the more the sentiment opposed to every aristocracy will be strengthened in Ireland; for it is the special hate which it inspires, that blights the privileges of birth and fortune in a country naturally disposed to respect both. It may thus be said, that the system of the Tories which tends to maintain the existing aristocracy intact and inviolable in Ireland, is at the same time the best calculated to ensure its complete ruin, and to prevent its transportation into any other aristocracy; whilst should such a change be made, it will be favoured by the Whigs, who, by reforming the Irish aristocracy, will render it less unpopular, and accustom the Catholics of Ireland to the injustice of privileges, by giving them a share of their advantages.

But if a Catholic aristocracy does not succeed the Protestant aristocracy, which is doomed to perish, what power shall then take its place? Will the government of Ireland become democratic? When we just now showed how the Tory party excites the hatred of the people against the privileged, we at the same time showed how the same party might, in certain cases, aid the development of democracy. But if this democracy triumphs, how will it be established? Under what circumstances? Will it be by a violent revolution, or by a slow and gentle process? Whether it should be by violence or by peaceful means, how can it be constituted in spite of England, who believes herself interested in resisting it? When we consider the passions of Catholic Ireland, it is hard to avoid coming to the conclusion, that the long obstinacy of the Tory party to maintain the privileges of the church and the aristocracy entire, will produce in that country the chances of a general insurrection. What will be the effects of such a revolt? How far will the passions of the people go? Will they attack persons only, or will they likewise assail institutions? And what will England do? How can she leave such an insurrection unpunished, and how can she chastise an entire nation? Supposing that a new government should emanate from tranquil progress or revolutionary changes,—what will be its form? what its principles? what equality will it give the citizens,—that belonging to despotism, or that peculiar to free institutions? Here is a multitude of questions which we can only state, and the solution of which belong to futurity.

But though we cannot tell what power will succeed the Anglican aristocracy in Ireland, we may assume it as certain, that this aristocracy will fall, and it seems impossible not to regard its overthrow as near and imminent. Vainly will the English government endeavour to avert this double ruin of the Protestant church and aristocracy of Ireland; whatever it may be, whether Whig or Tory, it will not have the power; it will succeed neither by prudent reforms nor by blind resistance, neither by wisdom nor by force.

England, no doubt, is far superior in strength to Ireland, and the latter would be mad to enter into a struggle of rivalry with the former. She would be insane, not merely if she wished to dictate laws to England, but even if she attempted to escape from her sovereignty: woe be to her, if ever she enters upon such a strife! But there is a great difference between the feeble engaging in an attack and making a defence. The weak, when oppressed, find a great auxiliary force in the sanctity of the cause, whilst the powerful oppressor is seriously weakened by the injustice which he practises, and of which he himself is conscious. Now England may believe it useful to her own interests to impose upon Ireland institutions pernicious to the latter; but she cannot think such a proceeding just, and the very doubt of her right is a source of weakness. On the contrary, when Ireland resists the violence offered her, she has the sense of the wrong committed towards her, and is sustained by the feeling. Thus, it seems, that a long system of injustice tends to equalise the power of the oppressor and the oppressed, and that the courage of the latter increases as the energy of the tyrant is diminished.

England would rise as one man against Ireland attempting to break the political chain by which both countries are united. But when Ireland limits herself to

resisting the persecutions and rigours of a political selfishness, when she causes
to be heard the mournful accents of the starving poor, and the groans of the suffering oppressed, England is divided, and the great people, which would be all
powerful to subdue a rebellious subject, wants strength to crush a victim. This is
the secret of English weakness when opposed to poor Ireland, supported by her
unmerited misfortunes. Here is the explanation of the past and the revelation of
the future. This is the reason why, even at the time of her greatest relative inferiority, Ireland has always been a source of embarrassment and a menace to England.

And the time is approaching, if it has not already come, when Ireland will
not be strong in her rights alone. Her population, which increases more rapidly
than that of England, increases the power of the weaker, and diminishes the
power of the stronger. Ireland is no longer the petty nation of eight or nine hundred thousand inhabitants, beaten down by the mere nod of Henry VIII. or
Elizabeth; she at present contains eight millions of inhabitants, full half of what
England, Scotland, and Wales, contain together: and the time is not far distant,
when England, taken by herself, will not be numerically stronger than Ireland.
Then, though the first will, doubtless, be infinitely more powerful than the second, we must not forget what a superiority of forces is requisite to exercise an
oppression, which weakens the one, and lessens the inferiority of the other.

Besides, let us take care not to look upon England and Ireland as two countries standing alone in the world, and everything to each other. It is very true,
that England is at present everything to Ireland, which as yet has only an existence relative to England; but the same does not hold good for England, who
has the care of maintaining the power which she has established in both hemi-
spheres. Thus, Ireland pursuing only one political object, the reform of her institutions, and in contact with only one people, that which opposes this reform;—
Ireland, I say, unites all her forces against a single adversary, and brings to the
combat, without diversion, truce, or relaxation, all her physical strength and
moral power; whilst England, in her political relations, engaged with a thousand
different interests, is forced to divide her strength. The resistance which Ireland
opposes to England is constant, and must increase; the force which the latter
brings to bear against the former is variable, and subject to very large reductions
in extraordinary times.

We must take these mutual relations of England and Ireland into our consideration to understand how a feeble nation has been enabled to contend successfully against a powerful people, and how it may reckon on similar success for the
future. Strong in its just cause, constant progress, continuous efforts directed to
a single object, and all the accidental embarrassments which arise to trammel its
adversary, Ireland advances steadily on her road; sometimes she obtains from
England an act of half justice, sometimes a valuable concession; one day a boon

is granted to her on calculation, which had been refused to her as a right; concessions are alternately made to the pity inspired by her misfortunes, and the alarm produced by her agitations; and thus England is led, half reluctantly and half voluntarily, to overthrow in Ireland the edifice she would wish to maintain. Should the future seem doubtful, let us consult the past.

England was not less anxious fifty years ago than she is now, to preserve in their integrity her aristocratic and religious institutions in Ireland; and at that epoch the relative weakness of Ireland was far greater than in our days. Still it is from this time that the greatest advantages obtained by England over Ireland are dated. From 1775 to 1793, that is to say, nearly twenty years, it would seem as if Ireland held England in check; it would seem as if the latter, which had hitherto refused to cede anything to Ireland, had taken the part of granting everything;—and why? Because England was then in all the embarrassments of her power; braved in North America, menaced in India, at war with France and Spain: hence the Irish emancipations of 1778 and 1782; England gave Ireland her liberties at the same time that the American colonies took theirs. On the day that revolutionary France, declaring war against Europe, made England comprehend the necessity of being at peace within herself, she gave new liberties to Ireland: hence the emancipation of 1793.

Finally, when England conceded parliamentary emancipation in 1829, she candidly confessed that she granted it, not because it was just, but because it was necessary. And what was this necessity? To prevent the general insurrection of Ireland, which seemed imminent.

The situation of England is doubtless deplorable, having neither the power to be equitable to Ireland, nor the strength to refuse her justice; merciless in the period of her power, and generous only in the days of her weakness; rejecting one day as impious and sacrilegious the reforms which she executes the next as necessary. She thus sees destroyed peacemeal, year after year, by concession after concession, and necessity after necessity, all the institutions she is anxious to preserve in Ireland. Every day must render this work of destruction more rapid and more irresistible. The nation to which concessions are made, not because they are just, but because they are necessary, learns an inevitable lesson. Warned that she has nothing to expect from the equity of her rulers, Ireland labours only to show them her strength; hence when O'Connell wants anything, he preaches agitation, and rouses seven millions of people as a Laputan flapper, proper to fix the attention of England.

And yet this sad system of concessions, wrested from fear or weakness, or sometimes from pity, seems the only one which under present circumstances England can pursue towards Ireland.

We have elsewhere seen for what reasons it would be impossible for England to execute peaceably and freely the reforms which Ireland requires. She cannot effect these reforms, because if one part of her population wished to render justice to Ireland, there is another part whose political and religious passions would require that the oppression of Ireland should be continued. Now these passions and prejudices, which would be roused against a logical and spontaneous reform, would yield to a reform imposed by necessity, and bow to superior force. England pardons her government for being weak, and even powerless, before the exigencies of Ireland; she would not pardon her government for immolating, merely at the wish of the country, the institutions entrusted to its care; there are reforms which the Whigs would not be allowed to effect as just and national, which England would allow to be accomplished by the Tories as deplorable but necessary.

Thus, the English institutions established in Ireland are crumbling to ruin, in spite of the efforts England makes for their preservation. These institutions must fall, and we may affirm that they will not be overthrown in Ireland, without the same institutions existing in England receiving a severe shock from their crash.

England would commit a great error if she believed that this mixed system of resistance and successive concessions will save her from the perils to which, perhaps not without reason, she believes that she will be exposed, if she openly and directly reformed the institutions of Ireland. She would strangely impose on herself if, because she insists on the maintenance of her institutions in Ireland, she believes that she will escape the irresistible contagion which is overthrowing them. A very little reflection should be sufficient to convince her that her own church and her own aristocracy will be more shaken by the slow and disputed overthrow of the Irish church and aristocracy, than by their immediate and complete reform.

Of what value is the fiction which supposes these institutions stable in Ireland, if England incessantly hears the blows directed against them, and the cries of alarm raised by their partisans? It is in vain that England, satisfied with her church and aristocracy, denies that Ireland ought to be similarly satisfied, if the miseries of the country murmur a perpetual accusation against the church and aristocracy, which finds an echo in England.

Fears are entertained for the English church, if that of Ireland should be overthrown; the latter, consequently, is preserved. But what is the consequence? Simply that England hears every day that a church exists in Ireland, detested by the people; a church gorged with gold, abuses, and vices, receiving enormous revenues for the benefit of a few Protestants, whilst the mass of the people, profoundly wretched, has no provision for public worship. England hears these discourses repeated in a thousand forms. One day it is the sinecures of the Irish church that are denounced; another, the enormous incomes of the bishops: sometimes a revolt of the people against the exactions of the clergy is announced; sometimes a dissertation is published, proving, without much difficulty, the legitimacy of the rebellion. When Ireland is insurgent, how will the revolt be appeased? All England asks the question of itself. Do the Whigs propose reform as a remedy? It must be discussed. Do the Tories propose coercive measures? They must be discussed likewise. Vainly is the question raised by these vicious institutions eluded; it returns on all sides in spite of every effort, and perseveres in troubling England in her repose: if violent means are adopted to quell the insurrection, the cries of sorrow from the scaffold in Ireland resound through England, and are more tormenting than conscientious scruples in favour of the church and the aristocracy.

It would be surprising if English imaginations, once directed to such a subject, stopped at Ireland. Many who do not see at the first glance the difference between the religious state of England and Ireland, are disposed to believe that the monstrous abuses in the church of the latter are not without a parallel in the church of the former. Is not the scandal of ecclesiastical sinecures the same in Ireland as in England? Do not the higher clergy possess inordinate wealth there also? Is not the 20,000*l.* a year possessed by the Archbishop of Armagh, less than the 30,000*l.* enjoyed by the Archbishop of Canterbury? Is it not as absurd in England as it is in Ireland, that edifices for the Anglican worship should be built and supported at the expense of Dissenters? Is it not equally bad in England and Ireland, that the church should have large landed estates fettered to sterility in its hands? Is it not a bad system, that ministers of religion should perform the functions of justices of peace in both countries, and throw into prison the person to whom they are appointed as spiritual guides and directors?

All these questions are now debated in England.—And how are they raised? By the state of Ireland, by the eternal complaints which that country raises, and her constant agitation to reject a religious system imposed by force, and maintained by violence. How many clamours, always followed by the same echoes, how many similar commotions, always producing the same reaction, will be necessary to shake the church in England, which is tottering in Ireland? We cannot tell; but may we not assert, that no institution is so firm as to resist such causes of ruin? And all these perils, which the political system pursued towards Ireland accumulates against the church, are not less menacing to the English aristocracy.

When it is incessantly repeated in England, that there exists a class of persons in Ireland called *the landlords*, or *the rich*, against which the hatred and the curses of the people are incessantly directed;—that these rich landlords use their wealth and power only to crush and plunder the feeble;—that, odious to the people, but friends to the church, they have made with that institution a selfish bargain, of which the ruin of the people is the object;—when England learns that the great Irish lords, who have no sympathy for the sufferings of the poor man, derive from his sweat and toil the means of their luxury and ostentation;—when every day she hears that men invested with the public authority arbitrarily imprison the citizens, administer the laws without comprehending them; —that, from want of moral authority, they know of no influence but that of the jailer or the hangman; and that from their ignorance, cupidity, imprudence, and selfishness, they have rendered themselves so odious to the nation, as to be reduced to the necessity of either flying a country that abhors them, or living there in constant fear when they do not fall victims to hatred or vengeance; when, I say, such facts, which the press invariably registers, and still further exaggerates, constantly reach the ears of the English people, is it not to be supposed that they, struck by the accusations against the aristocracy of Ireland, will be naturally led to inquire whether that of England is not subject to similar reproaches?

The English aristocracy is, doubtless, different from that of Ireland. But however good we may suppose it to be, it still contains within itself enough of vices, it is subject to enough of errors, it contains enough of selfishness, for Irish grievances to present some analogy with grievances in England; for whoever, in the latter country, suffers from an excess, a fault, or a weakness of the aristocracy, is induced to apply to its condition what is truly urged against the aristocracy of Ireland, and to be tempted to hate that institution at home as much as the other is odious in the neighbouring country? England, which, in order to continue Anglican and aristocratic, forces Ireland to remain so likewise, does not consider what danger there is in this solemn voice of a people, which incessantly exclaims, that the Anglican church is the most odious of all religious systems, and aristocracy the worst of all governments?

Thus, not only will England fail to maintain the Anglican church and aristocracy in Ireland, but the blows which she aims at that country will rebound against herself and shake her own institutions: and this influence of Ireland, which re-acts on England, and sends back hatred in return for bad laws, does not merely act in a moral and indirect way. Ireland, well aware that England would not violently impose upon her the rule of the aristocracy and the Anglican church, if such rule were not her own, labours to attack the institutions of England, and the important share she has in the parliamentary representation of Great Britain supplies her with the means.

The influence of the Irish members is, and necessarily must be, democratic; and it is natural that they should embrace every opportunity which is offered to them of assailing, by their votes, not only the aristocratic institutions of Ireland, but those of England: not that they are very eager for the ruin of the English aristocracy, but because they know that if it were overthrown, or even weakened, the factitious aristocracy of Ireland would fall to pieces of itself. Now this radical character of the Irish representatives exercises, and is calculated to exercise in future, the most extraordinary influence on the destinies of England.

We have already said, that England, if left to herself, would be disposed to preserve her own institutions, if not intact, at least nearly such as they are; and it is certain that, in the present parliament, the English members, if alone, would give the majority to the Conservative party. Whence does it happen, then, that this party is not in possession of the government? Because, in the nearly balanced state of English parties, the Irish representatives, by joining the Whigs, give the majority to their side. Thus England, which really holds Ireland under her yoke, is still forced, by the influence of that country, to renounce the government she prefers, and to submit to a party by which, on the whole, she is not represented.

Friendly as she is to repose, Conservative England would not remain motionless, if she could direct her actions according to her own pleasure. The nature of her government, her habits of liberty, the spirit of discussion which has passed from her religion into her habits, the varied interests she contains, which, too timid to yield very much, are too enlightened to refuse yielding at all, —everything would incline her to a slow, peaceful, and progressive reform of her institutions.

But whilst she wishes to advance mildly and prudently in the path of reform, she is forced to advance with rapid strides. Whence comes this violence? From the contingent contributed to her representation by a nation to which in other respects she dictates the laws. It is now very generally acknowledged, that the famous reform bill of 1832 would not have been carried by the representatives of England alone, and that its success is mainly attributable to the Irish members. And it seems that every day, the democratic influence of Ireland in the British parliament is on the increase. At the late election of 1837, England, which is in a reaction against reform, elected a greater number of Conservatives than there were in the preceding parliament, and Ireland more Radicals.

Everything seems to show, that for a long time the parliamentary representation of the two countries will follow these opposite tendencies, because the question will every day be more urgent between the grave interest which England has, not to hasten the democratic movement, and the imperious necessity which Ireland feels to precipitate it.

May not a formidable collision arise between the passions constant in their attack, and the interests determined on resistance?

Will not the singular desire that England feels to stop short in the road on which she is hurried onward by Ireland, produce in the long-run some extreme resolution in the English people? It is already evident, that England feels a secret reluctance to be dragged in the train of Ireland. The idea that she is subject to such influence annoys her; she feels her pride wounded, because an obstacle to her natural march arises from a people she is accustomed to despise. Besides, from the repetition of attacks, the conservative interests of England have taken alarm. Reforms always succeeding to reforms, and concessions to concessions, a time arrives when the aristocracy, right or wrong, deems that it should yield no further, and that henceforth it is reduced to the alternative of resisting, or ceasing to exist.

Might it not then, happen, that the party which by its nature is most attached to peace, may some day see that there is no safety for it but in war, and convinced that if it does not revolt, it will be killed by inches, it should engage its enemy by open force at the risk of a sudden and violent death?

It is not merely a collision between England and Ireland that is rendered possible by this conflict of interests and passions, but also an engagement between the English parties themselves, one of which is irritated by the support that Ireland gives to the other. Recourse to arms is not a proceeding familiar to political parties in England; it may be generally said, that all disputes in that country are solved constitutionally. Still, who can give an assurance that England will never swerve from legal paths?

Those who saw England in 1832 will, perhaps, hesitate in answering this question. At that time the resistance of the Tory party engendered such ardent and unanimous passions in favour of reform, that England might have been supposed on the eve of a revolution. Insurrection was openly mentioned, plans for a campaign were prepared, leaders were chosen; it is even said that generals were nominated for the national army. The aristocracy having yielded, the river has returned to its bed, but what would the consequence have been, were the national torrent resisted?

Now, would it not be possible that the English nation, having made a movement to obtain reform, should commence a new agitation to arrest its course? Already, in 1835, at the period when the re-action in England against the movement of 1835 began to make itself felt, the conservative party, impatient of the reforms announced by the Whigs, who still retained possession of power, raised the cry of *war*. Nothing less seemed designed than an appeal to the *Cavaliers* against the *Roundheads*. This challenge had then no result; but may not violence some day follow from such a menace?

It is thus that the impetuous wind from Ireland, breathing democracy over England, brings upon her the chances of civil war. It is thus that the attempt to support in Ireland a system of government which the country rejects, produces a sort of oppression to England herself. It is thus that England, whilst she forcibly imposes her institutions on Ireland, is menaced with their loss at home. A strange and grave situation, in whichever way it is viewed. To Ireland the more terrible, to England the more weighty in responsibility; more simple though more laborious for Ireland, because, having only one interest and one duty, she need not hesitate on the road she follows, though dragged along bleeding from wounds and tortures; more complicated for England, which, loaded with a thousand burthens, can neither carry nor throw off the weight of Ireland, —which, sure to conquer whenever she combats Ireland, gains only barren victories, and ruins herself whilst she ruins the unhappy country; and, in the midst of her rigours to the unhappy land, always dubious of her own cause. Stimulated by selfishness, and in turn restrained by conscience, she vainly tries to be always wise and always just. A situation vast and covered with darkness, in which the mind labours, wearies, wanders; where all that at present seems necessary to be undertaken, is found impossible; and for which we can discover in the future only sad and incomplete solutions, until the period, far or less distant from us, when the democratic principle, which is working its way through the world, and which reaches England not only through the passions of Ireland, but also the general movement of the whole human race, shall have overthrown aristocracy in England, and, by introducing into that country the only institutions which Ireland can endure, rendered possible an accordance between two people condemned to a common life, and which at present are no more able to unite than they are to separate.

Final Reflections

In the midst of all the miseries, all the perils, and all the complications of which we have drawn so mournful a picture, one consoling aspect is offered to our view.

Whence have these embarrassments, perils, and difficulties, which her greatest statesmen are all but unable to solve, come upon England?—From Ireland: from Ireland, unfortunate and oppressed; on which England formerly practised a severe and selfish conquest; which England cruelly attacked in her religious liberty, after having deprived the country of political liberty; from Ireland, held during centuries under a yoke of iron, and subjected, without relaxation, to the most odious persecutions ever invented by the most ingenious tyranny.

And it is this people, crushed by so much oppression, and degraded by so much servitude,—this people so often mutilated, broken, and trampled under foot by England; it is this people, a victim by turns to every form of calamity, foreign and civil wars, massacres and exiles, the sword that slays, the gold that corrupts, the law that persecutes;—it is this people, rent in sunder by eternal convulsions, and decimated by annual famines,—it is this people of paupers, this people of rags, this people of slaves, that now becomes to its tyrants a source of embarrassment and peril!

Assuredly, here is matter of grave meditation for rulers and for nations. Does it not show that violence and corruption are bad engines of government? Does it not show that every system of policy, to be good, must begin by being just, and that in the art of guiding nations, as in the science which serves individuals to guide themselves, no separation should be made between honesty and policy?

There are occurring at this moment, amongst the two greatest nations that ocean separates, two phenomena of the same nature, which deserve to engage the attention of the world.

The United States of North America are beyond contradiction the most fortunate nation on earth: in no country are the conditions of society so equal and so prosperous; no land advances so rapidly to the power conferred by wealth and industry; nowhere is the progress of humanity so constant and so extraordinary. Still, in the midst of this marvellous prosperity, shining with so bright a splendour, a frightful stain appears; this body, so young, so healthy, so robust, bears a deep and hideous wound. The United States possess slaves. Vainly in that christian land do religion and humanity devote themselves with admirable virtue to heal this fearful evil; the leprosy is extending, it is blighting pure institutions, it is poisoning the felicity of the present generation, and already depositing the seeds of death in a body full of life.

At the same time that the United States in America are making fruitless efforts to expel the negro race from their bosom, because their slavery troubles and humiliates them; the nation, which is probably the best skilled in the art of government in Europe, England, exhausts herself in useless efforts to shake off a nation which she took six centuries to conquer, and struggles vainly under the miseries of her slave.

And how have these two nations reached situations so sad and so similar?—By the same roads,—by a primary act of violence, followed by a long course of injustice.

America and England would indeed gladly abandon these pernicious paths which terminate in such frightful abysses. But it is not so easy to escape from the pernicious and dark road which has so long been followed; long deviations and tedious retracing of steps are necessary for such a purpose. When the solemn violations of morality and justice have been continued for centuries, the deep perturbation which they have produced in moral order must endure long after they have ceased. It is not sufficient that the tyrant, who believed tyranny useful to his interests, should recognise his error in order that he should escape the consequences of his iniquity. It does not depend on the greater or less intelligence of selfishness to suspend or prolong the responsibility of its actions. From the moment that oppression has begun to exist, the oppression has incurred the fatal penalty. This law is severe, but it is just and sublime; there is a happiness in recognising that selfishness, injustice, and violence bring with them retributions as infallible as their excesses.

There are those who believe that individuals and nations are led by fatality to crime. The opinion is false; it is injurious to humanity, which, by such a theory, cannot be acquitted of crime without being deprived of virtue. The crimes of nations, like those of individuals, are voluntary, not necessary acts. There is nothing necessary but the consequence of crimes; nothing predestined but their expiation.

Preface, 1863: A Report on the Present State of Ireland (1862–1863)

TRANSLATED BY TOM GARVIN

I: Introduction

In this book, first published twenty-four years ago and now going into a new edition, I attempted to sketch the condition of Ireland and the causes of its sufferings. I described a country that had scarcely recovered from the earlier violence of conquest by England when it was subjected to the rigours of a religious persecution that went on for centuries. I described a country that was punished for its continuing fidelity to the Catholic religion, a faith that her conquerors had deserted. I also wrote about a country that had to endure the double oppression of an aristocracy that was at once foreign and Protestant. I recounted how the deep-seated evil of a bad aristocracy was the first source of Ireland's woes, whether it be in the government of the country or in ordinary social relations, in the mutual relationships between rich and poor or between the landowner and the man who works the land. I described the landlord, indifferent and commonly absentee, taking his tenants to be members of an inferior race and separated from him. The tenantry in turn, defeated but unsubmissive, returned his contempt with hatred.

I attempted to draw a picture of this strange society that in ways is really two very distinct but intertwined societies, one of which is organised to oppress and the other leagued to rebel. The former has the upper hand by means of laws that are iniquitous; at the summit there sits an imposed official Church, a corrupt parliament, a government committed to the interests of the rich and the passions of bigots; lower down, to enforce the law, there are the judge, the policeman, the soldier and the hangman. Furthermore, in opposition to this official and tyrannical society, we see a terrible confederation of the oppressed, covering all of Ireland with its mysterious networks, plotting in the shadows and only revealing its existence by the lightning strikes of its fearsome justice. It opposes its laws to the official laws and its arrests to those of the judges; it strikes at people and at chattels and maintains a perpetual terror in the hearts of those whom it has not killed. I showed also the consequences of such anarchy: the progressive development of hatred and vengeance, the insecurity of life and property, the flight of proprietors and capital and the accumulation of all sorts of causes of ruin. In all, I described the creation of two things that are peculiar to Ireland: the first is a type of social misery unknown elsewhere, and the second is a kind of atrocious crime which is not found in the annals of any other people.

Having described the English tyranny in Ireland I reported the point at which this oppression began to be dismantled, and showed how England had decided to cure the wounds that she herself had inflicted. In the first place I recounted how, by successive reforms, particularly the granting of Catholic Emancipation in 1829, Ireland was pulled out of the abyss into which she had been thrown, freed from penal laws which had held her under the yoke of oppression and gradually called to the use of political and civil rights by the benign institutions which are inherent in the English political constitution. I demonstrated that these reforms were brought about not only by the use of new principles of government, but also at the instigation of one man who was himself for forty years the premier political institution of his country, a man whom Ireland has lost but has certainly not forgotten. The Irish still remember O'Connell, a man who was great during his lifetime, and who is destined to become even greater after his death.

It is over twenty years since I painted this picture. Is the portrait still accurate? In what ways are things still the same, and in what ways have they changed? Many things are as they were, but others have changed. I want to indicate in this essay those things in my book of 1839 which remain accurate portrayals of the present and also those which have been effaced or changed because they reflected a different and superseded past social order.

First of all an extraordinary and unspeakable event has happened to the Irish social order which has perhaps no parallel in any other country and which must above all be explained. In 1841, Ireland's population amounted to 8,175,000 inhabitants, but in 1861 there were only 5,764,000, according to the official figures in the most recent census of population. Ireland has therefore 2,410,000 fewer inhabitants today than she had twenty years ago. Furthermore, not only these 2,410,000 are missing, for, following the natural way of the world, this population should have grown during that twenty years by between one and two million people, which, added to the 1841 figure, would have given us a figure of about ten million for 1861. The real deficit is therefore about five million. This calculation follows the normal logic used by British officials in making their own estimates.

What could possibly have caused such depopulation? What scourge has struck this unfortunate land so as to annihilate perhaps half of its inhabitants? What new Atilla has stalked the fields of Erin and wielded a scythe of destruction and death on her miserable cabins? And if this ruin was not manmade what was, in fact, the cause?

II: The Famine in Ireland

There is a settled opinion among the Irish of today [1863] that the principle source of their problems has been overpopulation, and they must, by any possible means, bring the numbers down. The times in which the Irish aristocracy strained every effort to get the population to grow are long gone. There used to be no landlord in Ireland who did not try hard to increase the number of tenants on his demesne. Besides the fact that such increase fed his arrogance and extended his power, it also increased his rental income. The extraordinary fecundity of the potato, a tuber introduced into Europe in the eighteenth century, favoured his wishes. The potato has the characteristic that, given a fixed piece of land, it will generate more food for human beings than any other crop. The smallest piece of earth, seeded with potatoes, gives enough to live to the unfortunate man who occupies it, while the surplus of his labour is given over to paying the rent due to the landlord. Under the influence of this system, the population of Ireland multiplied mightily, and the land of Ireland was divided into an enormous number of little parcels, all cultivated in an identical way. Peasants, electors and hangers-on of all sorts thus surrounded the Irish landlord. The soil was damaged, broken up and reduced to powder; every grain of sand represented a family, a rent, or a client. But the economic consequence of this system was that eventually the existence of an entire nation depended completely on one crop.

One day a deadly blight struck this tuber, the only food of eight million people, killing the tuber or rendering it unhealthy to eat for those whom it normally sustained. This happened in 1845. A cry was heard all over Ireland, a cry that was repeated in England, a cry that echoed around the world: the potato is sick, and Ireland is going to starve to death. While this scourge was hitting Ireland, it had also arrived in the rest of Europe and in America itself. The potato blight came at the same time to Italy, Spain, France, Belgium, Denmark and Nova Scotia. However, in these countries people's very existence did not depend utterly on the potato, and the event was merely a nuisance. In Ireland, there was no alternative food and it was therefore a catastrophe. This is not to say that the potato was the only product of Ireland; the country produces grains and fruits of all sorts. In 1846, the year of famine, Ireland had a magnificent grain harvest. But, as Sir W. Routh, a senior officer of the British Government, wrote to Trevelyan, Secretary to the Treasury, "Wheat, oats and barley are not considered as food by the people." Ireland lived on potatoes and sold wheat to pay its rents. It is extraordinary that in the very moment of famine spreading over Ireland because of the potato blight, cereal exports from the country proceeded as usual.

Meanwhile the Irish cry of alarm did penetrate the British Parliament. The normal hatreds and animosities were stilled, pity replaced resentment in the members' hearts and the barriers that divided the parties were lowered. Peel and O'Connell, those two adversaries of thirty years standing (the years of both were, alas, numbered), shook hands. A single voice resounded through the vaults of Westminster, echoed outside by the press and heard throughout English society: "*Save Ireland!*" There was universal sympathy, and it seemed sincere; after all, were not England and Ireland sister countries? For at least a moment, it was believed that they really were; how could the one, so strong and full of life, not go to the rescue of the other in its hour of danger? England was the most civilised nation in the world, having a government which was the wisest and most enlightened on the planet; what greater occasion would England ever find to use her enlightenment and power?

However, there is a task that is beyond the science and the power of the most skilful and wisest of governments: the feeding of eight million people. Parliament voted emergency laws, but hunger worked faster and was far more pressing than any law. While preparations were being made in England, people were dying in Ireland. However, while the ships were crossing the Atlantic, people were already dying in Ireland. £400,000 was voted in parliament to establish workhouses with the intention of covering the island with these institutions. But, while these workhouses were being set up, the famine continued to rage. The unfortunates who were called upon to work were already so weakened and exhausted by their fasting that, when set to work, the picks simply fell from their hands. Anyway, how on earth can one construct a workhouse system to house an entire nation? The officials wondered whether one could, by means of these make-work projects, really deal with the needs that were going to be generated. The entire project was dubious, but it would have to succeed, or else death from starvation would be the result.

From November 1845 to February 1846, £852,000 was expended on famine relief, but still the famine raged in Ireland. Provision centres originally intended for the military were made available to the Irish poor, but the famine went on. I do not intend to describe the scenes of mourning that desolated the unfortunate island. These scenes horrified even the luckless Irish themselves, accustomed as they were to so much misery. I have looked at those same official reports given to the government by the special commissioners sent to these stricken areas to trace the progress of the scourge and to assess it. I have seen therein how a population attacked by hunger tries to fight off death. Firstly, the poor Irishman was reduced to two tiny meals a day, and, when the vice of misery tightened, he made do with just one meal. Children were harder to discipline, as they did not respect the limits set by scarcity and automatically went into the next day's reserves. At this point great suffering occurred. Some died immediately, and these were the lucky ones. More sickened and died somewhat later, sometimes very much later, generally of the illnesses brought on by hunger. It is a mistake to believe that the famine killed immediately those it had singled out to die; unfortunately the impact of the evil was not so prompt. Death, although certain, was slower to arrive. Fever, dysentery, typhus and inflammation of the intestines were the first effects of hunger. These were slow and cruel illnesses that provoked the eating of unsuitable foods in the absence of any normal nourishment. And saddest of all in this time of great public disaster was the infectious nature of these deadly diseases, generating an evil worse, perhaps, than that original evil that had caused them. Thus, in some of the hostels which had been opened and in many of the workhouses into which the unfortunates crowded, one man carrying a germ of one of these infectious diseases could infect the others, so that everybody in the workhouse perished. Ireland was covered with scenes of desolation and horror.

Everyone who saw these scenes reported that never had a people, condemned to such an ordeal, faced it with such a combination of sadness and resignation. This mournful resignation did, however, have its limits. One sturdy labourer from Clare said, "I can endure the hunger and resolve to die, but my children? When I think of them my heart breaks and my mind burns!" Can one wonder in any way at the acts of despair and violence to which some of these unfortunates resorted? No one should be surprised at the riots that burst out at Kilkenny, Listowel, Dungarvan, Sligo and Castleconnell. On one occasion, for example, a procession of unfortunates marched forward behind a black flag. What police force could possibly put down such a demonstration and spill blood on that funereal banner? On another occasion, people came down from the hills in which they were starving, to see fields full of a bounteous harvest and plains covered with huge herds of cattle. Farther off they could see wagons filled with cereals being carried to a neighbouring town. Following them, they saw the cereals being loaded on to boats bound for England. It is scarcely amazing that violence and looting occurred. However, this violence, though merely passing, made things worse, for the looting had no future. The baker closed his shop, and a boat forcibly prevented from departing discouraged the arrival of twenty others. Not only did violence aggravate the effects of famine, it provoked another evil, the necessary repression of the law: order was threatened, and it had to be restored. Eventually the police came, and after them the military. Blood flowed, and those who were not killed were arrested. Sad and horrible conflicts occurred in which the great crime of the guilty ones was misery, and in which the soldier, while doing his duty to the law by hitting back, had a doubtful conscience and a troubled heart.

In 1846 Ireland was covered in these scenes of mourning, and the year was not over when it became evident that the same scourge would continue into the following year. Earlier, as was customary at the time of the potato harvest, enough seed potatoes had been set aside for the following year's planting. However, under pressure of hunger, this reserve was attacked and the seed for the following year was eaten up. This guaranteed famine for the year 1847. On hearing the news of impending new disasters, the British government moved, and the experience of the year just ending was put to good use. The administration was now more knowledgeable, and the means of action were more readily available; an Englishman always does the job well if he is given time. All resources were supplied in enormous amounts. They can be judged by one single set of facts: there were more than 700,000 workers in the workhouses, costing twenty million francs per month; between two and five million free or below-cost meals were given out to the poor every day; the schools, converted into charity hostels, saved 176,000 children, and 285 temporary hospitals took in the sick. No one would dare to say that these efforts were in vain. Certainly, if the evil had not been fought in this way, it would have been even worse. It was, all the same, a terrible evil; the numbers dying in 1847 were perhaps even greater than they had been in the previous year. The scourge struck the bodies of people who were exhausted and half dead already.

We all know that in all English-speaking countries there is a public official called the coroner, whose task it is to report all violent deaths. During the Irish famine the coroner reported every case of death as though it had been a crime, and indeed the deaths were the crimes of an evil social system. There were many occasions in many localities when the coroner could not endure his work any longer, and asked for assistance. In many parishes, the graveyards were too small to contain all the dead. In Skibbereen, the carpenters and joiners, working night and day, could not satisfy the demand for coffins. The poor peasants of Mayo, whose piety towards their beloved dead was so moving, were too impoverished to buy coffins. All the statistics point to the conclusion that, in the course of two years, more than a million human beings died of famine or famine-related illnesses. This was the phase that preceded the departure of one half of an entire people violently torn from their domestic hearth. This was not any more the kind of voluntary emigration where one went freely to find other lands, other skies and other shores. I could see in this all the symptoms of violence and tyranny.

I saw a peasant, doubtless a coarse and ignorant man, but an innocent fellow, who first settled down as resident tenant on the word of a landowner eager to attract him at that time and determined to hold on to him; a poor peasant who, as long as he was able to, paid the rent of his plot and his cottage. He had built that cottage himself and at his own expense on the land of his master. Humble as it was, his house was his world. In his simplicity he knew of no other world. This little patch of ground, where he had passed his life, where his parents had lived and where his children had grown up before his eyes, was to him the best place in the universe. Having no other riches, he put his heart into it. The English do not understand, but the French know well, the passion that a tiny piece of ground can inspire in a man. In his primitive innocence, the poor Irishman was at length convinced that this land was his, and at the very least he believed he had a right to it. This right was chimerical, but he had been allowed to have this illusion over half a century. In other words, he had entertained it long enough for the idea of having such a right, by stimulating his work effort, to have rendered his belief useful to his master. But it also had the effect of making him resist eviction openly the day the field, poisoned by the potato blight, became good only for pasturage.

One day he received an order from a judicial official to clear off. He didn't understand, and stayed put. A second order followed the first. Then came the police, and he and his were forced out of their cabin. That evening the entire family returned. The next day they were thrown out again. The swarm, dispersed for a moment, reassembled once again. Armed men were needed to put down this tiny rebellion, and the family were overpowered. To assure the complete success of this expulsion, having hunted the people out of their home, the walls of the cottage were razed to the ground. When night came these unfortunate people came back again as though by instinct to the only refuge they knew, and they could be seen, like shadows, wandering in the darkness in the ruins of their cottages. The policemen and the coroners of Ireland could tell us how many of these wretched people died there and then of hunger and in despair. Those who escaped death emigrated, but in this case it was not true emigration, but a veritable exile. It all added up to a forcible and bitter exile from their motherland, a motherland more dear, perhaps, to the poor to whom it was their only valuable possession. It was a grief-stricken and despairing exile, without the promise or dreams of the free emigrant.

It may be that most of these poor Irish people, whom an evil law hunted out from their island, are happier now in a new land than they had been in Ireland. This is asserted, and I can easily believe so. What worse fate could they have had than that from which they had escaped? But, in God's name, what terrible evils required such remedies! More than a million Irish people, some freely, others under compulsion, all grief-stricken, abandoned their motherland. This was certainly a solemn exodus. This was a great migration of an entire people, but different from all other such events, and completely unprecedented historically.

It was a migration which perhaps stuck in one's imaginative memory less than those mass migrations of other peoples in mediaeval times because it was done slowly: day by day, family by family, individual by individual and, so to speak, drop by drop. This migration seemed to be far more extraordinary than earlier ones if the means by which it was done and the ends it achieved are considered.

III: Consequences: The Present State of Ireland

Emigration came to the aid of death. The famine exterminated a million Irish people. Two million more abandoned their country and settled elsewhere. Thus were the missing millions to be accounted for. The disappearance of at least three million people out of eight million amounted to a huge change in the social condition of the people. What were the consequences for Ireland of such a great depopulation? Did the number of poor decrease in proportion to the numbers dead or exiled? Has Ireland become peaceful and prosperous? Is it still in the shadow of scarcity? Are the hostile passions that divide the social classes, the rich from the poor, the landlord from the tenant farmer, the Catholic from the Protestant, extinct or at least appeased? Have agrarian crimes, mysterious murders committed in broad daylight by unknown hands, those crimes that everyone saw but which no one witnessed, ceased to make Ireland's soil bloody and cover it with horror?

The revolution that has happened to Ireland's population has advantages that should be neither diminished nor exaggerated. It is certain that death struck disproportionately at the most deprived. There are, therefore, a million fewer poor people in the country. If only the economic account is looked at, the benefit is absolute. As for the two million who left, there is no simple answer. Their emigration brought at least a temporary relief, and left a gap from which the remaining population benefited. These latter had more space to stretch out in and more air to breathe. Where emigration had been both heavy and carried out in a humane way, its effects could only be benign. But it would be wrong to think of the emigrants, those who settled elsewhere, as belonging entirely to the poor part of the population and therefore to be reckoned as a subtraction from the impoverished. It is now recognised that the migrants were generally the healthiest, strongest and less poor part of the population, and were those whom it was in the country's interest to retain at home. If the emigration statistics are examined, it seems that the counties that supplied the most migrants were not the poorest but those most shaken by agrarian agitation. The province that supplied the least number of emigrants was the poorest of all: the province of Connacht. The facts are in accordance with theory and experience. Normally the very poor did not leave the country. Settling in a new country required moral energy and material resources that the very poor did not have. Emigration is therefore not at all a sign of impoverishment.

As the means of emigration are commonly given free to many migrants, one might think at first that the poor, those who need this remedy most, would be those who got it. But that is not the case. No one in Ireland bent himself to the task of getting the poorest to emigrate. The kind of person who most wanted to migrate and set himself to do so with great zeal, was the small farmer who had a tenancy that the landlord wished to suppress and add to another tenancy. It was not a matter of finding the means of existence in Australia for a peasant who had such means in Ireland, but rather of clearing him off the soil of Ireland as being an obstacle to a more efficient agriculture. It can be seen how, in general, the tenant farmers went, and the very poor were left behind. In fact it is true to say that emigration was not so much a boon to Ireland as it was a boon to those who left. This benefit is undeniable, in view of the strenuous efforts made by the emigrants, once they had arrived in their new homeland, to attract their parents and other friends who had stayed behind. It is the case that after the beginnings of the emigration in 1848, in one year £1,000,000 was sent by the emigrants back to Ireland from Australia and America to pay for new departures. If they had been so miserable in their new homes in the new countries, they would not have called to their most loved ones to follow them at such a cost.

A psychological revolution had in fact occurred in the minds of Irish people as far as their attitudes toward emigration were concerned. This is a revolution that should be documented. It appears that their appalling misery, in tearing them from the only place they knew anything about, had pushed them on to a new path where new horizons were opened to them. Railways and steamships gave them an entire world, which offered itself to them suddenly, and widened their perspectives. A sort of courage that urged them on replaced the fear of emigration that had once filled their souls. Even nowadays this mood is a reflective and foresighted one. Young Irishmen can be seen, workers or artisans, working furiously to save money which they intend to use to pay the expenses of a long voyage and the costs of setting up on foreign soil. Such is the enthusiasm that these ideas ignite in them, that they abstain from every act of debauchery and drunkenness that might, by eating into their savings, delay the moment of their departure. It is a strange kind of social progress (if that is what it is) that is displayed by the Irishman in the form of an eagerness to get out of the country.

I admit to, and I share, the opinion of those who, while deploring the initial cause of emigration, recognise the effectiveness of the remedy that it offers to the misery that generated it. But I must state that I do not understand the language of those who, in their enthusiasm for this heroic remedy, bless as a providential benefit the self-same necessity that drove half of a people to abandon its motherland. Besides all that, even if famine has receded in Ireland, the problem is still a dominant one. The sickness of the potato hangs over people's heads like a perpetual menace. It is the subject of all worries and conjectures. Each degree of misery that might make the blight more or less serious is known and noted in advance. It is known that if one quarter of the crop is gone, there will be suffering, distress if one half fails, and if three quarters goes, there will be famine. The slightest intemperance of climate, the tiniest seasonal shift that seems capable of damaging the potato harvest, a rainy day, an early frost, an abnormally early spring are the subjects of commentary in society, the newspapers and in parliament.

I put forward in 1839 some conjectures concerning the appalling effects of the poor law which had just been introduced to Ireland. I never suspected that my predictions would be surpassed by reality. In all countries where the fate of the poor has occupied public attention there has been unanimous agreement that the most genuinely effective assistance for the indigent is that received at home. This method is the only beneficial and moral one. It does not break up families. It is not a misfortune to those who accept it. It does not make the poor become public beggars. Even in England where the abuse of legal charities has occasionally made it necessary to render the workhouse unattractive, these strictures are very exceptional and home assistance remains the common law. In Ireland, assistance in the Beggars' Depot [i.e. workhouse] remains the rule, and home assistance is unusual. In England, six out of seven poor people are assisted at home, in Scotland 19 out of 20, but in Ireland the figure is one out of 50. This explains why in Ireland those for whom assistance would be far more desirable if applied to a limited misfortune never apply for it. It also explains why it is only resorted to by utterly miserable and desperate people who have no other recourse whatsoever. This also explains why in Ireland, where there are many poor, there are twenty times fewer assisted poor than in England, where their numbers are relatively low.

Even if differences in political and social conditions between England and Ireland make for some diversity in applying a charity law based on similar humane principles, it cannot be denied that in the long run the stubborn maintenance of such a stark contrast is injurious to the Irish. It is clear that of the two relief systems, one is benign and the other corrupting and evil. Why is one applied to the English and the other only to the Irish? Evidently, rather than admit that the Irish are inferior human beings to the other inhabitants of the British Isles, we must look at the true motivation behind this contrast. The reason is, if there were no obstacles put in the way of relief, too much assistance would be asked for; in other words, less relief is given because more relief is necessary in Ireland. Deep down this Irish poor law is a false charity; it is the official sign of a relief that is not to be given.

It had been believed that, in burdening landowners with a very heavy tax, it became in the interest of each of them to ensure that pauperism was prevented so as not to have to pay for poor relief. However, it made a different calculation come into their minds: to suppress misery, you suppress the poor. From this came the resolve that led a large number of landlords to evict all those tenants who, because of poverty, threatened to become a charge on them. Also they resolved not to permit anyone who looked like they might become indigent to be made one of their tenants. In the light of all this, I do not think it is in Ireland's interest that the poor law be abolished. The principle behind it is a fair one, and it is the application of it that is evil, and that has to be changed. It seems impossible to maintain for a long time two such different ways of applying a law which is in itself fair and humane, but which operates in a benign way in England while in a malign way in Ireland.

The character of the crime is always the same. When you hear of one of them, you need not enquire as to the motive. It is always about land. The cause of the crime is always some tenant being driven off his plot, or believing himself to be. The victim is invariably the landlord or his agent, the murderer an unknown person who commits the crime openly and is fairly sure of getting away with it. It has been like that for a century. Always it is the same. Among the victims of successful murder attempts were two whose fathers had been killed in the same way as their sons. Crime in this country seems to fill the morgues rather as the sea does on its shores, where every maritime family can count several members who have been victims of the fury of the ocean. It is only fair, however, to recognise that although agrarian outrages are still characteristic of Ireland, the zone in which such crimes are committed has shrunk. If the counties of Tipperary, Limerick, Cork, Kerry and Roscommon, areas where attacks are common, are taken out of the reckoning, crime of this kind has become more and more rare throughout Ireland.

What is really unfortunate is something that is the same as ever and still very widespread, and that is the tolerant mood with which these crimes are accepted, or, to put it better, the extent to which the perpetrators are protected by popular opinion. If the number of such crimes has lessened, their suppression is still as difficult as ever. Mr. Larkom, chief officer of the Royal Irish Constabulary (the *gendarmerie*), has remarked that their greatest problem in arresting the guilty is that the people take the side of the assassins. Everywhere the silence of witnesses is guaranteed to the killer, and punishment is assured to whoever might help justice to recognise the guilty party. Secret societies maintain a reign of terror everywhere in the hearts of the population. These societies, of which only the names have changed, are still plentiful in the country, and their secret power is still effective. These societies are pursued relentlessly through the courts, and every opportunity is taken to strike at them. They are denounced daily from the pulpit by the Catholic Church as being the most dangerous sources of crime. These societies now make themselves felt by a lesser number of attacks than of old. But if a crime is committed under their deadly direction, they bring to bear all their powers of intimidation on witnesses and sometimes on juries as well.

They make themselves felt on other matters besides attempts by the authorities to put down agrarian crime. It is because of their evil influence, and the habits of mystery, violence and perjury that the population have absorbed from them, that it has become very difficult for justice to be done to all kinds of crime. There are an extraordinary number of everyday offences of which the perpetrators remain unknown. In England and Scotland three quarters of accused people are condemned, but in Ireland the figure is only one half.

The habitual activities of this secret confederacy are also the source of a type of crime that, although known elsewhere, may be looked upon as an Irish speciality because it is so common there. This is the posting of notices threatening death, or the sending of menacing letters, commonly decorated with funereal emblems, and usually with some agrarian connection. It is insufficient to say that there is a lot of crime in Ireland; crime is everyday. It bothers everyone and is on everybody's mind. The government applies all its strength to re-establish the realm of law in Ireland and to make sure that crime is put down. One of the most appropriate and noble ways in which the government could bring in the rule of law would be to have justice done by judges who deserve the trust of the people. In this spirit it has put through important reforms, of which there is certainly none that produced a better impression of the bench than that which put on it more men of their own religion. However, it takes more than a day for wounds like that to heal, and it is easier for an enlightened and just government to reform its laws than it is for a people to reform habits corrupted by iniquities that have persisted for a very long time. Furthermore, despite the changes that have been made, criminal justice in Ireland is still somewhat barbaric. To prove this, all you have to do is point out that criminal courts still think themselves obliged, as in the past, when they wish to convict the guilty, to retreat to the use of paid witnesses ("approvers"). This amounts to the most immoral and dangerous procedure which human justice could employ. Such devices guarantee oppression. They will not make that sense of justice and respect for the law grow, a sense and respect that is so urgently needed to be re-established in Ireland. It is to be wondered how many disgraceful acquittals have been made for each possibly unjust condemnation pushed through by these means.

The persistent way in which the most honest Irishman will shield the most criminal, because in his eyes his only crime is to be at war with society, demonstrates how deeply the mind of the Irish, after centuries, has internalised over the generations the notions of justice and injustice. In Ireland, not only is crime unpunished; it is honoured. Quite recently, the murderer of Mr. Fitzgerald, condemned by the verdict of his fellow citizens, had scarcely paid the penalty for his crime when he was glorified as a martyr in the city and county of Limerick. If an Irishman ever saw the spectacle of a pure and straightforward justice, possibly he would accept it. Until such an acceptance has entered his mind, he will evidently deal with the present "justice" by means of trickery and violence. Moreover, even if the hunger for land is nowadays less often a source of criminal behaviour, this hunger still persists and its nature has not changed. The land and its occupation are still the supreme goal of the Irish or, more accurately, the one goal worth seeking in this world. An Irish small tenant farmer said, "I am on this piece of land, and it is I who made it what it is. I'm staying here and I'll kill anyone who tries to throw me off it!"

Not only does the Irishman imagine no other existence on earth, he understands no other way of achieving happiness. Even in exile, his imagination dreams from afar of possessing a piece of land. Land does not only take over all his mental faculties, it also takes full control of his emotions. It alone fills the hearts of the working population, and it also obsesses those who have spare time by the ceaseless terror that it provokes. The poor think of nothing but of the possession of land, and the rich only of the dangers of such possession by the poor. Land and its terrors are, in the aftermath of the Irish famine, the constant subject of any conversation in which Ireland is involved. All thought, all interests, all passion, all entreaties, all writings, all argument, all crime are connected with it. These passions, which I saw in Ireland twenty years ago, are still there, as alive as ever. The enemy of the Irishman is still he who, sooner or later, might take away the land he occupies, dispute title to land that he covets or take away from the Irish market land that is available for commercial exploitation. This enemy is first of all the landlord who, to increase the size of his tenancies and create large agricultural concerns, suppresses small tenancies and, in getting rid of tenants, increases the number of claimants for the land.

There has existed for a long time in both England and Scotland an economic doctrine which, when applied in Ireland, probably has some influence on violent crime. This doctrine is apt to instil alarm and despair into the hearts of the Irish poor. According to this doctrine, the land is essentially a factory like any other, and the tiller of the land is best seen as a machine. The ideal goal of agriculture seen as an industry is to get from the land the greatest output for the least amount of human effort. The landowner should act like any other manufacturer who, in pursuing his interest, prevents mechanical threshing and even stops threshing machines and dismisses men as some other person might change his skills. In the north of Ireland, near the Donegal coast, there is a little island called Arran that had, a few years ago, a population of 1,500. They were all poor tenant farmers, growing potatoes. Potatoes were their only diet and also the source of their rent. When the potato failed, some of these unfortunate people starved to death, while the rest emigrated. The houses were demolished, and where there were 1,500 people there are only cattle and a cowherd. Here there is a strict application of the doctrine, and the doctrine which equates agriculture with other industries is indeed true in strict terms. I do not intend to deny this, even though there are some differences between the skills needed in a factory and those needed for working in the fields. There is an obvious difference between a steel spring which has been stressed, broken and thrown away without feeling anything and this thinking machine which, in working the land, comes to love it and is grieved by being separated from it. I do not deny the basic doctrine even though the air of a factory might be poisonous for the worker and humanity may be willing to accept a political economy which puts as few people as possible to work a machine in the depths of a mine and welcomes the fact that a few poor families, even if their smallholding is overpopulated, at least live out their lives there in fresh air and sunshine.

I dismiss these objections to the doctrine and accept it as fair and generally valid. I merely request that it be applied strictly in Ireland. After all, political economy has used the best and most appropriate procedures to reduce and nearly wipe out the agrarian population of a country in which, over centuries, the same science, driven by a different principle and using different calculations, had set itself to permitting the population to grow to infinity. This system, whose present purpose is the wiping out of all smallholdings, is on the way to achieving its objective in Ireland. Every day it is reported that another crowd of impoverished tenants has been evicted and their tenancies converted into pasturage. Strong farmers are being imported from Scotland to replace them. Unless I am mistaken, this conduct of great landowners is one of the causes of trouble in Ireland and provokes the very agitation from which the country suffers. However, the land issue is not the only thing that disturbs Ireland; for these other things we must look elsewhere.

IV: England Must Decide to Recognise That Ireland Is a Catholic Country

The more I examined the causes of the extraordinary agitation that continually troubles Ireland, the more I became convinced that one of the principal causes is a religious anarchy which is generated by the law itself. This is the law, which establishes the Protestant Church as the officially established faith in a country that is profoundly Catholic, and the imposition of payments to that Church on a population that does not profess its faith. However one tries to excuse the maintenance of such an established Church, there is, and can be, no way in which it is not seen as a permanent assault on their own religion in the eyes of the common people. To require them to be associated with such a thing is seen as an injury, and to force them to co-operate is seen as an assault. The persistent nature of this attack is seen as a persecution.

I am sure that all those people who claim there is no religious persecution in Ireland are quite sincere. They think the country is happy and free, because it is no longer subjected to the violence of Cromwellian soldiery or the everyday oppression of the penal laws. But persecution varies from era to era. There are persecutions which, although gentler than they used to be, still hurt as much because custom has also become gentler and people have become more sensitive. It is a very painful thing for an Irish Catholic to hear every day the law that he is bound to obey proclaim the superiority of a faith which his conscience forbids him to recognise. It is painful for him to hear something declared legally true which his own religion tells him is a lie, and to pay to the state a tax for the maintenance of people whom the law declares to be the ministers of the Church of Ireland and who for him are merely the apostles of error. It is understandable, and unnecessary, to justify one religion seeing itself as superior to another, and perhaps the majority faith may be justifiably established. But what is not justifiable or understandable is for the faith of a few to be established solemnly and legally over the faith of the great majority. Here oppression is allied to insolence. On the occasion of the recent death of an Anglican prelate it was calculated that in the course of a long ecclesiastical career that lasted at least sixty-five years, he received as reward for his various religious duties about 19,000,000 francs. All this was paid out by a Catholic country and by a poor population!

The census of the population of the country before the famine came up with the following results. The total at that time was 7,943,000, of which 6,427,000 were Catholic, 852,000 were Anglican and 642,000 were Dissenters. Today there are 5,764,000 people in Ireland, comprising 4,490,000 Catholics, 678,000 Anglicans and 596,000 Dissenters of various sects. The figures make it clear that, although the famine and emigration changed the total, the proportions adhering to each faith have not changed very much. Thus the same minority faith is still imposing itself on everybody else. It can be imagined that the existence of certain abuses which have attached themselves to the Anglican Church have made it a source of trouble in Ireland. There were two in particular which were strongly criticised. The first was a property tax (church rates) that was levied on everyone by the Anglican parish for the maintenance of the Anglican clergy. This was abolished by parliament in 1833.

The other abuse is the tithe that Protestant ministers collect from lands cultivated by Catholics. The tithe has been an issue which has provoked continuous quarrelling and murderous encounters. In 1838 parliament abolished the tithe, but substituted for it a means of payment which, while being less vicious than the tithe, took the form of a rent conferred on Anglican clergy and paid by

Catholics to the rent collector in the form of a tax. These reforms were benign, but they were virtually fruitless. The anger at the establishment of the Anglican Church caused in Ireland has never died down. In fact, whichever way the present mood of the country is examined, it is obvious that this anger has never been stronger than it is at present. This is because, in abolishing the Church rate and reforming the monstrous abuse of tithing, the supports of an institution which itself is the central evil have been taken away. The evil is the imposition of the Anglican Church on an entire people who wish to remain faithful to their own religion.

I could say that the hostility to the Anglican Church has never been stronger, nor Ireland ever so agitated about this issue. It would be difficult to communicate to French people any notion of the intensity of the hostility which divides Catholic and Protestant Ireland. Looking at the gap between the two sides and the eager proselytism which excites the combatants, you would think you were in the early sixteenth century. It is not quite warfare, but it is quite close to it. In the press there appear angry controversies and from the pulpits issue denunciations and mutual insult. Even in open country there are meetings where the champions of each faith meet, rather like a tournament, to fight for their cause with popular passion as witness and judge! And these are just the peaceful contests. Only a few years ago, were it not for the intervention of the British Army, Belfast, capital of Ulster, would have witnessed the mutual violent aggression of Catholics and Protestants degenerate into civil war.

Some believe that England long ago gave up trying to convert the Irish to Protestantism. I thought so myself twenty years ago. In general people who thought like this assumed that the English defended the status of Anglicanism only because it was the existing state of affairs, and because to desert the Protestant banner in the face of the Catholic Church would injure their pride. Perhaps that is the way most English people in England think. However, this is assuredly not the way in which those English who defend the Protestant Church in Ireland think. These people certainly wish to convert Ireland. Not only do they attempt to do it, they hope for success. This hope was apparently revived by the terrible tragedies that emanated from the famine of 1847 and which, reaching the poor, hit the Catholics far harder than the Protestants. Never have there been more Protestant schools founded in Ireland than those established recently by associations and individual subventions. Never have more bibles been distributed nor churches built.

The recrudescence of a proselytism, in the form of an enthusiasm that inflames the Protestant party in the country, is very visible and is particularly so in the national school system. Thirty years ago the British government had a political vision that certainly had some originality and grandeur. This was the idea of building a system of general education for the populace for all religious persuasions without exclusion or privilege. Children were all to be taught the things generally needed to be known by human beings, but they were to be segregated from each other for purposes of religious instruction. For literature and science they had the same teachers, for religion, each faith had its own teacher. It was on this basis that the national schools were set up in 1833. In the same spirit, the government established the Queen's Colleges in 1846, in Cork, Galway and Belfast during the ministry of Sir Robert Peel. These were superior schools intended to take in students of all religions, Catholics as well as Protestants, where it was hoped that instruction that was free of bigotry and partiality would give the Catholics a confidence that the University of Dublin could never inspire. However, these colleges have never obtained that trust, and the national schools, which were trusted at first, are in danger of losing it. The national schools attracted the Irish people to them on the strength of a promise of complete religious impartiality. Despite all attempts to contain it and disguise it, proselytism has become visible, and resistance to the system has grown.

Eventually the Catholics of Ireland concluded that the spirit in which children were being taught in these schools was hostile to their religion. The Catholic clergy of Ireland also gave the alarm. This happened in 1852, and from then on a mortal blow would have been struck at the schools had not the British government hurried to give guarantees to the Catholics of Ireland as to the impartiality they had asked for. These guarantees have enabled a compromise to be made and given a respite, although it is not clear that they will work in the long term. Furthermore, if the guarantees satisfy the Catholics, they may not satisfy the Protestants. A system, which is very moderate and sensible, may not be imposed easily in a permanent form on parties that have such fiery passions. When the narrow distinction which exists between religion and teaching is considered, between the light that guides one's reason and the principles which form one's faith, it is astonishing what bravery it must have been which placed together side by side in one school children of different religions, so that they might learn the sciences together while allowing them to profess different faiths. And it seems unclear how to separate, in a way that they will not get mixed up, the general elements of teaching with the particular basic principles of each religion.

It can be imagined that such an enterprise would find ready acceptance in a country where religious indifference gives tolerance its melancholy guarantee. But how could one hope that, in a country where fiery religious passions run wild and a kind of insensate proselytism reigns, the limits of impartiality would not be broken? It was only on condition of these limits being respected that the national school system could be maintained. Certainly we can understand the extremism that is penetrating the great conflict between the two religious parties into which Ireland is divided. Seen from a distance, this great conflict, deep down one of morality and intellect, has some grandeur, despite the violence. It

raises up the soul and releases it from the monotony associated with most societies, absorbed as they are with mere material interests. But the more impassioned the conflict becomes the more difficult it seems for the schools to observe
a strict religious neutrality. We have seen Protestant proselytism run amok. It is
not alone in its excesses, and I am sure that Catholics will not escape going
astray much as have their adversaries, given a country that is aflame with religious controversy. I am even more certain of this now that I see the Catholics
getting more powerful.

There are, however, two contemporary facts which I think are demonstrable,
and which look as though they might exonerate Catholics of excesses while ac-
cusing their opponents of them. In the first place, Protestants who convert to
Catholicism tend to come from the higher classes in society, while Catholics
who convert to Protestantism generally come from the lowest and poorest social
orders. To explain the conversion of a rich and enlightened Protestant one needs
only to point to his own free will and choice. The conversion of a poor and ignorant Catholic needs more explanation; in explaining his desertion of his religion, it is natural to suppose some illegitimate pressure that he has given in to. It
is the case that many children who go into workhouses as Catholics or of uncertain religion, come out as Protestants. There are estimates of some 10,000 con-
versions per year, which seems an exaggeration.

It is certain that during the lethal years of famine a number of unfortunate
Catholics did indeed desert their religion. Their priest whom they had supported, but who now had insufficient bread for himself, no longer sustained
these poor people. They had met some prosperous Protestant whose charity had
saved them. Beside the Protestant mansion where their misery had become
housed they found a Church that they entered and stayed in. This was the terrible ordeal of poverty. In this melancholy time the tortures of the body and the
agony of the spirit mingled, doing good became confounded with seduction and
charity, that gentle sister of faith seemed to become the accomplice of apostasy.
In the midst of the passions that inflame them, Irish Catholics forgive those
whom the famine separated from them in this way, but they do not forgive the
Protestants whose charity they see as a trap. They see this generosity as purely a
snare laid by the enemies of their creed, a snare into which one of their brothers
has fallen. They react even more violently against this conspiracy by which they
feel surrounded, and which seems even more dangerous because it is disguised
as charity. If the passions of Catholic Ireland are such that it sees alms, perhaps
motivated by simple charity, as a hostile act, what can one expect those passions
to be like when its religious enemy does not bother to disguise itself? When, for
example, it happens that a great landowner, having founded a Protestant school,
calls the children of his Catholic tenants to attend it, while threatening to evict
the fathers of those children who do not attend. There you can see unfortunates

dragged out of their cottages and flung on the roadside without any food, unfortunates whose only crime was to stay faithful to their creed and to fear less the deaths of their children than the loss of their faith. Attacks of this kind mean that Catholics have to recognise that there are implacable enemies of their religion, whether they come in the form of violence or the form of charity, or even in the more everyday but dangerous form of daily common teaching in school.

It is not surprising that Ireland is on fire, that the population is up in arms or that Catholic priests, seeing danger, give the alarm. A people that sees its religion under attack surely has the right to defend it and react against those who assault it. It is unsurprising that the Catholics now want their own schools, reject mixed schools and want a Catholic university. It is also unsurprising that Irish people are more divided, more agitated and even more hostile to England than ever before. There are causes of agitation in Ireland that long precede this religious issue, as we have seen. But this is the one that fuels all the others, and every time the fires look like they are being quenched, this one revives them and fans them.

Certainly, it is evident that the bizarre condition of this unfortunate people, whose woes seem to defy the craft of political science, poses problems that are difficult to solve. There is no trickier set of problems than those connected with the Church of England. The Anglican establishment can no longer be maintained in Ireland; that is obvious. But how is it to be abolished? The abolition has to be wished for by a government, by a queen, by a House of Commons, by a House of Lords, all of which are Protestant. Religious equality must prevail in Ireland, that is certain, but it is not obvious how it can be done. These are the hard questions which one would have to be blind not to be aware of. I am not going to discuss at all the issues that I have dealt with elsewhere in the book. I wish only to point out that the first condition for tackling their assessment with any hope of success is to recognise first of all the self-evident fact that Ireland is a Catholic country, that it is determined to stay Catholic and that the maintenance of the Anglican Church as the official religion is an incessant symbol of proselytism and a permanent stimulus for agitation. This is what the British Government must see and recognise. After that, the difficulties will not be solved, but it will become possible to solve them. The obstacle that makes them insoluble shall have been pushed aside.

V: How It Is That Ireland Is Making Progress, Despite Being Still Poor and Agitated

Despite the evils from which Ireland suffers and the stormy agitations that persist, the country is making progress and a better future lies before her. This future does not involve separation from Britain and an independent political existence, but rather a people united with England, a free people, and a people free with England and freed by her. There are people in France who believe that it only needs a foreign military invasion of Ireland to see the flag of green Erin fly together with the foreign flag. They believe that the Irish people are waiting impatiently for their deliverance. I have said elsewhere that in my view this is a complete illusion, and I still believe so. I am rather inclined to believe that the presence of a foreign military force on Irish soil would actually rally to the British flag many Irish people who at the moment have little affection for England. What certainly is beyond doubt in my opinion is that, were such an invasion to be launched and to succeed, and if, somehow, the country, having got rid of one link and not having fallen under the control of its liberators, Ireland, having become master of her own destiny, would also find herself abandoned to her own weakness and internal divisions. Ireland would have less chance of a happy future as an independent country than she has if she stays a dependency of the British Empire.

Even though it is the case that some improvements in Ireland are more apparent than real, it has to be said again that some real progress is also being made there. In particular, perhaps one improvement in particular takes the form of a new institution designed to deal with the redistribution of landed property in Ireland. This is an event that is very important and deserves our immediate attention. In the course of this book I argued that the chief ambition of the Irishman is to own a piece of land. I demonstrated that the chief obstacles to this ambition were the aristocratic spirit of the laws that, in Ireland, govern the inheritance of land and the uncertainty of property titles that, by only conferring rights of litigation, make commercial use of land nearly impossible. Nowadays, thanks to reforms in the law, these obstacles have ceased to operate, and traffic in land has become far easier, surer and more frequent; in the past it was precarious and unusual.

The way in which this change, one from which will flow great consequences, occurred is of interest. The sight of Irish misery in its extreme form provoked the first proposal of this reform, a reform that, more than any other, goes directly to the heart of Irish woes. On 25 January 1847, just when public sentiment in Britain and in the rest of the world was shaken by the cries of lamentation that famine was causing in Ireland, one member of the government, Lord John Russell, said in parliament that there were in Ireland over four and a half million acres of unused land which were capable of being cultivated. The government proposed, he went on, to devote £1,000,000 to this project. Furthermore, it proposed that if the owners did not exert themselves to improve the land and refused also to sell it, the government would claim the right to take possession of it. When the land had been reclaimed, the government would divide it into allotments of a modest extent, say 25 to 50 acres, which would be sold or rented on condition that they eventually be sold. Russell thought that the plan had great advantages, if adopted. He felt that a great number of people who were in despair and sometimes driven to crime because of land hunger, would be able to make their living from these new holdings. In this way the government intended to create a new class of smallholders who, by their work and independence, would create a new era of social conditions and a bright future in Ireland.

By these words Russell was saying two things. Firstly, the British government intended to create a class of smallholders, and would resort to expropriation to do so, an expropriation for public purposes of the lands of the landlords of Ireland. This resort to revolutionary means was proposed in the heart of an assembly of rich English landowners, and this fact attests to the mood of exaltation and alarm that the terrible sufferings in Ireland had generated in England. Afterwards this particular solution was abandoned but not the basic purpose. Other means were proposed to create a class of smallholders. It would be wrong to believe that to accomplish the liberation of the soil in Ireland would involve a large number of new laws, to abolish primogeniture, entail, etc. A close study of English law and its interpretation makes one recognise that neither in England nor in Ireland are entails ever permanent; they can be extinguished by those who have profited from them. Entail in England has always been regarded with hostility by kings who see in it a resource of the nobility and an obstacle to confiscation, a strategy which kings wish to be able to use liberally. Entails irritate also many of those whom they are intended to protect. Also, after centuries in which many statutes have been passed introducing a horde of exceptions under which entail can be extinguished, things arrived at the point where the Court of Chancery could always, in the name of a third party, either at the request of the landlord or his entailed tenant annul the entail that blocked freehold of land. The land of Ireland was certainly not inalienable under law. Any obstacle to its alienation came not from law, but from custom and jurisprudence.

Most commonly the proprietor of a demesne, even entailed, had the right and the wish to sell it. However it was unclear how he could sell land that was covered in debts, mortgages, loan pledges, personal credit notes, agreements of all sorts, often contradicting each other, all secret, and all impossible to verify with any certainty. Most Irish land was in a state where, in the midst of all this confusion of title, there was always the insoluble problem of knowing who actually owned the property and therefore the right to sell it. Everyone knew that if you wanted to buy Irish land, you also bought a legal process with the possibility that even though you had already paid for the land you might be made to pay for it all over again. And if you went to the Court of Chancery to get what was needed to sell entailed or mortgaged land and had got title to the land under the seal of that Court's authority, there were so many formalities, inevitable delays and enormous expenses that generally the enterprise was not carried through, and when it was successfully completed it resulted in your ruin. It can be said that, even if Irish land was not inalienable in law, it was in practice, protected as it was by the miseries of the country and its judicial traditions. Private sales were effectively forbidden because title was uncertain. Judicial sales, the only ones that had some authenticity, were unaffordable because they were ruinous.

The British government, wishing to ensure that Irish land could be bought and sold, did one thing only; it changed the legal procedure which made it impossible to make a free sale safely. However, to change the jurisprudence, the judge had to be changed. This was done. In place of the Chancery Court, parliament established in 1848 the Encumbered Estates Commission, later on to be termed the Landed Estates Court. This was a commission or court of justice which, without using any laws not used by the Chancery Court but applying them in a different spirit, rapidly proceeded to transfer all land which interested parties, often the landlord himself, asked it to do. These lands could be divided into allotments in accordance with people's wishes, carry out auctions, value the lands and confer watertight titles on the purchasers. These titles have been dubbed "parliamentary titles" because of the origins of the Court that issued them. During the discussion in the House of Lords on the bill that made these reforms, when a member protested against the exorbitant power which was being given to the Commission, the Lord Chancellor, Lord Campbell, admitted that it was indeed a somewhat arbitrary law, but that the state of Ireland made it absolutely necessary.

It has been estimated that by 1855 one fifth of Irish soil was in the hands of the Landed Estates Court. The amount paid to bidders by the Commission amounted to £25,000,000 even by 1859; this amounts to a revolution in the Irish land question. Under the external appearances of a simple procedural law, we have here the germ of a social revolution. The land of Ireland is thus going to change ownership in a few years, passing from ineffective and discredited owners to new owners who are capable and solvent. The sales of estates involved very high prices, so that immense amounts of money were put into the land of Ireland, thereby demonstrating that it was not capital that was lacking in Ireland, but rather the security that capital needs. It also proves that the state of Ireland is beginning to inspire a confidence in the future that had never previously existed.

It is strange. For a long time it was believed that Irish land was protected by law which rendered it inalienable, and that to give it back its true value it would have to be freed up for sale. However, it was the English landed aristocracy which, having maintained in Ireland a regime which was hostile to land sales, at last turned around and gave land an extreme mobility; Ireland went from being a country where land sales were systematically blocked to being one which permitted the easiest expropriation of land in existence on the European continent. It has been calculated that the farms sold off in Ireland averaged between 200 and 300 acres and were distributed between 8,000 and 9,000 owners. A new middle class of farmer is being formed, destined to form a social stratum that has been hitherto almost completely missing in Ireland. Furthermore, it is not just that the land is passing into the hands of new owners; these new owners are by and large Irish, who are replacing English landlords. In the past English people owned almost all of the land of Ireland. Furthermore it is worth knowing that most of these new owners are Catholic; basically, it is that Old Ireland, feudal, English and Protestant, that is falling apart on its last bastion, the soil of Ireland. It was not so much a matter of demolishing a building; rather, in striking it once, it became evident that it was already a ruin. It fell down because it could no longer stand up. A new life has been given to that which was about to die, and this renovation has been done without violence. New landowners have been created without attacking the principle of private property.

What is happening in Ireland today is analogous to what happened in France after 1789, when the sale of goods belonging to *émigrés* and clergy put into circulation a great chunk of land that had up to then been kept off the market. However, there are also differences which I see, among them this: the selling off of French land did not only make for a middle-sized farming class, it also created a class of small farmer. It does not seem to be proposed to create the latter stratum in Ireland. When the condition of Ireland is considered, and the land hunger which exists there, the danger which this hunger gives rise to and the agrarian malaise which pervades the country, it is to be thought that the cure has to be agrarian, and that that cure should consist of the creation of a class of small landowners. The breaking-up of the land into small parcels is everywhere a useful guardian of property rights and in Ireland is perhaps a necessary guardian of such rights. In Britain it is not really understood what effect the transformation of the present class of tenants into owner-occupier farmers could have on the public peace in Ireland. It is scarcely understood even in France, where the division of the land into four or five million little parcels protects ownership. France is the country where, in 1848, the rights of property had been breached by anti-social doctrines. Private property would have been imperilled had it not been for the firm defence afforded to it by the rampart of extreme land division. The Irish small tenant farmers, who nowadays think only of attacking the property of landowners, could be turned into small landowners. They would then become amazingly conservative and develop a great respect for the law. Those who are now the implacable enemies of the police and soldiers would overnight be themselves transformed into policemen.

To get them access to the land of Ireland it would not be necessary to give them it for free, as dangerous theories suggest. It would suffice to sell it to them.

Other reforms have occurred also. In 1835 Church rates, paid by Catholics to maintain the Protestant religion, were abolished and their own Catholic religion was recognised. In 1859, tithe laws were reformed because they provoked a rebellion of heart and conscience expressed openly by a free people. Again, the reform of municipal corporations went through in 1841, and that old monopoly of the Church of Ireland collapsed under the assaults of the logic of Robert Peel; he remarked in parliament that if British local government was being reformed, he could scarcely refuse such reform to Ireland. This is the freedom, which, in a country that is legally Protestant, protects the Catholic religion. Having assured that religion its autonomy, it will get it the only other thing it lacks, which is equality and will dissipate as a vain phantasm that fiction of Anglican supremacy. When it goes, it will be impossible to understand how it managed to persist so long. It is extraordinary that, in Ireland, only liberty restrains any reaction by Protestant fanatics. When, some day, Catholics, in their equal status try to become dominant over Protestants, that same liberty will prevent the oppression of Protestants.

That freedom, having allowed Catholics to recover their religious rights, assures them of the eventual achievement of all civil and political rights. It has permitted the expansion of national education; twenty years ago there were 500,000 students in school, and nowadays about 600,000. Freedom encourages a friendly competition between schools, raises daily the levels of instruction, while religious education raises the general level of morality, allows all Irish people regardless of their religion to participate in the public affairs of the country, particularly at the local level where they are already in the voting majority. It permits them to get established in the courts of justice and start to penetrate the grand juries. Because of a set of rules which reward ability and encourage the claims of superior ability the highest dignities of the state are nowadays awarded to men who, a generation ago, would have been excluded legally even from subordinate employment. Thus, of twelve high court judges in Ireland, eight are Irish Catholics. This remarkable figure bears witness simultaneously to the merit of the candidates, the impartiality of the British government and above all the power of free institutions. It is these free institutions which, by maintaining a certain peace in Ireland in the middle of a ceaseless disturbance and discord, permits all Irish people, whether Protestant or Catholic, to achieve riches through effort. By these riches they can achieve ownership of property. By this freedom they can also get access to land, an access accorded to them by the Landed Estates Court. From this originates middle-class ownership. This freedom will create a class of small farmers on the day when public opinion, the only sovereign in a free country and the only one suited to an enlightened country, imposes such a measure on parliament.

In sum, it is this liberty, a great and noble political liberty, which quite recently, in the midst of the terrible ordeals to which an unspeakable catastrophe condemned Ireland, strengthened the country in the face of an inexorable fate and filled Irish hearts with a new resolve. Again, it was this freedom which, strengthened by extraordinary inner resources and the individual energies which it developed in people, the enlightenment which it spread, the solutions which it suggested and the co-ordination of effort which it encouraged, finally raised up a beaten people and gave them courage by giving them hope. This was a sight worthy of contemplation. England in Ireland gradually undermined the old social system even at the risk of shaking by its underground activities the entire aristocratic and religious apparatus that it shared with Ireland. Motivated by a moral imperative which cannot be admired too much, English freedom, that slave of English justice, forced England to abolish the institutions with which England had oppressed Ireland. Perhaps this reform may some day attack those institutions that England wants to preserve at home!

Many people, even though they recognise that England has given Ireland free institutions, deny that this is to Ireland's advantage because Ireland is still miserable in the midst of freedom. This is to make the same mistake as those who see a country prosper under despotism and attribute that prosperity to that despotism. There are countries which have lost the freedom which they once had and miss sorely its benefits long afterwards. This is rather like land that is fertilised by a river whose source has dried up. Everything is desiccated and stigmatised near that source. However, farther away from it, people think that the river is flowing as usual and that the clean water that passes by will continue to encourage plenty in its passage. The soil it waters is still fertile and everyone sees that it has a good and enlivening impact. The appearance of life hides the germ of death.

There are other countries where there can be seen all the evils of a long-lasting tyranny but where freedom still exists despite all. Here the river's source spouts forth, but the river has not yet started flowing. Far away from the source everything is still desert, dried-up and arid. Everything looks as though it is going to die, but the wave that is to give it life is about to flow. This is the picture that Ireland offers, an Ireland with free institutions which have not yet fertilised the land but which have the source of that enlivening, and which will be the font of the country's riches and prosperity.

Chronology
Index

Chronology

1778-1782: Beginning of Irish Volunteer activities

1782: Independence of the Irish Parliament ("Grattan's Parliament")

1789-1799: French Revolution. Various plans exist to weaken Britain by invading Ireland and supporting Irish rebels

1798: Rebellion of the United Irishmen

1800: Irish Act of Union. Estimated population of Ireland: 5,000,000

1801: Act of Union comes into effect. Pitt resigns as prime minister over veto on Catholic Emancipation

February 6, 1802: *Gustave de Beaumont de la Bonninière born at Beaumont-la-Chartre, Sarthe*

1803: Crushing of Irish rebellion led by Robert Emmet

July 29, 1805: *Alexis de Tocqueville born*

1821: Irish Catholic Emancipation fails in House of Lords

1825: House of Lords again rejects Catholic Emancipation Bill

1825: *Beaumont meets Tocqueville when both are serving as* juge-auditeurs *in the court of Versailles; Tocqueville and Beaumont develop an interest in political economy*

1828: Daniel O'Connell elected Member of Parliament for Clare

1829: Catholic Emancipation Act

1830: July Revolution brings Bourbons' reign to an end. Beginning of the monarchy of Louis-Philippe. *Beaumont takes oath to support July Monarchy but is uneasy about intentions of new regime*

1831-1832: *Beaumont and Tocqueville travel to America to study prison system*

1832: British Reform Bill increases Irish representation in the Westminster Parliament

1833: *Tocqueville and Beaumont's report published as* The Penitentiary System of the United States and Its Application to France

1834-1835: O'Connell introduces debate on Repeal of the Union. Alliance between O'Connellites, Whigs, and Radicals

1835: *First part of Tocqueville's* Democracy in America *published. Tocqueville and Beaumont travel to Ireland July 7 to August 16. Publication of Beaumont's* Marie, or Slavery in the United States.

1837: *Beaumont elected to French Parliament seat for Sarthe. Beaumont travels to England and Ireland to gather material for his book* L'Irlande

1838: English Poor Law extended to Ireland

1839: *Publication of Beaumont's* L'Irlande: Sociale, politique, et religieuse. *Beaumont receives Prix Montyon*

1840: *Second part of Tocqueville's* Democracy in America *published*

1841: Irish census counts a population of 8,175,124

1842: The Young Ireland movement, which is critical of O'Connell's politics, emerges

1844: O'Connell is convicted and sentenced to one year in prison. Verdict overturned by House of Lords

1845: Potato blight first noted. Beginning of the Irish famine lasting until 1849. Estimated death toll between 1,000,000 and 1,500,000. Beginning of mass emigration mainly from the west and south of Ireland

1846: Public health acts introduced to cope with Irish famine crisis

1847: 105,000 Irish emigrants arrive in the United States. Death of O'Connell

1848: Revolution and beginning of Second Republic in France. Louis Napoleon elected president

1850: Franchise Act widens franchise in Ireland considerably

1851: Mass migration from Ireland reaches its peak with 250,000 people leaving in one year alone. The Irish census reports a population of 6,552,385

1851: Louis Napoleon seizes power. *Beaumont and Tocqueville imprisoned for opposing the coup*

1858: Irish Republican Brotherhood (Fenians) is founded in Dublin

January 16, 1859: *Tocqueville dies*

1861: The Irish census counts a population of 5,798,967

1862-1863: *Beaumont writes a new foreword for the seventh edition of* L'Irlande.

1863: *Beaumont delivers a speech on the present situation of Ireland to the Academy of Moral and Political Science*

February 22, 1866: *Beaumont dies in Paris*

1867: Fenian disturbances in England and Ireland

1869: Church of Ireland disestablished

1870: Number of people to leave Ireland since 1845 reaches 3,000,000

1871: The Irish census counts a population of 5,412,377. Most Irish emigrants went to the United States

1872: Secret Ballot Act

1875: Charles Stewart Parnell elected to Parliament

1877: Parnell becomes president of Home Rule Confederation

1879: Formation of National Land League

1881: Irish census counts a population of 5,174,836

1885: Ashbourne Land Purchase Act

1886: Gladstone adopts Irish Home Rule

Index